DOG SHOWS
Then and Now
An Annotated Anthology

ANNE M. HIER

IMAGES IN PRINT

DOG SHOWS
Then and Now
An Annotated Anthology

ANNE M. HIER
IMAGES IN PRINT

Published by Images in Print

Inquiries should be addressed to:

Images in Print
P.O. Box 37
West Redding, CT   06896
or via website:
http://www.imagesinprint.com

Manufactured in the United States of America

ISBN 0-9673801-0-3

Dust jacket design: Anne M. Hier
Book design and typography: Anne M. Hier

Table of Contents

Introduction

Dr. James W. Edwards

The commoners, the nobility, the saints, and the gods—she will offend all at some point and some at many points in this book. However, she came from—among others—two U.D. Bulldogs bred, and finished, a decade apart. When one begins with real dog credentials, the ending (in this case the present) is of interest to all real afficionados with real canine contributions. They will say about her that she was direct, noisy, gruff, frightening, ruthless, overbearing, misguided, misdirected, misinformed, ingratious, incorrigible, incredible, incredulous, unkind, unforgiving, unbelievable, uncaring, and uncooperative. In so doing, they will reveal the truth: fault judging always fails—for it is the virtues we must always seek. For she was and is first and foremost a serious student of dogs, art and scholarship; and when you read this book you will realize how serious a student she was and is. Other opinions, of course, are both welcome and wrong.

Woops—I almost forgot—sometimes she fails to complete work on time. :)

CH. MAGICIAN
The first Bloodhound to win a Best in Show in the USA
Breeder, Lewis B. Strong
Owner, Dr. Knox
Artist, G. Muss-Arnolt
1906

Preface

Anne M. Hier

It is impossible to completely understand the Victorian concept of the dog show without learning a great deal about three key 19th Century English breeds—the Bulldog, Smooth Fox Terrier and Bloodhound. Almost without exception the early members of the Kennel Club were actively involved in ownership and breeding of one, if not all, of these unique breeds. Fortunately for me, my original breed is Bulldogs and this study has not been a hardship. However, whether one has any particular personal interest in these breeds or not, understanding more about them, and their owners, contributes to our appreciation of the cultural phenomenon known as the dog show.

My original intent in creating this anthology was to produce a reference and learning tool for dog show judges and those passionately involved with dogs and dog shows. I was initially surprised to discover very few books on the subject of dog judging other than some which cover the mundane mechanics of ring management, filling out a judge's book, and so on. Various breed books usually have chapters, or at least a few paragraphs, to guide one in adjudicating a given breed, but most of the truly extraordinary writing on the subject exists, or originally existed, in periodicals. Sadly, a century has taken its toll on canine information conveyed on acidic newsprint. Most of what remains is now disintegrating and crumbling on shelves or in garages, basements and attics. Furthermore, many of the most valuable dog books of the last century are now quite scarce because the lovely drawings and color plates have been stripped out and sold individually by Philistines who do not understand the priceless historic value of the corresponding written word. One of the advantages of today's computers is the capacity to enhance degraded newsprint images which a few years ago would have been considered worthless for reproduction. In this regard, while the illustrations in this book are beautiful and decorative within their own right, the majority were utilized within the context of why they were initially created. I have been extremely fortunate in my research (in actuality, an exciting treasure hunt), to find images which elaborate and expand upon the corresponding critiques and articles. Hopefully, this marriage of text and image will help revive some of the original meaning of both.

It is rather painful to concede that most Victorian writers had more vivid and educated pens than those of us today. Many articles in this anthology have been printed in their entirety with very little editing and in all I have tried to maintain the color and flavor (or colour and flavour) of the authors. If one reads most of these articles without checking the dates of publication it will be obvious they could have been written today. What does this mean? Well, one conclusion is dog shows have been able to continue on their initial momentum—whether or not we solve any problems or finalize any discussions.

In determining the fine line between

scholarly writing and readability (not that they are necessarily incompatible), I have not included any footnotes. I am aware this lack will be particularly irritating to real scholars. The other reason for not including footnotes, a more personal one, has been my persistent frustration with the general sloppiness of many who write about dogs. Researching this volume over three years has been a joy from the discovery aspect but, on the other hand, a true nightmare in terms of desiring accuracy and diligent information verification. It would seem the majority who write about dogs rarely verify facts, dates, proper spelling of names or accreditation of source materials, gladly plagiarizing with impunity the work of others, both written and pictorial. Thus, rather than spoonfeeding footnotes and exact dates of magazine publication of included articles to the above referenced canine contingent, I kindly refer them to the bibliography. By engaging in independent research they will, no doubt, discover something exciting which I overlooked.

As a visual artist it is extremely important to me that the illustrations in this volume be given their proper historical context via dates, when known, in conjunction with the name of the artist. If I could not ascertain a work's exact date, the appendix lists the date of the publication from which it was extracted. This is not an entirely satisfactory reference system. However, it truly amazes me how much information can be lost in only one hundred years.

I first became interested in dogs as a child in 1964. Since I like to think I have read everything pertaining to dogs since that date, I decided to use 1964 as the cut-off date for articles in this volume. Interestingly enough, the first dog book I ever purchased was a children's book with color drawings of all the AKC recognized breeds. When I started this anthology I reviewed that book once more to discover that the section on showing dogs was written by Laurence Alden Horswell. There are five articles in this book by Horswell and it was extremely difficult to edit his contributions down to that miniscule

amount. The majority of his written work was published in magazines and as a sad consequence will be unknown to many. Yet, to my mind, he clearly stands out as the premier 20th Century American canine writer, because of his ability to see the real issues at hand and to convey his conclusions in an entertaining and thought provoking manner.

Another significant reason for terminating works at 1964 is to avoid those people still living. I consider this anthology to be an historical tome and judgment is still out on contemporaries. Many of the authors and artists in this book, though from another place and time, have become my close friends through their works. There is much greatness in their efforts to advance and celebrate purebred dogs. We need to reflect on those who have gone before, for their contributions have lived beyond their physical existence. If we understand the "then" of dog shows we will, hopefully, be able to make sound, purposeful judgments for the "now."

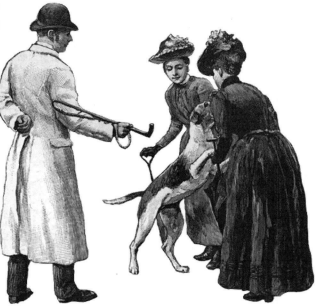

p.s.—There is no appendix with answers to the "Questions for Consideration." It is presumed those reading this book will, through thoughtful discussion and meaningful action, provide the correct solutions to insure the viability of dog shows in the future.

Judges and Judges

"The Fox Terrier Chronicle"
1904

There can be no doubt about the dissatisfaction felt at the varied placings of the Fox Terrier judges at shows held this Spring. That the placings have been satisfactory no one can for a moment contend; moderate dogs have won championships, good dogs have been passed over, bad dogs have been placed too high; in short, the year 1904, as far as it goes, distinctly holds the record for judicial errors. That we shall ever get anything like uniformity in awards is as unlikely as it is perhaps undesirable. Once introduce the element "certainty" into dog showing, and the degeneration of the pursuit is certain. We have no possible objection to two, three or four judges placing four different dogs in different relative positions at the heads of classes at different shows, but we do protest against the "experimental aspect" that the appointment of judges has assumed of late. "Novelty and not efficiency" seems to be the watchword of those responsible for the selection of the judges. It would be needless to mention the instances of bad judging that have recently occurred; all our readers, or the majority of them, have suffered. But it is not to persons, but to practices, we wish to call attention; the fact remains the best dogs are not winning, and as long as that is the case the great motif for the existence and continuation of dog shows is a dead letter. This state of things is unfortunate, it is detrimental to the best interests of the fancy, it materially affects the status of the breed, and it creates a feeling of distrust and discontent that cannot help the working of considerable harm to the breed. The remedy is hard to seek, but all readers can do something toward remedying this undesirable state of things, by bringing all the influence they can to bear upon committees to induce them to make none but sound judicial appointments. Such efforts, however well directed, will not entirely remove the cause for complaint, but it will at least mitigate what is the greatest evil the Fox Terrier man has at the moment to complain of.

Questions for Consideration

1. Why would it be acceptable for different judges to place the same four dogs differently in order of merit at separate shows?
2. When the same four dogs are always in the ribbons, what does that situation say about the current state of a particular breed? About the current state of judging?
3. What constitutes a sound judicial appointment?
4. Can you name a year or particular event that, in your opinion, "holds the record" for judicial errors?
5. Are judicial errors the same thing as procedural errors?

Judging the Judges

Harding Cox

"The Kennel"
1912

It is a good thing that everyone does not think alike. If such were the case the peculiar fascination of dog breeding and dog showing would assuredly filter out, until only a very tame and unsatisfactory consummation was arrived at. The glorious uncertainty of war, women, cricket and other problematical endeavours, is the great incentive to competitive effort. Given an infallible judge—or compendium of judges—the dull spectre of certainty would wave away the votaries of the show ring, and a monotonous repetition of placings would be destructive of that hope which is wont to spring eternal in the heart of the disappointed exhibitor.

It would never do for the committees of shows to confine their appointments to a strictly limited circle of tried and proved judges. Such policy would be suicidal for the reasons indicated; so that it behooves executives to search fresh fields and pastures new for likely novices at the game. Everyone must have a beginning, even a dog show judge, and it is impossible for those who are responsible for appointments to the judicial list to gauge the merits of their neophytes before hand. They can only go on what capacity these gentry have shown as successful breeders and exhibitors, which is, in reality, a sorry recommendation, *per se*, for judicial duties. A judge is born, not made. That is to say, he must be fully equipped with those natural and inherent faculties which are *sine qua non* if success is to crown his efforts. Experience and academic knowledge are very useful adjuncts; but they are valueless without the special attributes which command the appreciation, the respect, and the confidence of the general body of exhibitors.

And what are these same desirable faculties? They may be enumerated as follows: (1) comparison; (2) critical analysis; (3) form; (4) concentration; (5) continuity; (6) consistency; (7) freedom from fancy bias and prejudice; (8) physical courage (especially when dealing with those classes chiefly patronized by the fair sex); (9) self-reliance; (10) method; (11) patience, and; (12) promptness (in disappearing as soon as ever the last class in the judging book is disposed of!). *n.b.*—It is an immense advantage to a judge, if he is something of a sprinter, and is really smart off the mark!

It is given to few to possess the bumps of criticism and comparison in fully developed measure, and without them the whole equipment goes by the board. A man, and for that matter, a woman, may be an expert breeder and exhibitor whose successes have been conspicuous and continual. Such may have an intimate knowledge of the breed they affect, may know every positive and negative point in its minutest detail, they may be able to tell the exact quality and value of any particular specimen of that breed that comes to their notice; but when the time arrives for them to take up their judicial position in the ring they are more often than not in a hopeless tangle before they have dealt with the first strong class that comes before them. The task of awarding the prizes in the minor competitions has been an easy one, there have been only three or four entries in each. A novice of exceptional excellence has made its debut. One that stands out by itself, and then runs through the preliminary

classes. Then there is a puppy of considerable promise, which is streets in front of the remaining competitors, and the only difficulty is to determine which of the latter shall be third and which shall be consoled with the barren honour of reserve. This is practically a toss up, and whichever way it goes our judge's conscience will be at rest.

But now comes that plaguey Limit Class, with nearly a score of entries, half of which are accredited prize winners at other shows. The task of separating the wheat from the chaff is not a very arduous one; though even here a timorous judge, deficient in self-reliance, is apt to make the grievous error of overlooking merit, which for the moment is endeavouring to conceal itself—if

not beneath a bushel, at any rate between the legs of an owner, who is not an expert showman. He (the judge) thinks to pick out four, or at most, five, of the candidates whose claims to recognition are obvious, send them into the corner of honour, and then dismiss the remainder with a few cards distributed according to the standard of merit which he has fixed in his own mind. But when he has gone over the whole bunch, he finds he has nearly a dozen in the corner, and has only been able to discover two or three "impossibles" that could be dismissed without recognition. Now this is where the true faculties of criticism, concentration, and comparison come in. Alas! for the judge who lacks them; for he is assuredly in for trouble, and before he has walked his select little band round the ring a couple of times his brain will begin to reel, and he will wish himself anywhere but where he is. But a selection has to be made, and so he has a dash at it, and prays to Providence that he has not committed any particularly glaring error. Nowadays exhibitors are, for the most part, very amenable, and know how to bear the whips and scorns of outrageous fortune without taking up arms or raising abortive squeals. Like the proverbial parrot, they don't say much, but they take the liberty of thinking a lot!

There is one type of judge which, although lacking the three cardinal faculties, yet manages to steer clear of preposterous misplacements, and more often than not gives tolerable satisfaction. This is he who judges by rule of thumb, and who is guided by a hasty inspection of the general characteristics of each competitor. His mind is quickly made up as to their qualifications, and he ticks off the prize winners in his judging book according to his idea of their respective merits, without any minute comparison or appraisement of point values.

In the old days this happy-go-lucky method was very much in vogue, and at its worst is certainly preferable to the abortive attempts which from time to time have been made to judge by actual point figures, written down and added up. In this respect one of the greatest fiascos I ever remember was when Mr. James Berrie, the respected first president of the Bulldog Club, signalized our first show by resorting to this expedient.

On the other hand there were men with a fine eye for a dog, who invariably practised the "judging at a glance" system with conspicuous success, and as an example of this type I may mention the late Mr. William Lort, whose judicial verdicts were often surprisingly short, sharp, decisive, and seldom erroneous. The modern craze for specializing is responsible for much that

> *"I think the most difficult task for an 'all-rounder' is the judging of variety classes, especially where there is a dead level of transcendent merit in specimens of several breeds, whose characteristics are diametrically opposed to one another."*

is unsatisfactory. A specialist in one particular breed, or group of breeds, is always prone to ignore general canine structure and symmetry. He is so obsessed with the standard of his own hobby that its details and fanciful points become exaggerated and segregated in his mind, so that he is inclined to consider each point separately without taking into consideration general balance and symmetry. Thus it often happens that he will "carpet" an exhibit because it displays a fault which offends his eye, but which is not a disqualifying one; whereas an "all-round" judge would only penalise it to the extent allowed for that particular item in the scale of points.

The wide-spread institution of specialist clubs, especially of such as keep a list of judges, the names on the rota of which are strictly confined to their members, is responsible for a great deal of the unsatisfactory, not to say incompetent, judging that a long-suffering body of exhibitors has to put up with. Your special club judge knows every exhibitor and every dog in the breed for he sees them at almost every show, and he goes into the ring unconsciously biased; and though he may be entirely innocent of the fact, and righteously determined to make his awards without fear or favour, he is unable to avoid the result of his own preconceived knowledge.

But as I pointed out at the commencement of this article, it is necessary that fresh blood should be introduced. *Experientia docet.* It would be a grand thing if there existed some vile bodies, on which aspiring and perspiring embryo judges could try their 'prentice hands, but I fear that a school for such is outside the pale of practicability, and the Kennel Club can hardly be expected to institute pass examinations before granting a judging certificate, though I fancy there would be lots of fun to be had out of the enterprise!

CHAMPION CRIB
Owned by T. Turton
Born 1871
Breeder, F. Lamphier
This dog won the first Bulldog specialty
show at which Mr. James Berrie
evaluated the dogs on "points." Cox
refers to his method of judging this show,
and the results, as a "fiasco."

Happily there is available a sturdy band of highly tried and dependable "all-rounders" to leaven the host of raw and green novices.

I think the most difficult task for an "all-rounder" is the judging of variety classes, especially where there is a dead level of transcendent merit in specimens of several breeds, whose characteristics are diametrically opposed to one another. Of course the idea is to place in ascendancy that dog which is most perfect as a specimen of its particular breed. But supposing there are half-a-dozen champions, with scarcely a fault between them—what is to be done? My custom has been to select the most perfect specimen of that breed, which itself has been brought nearest to its recognised ideal; and my theory has worked out pretty well. But I have been challenged thereon, and it has been held that pride of place should go to the best specimen of the breed that is of the highest intrinsic value! To my mind such a procedure borders on the sordid, and is assuredly unfair to the representatives of the humbler breeds, whose owners, having paid their entry fees, surely have a right to be allowed to compete on even terms with the most costly exhibits, and those which are sold by the yard, or the hundredweight.

But since these experiments with judges serving their novitiate are unavoidable, a survival of the fittest is the best that can be hoped for.

Questions for Consideration

1. Can you think of any reasons why a knowledgeable, experienced, successful breeder would have difficulty making decisions as a judge in the ring?

2. Can accurate judicial decisions be reached by judging on first impressions, i.e., assessing general characteristics "at a glance?"

3. Even though he was a founding member of the very first specialist club, Cox claims that the rise of specialty clubs has produced much unsatisfactory judging because he feels specialists cannot help being biased. Agree or disagree?

4. Do you agree with Cox that the most difficult classes to judge are the Variety (Group) classes? Elaborate.

5. Cox enumerates twelve attributes which he feels judges should possess. Prioritize and prepare your own listing of the qualities which constitute a qualified judge.

6. The system of judging on points is criticized by Cox. Yet, he claims that specialist judges have a tendency to fault judge, whereas an all-rounder would only deduct up to the maximum of points allowed for a particular feature. Can you reconcile these conflicting statements?

Judging by Catalogue

"Field and Fancy"
1906

Catalogue cover from 1906

There has been something of an outcry because at the Leicester show Mr. Sprague judged with a catalogue in hand. Both the *Dog Times* and *The Illustrated Kennel News* have something to say on the subject, the latter paper remarking, "An innovation we should not like to see become general." Why not? I take it that the first consideration of a committee when selecting a judge is that he is an upright and honest man as well as a good judge. Satisfied on this point, what possible objection can there be to allowing him to look at a catalogue if he wishes to? This is one of the pet fads of the English kennel world—a judge must never see a catalogue of a show before he makes his awards! Bearing in mind the frequency with which certain men judge and their obvious recognition of the most prominent dogs that are brought before them, a glance at a catalogue would be in their cases entirely superfluous; therefore, on the same principle of debarring a judge from looking at a catalogue, judges who recognize the dogs brought before them and know them by name, know their history and their owners, should be objected to as being likely to be biased in making their awards! It is ridiculous, of course, but not more so than objecting to a judge looking at a catalogue. The moral is, if you can't trust a man to look at a catalogue and then make his awards, don't trust him at all and choose someone else!

Questions for Consideration

1. What possible objection can there be to allowing a judge to look at a catalogue?

2. What possible objection can there be to knowing the previous day's placements of a breed one is to judge?

3. Does knowing a particular dog on sight and its show record automatically imply bias on the part of the judge?

4. Should judges look at advertisements of various winners in the dog magazines?

The Canine Press

from the Minutes of the Quarterly AKC Delegates Meeting

"American Kennel Gazette"
1904

The Secretary: (A. P. Vredenburgh) I have just received this resolution:

1. Resolved, That the Secretary of the American Kennel Club be and hereby is instructed that on and after this date no official business or communication connected with the affairs of the American Kennel Club shall be given out until such time as same has been published in the official organ of the club, namely, The American Kennel *Gazette*.

G. MUSS-ARNOLT

May 20, 1904   Delegate, Great Dane Club

Mr. Moore: I second the motion.

Mr. Muss-Arnolt: I am not very much of a business man, but I cannot see why we should permit our communications to go out when we have a paper which is really sustained and supported by this club, in which our official business and communications are published. It is not a readable paper in general; it is simply a paper which contains our proceedings, etc. We are running this on charity, I suppose. Usually everybody is anxious that we hoard up all the money we can, and in this way of handing over our affairs for publication by the press, we are throwing it away. Why do we publish the *Gazette*? We can read the matter that is in it weeks ahead of its appearance in other papers. I think it is very bad business, that we should give out our very substance that we can print in the *Gazette*. If we do not want that, let us stop the *Gazette*.

Mr. Moore: My reason for seconding that motion was that I noticed that these go out to the

COVER *of the May, 1904 issue of the "American Kennel Gazette"*

press, and sometimes they look pretty rocky. I think directions should be given to the Secretary to look over the report of the stenographer before it is given out to anyone to print, and that would be the case if it was published first in the *Gazette*, and I think that being the official organ, it should first appear there.

Mr. Carnochan: I would like to ask Mr. Muss-Arnolt to what report he refers.

Mr. Muss-Arnolt: I refer to everything that is official business.

Mr. Carnochan: Do I understand that the

Canine Newspapers

Dozens of newspapers devoted in whole or in part to dogs came into existence in the late nineteenth and early twentieth centuries. The increasing popularity of dog shows, recognition of new breeds and unique patronage by Queen Victoria helped make activities concerning dogs "news." Even journals covering other topics had correspondents submitting bench show and field trial reports. Each newly introduced breed was an item of curiosity which everyone wanted to both read about and see. Although photographs were taken of many of these dogs, publication capabilities were not as advanced. Thus, printing of half-tone images was very expensive. "The Fox Terrier Chronicle," the first specialist magazine, affixed actual photographs of the featured dog on the front page from 1883-1892. Mass consumption newspapers could not afford to do this and until the perfection of the rotogravure technique engravers were relied upon to make copies of photographs or paintings for publication. However, dog shows necessitated quick depiction of the top winners, opening the way for talented pen and ink artists. In England, the best known of these sketch masters was R. H. Moore and in the United States, G. Muss-Arnolt.

A very popular English paper, "The Field," was edited by J. H. Walsh, well-known for his dog books under the nom de plume, "Stonehenge." The oldest newspaper highlighting kennel activities was "The Stock-keeper," published in London from 1880-1906 and flourishing for almost 20 of those years under the extraordinary editorship of George R. Krehl. Unlike other canine papers, "The Stock-keeper" focused primarily on the "fancy," covering all aspects of the dog show social scene and introducing the public to the finer points of new and established breeds and dog shows. In the United States, "Field and Fancy," edited by James Watson, was modeled on "The Stock-keeper" and continued for many years, finally evolving into "Popular Dogs" in 1928. Watson was also the first editor of "The American Kennel Gazette." Initially, most of the early weeklies did not rely so heavily on advertising revenue as newsstand sales and subscriptions, functioning as true newspapers with a combination of news, in-depth reportage and, of course, the controversy of gossip and lively letters to the editor sections which always contained much discussion about the quality of dog show judging. In contrast to current canine magazines, and of particular importance, is that the majority of these papers were edited by active judges with truly expert writing on the subject at hand. Today, except for the hundreds of specialty breed periodicals, most public consumption dog magazines are now directed at the pet owner. Though the corporate monthlies still exist, such as the "Kennel Gazette," AKC's "Gazette" and "The American Field," virtually all of the weeklies have disappeared. Sadly, of those extant, most intellectual writing has given way to endless photographs advertising show winners, making the task of those who wish to research canine progression and development in our times very difficult, indeed.

motion would rescind a motion passed here that all documents of the American Kennel Club are obtainable by the press if they apply for them?

Mr. Muss-Arnolt: Certainly, because it should not be obtainable for publication before it is first published in the *Gazette*.

Mr. Carnochan: You know that there was a resolution of that kind here, do you not?

Mr. Muss-Arnolt: Yes, but I stand by what I have said. I do not think it is right, for why should we have an official paper?

Major Taylor: I understand that one of the best stenographers in New York is employed here, and that this matter goes before the Secretary before it is sent out, and I do not see why it should not go out in good shape.

The Secretary: That is so. I have got to have copies to revise. I usually get them the day on which they have to be mailed to the West.

Mr. Mortimer: I do not think that the American Kennel Club can be blamed for the language that is used in any publication. I think it would be very poor policy on the part of this club if it withheld its information. The *Gazette* is published once a month. Very often matters of business are transacted in connection with which no harm can be done by giving it to the public press.

Mr. Muss-Arnolt: I think it does harm in regard to our business.

Mr. Mortimer: So far as the business is concerned, the American Kennel Club is getting wealthy. I do not know what more you want.

Mr. Buckley: May I ask whether the information given out to these papers is recorded and noted in any paper in which it may be published as unofficial, or whether it is the official report of the meeting?

The Chair: (August Belmont) The *Gazette* is the only official organ of the American Kennel Club.

Mr. Buckley: Is it so noted in the papers in which it is published?

The Chair: I am not responsible for that; I do not know. I very rarely have an opportunity to read them.

The Secretary: They are unsigned reports.

Major Taylor: The treasury would not seem to show that it has been very seriously injured by the press abroad.

Mr. Hopton: I think by the press copying the reports of the meeting of the club does the club much good, because numbers of people read it, while lots of people do not subscribe to the American Kennel *Gazette*.

Mr. Moore: In view of what has been said I withdraw my second of that motion.

The Chair: The matter is not before the house if it is not seconded.

Questions for Consideration

1. Should all AKC documents be obtainable by the press if they apply for them?

2. Should official AKC business be published in the *Gazette* before it is obtainable elsewhere?

3. Because rule changes and revisions of breed standards are printed in the *Gazette*, should conformation judges be required or expected to subscribe to it?

4. Although judges are no longer permitted to edit or publish magazines which accept kennel advertising, they may contribute articles to dog related publications. Is the level of discussion helped or hindered by not allowing the most experienced and knowledgeable group of dog fanciers full control of their ideas through editorship or publisher status?

5. Modern printing techniques permit canine newspapers and magazines to overflow with pictures of show wins. To whom are these touts directed and what is their relevance, significance and contribution to the future of the sport?

Following the Judge

"The Stock-keeper"
1902

That certain Bulldog men object to a fair and honest criticism of their dogs daily becomes more evident, and the latest recruit to the ranks of those who have apparently banded together to attack my articles in the endeavor to hide the truths contained in them and to minimize the effects of same truths is Mr. Vicary, the owner of Primula, and the secretary of the Bulldog Club, Incorporated.

Mr. Vicary, in a letter to *The Stock-keeper* of August 15, takes exception to what I wrote about Primula, and makes a great fuss of the last Bulldog Club show, which he calls the greatest show on earth.

Primula has won three championships, and is entitled to be called, "Champion." But, when I point out that all three championships were awarded by the same judge, Mr. Woodiwiss, and that Mr. Vicary seldom if ever shows Primula under any other judge, the value of such championships is far below what one might think if one did not know the circumstances.

Mr. Woodiwiss is, of course, entitled to his opinion, and I do not for a moment complain of his mistakes, as they are, I believe, made in good faith. And, Mr. Vicary must be accounted lucky to have found a judge who officiates frequently at the championship shows to hold such an opinion of his bitch. But Primula has had to wait for her honors until her seventh year, and until those bitches which Mr. Woodiwiss preferred to Primula were either in America or absent from the show or dead.

Primula won her last championship at Darlington, a town right in the north of England.

Mr. Vicary has never been known to take such a journey before with his bitch and the only times that he has ever taken her out of London have been those occasions on which Mr. Woodiwiss was down to judge.

On reading this the public may ask why Mr. Vicary, if he has so high an opinion of his bitch, does not show her more frequently and under other judges. The answer is obvious. He does not wish her to be beaten, as she has frequently been in days gone by. Nearly every disinterested Bulldog man agrees that she has always been much overrated and that the dissatisfaction at the Bulldog show was general when she was winning everything.

I have referred to several of my articles in which I mention Primula and I find that I have spoken well of this bitch, and have certainly handled her with kid gloves. There are several things to admire in this bitch but the main thing which carries her through is the splendid condition she is always in, her coat being always spick and span, which does credit to her owner. She is generally shown too fat, which makes the worst of her hindquarters, which are beefy at any time. But she is a bitch that cannot well be shown thin, as her other faults would then stand out more prominently. Notwithstanding her faults, she is as I said before, one of the best we have. At the same time, this does not put her on a pedestal as a "flyer."

These remarks are called forth because my judgment has been questioned by Mr. Vicary and others. But this questioning of my judgment has only taken the form of abuse, and never has any single argument been put forward pointing out where my criticisms are wrong. It has been said I am biased, but the number of dogs I have spoken highly of should dispel any such idea. I hold no brief for any kennel and whenever I see a dog of merit I shall write well of him, and whenever I see a poor or second-rate specimen put into very high position I shall speak about it, no matter whom the owner may be. Mr. Vicary draws conclusions as to the relative merits of Primula and Mistress Penfold—a bitch I spoke well of. I've not drawn comparisons, nor do I intend to, but I must say Mistress Penfold has proved herself all I said she was, and under more than one judge.

Questions for Consideration

1. What is the difference between a mistake made "in good faith" and a mistake?
2. Is it ethical to travel great distances to repeatedly show under a judge who happens to like your dog?
3. What should judges do when an exhibitor repeatedly shows the same dog under them at every possible occasion in all parts of the country?
4. Is a dog's merit increased because numerous judges put it up, or is merit constant?
5. Are exhibitors being bad sports if they do not choose to exhibit under judges who probably will not put up their dogs?
6. How far would you travel to show your dog under an acknowledged breed expert?
7. Is it anyone else's business where exhibitors decide to show their dogs or how far they travel to do so?

The article on the following page is a recollection of the above events with a commentary on judging by Mr. Sam Woodiwiss from the book, "Bulldogs and Bulldog Men," by H. St. John Cooper. Pictured below are the famous winners which Mr. Woodiwiss mentioned.

CHAMPIONS BLACKBERRY, BARON SEDGEMERE, BOAZ and BATTLEDORA (left to right) breeder/owner, Mr. Sam Woodiwiss. The Kennel Club Stud Book records reveal Mr. Woodiwiss was not exaggerating when he claimed he was taking practically every prize with his string of dogs. At a time when breeders were concentrating on either head or body properties, Sam Woodiwiss was consistently producing dogs which excelled in both.
Artist, R. H. Moore
1899

In the years 1897 and 1898 I was a constant exhibitor at shows all over the country with my team of home-bred ones, consisting of Champions "Blackberry," "Baron Sedgemere," "Boaz," and "Battledora." I took practically every prize that was offered; in fact my success became absolutely monotonous. I said to myself —I cannot possibly do better than I am doing, and if any change is made it must be for the worse. I also found that when I was invited to act as a judge I was somewhat hampered by the fact that I owned a big kennel of Bulldogs myself, for with every desire and intention of going straight, I was conscious of the fact that certain Bulldogs appealed to me rather more than others, because of the similarity of their type to the type of my own dogs. I therefore formed the intention of disposing of my kennels and of breeding no more. This I did, and now I find that I can take up my position in the judging ring with an absolutely open and unbiased mind and a feeling of far greater confidence in myself and much more comfort than I experienced when I was in the thick of Bulldog breeding. I do not think that any man gets the same contentment over judging as I do, for nowadays I do not own a Bulldog, and I know practically nothing of the present day celebrities and of their owners. As an instance of this I may recall that at the late show of the Bulldog Club, Incorporated which I judged, I selected a certain bitch which I had never seen before for high honours. I gave her a number of prizes, and it was not until the judging was over that I discovered that she was a well-known winner, and had something like seventy prizes to her credit.

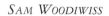

SAM WOODIWISS

Questions for Consideration

1. Woodiwiss expressed concern about being biased when he judged because he was still an active breeder and exhibitor. Is it necessary to give up breeding and/or exhibiting to be a successful judge?

2. The article from *The Stock-keeper* implied that Primula was rarely in the prizes until Mr. Woodiwiss first put her up. In making reference to his judging at the Bulldog Club, Incorporated show, Woodiwiss claimed he had never seen the bitch before the day and after putting her up discovered she had won numerous prizes previously. How does one account for this discrepancy in reporting?

3. At the time he became a judge, Woodiwiss was the most successful breeder and exhibitor of Bulldogs in England. Since he had given up active breeding and claimed to no longer keep up with the current winners, can you think of any reasons why he would repeatedly put up the bitch Primula each time she was exhibited under him?

4. When either judging or giving commentary upon judging what is the difference, both in implementation and results, of rendering an opinion, an informed opinion or an expert opinion?

Who's Running the Show?

"Nutcracker"

"The Stock-keeper"
1891

"Nothing is hidden that shall not be revealed, and nothing secret that will not become known. Therefore, whatever you have said in the dark will be heard in the light, and what you have whispered behind closed doors will be proclaimed from the rooftops."

Luke 12:2-3

I have been intending for some time to write you a history of the American Kennel Club, how it came to be formed, by whom conducted, and its achievements. The time now being ripe, I will state all as briefly as the circumstances will admit of, and then allow the English doggy men to draw their own conclusions.

The first large dog show ever held in this country was during the Centennial Exposition in 1876 at Philadelphia, and dog shows did not commence to bloom forth till some two or three years afterwards.

The Westminster Kennel Club was the first formed, and its show being held in New York, the projectors being wealthy men, it was boomed for all it was worth, while Mr. Charlie Lincoln (of England) conducted all the preliminaries, selected all the judges, etc. The power of the Westminster Kennel Club began to be felt, and as their show was the largest, they soon were consulted by the smaller clubs as to who ought to

CHARLES LINCOLN
First Dog Show Superintendent

superintend the shows and judge the dogs. Correspondence being opened, Mr. Lincoln, as Superintendent, gave them all the necessary points, and, of course, strongly recommended those judges who were in favor with his biggest employer, the Westminster Kennel Club. This wire-pulling resulted in The Hon. J. S. Wise, Major J. M. Taylor, Messrs. Sterling, Munson, and later on Messrs. Tracy and Donner being brought well to the fore, and by the influence of the Westminster Kennel Club, they were kept there for years.

Finally, Mr. John Davidson, known then and now as "Honest John," did quite a deal of judging all round, but as I stated in a former letter, he got into trouble with a reporter of *The American Field*, who was judging with him at the field trials. As Charlie Lincoln was in mortal fear of the paper and its influence with the Westminster Kennel Club, for policy's sake he quickly dropped Mr. Davidson, as soon as *The American Field* opened fire on him, and left the judge to take care of himself as well as he could. Things ran somewhat smoothly for some years, the Westminster Kennel Club's power gradually increasing, and their opinions being much sought after, especially by newly formed clubs, who almost invariably had Charlie Lincoln superintend their shows, he, in the mean

Sensation

When the Westminster Kennel Club was organized in the early 1870s, one object was to establish a kennel of Pointers and to this end, elaborate facilities were constructed in Babylon, Long Island. With a huge influx of money, the club did much for the promotion and acceptance of the breed in this country. In 1876, they imported from England the lemon and white dog, Don, and registered him with a new name, Sensation. The dog and his record were exactly as Charlie Mason revealed, particularly unremarkable, and anything but a sensation.

With WKC backing and many of their members conveniently serving as judges at the shows, the dog amassed a successful bench show record but most objective accounts found him much less than the "great classic beauty" his owners claimed him to be. A. F. Hochwalt, in his book, "The Modern Pointer," described the dog as being, "very faulty in head, and while he was quite good in front, shoulders and chest, his rear parts were entirely too light to correspond, and in our day he would be considered a rather badly balanced dog, especially by practical men, who demand strong loin, quarters and stifles, as this is where the driving and staying power of a field dog comes from."

Sensation had a lack-luster record in the field trials, with only one credited win, a third place in an all-age stake in 1880. Reports of his performances in the field consistently described him as wanting in spirit and dash. But, because there were few English imports at the time and with the promotion of the biggest club in the nation, the public flocked to the dog, sending bitches for breeding from every part of the country. Not surprisingly, Sensation was also a failure in this department, with only a very few of the hundreds of puppies he sired ever credited with either a bench or field win.

As Hochwalt concludes: "It is rather unfortunate that the Westminster Kennel Club did not secure a better dog as their first importation, for he would have done the breed an incalculable amount of good at that period."

time, being looked upon as the only man in the country who could do that work successfully. It was noised about that Mr. Charlie H. Mason was to report the Westminster Kennel Club show of 1881, and I have repeatedly heard it stated that when Charlie Lincoln, the Westminster Kennel Club Superintendent heard that Mr. Mason did not like the club's great (!) Pointer, Sensation, as well as heard his glowing accounts and opinions of Faust, Bow, and other dogs of that type, he was advised by the Superintendent that he ought to try to like the dog! When the show opened Mr. Mason discovered in the £1000 Pointer Sensation none other than Mr. Humphrey's old dog Don that took second prize in a class of some four Pointers at Birmingham, and catalogued at £20,

had no takers. Mr. Mason thereupon disclosed to the public the true state of affairs, warned all intending breeders not to use Sensation's services, which caused a little Kansas cyclone. The breeders did not heed the warning. The dog was bred to about every good bitch in America, and there is not a good pup by him. This all was the beginning of what shook the foundation of American dogdom. The only one who openly endorsed Mr. Mason's course was Mr. James Watson, for which honesty, I regret greatly to say, that the Westminster Kennel Club went for both most vigorously, and did all it could to prevent these two from judging at any of the shows. I have related the foregoing just to let you see how it all came to pass.

In 1884, the National Breeders' Show was held in Philadelphia, and, *mirabile dictu*, Mr. Lincoln was not invited to officiate, nor was he consulted at all, to the utter consternation of everyone who looked upon the Westminster Kennel Club as the Grand Mogul of American dogdom. Here a row began, and for years it has waxed furious and hot. The Westminster Kennel Club and its adherents would not have it. They kicked vigorously, they kicked all ways, and Dr. Rowe, the editor of the then, *Chicago Field*, pitched into Mr. James Watson, known by his caustic writings as "Porcupine," claiming in sum and substance that Mr. Watson had arrogated to himself the right to run a dog show, whereas Mr. Lincoln was the only man who ought to be accorded that privilege—by right of being backed by the Westminster Kennel Club. At this the independent clubs began to think for themselves, realizing how they had been led about by the nose, and soon turned against the Westminster Kennel Club, calling it a clique, and as being run only in the interest of a few to the detriment of the many. This revolutionary movement was headed by Messrs. C. H. Mason and James Watson. The independent exhibitors and clubs as well began to ruminate, which resulted in the conviction that others besides Mr. Lincoln could run a dog show successfully, and that the dogs that were hoisted up as typical specimens were not such, that it was about time for a change, and that they were tired of Westminster Kennel Club men judging their own dogs. This state of things had grown monotonous, and a remedy had to be found.

Then, the Westminster Kennel Club, recognizing its power was on the wane, and that the other clubs were striking out for themselves, resolved to make a bold move. The National Breeders' Show brought back Mr. Davidson from his "retirement," which was a direct fling at Messrs. Rowe, Lincoln, and the Westminster

> *"The result is we really have no American Kennel Club, simply having a Westminster Kennel Club with an alias of 'AKC'."*

Kennel Club which, too, was keenly felt. Things were getting desperate, so the *Kennel and Gun* was started, with Luke White as editor. As he was not a man of means in any way, it was generally believed he was backed by the Westminster Kennel Club. He not only handled the Westminster Kennel Club's dogs at the field trials, but boarded some of the members' dogs at his kennels. White therefore bolstered and puffed up Westminster Kennel Club men every week, advocated Mr. J. Otto Donner, of the Westminster Kennel Club; Mr. Tracy, the artist for the Westminster Kennel Club; and Mr. F. R. Hitchcock, one of the foremost members of the Westminster Kennel Club, and advocated them very strongly as the proper persons to judge sporting dogs at the shows. The articles appearing each week were marvels of literary productions. Finding the venture was not a roaring success, and White could not make it go, it was sold to Mr. Rendle.

About this time, it was proposed to start a kennel club to offset the National Breeder's Club, which was gaining strength each day to the detriment of the Westminster Kennel Club. Those who were doing most of the judging at that time were Messrs. Mason, Barlow, Kirk, and Watson. These did not suit the Westminster Kennel Club for many reasons, one of which was the awards were in accordance with the relative value of the dogs, and not as "Espan" says of some of the specialty clubs, that they want judges who know the owners. When it was proposed to form a kennel club, a meeting was called at Philadelphia. If I remember rightly, a powerful delegation from the Westminster Kennel Club was on hand which tabooed the idea of individuals being in the club, desiring only a club of clubs. This practically put the entire governance of all things canine into their own hands, as they were the only real, strong and influential club. By their action they formed the American Kennel

James Mortimer is hired as WKC kennel manager

Club, to which one Delegate from each of the contributing clubs was to be recognized as a unit, and not like the Kennel Club, which is composed of individuals, most of them doggy men and judges. Instead of framing the constitution so that one man could only act as Delegate for one club, they manipulated so that he could represent a dozen by using proxies or by being regularly appointed by the clubs of outlying districts or cities. You must bear in mind our country East and West is 3,000 miles, and as clubs exist in New York and California, the latter could not send its Delegate to New York. If the AKC had been desirous of being both impartial and

James Mortimer becomes a Superintendent

James Mortimer hires himself to judge

August Belmont, Jr., AKC President, exhibits his dogs under judge James Mortimer. His dogs win!

national in the full sense of the word, it would never have permitted more than one member of a club to act as Delegate for any other club at its councils. They evidently left the loop hole in

order to further the Westminster Kennel Club, as it being in the Empire City, where all meetings are held, that club being the stronger could recommend for far-off clubs such Delegates to the AKC as were in favor with them and their ideas.

The result is we really have no American Kennel Club, simply having a Westminster Kennel Club with an alias of "AKC." The annual meeting of the AKC is held during the Westminster Kennel Club show. Now, take the meeting of Thursday, February 26, 1891. Mr. Thomas H. Terry, AKC Vice-President was in the chair. He is the Secretary of the Westminster Kennel Club. The Secretary as well as a prominent member of the Westminster Kennel Club had an office adjoining that of the AKC, or rather at one end of it. The Delegates of the Associate members to the AKC are Messrs. J. L. Anthony and L. F. Whitman. The former is and has been for years hand in glove with the Westminster Kennel Club members, but whether he is a full fledged member of it or not I cannot say—in fact, no one, as far as I can find out, knows exactly who its members are, as it is stated it is not incorporated. Mr. Anthony is Mr. Belmont's henchman, and nominated him for President again this year with a great flourish of trumpets. Mr. Whitman goes to New York about once a year, and in Chicago is agent for the sale of the *AKC Gazette.* The Kansas City Kennel Club Delegate, Major J. M. Taylor, to represent them at the councils. Some years ago he bucked against the clique.

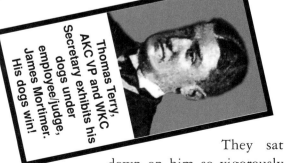

Thomas Terry, AKC VP and WKC Secretary exhibits his dogs under employee/judge, James Mortimer. His dogs win!

They sat down on him so vigorously

James Mortimer hires more WKC members to judge

that he evidently repented of his action. Now he is in favor with them, and all see how the wind blows. Virginia Field Sports Association selected Mr. J. S. Wise, who is, and ever has been, a Westminster Kennel Club member and its champion. The Westminster Kennel Club recognizes Mr. Thomas H. Terry, and he bows to the AKC as he presents his credentials. The South Carolina Poultry and Pet Stock Association relies upon Dr. H. C. Glover to see all things are done in order. In his recent articles in the newspapers he signed himself, "Veterinarian to the Westminster Kennel Club."(!!) The Mascoutah Kennel Club of Chicago dotes on Mr. James Mortimer as their Delegate. He is the kennel manager of the Westminster Kennel Club as well as the Superintendent of the Westminster Kennel Club show. Mr. A. D. Lewis, at one time partner in dogs with Mr. T. H. Terry (Secretary of the Westminster Kennel Club), and who even now is said to be such, is Delegate for the St. Paul and Minnesota Club. Mr. George La Rue, the very strongest partisan of the Westminster Kennel Club is on hand at the AKC meetings to see that the Pointer Club of America secures its rights. Mr. A. H. Vanderpoel, a member of the American Fox Terrier Club, of which the President of the AKC is also President, stands for the Louisiana Poultry and Pet Stock Association. Out of forty-seven Delegates to the AKC, twenty-six were pre-

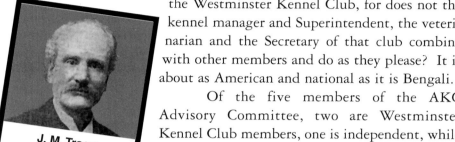

J. M. Tracy, WKC member and artist is hired to judge

Thomas Terry, AKC VP and WKC Secretary exhibits his dogs under fellow WKC member, J. M. Tracy. His dogs win!

Someone hires "Honest John" Davidson to judge in Pittsburgh. No WKC dogs are exhibited.

sent, out of which twelve are known to be either Westminster Kennel Club members or henchmen of it, seven believe the Westminster Kennel Club can do everything just about right, while seven are independent. That is the combination the seven independent clubs have to face at every meeting, and their chance of doing any good is about equal to a snowball melting in Tibet. We have no American Kennel Club. All we have is the Westminster Kennel Club, for does not the kennel manager and Superintendent, the veterinarian and the Secretary of that club combine with other members and do as they please? It is about as American and national as it is Bengali.

Of the five members of the AKC Advisory Committee, two are Westminster Kennel Club members, one is independent, while Mr. Anthony sees everything through Mr. Belmont's glasses. This centralization is all wrong. Not more than one member from any club should be permitted as Delegates.

Let Mr. Donner, for instance, act as Delegate for the Westminster Kennel Club, dispensing with the valuable services of the Westminster Kennel Club veterinarian, Superintendent, and artists (Messrs. Tracy and Muss-Arnolt).

During the two months preceding the Westminster Kennel Club show, the Superintendent and his staff of clerks used the AKC offices for

E TCETERA!

Dealing in Dogs

MAJOR JAMES M. TAYLOR
First AKC President

The greatest contrasts between the founders and active early participants of the Kennel Club and the American Kennel Club are visible in the character of the men involved and their motives for forming each organization. One has only to read the biographies of those in the Kennel Club to find that most were university educated, professional people, including well-known doctors, lawyers, ministers and writers—many making significant contributions to other aspects of society as a whole, apart from their interest in dogs. Collectively, this group had a passion for the dog and their goal was the improvement of all breeds and the elevation of the dog's status within society.

Conversely, those in control of the canine political process in America had personal vested interests to protect and promote, many making their livings, in whole or in part, from dealing in dogs. Initially, a strong coterie of sincere breeders attempted to be actively involved, but they were quickly out-maneuvered with blatantly undemocratic tactics.

In 1905, E. B. Jacquet wrote, "The Kennel Club: A History and Record of its Work," detailing the first 25 years of that organization. This is a particularly valuable resource as it was printed when many of the principals mentioned were still available to verify the facts published therein. However, anyone researching the early years of the American Kennel Club has a much more difficult time finding the truth because the most readily available materials appear to be sanitized, corporate justifications of long-gone events. Those who go further discover the term, "sportsman," when listed as a "profession" means someone who deals in dogs, as can be ascertained from the frequently run advertisement of J. M. Taylor, AKC's first President. Elliot Smith, the first Westminster Delegate and AKC's second President was also a "sportsman" of this ilk, being a close associate of Nicholas Rowe, editor and publisher of "The American Field," and also Charlie Lincoln, the first professional dog show superintendent in America. While there were many well-known dog dealers in England, it was simply considered a matter of British fair play that these professional biases would preclude one from management of Kennel Club affairs—even the affairs of a self-elected oligarchy.

J. M. Taylor, a Kentucky native, expert on guns and a Civil War Veteran, was considered an authority on several breeds, particularly English Setters. Apparently, he was also considered an authority on heavy drinking and during a time when the press seemingly had no compunctions against printed character aspersions one of the more polite references to his personal habits said, "...he is conceded to be one of the best judges of whisky in the country, and certainly his experience has been vast and comprehensive, nearly as great I should say as that of Hugh Dalziel, who, if he had remained in America much longer last year, would have carried off the championship." Nevertheless, Taylor not only bought and sold dogs for others, but wrote favorable critiques of them as a "reporter" for numerous journals, judged dogs owned by those for whom he had purchased animals, remained active in doggy politics, and, for several years his business office was conveniently located next door to the AKC offices. While his fourteen month presidency of AKC was termed in one leading newspaper as, "woefully incompetent," he afterwards served three years on the Advisory Committee, forerunner of the Board of Directors, and continued as a Delegate until 1909, the year preceding his death.

This principal of blatant partisanship became ingrained within the system and perfected in the form *of James Mortimer, who wore all hats available simultaneously. He was initially hired as the kennel manager for WKC and Charlie Lincoln soon was asking him to judge. After Lincoln's death in 1884, Mortimer came to the fore as a professional superintendent and dog dealer, matter-of-factly announcing through the pages of "The American Field" his numerous trips to Europe and availability to purchase dogs for others. Unlike Taylor, who only adjudicated Sporting and Hound breeds, Mortimer became a self-proclaimed, "all-round" judge and was able to give himself numerous assignments at the shows he superintended. He also was an AKC Delegate for over 25 years and served two consecutive terms on the AKC Board of Directors.*

Because so many Westminster Kennel Club members were also AKC Delegates, it is not difficult to grasp the public perception that the two organizations were one in the same. Further, quite a few WKC members were not individual dog breeders, per se, but merely collective owners who liked to go out for an occasional afternoon of hunting. To off-set the expenses of maintaining a large kennel with its attendants, grounds and club house, the dogs were expected to be a paying venture and thus, wins at field trials and bench shows were of great importance to increase the value and demand for the animals.

Quite ironically, the Westminster Kennel Club, founded as a sportsmen's club, is probably the most responsible for the creation of the great chasm which exists today between the field trial and conformation factions. Because of the lack of formal breed standards and any official requirements for judges, from the first WKC benched show in 1877 (the idea of Mr. Tiletson of "Forest and Stream" who met an early demise when a brick wall fell upon him in 1880), it became very clear that conformation judging was based, quite largely, on personal opinion. Field trials, on the other hand, required performance which couldn't be manipulated as easily by merely installing the "right" judges. Thus, when a large circuit of field trials was officially established in 1884, this gave further impetus to the birth of the American Kennel Club, formed with the specific requirement for membership being the holding and promotion of benched shows.

By 1892 it was quite clear that WKC dogs could not consistently do any significant winning at field trials, and because most of the WKC members were not true breeders, the decision was made to keep only the stud dogs and dispose of all the Pointer breeding stock. A total of 35 animals, plus several litters of puppies from two to four months of age, were taken to the American Horse Exchange in Manhattan to be auctioned. Little publicity had been given to the sale and all the dogs went for giveaway prices, most between ten and twenty-five dollars—none at true market value. For a kennel that had done so much breeding, only one champion was in the lot, Ch.

Lass of Bow. Westminster Kennel Club had been so anxious to purchase this bitch that she had originally been sold to them for the then phenomenal figure of $1,750, cash. Her selling price at auction was a mere $125, and that only because her previous owner and importer, Charles Heath, of the Graphic Kennels, received word of the auction and made the trip to New York. Although at the time Heath had 40 dogs in his kennel and said there was room for no more, he started the bidding on his favorite at $100 and was quoted as saying, "The old gal's got one friend, yet."

their own work. Truly! They have all things between their finger and thumb, and do as they please. The Westminster Kennel Club kennel manager judges at Baltimore! And the fact is now revealed that the Secretary of the Westminster Kennel Club sent his dogs there to be judged(?) by his own employee. Before a year passes I shall not be surprised if I see one of the lot in veriest flesh and blood judging his own dogs. It is coming to that quickly. Let it hurry up, so when the crash comes, "Nutcracker" can wink and whistle, "I told you so." When any critic exposes the peculiarities before mentioned, he is at once sat upon by the entire lot, and if they can, they will crush him. They deny anyone's right to criticize their actions or the motives that prompt them.

At the last New York show, Mr. R. F. Mayhew, who had acted as Chief Clerk to the Superintendent, judged Mr. F. R. Hitchcock's dog and gave him first prize, that gentleman the while being one of the most prominent members of the Westminster Kennel Club! Mr. Mortimer superintends the Westminster Kennel Club show, for which he receives always a valuable consideration, and in addition is manager of the Westminster Kennel Club's kennels at Babylon. He judges at Baltimore. Mr. Terry, Secretary of the Westminster Kennel Club and Vice-President of the AKC, sends his dogs down to Baltimore to be judged by the club's employee. The question now is, "Is the American Kennel Club what its name implies? Is it not rather the Westminster Kennel Club?" I would ask another question. Mr. James L. Anthony, who is hand in glove with all the Westminster Kennel Club members, who always monopolizes the floor at the AKC meetings, when everyone wants him to sit down and keep still, and give someone else a show, a man who is thoroughly intoxicated with

> *"When any critic exposes the peculiarities before mentioned, he is at once sat upon by the entire lot, and if they can, they will crush him. They deny anyone's right to criticize their actions or the motives that prompt them."*

his own importance. Why is it, in all his vaporings he never has a word to say about what everyone sees, yet is powerless to check? If he is such an exponent of exceeding virtue, why does he not object? At the time when he was not on friendly terms with the WKC-AKC "gang," he denounced it as an outrage for Westminster Kennel Club men to judge at field trials any dogs they were interested in. If it was an outrage to judge them at field trials, is it not an equal outrage to judge them at dog shows? How did the Pointer Club judges get their appointments, and why was the wretched thing dropped? Was it not because certain members of the club denounced it, threatened to leave it instantly rather than have a grand breed of dogs sacrificed by such scheming? Explain, if possible, the ill-feeling (to draw it mildly) caused by Mr. Tracy (judge) placing Mr. Terry's dogs over Mr. Heath's? How did Robert le Diable come to get placed over Duke of Vernon at New York under Mr. Tracy, and why did not Mr. Terry show the dog at Pittsburgh where Mr. Davidson judged, and where he would have met both Duke of Vernon and Graphic? It is no more nor less than the old racket that was in operation in the days of the Pointer Sensation, and yet Messrs. Belmont and Anthony sanction it all by looking on and uttering never a word of protest. Where are we going to land, is the momentous question of the day? For the papers to try to correct all this is useless. Most of them (in charity I do not say *all*) are scared out of their wits to ventilate all they see and hear, and denounce publicly what they do privately. They know full well if they do it it means loss to them of dollars and cents. The first intimation of the clique's displeasure appears in the form of numerous letters withdrawing advertisements and stopping at once subscriptions to the papers. This is not idle talk. *It has*

The Company Artist

Dog shows and field trials created an increased demand for canine portraiture at the turn of the last century. The axiom that "a picture is worth a thousand words" was not lost on owners who realized that public perception of their animals could be molded favorably by the right image. The Westminster Kennel Club had two prominent artists within its ranks, G. Muss-Arnolt and J. M. Tracy. But, because Muss-Arnolt was himself an active breeder of Pointers, he routinely declined to judge the breed and made it known to the club that he would not adjudicate members' dogs. As a result, the majority of the work of depicting Westminster owned dogs was given to Tracy.

Three Artists View the Same Dog

GRAPHIC — as seen by J. M. Tracy, G. Muss-Arnolt & A. W. Roberts

Hailing from St. Louis, John M. Tracy earned early recognition in 1878 when his first canine painting of the Irish Setter, Berkeley, came to the attention of Nicholas Rowe who then had him create the masthead for "The American Field." Subsequent commercial work followed, but Tracy could still barely make ends meet. Rowe encouraged him to move to New York and assured him he would be able to secure numerous clients for him there through his connections in both the dog and racetrack worlds.

Tracy limited his artwork to horses, dogs and cattle. Overly sensitive to any criticism of his work, his technical skills and artistic vision were equally as limited, being rote, wooden presentations with little imagination or feeling transferred to the canvas. To bolster his reputation, judging appointments were secured but his judicial abilities were also found lacking. He was severely criticized in the dog press for being only an owner, rather than a breeder, and basically a beginner in the sport. In another attempt to establish Tracy's credibility, arrangements were made for him to write and illustrate a series of articles for "The American Field" entitled, "Studies of Great Dogs." Unfortunately, he used this vehicle to puff up Westminster owned dogs and to severely critique those dogs he had put down as a judge. His non-commissioned portrait of Graphic, on the left, is probably one of the most unflattering paintings of any dog of the time. Compared with the wood engraving by A. W. Roberts, it is hard to imagine they are of the same dog. Tracy actually criticized Graphic for having a look of "exact balance and smoothness" which he claimed was not "workmanlike," and not of the correct type. Yet, Hochwalt says, "Graphic was remarkably well balanced, showing finish and quality from head to stern." While he faulted him as not in the top class of field dogs, he felt this dog essentially helped establish correct type in America and commented that he was the successful sire of numerous field and bench winners.

Tragically, Tracy had been invited to exhibit his paintings in conjunction with the World's Colombian Exhibition in Chicago in May, 1893, but the majority, representing his life's work, were destroyed in a fire in December, 1892. Working feverishly around the clock to recreate the pieces, he died in March, 1893, from what his obituary described as "nervous prostration." Consequently, very little of his oeuvre, including oils, drawings and a few prints is in existence today.

The Associate Members

Although AKC is thought of as a "club of clubs," few people are aware that in 1888 a provision for individual membership became part of the Constitution. Because there were very few dog clubs in the early years of the sport, Associate membership allowed representation through an elected Delegate to individual fanciers not serviced by an organized kennel club in their area. However, the principal motivation for this change was to counteract the individual memberships offered by the rapidly growing National Kennel Club of America.

In 1889, as the result of meetings of the Associate Members, the rules regarding this sub-organization were more clearly defined within the official framework. Amazingly, these rules provided for an independently governed, democratic unit within AKC. For example, membership did not require approval of the Advisory Committee but only for one to be vouched for by either two members of a recognized club or two members of the Associates. Upon payment of the $5 annual membership fee one was entitled to a subscription to the newly created "American Kennel Gazette," the "Stud Book" and two free registrations. The Associate Members also had their own officers consisting of President, Vice-President, Secretary and a Delegate for each 100 members. The President of the Associates was automatically a Delegate and member of the Advisory Committee (later to become the Board of Directors). To prevent any appearance of conflict of interest, no Associate could be elected an officer of that group if a member of any other Member Club, except specialty clubs.

The Associate Members' Annual Meeting was held the day before the AKC Annual Meeting with the main order of business the installation of new officers. The Constitution specifically provided for the innovative method of voting in advance by mail ballot. If there were any tie votes, the matter was to be decided at the Associates' Annual Meeting by simple majority. If an elected party declined to serve, the next highest recipient of votes was to fill the vacancy. The current nominating committee procedure which is used for AKC's annual board elections was originally instituted by this group to facilitate the mail-in vote. Also in 1889, it was further voted that $100 received from Associate Member dues was to be used to pay the travel expenses of their Delegates to attend the quarterly meetings.

After attending their Annual Meeting, some Associates generally stayed as spectators at AKC's Annual Meeting the following day. Any member in good standing of a Member Club or the Associates had always been permitted to hear the proceedings. In fact, various canine press reporters were also allowed to attend and take notes. However, it was August Belmont, Jr. who took the steps to clear the house of anyone whom he did not want present. In 1891 to prevent one particular reporter from having access to the proceedings he had the Delegates vote to exclude anyone from the room without credentials. Other "approved" reporters simply stayed in the room. Unfortunately, quite a few Associate Members interpreted the vote to indicate they should also leave and this started a damaging rift within the organization.

No one could have possibly anticipated the extraordinary growth of the dog sport in America before World War I. As the Member Club roster grew so did that of the Associates and their increased representation became a great cause of concern to the few powerful kennel clubs who could see some of their complete power giving away to more democratic ideals. In 1889, the first women Associates joined but they could not be Delegates or run for office. With the ratification of the 19th Amendment in 1920, AKC was under increasing pressure to allow women full privileges. However, there were not enough Delegate votes available to secure this type of radical change, though many Associates favored it. The AKC Board of Directors was becoming increasing irritated with the demands for reform and accountability continually put forth by the Associate Members at each meeting. Finally, in 1923, after counting the house, they were able to successfully deal with this "problem," voting to abolish the Associate Members.

been done time and again; so now we may say the press is muzzled through fear of the Mafia gang, that will have its own way, right or wrong. It is therefore quite out of the question to expect any paper to bring financial ruin upon itself by exposings, and many men have made bitter enemies of influential members of the clique by making simple reference to what they knew and saw themselves. For instance, Mr. James Watson surrounded himself with the bitterest kind of enemies because he called public attention to the disreputable Sensation medal affair, which took place at the Boston Show, if I remember rightly. Some years ago the Westminster Kennel Club entered their Pointer Sensation at Boston in a class in which he was not eligible to compete. He won the prize. Mr. Watson discovered the deception, publicly called upon the Westminster Kennel Club to refund or return the medal, which they persistently refused to do. They held on to it like beeswax to a shoemaker's trousers, and hold on to it yet—at least, I have never heard of it being returned, nor do I believe it ever was. Is this a proper example for any club to show, particularly the Westminster Kennel Club? And why dare they brave public opinion? Simply because they control, or rather virtually are, the AKC, and if anyone dared to propose the disqualification of the Westminster Kennel Club for anything whatever, the entire crew (ever on hand) would hustle him out of the room or out vote him. For this piece of honesty and endeavor to right a wrong it took Mr. Watson four or five years before he could even be on speaking terms with the men who owned the dog he would have disqualified. Everything points in but one direction. The Pointer Club was formed by the Westminster Kennel Club; its list of judges were Westminster Kennel Club favorites, while the real Pointer men were left off

*The Westminster Kennel Club's
Club House
Babylon, NY
1893*

the list, everyone of them, without exception. Think of such a man as Mr. La Rue being placed side by side with such real judges as Messrs. Statter, C. H. Mason, Lord Down, and Mr. Garth! Why was Mr. J. H. Winslow's name left off the club's list? Surely he has forgotten more about Pointers than ever all the judges on the list knew. How about Mr. J. H. Phelan? Surely no one would class him as a judge with Mr. La Rue! How about Mr. J. H. Wilms, and "Billy" Tallman, and Mr. John Davidson? It surely can't be one the score of integrity, for has not the Pointer Club offered one of its cups to be competed for at Boston, where the latter judges?

The American Kennel Club is run by the Westminster Kennel Club!!! It tried to run the Pointer Club, and would no doubt have succeeded, and but for the bungling work of Mr. Tracy at New York, the list of names would still have been held up as judges, and the Pointer Club's cups would have been offered only to such shows as engaged its favored candidates. How was it Mr. Winslow fell from grace in the eyes of the Westminster Kennel Club? No one knows, but everyone knows that once at Boston he did not make a farce of judging Pointers. He judged dogs, not men, and so placed Graphic over the Westminster Kennel Club's Lad of Bow, gave the Westminster Kennel Club third prize in bitches, and landed their puppies the other side of nowhere—just placed each where he belonged.

The Associate Members of the AKC recently held an election of officers. This tail end of the AKC consists of 361 members, according to the *Gazette*. Yet, who can tell how the present Secretary, Mr. Bernheimer, was elected, how many of the votes cast were for him, who voted for him, and last, but the most pertinent question, *who is he?* Everyone is asking who is he? No one knows. Ergo, how did he get there? Solve me the riddle, I pray you, for we cannot.

Gentlemen, you have the history of the AKC (?) in a nutshell, though perhaps a pretty big one! Think of it, Mr. Stock-keeper! You, a handful of your friends, and I form a kennel club. You elect me Superintendent of the Kennels, refuse to show your dogs at any show except where I judge or one of the club. Would such rot-tenness be tolerated in England? Methinks not. Think of it again. A club composed of owners who use their influence against a judge or two, not because they are dishonest, but because they cry down incompetency and all other things that bring scrubs, skates, and wastrels to the very highest pinnacle of fame, crushing the while the typical and rare good dogs.

Questions for Consideration

1. How do you suppose AKC would be structured if individual memberships were available at five dollars each? Do you think it would be more democratic? Can you think of any good reasons why the Associate Member classification should not be reinstituted?

2. Is the system of having a "club of clubs" workable with a current membership roster of over 500 clubs?

3. Currently, there are over 3,500 Licensed Clubs, without voting privileges. What would happen if all 3,500 applied *en masse* for membership status? If 2,000 applied? 1,000?

4. How could, or should, the AKC Constitution be restructured to make it more representative of all exhibitors and breeders throughout the country?

5. Is it reasonable to expect that AKC can function democratically today as currently structured, or is it run in the manner of a 19th Century men's club?

6. Should the AKC Delegates pass a resolution to restrict the numbers of members of the same kennel club elected to sit on the AKC's Board of Directors at any one time? Is it in the best interests of the Delegate body and the fancy at large to have more than one member of any particular kennel club seated and serving on AKC's Board of Directors concurrently? How many members of the same kennel club should be allowed to be AKC Delegates?

7. To remove any appearance of conflict of interest, should those who serve on the AKC Board of Directors take a leave of absence from such things as judging assignments and positions as show chairmen while in service to the organization?

8. Because AKC has now grown into a multi-million dollar not-for-profit corporation, should Delegates who are members of for-profit clubs be allowed to be seated on the Board of Directors? To avoid any real or perceived conflict of interest, should these proprietary clubs be forced by AKC to come into compliance with the vast majority of Member Clubs which are not-for-profit organizations, as is AKC?

9. Should certain Member Clubs be given preferential treatment in their dealings with AKC or should all clubs be treated identically?

10. Has human nature changed for the better in regard to dog show matters in the past hundred years or so? What, if anything, can we learn from the past?

11. How have the cumulative actions of those in the past impacted and affected the sport of dogs in our time?

Great Dane Type & Theories

Letters to the Editor

"The American Field"
1894

EDITOR—When the owner of the Lawrence Kennels told me in New York that he could not see why I at Chicago and Mr. Arnolt ever since picked dogs too small as winners, I thought he would endorse my Newark decisions, where I selected a somewhat coarse, large specimen, with enough type, expression, movement and temperament to be very useful to the breed. There are many Great Danes, old and young, American-bred and German-bred, in America today that can compete and win their large share in any country of the world and in three years hence we will be able to take our own American-bred stock and beat on any bench the Great Danes of any other country.

If you follow Arnolt's doctrine, three years hence you will blush to point out as Great Danes the offspring of such Greyhounds as now win. When I had to select type at Chicago and took small dogs for second prize, I was obliged to because there was no trace of breeding in the large ones. The first prize dogs were over 150 pounds with the exception of one little bitch, eleven months old, in the Puppy Class, which also won in the Open Class. I said distinctly that there was nothing shown that could be called a good specimen.

It is high time my advice was heeded, like once at Chicago when I put my shoulder to the wheel and endured all the abuse that came from my efforts. Stop the breeding of calves called

A. H. Heppner

Great Danes. The breeding and prizing of Greyhounds such as Mr. Arnolt endorses as Great Danes, all the time neglecting imposing specimens, should also cease. There is no necessity to go to the extremes this judge indulges in. When I approved the defeat of Melac by Wenzel the latter should never have climbed so high with Earl of Würtemburg, V.H.C. or H. C. in Vienna, and in Europe was denounced as a Greyhound. He is represented to us as a grand dog at New York a few months later because the judge indulges in phantasms.

A good authority informed me of the denunciation by the German fancy of Wenzel at the time and warned against endorsing such a specimen. All parts of Germany and other countries buy dogs from Würtemburg, and the largest and some typical dogs that went to England came from there. There must be bone and muscle, which were entirely absent both times Portia Melac took first at New York. Leaving her size out, her houndy proportions are at fault. Hepbern Vera was not bought as a brood bitch, nor did Mr. Arnolt ever recommend her as such, but claims so now after seeing her offspring. He again wants to take credit which is not his due. Vera would easily have been the winner at New York in 1893 (under a competent judge) and Mr. G. Lang pronounced her a first-class specimen for a European show. Even Mr. Arnolt in his report predicted her winning career, which

MELAC
1892

In Challenge Class, Melac, of course, beat Pedro, the latter being only fair in type and not sound and true, his tail being in such condition as to be an eyesore. Open Dogs brought out a good blue, Wenzel, of correct type in general, although a bit cheeky, wrong on top of skull and bad light eyes, but has beautiful proportions, wonderfully arched, clean and long neck and good legs, feet and body; hindquarters a bit soft. I should be not a bit surprised if Stanley, the fourth prize winner, would, under judges whose first consideration is size, beat those I placed above him, although I certainly prefer size if combined with correct character and proportions and with good movements, which is my next and almost just as necessary demand from a Great Dane of correct form. Stanley is wooden in head, not clean in neck, not true enough in front legs, poor movement, and coarse tail, his hindquarters are weak. Major McKinley, very much improved in hindquarters and action since last year, but gone slightly coarser in head and more throaty. The Newark winner, Yarrum, is a gigantic dog, but inclined to be too round in skull and coarse all over. In bitches, Portia Melac is a beautifully made animal of the best type, and if she could be enlarged 10 per cent, would be the best Great Dane in this country. She is a feather in her sire (Melac's) cap. She is a racily built, grand moving bitch, and had she a trifle more bone and substance and sounder pasterns and feet she would be difficult to beat. She has a fair head and only one point, outside of size, is really against her and that is her expression is marred by the faulty carriage of one ear. But, as this is a wrong crop and not a structural fault I think it will only count in the closest competition. Her color is a good orange brindle, although her coat in bad condition. Hepburn Vera seemed an easy winner till I had her move and saw her from behind, and though she has a beautiful head, excellent muzzle, good neck, feet, body and color, I had to object to her for first and second honors on account of poor moving behind, as I will not tolerate it. The Reserve, Nora, a frequent winner before, is short in head and was shown more as a prize pig than a Great Dane. The special between Major McKinley and Portia was awarded to Portia Melac, but McKinley was the favorite of onlookers and the consensus of opinion was in his favor. McKinley towers head and shoulders over Portia, and is especially strong in bone, legs, feet and pasterns. Wenzel easily defeated Melac for Best of Breed. He is a round dog and fairly typical. Active and sound on his pins as a terrier. He was an inch taller at shoulder and three inches longer in neck than Melac but could have had a more chiseled head, but in that respect he is certainly streets ahead of Melac. Melac has a grand body and limbs, almost perfect in that respect, but his neck and head are about one-third too large, having too much skin on neck and head, too coarse, which is not as good as Wenzel in character.

HEPPNER

MUSS-ARNOLT

"A Greyhound."

"Again I say, type means beauty combined with size and Wenzel is not such a dog."

"Parlor ornament."

"Grand, typically cut 120 pound dog."

"I do not consider a Great Dane of less than 140 pounds a first class specimen, no matter how typical otherwise he may be."

WENZEL
*Best of Breed at Westminster Kennel Club, 1893
Judge, G. Muss-Arnolt*

"A round dog and fairly typical. Active and sound on his pins as a terrier."

"Why I put Wenzel first was my desire to check the tendency to promulgate the English craze for enormous 'cripples'."

"He was an inch taller at shoulder and three inches longer in neck than Melac; but could have had a more chiseled head, but he was, in that respect, certainly streets ahead of Melac."

"If this dog had been brindle instead of blue he would have been considered by all a crack."

proves how far he differs from the correct perception of judging and breeding.

Is the degeneration of the breed going to be stopped?

To come back to Würtemburg it differed, contrary to Mr. Lawrence's target idea of only doing one thing at a time, by trying for the correct thing at once. This correct thing I will outline after giving Mr. Lawrence his target problem in a different parallel. If I want a package of tobacco, a cigar and some cigarettes, I do not send an errand boy three times to the same store but tell him to get me those three things at one time. If we want Great Danes with good color, size,

type (i.e., form in this sense), we must try to master the obstacles in the same process, all at the same time, or we will with success in one direction only have glaring faults in two others. If I said three years ago, when we firmly fix the type size will come, I meant just what I said, but I did not expect that breeders of Mr. Lawrence's ability would simply inbreed until there was nothing left but type `a la Greyhound, or as he seems to have done, simply worked out, as he puts it, "beauty." Of course, that alone describes the thing to the satisfaction of everybody except those that differ from his idea of beauty—long clean heads, long arched necks, graceful movement and Great Dane outline—the above qualities do not make a Great Dane. We want clean colors and substance, by which I don't mean alone weight and height, but proportioned heavy bone and strong, imposing features with the desired quality of grace.

I saw the danger of Mr. Arnolt's eccentric judging from his beginning in 1893 at New York, since which time I think he has endeavored to become more and more a sensational judge and extremist. Where would we be if we were to take a finely cut, houndy bitch, with a snipey muzzle and Greyhound make-up, with a grand, typically cut 120 pound dog? We would get something like a Pointer or a large hound, something as fit for a watch charm as he would be a representative of a noble, commanding, grandly formed Great Dane.

Again I say, type means size, not in the sense of inches and pounds so much, but in proportions. The bones must be heavy and straight, the joints strong. We must preserve enough of the Mastiff type to make the dog imposing. In 1892 I wrote, "If bred for height only, he will soon get too narrow in chest, light in bone and snipey in head. Breeding for heavy bone and a wide chest primarily, you will naturally get a Great Dane that is likely to stand crooked on his legs, or whose legs are simply able to carry

weight, but not to move it as desired in a Great Dane. He will be throaty, have a short, thick head and neck, and will likely be cheeky. If you desire the combination of both, i.e., height and substance, content yourself with at the utmost, say, 33 inches."

When you judge, explain the value of the respective merits in your report. Is a dog bad because he has size? Decidedly, no! We can't get them big enough, but they must be of the right sort. We will and should make certain allowances for a coarse, unclean neck, a moderately enlarged head, and lack of grace with a 200 pound dog, and should remember that a good one which is large is our aim. We should not discard them as long as there is enough type, i.e., correct form. In passing over in the ring a large dog like Major McKinley, as though he had the smallpox, when as judge he admires the full sister Portia Melac, Judge Arnolt discourages the main point at this juncture in Great Dane breeding, i.e., size, now that type is established. We can breed for size and type, which are one and the same thing, and here is where the golden path of moderation has been missed during the reign of Judge Arnolt. He is to be blamed if our breeders aim for good ones, no matter how small, because he passed fairly typical large specimens seeing on them a little loose skin under the throat and they

---

WHY THE EX-PRESIDENT OF THE GREAT DANE CLUB WOULD NOT JUDGE GREAT DANES AT CHICAGO

"How happy could I be with either, were t'other dear charmer away."

Mr. W. F. Fox was scheduled to judge Great Danes at the Chicago show in 1892, but cancelled at the last possible minute and A. H. Heppner was given his first judging assignment to replace him. The Challenge Class competition in Great Danes was of interest to many in the fancy as it was known that the two big winners of the day, Melac, on the left, and Imperator, on the right, would meet in the ring for the first time. This cartoon, which appeared in "The American Field," implied that the reason Mr. Fox chose not to judge was because he would be incapable of making a decision between the two dogs.

Gustav Muss-Arnolt *was clearly one of the most colorful and outspoken dog fanciers during the late 19th and early 20th Centuries. He served continually as an AKC Delegate for 14 years, representing at different times the Pointer Club of America, the Great Dane Club of America and the American Dachshund Club. He was also a member of AKC's Board of Directors, Class of 1909.*

Muss-Arnolt grew up with dogs, his father being a Great Dane breeder in Germany. Generally considered a fair and impartial judge in the ring, he adjudicated numerous times in America, England and Germany. Muss-Arnolt was further regarded as an expert and an early "all-rounder," but he detested that term, feeling most people who had acquired this lofty status had neither particular experience nor expertise on the individual breeds. The first judge to publicly state that type was the most important consideration in properly evaluating dogs, he backed up that belief with his decisions in the ring, regardless of public opinion to the contrary. Muss-Arnolt was also the first person to advance the notion that dogs had to be judged on the day—not on any knowledge of previous record, former condition or how the dog might appear in the future. Further, he chose not to judge breeds with which he was actively involved, most particularly, Pointers. His show critiques were extremely straightforward and blunt, and apparently, they were also deadly accurate as well, which did not endear him to those whose dogs did not win under him.

Numerous reports of the minutes of the quarterly Delegates' meetings would also indicate that Muss-Arnolt was equally as outspoken, not only on issues which concerned him, but in expressing in sometimes caustic and sarcastic terms his contempt for those who lacked his knowledge of dogs. In particular, the exchanges between Muss-Arnolt and A. P. Vredenburgh, clearly show a mutual distaste.

However, Muss-Arnolt's emotions were best expressed as a professional artist, specializing in canine portraiture. His principal media were pen and ink drawings and oil paintings. He created numerous drawings for the "American Kennel Gazette" of some of the top show dogs of the day. Most of his better known paintings depict sporting dogs in the field. His works are historically significant because almost all are of specific dogs which were exemplary representatives of their respective breeds. Besides mastery of form and anatomy, the works exhibit evidence of being created by someone who not only loved dogs, but understood their very essence as well.

Muss-Arnolt's portrait of his own dog,
CH. BRACKET
1889

were not quite as gay as the judge liked in moving within the ring.

To indicate what judge Arnolt wants in the neck of a Great Dane, he told me to look at a Pointer. Now, I say he can never get a fair sized dog and have him like a modern Pointer in form. Such type (without size) one can get in three years by inbreeding, if that is all that is desired. I may submit the following quotation from one of my letters to the present state of things:

"Again, I say type means beauty combined with size, and a Great Dane like Wenzel as seen last by me is not such a dog. The most successful Great Dane judge will not pick specimens of that combination. In order to make myself more clearly understood I would like to draw as a parallel the situation in Setters. Some judges will look for a show form in conformity with their own conceptions of beauty as to coat and make up. Others, perhaps enthusiastic field trial men, will choose in a bench dog as their idea such forms as indicate speed and ability for practical work. Just so in Great Danes. The one wants a big dog adapted for watch purposes, a dog that will paralyze a man by the expression of his face and is able to knock the bark off a tree by the wag of his tail, while the other would only appreciate a dog sufficiently pretty and diminutive to be suitable for a parlor ornament.

The successful judge in Setters is one who picks out dogs with field trial make-up, yet at the same time satisfactory in regard to beauty. The successful Great Dane judge, on the other hand, will pick a dog of type and high breeding and will remember that the word "type" implies a certain height and substance. I for one do not consider a Great Dane of less than 140 pounds a first class specimen, no matter how typical otherwise he may be."

A. H. Heppner

Mr. Muss-Arnolt Replies

EDITOR—With great reluctance I reply to Mr. Heppner's article in your issue of October 20, and only self defense against unfounded accusations makes me take it up at all. Mr. Heppner is doing precisely now what he attacked before, that is, promulgating his preference of what he used to term himself, "butcher dogs."

If Mr. Heppner had come out with a plain and straight criticism of my judging in 1893 and 1894, and he had every opportunity to do so, I should have respected him for it, no matter how far we might have disagreed; but now he prefers covert attacks and malicious insinuations, as for instance, his remark about my trying to pose as a sensational judge and extremist. I think it is safe to leave your readers to try this shoe where it

properly fits. I hardly think all my writings on Great Danes together would cover one average article of Mr. Heppner's and many of them have been written in defense of him. If Mr. Heppner had, after my judging, come out with plain and direct criticism, where and why my judgment was in error and which dogs and for what they should have been placed differently, it would have been manly and of value to the cause; but months later, after being incidentally found out, that he supplied notes in two different, that is opposing, lights, he comes out with a mass of incoherent random assertions, which have no more value than they bear on their face. Why did Mr. Heppner rush over the whole ring at the '93 Westminster show with outstretched hand, when

> "Yarrum, his last choice, should never appear in public without skates on his hindfeet, as an excuse for his movement."

I decided the special between Melac and Wenzel in favor of the latter, and declare aloud, "Arnolt, if you had decided the other way, we would have had nothing in common about Great Danes?" I, of course, asked Mr. Heppner to desist from such out-of-place demonstrations in the ring. Why was Wenzel no Greyhound then? I enclose for you this photograph of Wenzel as he was then, and say that if this dog had been brindle instead of blue he would have been considered by all a crack. He was one inch taller at shoulder than Melac and three inches longer in neck; but could have had a more chiseled head, but he was in that respect certainly streets ahead of Melac.

The only criticism Mr. Heppner made to me about Portia Melac in '93 was her size, and I replied then as I have stated repeatedly in my reports that I wished there was some more of her. But I wish to ask Mr. Heppner, or any other Great Dane judge, if Portia is below the standard, or why she ran Neverzell—the highest class Great

The Dog Show That Never Was
The World's Colombian Exhibition's Benched Show — 1893

W. I. Buchanan

Who should run a dog show? Who should pick the judges? Less than 10 years old at the time of the World's Fair, AKC had taken the lead in sanctioning and recording shows but was still decidedly nervous about any independent event which might be considered a threat to its authority, if successful. As mentioned in the previous article, the first large dog show held in this country was in conjunction with the Centennial Exposition in 1876. It seemed only logical that when America was to host another World's Fair a dog show would once again be conducted as one of the events.

In 1891, the AKC Secretary, Alfred P. Vredenburgh made a trip to Chicago to meet with representatives of the Mascoutah Kennel Club, the AKC recognized Member Club in Chicago and W. I. Buchanan, Chief, Department of Agriculture, who was in charge of arranging the livestock exhibits for the exposition. Buchanan was aware that to attract exhibitors from all parts of the country it would be necessary for AKC to sanction the awards and officially record them. This had been done numerous times in the past by AKC for non-member clubs. However, Vredenburgh informed Buchanan that Mascoutah Kennel Club would have to give up their spring date in order for AKC to recognize the awards at the World's Fair Benched Show which was to be held in June. Mascoutah KC agreed to do this. Vredenburgh then suggested that Mascoutah KC be allowed to consider the dog show at the Colombian Exposition as their event for 1893, but Buchanan objected, stating that this was to be considered a World's Fair show and not a locally sponsored exhibition. His preference was for AKC, as a national registry, to support the event. The meeting ended with Vredenburgh agreeing that AKC would not back the show financially but would recognize the awards given.

James Mortimer, Mascoutah Kennel Club's non-resident AKC Delegate, contacted Buchanan to offer his services as Superintendent for the dog show. As benched shows usually lasted four days, it was no mean effort to have one. Thus, the professional Superintendent was a necessity and Buchanan was grateful for the offer. At the time, it was a routine practice for the Superintendent to select the judges but there seems to be no indication that Buchanan and Mortimer ever discussed this until very late in the game. Buchanan was one of the speakers at the Westminster judges' dinner in March, 1893 and shortly thereafter it was discovered that he interpreted the job of the Superintendent as that of a facilitator—setting up and managing the show only. On his own initiative, Buchanan had contacted all the recognized parent clubs to ask them to submit the names of those persons their membership felt most qualified to adjudicate, further indicating to Mortimer that it would not be proper for him to both Superintend and judge at the same show. Outraged, Mortimer had exhibitors initiate a letter writing campaign to "The American Field" against the judging selections in many breeds. Minutes of the AKC Delegates' Meeting then indicate questions about whether awards should be recorded for organizations (specifically the World's Fair) which were not recognized clubs.

On the day the benching arrived in Chicago, Mortimer announced he was resigning as Superintendent. In an attempt to salvage the show, Buchanan postponed it until the end of September. Next, AKC reneged on their agreement to record the awards. Thus, most exhibitors could not justify the expense of an arduous trip to Chicago. When entries closed with less than 900 dogs, the show was cancelled. Over 27 million people attended the fair, an amount equal to half the population of the United States at the time. But, apparently, even the United States government could not expect to stage a dog show without the approval of AKC and there has been no suggestion of holding one in conjunction with a World's Fair since.

The Judges for the World's Colombian Exhibition's Bench Shows

"The American Field"

1893

When it was decided to have a dog show in conjunction with the World's Fair held in Chicago in 1893, the Hon. W. I. Buchanan, Chief, Department of Agriculture, was put in charge and set about to appoint an appropriate judging panel. At the time, the standard procedure for all-breed shows in America was to have all arrangements for judges made by the Superintendent, taking into account a kennel club's specific requests. However, in what was considered a novel approach, Mr. Buchanan decided to contact all recognized parent clubs and ask them to submit the name of the person their membership felt most qualified to adjudicate their particular breed. This caused quite a shock to many and "The American Field," being based in Chicago, was the logical choice for letter writers to let their views be known on the subject.

EDITOR—Mr. Harry L. Goodman comes out rather "flat-footed" in a protest against Mr. G. Muss-Arnolt being appointed judge of Great Danes at the coming World's Fair dog show. Now no man living today can judge Great Danes to the satisfaction of all. The breed in this country is too new and we have not as yet come to anything like a recognized standard that shall be apparent to all, though that is what we are striving for. Mr. Muss-Arnolt claims that type is all important, the first thing to be looked for in a competition, if we wish to develop the ideal dog. Size going with type makes it so much the better, but massive bone and muscle should not be allowed to count for more than grace and beautiful outlines. Mr. George Raper seems to go to the other extreme and favors the heavy dog. Wenzel would hardly be recognized by him in a large competition, and so many other judges might be mentioned, all of whom have stirred up hornet's nests by their decisions. Seeing your dog judged in a ring can be compared to nothing better than a game of chance, where one man wins and all the others lose. We go away from the show thinking that the poor misguided judge may be honest, and mean well, but we won't show before him again.

Mr. Muss-Arnolt has taken a bold stand in his decisions and should be supported by everyone who desires to see a man judge conscientiously and according to his convictions, and where favoritism is the last thought in his mind and especially by those who have the future interest of the Great Dane in this country at heart. In spite of the fact that his decisions in New York were directly contrary to the opinion of most of the exhibitors at that show, those same exhibitors, or at least many of them, endorsed him as their first choice as a judge of Great Danes. At a meeting of the Great Dane Club of America held a few evenings subsequent, when the question came up of recommending certain judges to bench show committees when requested, Mr. Arnolt received quite a majority of the votes for first place on the list over A. H. Heppner, James Mortimer and John Davidson.

I think that the specialty club should be the first to be consulted in the matter of selecting a judge for this very important event; in this way the opinion could be reached of a very large number of any particular breed and any judge thus appointed could hardly be criticized, except by some disappointed exhibitor.

W. H. Shepard,
Secretary, Great Dane Club of America

The Judges for the World's Colombian Exhibition's Bench Shows
"The American Field"
1893

EDITOR—The situation as to the selection of judges at the World's Fair dog show was evidently too much for the capacity of Mr. Harry L. Goodman's conception.

The World's Fair is not a local show at Nashville, Tennessee; it is an international affair. It is not the question of how "many" dogs will be shown, but how great is the quality and merit of the dogs shown. Mr. Goodman may promise a bigger entry, but he cannot promise an entry of merit for an international show, judging by what I saw from his kennels at the Philadelphia show. Such ideas as having the leading kennels in American may do for Nashville, but I have no reason to doubt that this Nashville kennel will not be in the running with the English and German kennels, which will certainly come over if Mr. G. Muss-Arnolt judges, and I think here is Mr. Goodman's point—under Mr. Raper and Mr. Mason, German competition will be very small; under Mr. Muss-Arnolt it will certainly be large. If this supposition is not correct then there is but one conclusion left and that is a grudge of Mr. Goodman against Mr. Arnolt because the latter justly downed Melac in competition to Wenzel.

Oscar Beck

EDITOR—Mr. Harry Goodman calls upon intending Great Dane exhibitors at the World's Fair dog show to come out and state what reasons they have against Messrs. C. H. Mason, George Raper and John Davidson as judges for Great Danes. Now why does Mr. Goodman not lead us with a good example and state what he has to say against Mr. G. Muss-Arnolt as a judge and as a man? The fact that a judge does not like a certain dog does not disqualify that man from judging at the World's Fair.

My individual interest as a breeder and importer of Great Danes would demand just exactly the same action as Mr. Goodman has taken in denouncing Mr. G. Muss-Arnolt as a judge. I, too, would prefer Mr. Mason or Mr. Raper, or best of all, Mr. Mortimer, because the Hepburn Kennels easily won first under two of the above judges, where they could only get a third under Mr. Muss-Arnolt. But to lower myself so far as to attempt to run a man out because he does not like my dog has never entered my mind. I have imported just such stock as Mr. Mortimer, Mr. Raper, Mr. Mason and other judges with Mastiff ideas for a Great Dane seem to desire, but when I once import a real Great Dane of German fame and breeding, I would rather show him under Mr. Muss-Arnolt. The more such dogs as the grand Cesar Hansa, imported by Mr. Mortimer, come here, the faster the judgment of John Davidson, Mr. Muss-Arnolt and Dr. Shepard will be proven as the correct idea. And when Mr. Bernheimer and myself have procured leading specimens of both strains, heavy and light, we will show them and let public tests decide which is to be preferred.

A. H. Heppner

Dane ever owned in this country—such a close second at Chicago this spring, so that some reports thought she should have beaten the old bitch under the conditions? And yet he designates her a watch charm! Charming she is, no doubt, and watching she does also, I suppose. Why I put her and Wenzel first was my desire to check the tendency to promulgate the English craze for enormous "cripples," as it would be absolutely ruinous to the breed and besides ridiculous to foster a third breed of shuffling, dragging, sloughing, big cripples, like most St. Bernards and Mastiffs are, and which is plainly demonstrated in dogs like his Hepbern Vera,

G. Muss-Arnolt on *The World's Fair Dog Show Judging Appointment*
"The American Field"
1893

EDITOR—I am awfully sorry I cost some men who own Great Danes so much trouble and your paper so much space, as the whole matter emanates only from a selfish desire. Mr. Goodman ought not to pose as a defender of the Great Dane in such an authoritative style, for where did he get his knowledge of them? From being employed to show a dog, Melac, good enough as long as nothing better is shown, and as regards body a very superior specimen; but every cur on the street has this as a rule, good body and legs, etc. But the breed and type of any race is, to my incompetent mind (as the writers assert), determined by the superiority of an animal's head and tail, and I am not in the least afraid of having to disagree with a number of other judges, whose principal knowledge is attained from having been judging this same dog, and no doubt sincerely and at most times in default of something better, correctly judged this breed, which their profession of all-round judges compelled them to judge, if they knew much or not. Of course, Mr. Goodman has the absolute right to express his ideas; but he is allowing himself rather much, by pronouncing me, just like Mr. Maenner, because their dogs did not win under me, incompetent. Mr. Mortimer, no better judge than the all-round, has differed with me, no doubt, so have I with him, when I put that immense calf, McKinley, with his weak hindquarters and block-chopped head, in the same place, VHC, and if Mr. Mortimer was not Mr. Mortimer, with his reputation, in most instances justly, so exalted that he hardly cannot do wrong, neither Mr. Goodman nor his associates would have opened their mouths and fought behind his broad back. I am a warm admirer of Mr. Mortimer personally and as a judge of most breeds, but it is an audacity to assert that he or anybody else can be up in all breeds.

Why is Mr. Goodman afraid to have his dog's photograph reproduced side by side with the dog I consider a better all-round specimen? He has not sent me the photographs I have asked him to send me for this purpose, and as he promised to do, so everybody could decide without so much wrangling. Because Mr. Goodman has a business interest to have his dogs win, does not prove that they are the correct type.

I never had a thought of or any connection with my name being put on the proposed list of World's Fair judges, and it was as much a surprise to me as anybody else; I do not care for it either, the show being bound to be a failure by the grab-all principle which has brought on this public judgeship wrangle.

G. Muss-Arnolt

Major McKinley
1893

Heppner declares I want a "Greyhound-Great Dane!" How does he know that? Because I put two round dogs, which were accidentally, or better naturally, no giants, at the head of their classes? What did he do in Chicago in 1892, which maiden effort of his he so often describes as having stood "in a howling mob, almost afraid for his life, and demonstrated why he put small, typical dogs over big brutes!" But as he has neglected to take out a copyright for this, his phenomenal performance, he must permit others to follow their own judgment unembarrassed by his solitary effort in this direction, as his subsequent judging in Brooklyn in 1892, where he beat a very fair all-round bitch, Podyn's Nora, by the then butcher-dog-like Melac, and also putting a not absolutely untypical, but absolutely coarse specimen like Yarrum, as his selection at Newark, makes his object lesson of Chicago appear of very little consistent value. Yarrum, his last choice, should never appear in public without skates on his hindfeet, as an excuse for his movement. Major McKinley is a grand dog in comparison with Melac and Yarrum, and Mr. Heppner's reference to my passing him like smallpox is funny, too, as I gave him the blue in his class and beat him for the special by his own litter sister. Very inconsistent and queer that, is it? I don't think so, especially not when I remember his own criticism of

Earl of Würtemburg, Count Frederick, Major McKinley, Stanley or his latest effort in judging—the Newark winner—Yarrum.

Portia Melac and Wenzel are both round dogs and fairly typical, but of course not so hypertypical as Earl of Würtemburg, but either could have run rings around the Earl or Hepbern Vera, and that is what the Great Dane in Germany is, active and sound on his pins as a terrier, except he is, here or there, a kennel-raised

> *"A judge for Great Danes must be an educator or he is of no value for us,*
> *for there are too few who really do know what is at issue;*
> *if they did some diatribes would be cut shorter."*

size premium, as Mr. Heppner seems to foster now. How little it is of Mr. Heppner to denounce me, as claiming honors where they are not due, etc., in regard to my statement of Hepbern Vera as a brood bitch. He must of course have read my report of Great Danes at the Baltimore show, printed in a contemporary, March 16, 1893, where I said of her, "She (Vera) would do her owners better service as a matron than on the bench," but it was useful to him and he ignored this. Mr.

Major McKinley at the Philadelphia show, where he beat his flatheaded, though of good type and excellent body and quarters, but Dachshund fronted, Hepburn Hero. There he was only a big calf, with a pig's head and too weak to lift his hindlegs from the ground, cut out of wood, and what else, this and sundry other remarks about Mr. Mortimer, the judge at Philadelphia, "how ruinous his ideas were to the breed," etc. But then, Mr. Heppner's dog was beaten by McKinley

35

and now he owns no competitors; otherwise both dogs are relatively now as they were then at Philadelphia in 1893. Mr. Heppner's correct perception of typical specimens like Hepburn Vera and Earl of Würtemburg which, when both were so weak in hindquarters at the Westminster show in 1893 that they could not lift their hindlegs off the ground and he took Vera away right after judging, because she was so weak, would ruin this, the only big breed, which is, or ought to be, sound and active, standard size as granted. Yes, the Earl and Vera were the best specimens at the show, as long as they remained stock still, but their dragging, shuffling, cow-hocked hindlegs were enough for the worst Mastiff or St. Bernard one sees so often. A judge for Great Danes must be an educator or he is of no value for us, for there are too few who really do know what is at issue; if they did some diatribes would be cut shorter.

G. Muss-Arnolt

OSCEOLA NEVERZELL
Artist, G. Muss-Arnolt
1892

...One More Letter to "The American Field"—1893

G. Muss-Arnolt described Neverzell as, "the highest class Great Dane ever owned in this country."
Her owner wrote the following letter in response to reading a show reporter's negative description of her.

EDITOR—I always was of the opinion that I knew what constitutes a good Great Dane, but I see that I can learn something from your reporter of the Chicago show. To be candid, I must say the gentleman has either looked the class over very lightly or he does not know a Great Dane. I agree with your reporter in general, but cannot see how he could overlook the throatiness of Major McKinley, winner of first in Open Class; besides, Major is weak behind, but will outgrow it. Prince Victor, winner of second in Open Class, is given a good head by your reporter when, indeed, the head is the most faulty part of the dog. His head is cheeky, has too deep a stop and too much skin under the throat, while the body is A No. 1. Had he McKinley's head I should like him far better than the winner. Neverzell, winner of first in Open Bitches, shows age according to your reporter. She is four and three-fourths years now and I hardly believe that your reporter has seen her before. Could he see her here on a hundred acre lot, chasing rabbits, he would think she showed youth. Where her supposed throatiness comes in I cannot see; if not the cleanest, she is certainly one of the cleanest Great Danes in America today. Major McKinley and Victor are not reported as throaty while Neverzell is—this opinion ought to be reversed. I know very well the shortcomings of my bitch, and I am convinced she was lying in her stall and looked drowsy (hence old age). Had she been properly led before your reporter, he ought to have seen that her tail is too long and that it is not carried correctly, and that she is a little too low behind the shoulders. I do not wish to have any controversy with either the owners of the above dogs or your reporter, but I have bred Great Danes for ten years, and I looked the winners at the Chicago show over very closely during four long, long days, and I must say it hurts me when I find the prize winners so wrongly criticized.

Gustav Hansen

Questions for Consideration

1. After a well-known Great Dane breeder criticized him for his choices (putting up smaller specimens) when judging in Chicago, Heppner states he purposefully chose a larger, coarse dog when judging in Newark and was surprised that his critic did not endorse that decision, either. How should judges respond to criticism of their judging, especially when it comes from knowledgeable breeders?

2. Heppner states that type is size in this breed. Can particular breed type be consolidated into one key element? Is type breed specific?

3. Heppner feels that in breeding for size and substance the judge must make allowances for coarseness. Do you agree or disagree? Is it possible to breed typical dogs of great size with soundness and elegance?

4. Heppner criticizes Messrs. Lawrence and Muss-Arnolt for only concentrating on certain traits rather than the total dog in their breeding programs. Is it possible to fix more than one trait at a time?

5. Does Mr. Heppner have the same prioritization system for evaluating Great Danes as Mr. Muss-Arnolt? Where do they differ?

6. If Muss-Arnolt believed that type was the most important consideration in judging, why was he so concerned about selecting dogs which were sound? Is soundness a consideration of type when judging a breed or is it a separate entity?

7. Allowing for the fact that more than 100 years have elapsed since the decision in question was made, and that you only have one photograph for your evaluation, with whose assessment are you in most agreement regarding the dog, Wenzel—Heppner or Muss-Arnolt? Elaborate upon your reasons.

8. Over 100 years ago, it appears that color was an issue in evaluating Great Danes. To the best of your knowledge, is color still an issue in this breed today? Why or why not?

9. Based upon your knowledge and observations of Great Danes, would you say the breed today is more akin to the type Heppner promulgated or that desired by Muss-Arnolt? Give specific examples.

10. Although specialist clubs in Great Britain keep lists of club approved judges for their particular breeds, it is not done in America. Should kennel clubs be encouraged to seek the advice of the parent clubs in making their selections for judges? How does Dr. Shepard's viewpoint compare with that of Harding Cox on the same subject?

11. Does Mr. Hansen's analysis of his bitch Neverzell seem accurate? How much credence should be given to published reports of dogs in competition written by persons other than the judge?

12. Mr. Hansen stated that had the reporter seen his bitch at her own home his opinion of her would be entirely different. Is the dog show always the best forum for analyzing the true character of a particular dog? How important is showmanship?

13. Our current system does not allow judges to openly criticize each others decisions in the press. Do you feel this would be helpful to understanding what each judge's priorities are in different breeds? Is a system of gossip and innuendo better than a system of allowing judges to write opinions of specific dogs? Do you feel exhibitors today would want their dogs as critically and publically analyzed as occurred in these letters?

Criticism

"Popular Dogs"
1938

On the whole, American exhibitors are a grand lot of good, clean sportsmen who not only "play the game" but benefit the game. Big and little fellows alike, they show their dogs fearlessly under any and all judges—no matter how formidable the competition, how far the distance to be traveled or how great the expense entailed. They accept the decisions made in the ring with admirable spirit, and they abide by the rules without grumbling. Their enthusiastic participation in shows and their keen support of all purebred dog interests, with little thought of personal profit, are the real reasons for the amazing growth we have enjoyed in every activity of the American dog world.

But when it comes to criticism of their dogs in print, whether the offending reference be found in a judge's critique or the writing of a breed or show reporter, American exhibitors must yield a point to the English.

As proof that our friends overseas can take it, one has only to read their show reviews. Over there reporters and judges are free to call a spade a spade and do not hesitate to do so; their criticisms have the benefit of being impersonally made and impersonally accepted by those concerned. The English well know (as we do if we would only admit it) that the makeup of every dog—even one's own—

Smooth Fox Terrier
DAME FORTUNE
Artist, Arthur Wardle, 1895

includes points both good and bad; and since the purpose of dog shows is the comparison of each entrant's qualities with those of his competitors, they believe that a carefully weighed estimate of these points arrived at in public by the judge should also be passed on through the press to those of the fancy who may not have been present at the show. Dogs competing at shows are in the public eye; if they are out at shoulders, bad in feet, long in body when they shouldn't be, these items are mentioned along with their good points, not with intent to down the dog or its exhibitor but for the good of the game, and especially its breeding phase in which Britain has long excelled.

Not so in America—far from it! Our exhibitors don't like published criticism of their dogs, even though they know the critic to be an intelligent, well meaning person whose opinions are of value to the fancy, even though they know the statement to be perfectly true and justified; and to print any uncomplimentary reference to the pride of their kennel is a sure way of incurring their wrath. Every American kennel publication receives its share of letters to the editor pointing out in no uncertain terms the awful injustice done by some such remark in its columns. They usually end in this wise: "Cancel my subscription," or, "Take out my

Critical Analysis

Americans tend to think of criticism as a negative concept but, at its best, the critique gives both positive and negative commentary with insights into the judging process. Specifically, knowledgeable, honest, written assessments are particularly informative to analyze dogs of the past and present, further amplifying and helping interpret photographs and artists renderings of famous winners.

LYONS STING

Excerpts from the Judge's Report—Fox Terrier Club Show
Judge (Smooths) Mr. J. B. Dale
"The Kennel Gazette"
1894

I daresay most judges go to a show with some sort of idea that such and such a dog or bitch will win pretty easily, and I certainly expected that Venio and that lovely bitch Lyons Sting would head their respective classes, and was extremely surprised when I saw them, especially the latter, as she is quite young, and her fault simply lay in the fact that she was pig-fat and showed listlessly and badly, never once getting her tail up or standing well in the ring that I could see. It was therefore a great disappointment to me to have to give her her first "put back," I believe. However, I am sure her owner will take care that the next time she appears in public she will be in form, when I feel sure she will be placed in front again.

Apropos of big terriers winning, a good deal has lately been written; but it is one thing to write about it and another to judge them, as when it comes to the point, I fancy most judges (as I do) find it extremely hard to get away from a really good big one.

In the Bitch Classes, I was introduced to a real flyer, but I will speak of her later on. The Open Bitch Class contained four wonderful ladies. Meifod Molly I consider won fairly comfortably. A lovely terrier, with hardly any faults; full of life and fire, and I like her head and expression although one gentleman afterwards told me she was the worst in the class. However, I thought otherwise. Chumleigh Topsy is a wonderful sort, and hard to pass over. She is a very masculine bitch, and one I should like to breed from. Mr. Raper's Greno Jewel is another very high-class terrier, but wanting a little in character, and a shade high on the leg. Many more good bitches were shown, amongst which Mr. Raper's Richmond Sanctum and Mr. Hargreave's Dame Gallantry were the best, but of rather different type. The former excels in quality and style, and the latter is a grand stamp of bitch, with a long punishing head, good bone, legs, and feet and a hard coat. Her marking is too heavy which somewhat detracts from her general appearance. Anyhow, she is a good one.

In her class Dame Fortune won hands down. I cannot speak too highly of her, and when I say that to my mind, barring being a shade full in cheek, and lacking a little more marking, which at first sight is apt to give an impression that her expression is not altogether what it might be, she is absolutely perfect, I mean to say a good deal. She has the most extraordinary legs and feet I ever saw, and the quality and roundness of bone is marvellous. She is also faultless in body, size, set on of tail, shoulders and neck, and her head is a great length with her ears right size and well carried. She afterwards beat Vice Regal for the Challenge Cup. He only beat her a little in head and expression and a trifle in coat; but she smothered him in legs and feet, size and type.

Show Reports

Mrs. Neville Lytton
"Toy Dogs and Their Ancestors"
1911

I wish the editors of newspapers would institute a reform in their show reports. How often have I heard it said: "Oh, Mrs. So-and-so, I am so dreadfully busy, and you know I am not a specialist in your breed, just write my notes for me, will you, and I'll forgive you anything you say about your own dogs."

Mrs. So-and-so is, of course, delighted, and instead of being put on her mettle to be extra generous to her opponents, she writes a flaming account of her own exhibits and runs down those of anybody against whom she has a grudge. The reporter rushes up, stuffs the reports into his pocket with effusive thanks, and publishes them with his own name, without having time or opportunity to verify them by personal examination of the dogs, and as he can't acknowledge what he has done, he stands by them in public afterwards because he can't help himself. Should he be brought to book for some downright misstatement he can always apologize and say he mistook one dog for another. The press is much imposed upon by some of these professional trumpeters. Occasionally they sign their names to the reports of the classes at which they themselves have been exhibiting and do not blush to run down their opponents' dogs and praise their own in unmeasured and perfectly unwarrantable terms. The ladies who sign their reports are, however, in a minority. An excellent trumpeter of my acquaintance writes anonymous reports of her own dogs at all the important shows, and most wonderful they are. If her dogs lose, the lady "cannot follow the placing," and writes a panegyric of the losers; if they win, they have won in the strongest company ever got together.

I have occasionally written official reports myself. In spite of the fact that I have expressly stated that I would not write unsigned reports, my signed reports have twice been altered and the signature suppressed, and so long as this is done it is hopeless to expect any independence of criticism. I know that it is very difficult to be strictly impartial. An acquaintance, possibly someone who is going to judge your own dogs shortly, comes up and says, "You won't mention Jacky's defect of action, will you? Give me a good report and I shan't forget it." To harden one's heart and say firmly that Jacky is not sound requires considerable determination, and sometimes entails a VHC card instead of a championship for one's most valued dog at his next public appearance. These, however, are the natural risks of reporting. Reporters should make up their minds whether they can bear the onus before accepting their official responsibilities, but to be coaxed or bullied into betraying the trust is unpardonable. I notice that whenever a judge has made more than the usual hash of his classes and the exhibitors are angry enough to lynch him, the reporter always mentions in print that, "the awards gave general satisfaction." This is so invariable that I generally can tell how the awards have gone before I look at the list, and it has always appeared to me an absurd farce.

My parting exhortation to reporters is, "Speak the truth and shame the devil." Write your own reports, and don't try to pat every dog on the back, and always sign your name in full.

advertisement," or, "I never want to read your paper again," or, "I demand you publish an apology." Sometimes the offended one will even round up his friends to contribute their opinion on the matter via the mailbag. In one case, we remember, a writer said a certain dog could have been shown in better condition. Now that certainly was no cardinal condemnation, but it netted up nine or ten letters, each one pages long, from the owner and his confreres. And later, their ire or their interest in the situation having died down, the majority of these folk thanked us for not publishing scathing communications whose appearance in print over their signatures they had previously insisted on.

A well-known member of our exhibiting fraternity recently summed up his difference of attitude between the Americans and British thusly: "The Americans are dog lovers and the English are dog fanciers." There you have it. That's why we can't take criticism and they can; that's why editors in this country are on occasion asked to enforce a muzzling procedure out of keeping with American ideals. Our dogs and their records are almost too much a part of us. We resent making public anything but praise of them just as we resent making public anything but praise of ourselves or our children.

This love of dogs is an excellent thing—don't doubt that. But if it could only be combined with the fancier spirit, then would criticism point the way to improvement and progressive breeding rather than indignation; and greater would be the game and the sportsmanship of those who take part in it in all other respects as true "good sports."

Questions for Consideration

1. Are written critiques of dogs in competition useful? Should they be encouraged?

2. Is the refusal to publish or encourage open discussion, frank critiques and rational discourse of any dog entered in public competition anti-American as the writer asserts?

3. Do you feel most judges are capable of giving accurate, meaningful critiques? Do you believe most judges want to be able to give critiques?

4. Is there any correlation between the decline of written critiques at American dog shows and the rise of the professional handler as an integral part of the sport in this country?

5. Do American exhibitors want to either hear or read critiques of their dogs? Why or why not?

6. What is the difference between a dog lover and a dog fancier?

7. How valid are show reports written by other than the officiating judge?

8. From reading Judge Dale's critique, can you determine his priorities in judging Fox Terriers? For example, is condition important to him? How does he feel about big Fox Terriers? Does he like doggy bitches?

9. Because of his familiarity with the breed, Mr. Dale admitted that he thought he knew which dogs would win before he ever entered the ring. Do you feel this is a common occurrence among most judges?

10. How would you evaluate Mr. Dale's handling of the disgruntled exhibitor? Does it appear that Dale had confidence in his decisions? How should judges deal with exhibitors who verbally dispute their decisions?

11. Compare Dale's critique of Dame Fortune with the painting of her by Wardle. Do you feel both the written and visual descriptions of this dog are in agreement? If not, where do they differ?

Making a Statement in the Ring

Sydney H. Deacon

"Show Bulldogs"
c. 1919

CHAMPION GUIDO
Owned by Mr. J. H. Ellis
Born 1889
Breeder, J. Billingham

Champion Guido, the property of that genial fancier the late Mr. Jack Ellis, was a grand-headed dog, but he was not of the low, cloddy type, being rather stilty in shoulders and lacking spring of ribs, besides having plenty of daylight under him. It was a big blow to his owner when Mr. Richards, at the South London Bulldog Society Show in 1894, left him out of the money in the Open Class; but it was purely a question of the low, thick-set sort being in front of those with grand heads but lacking the necessary lowness to ground and massive formation. Mr. Richards at the time came in for a lot of criticism, as he stuck religiously right through his judging to ignoring dogs that were leggy or lightly built. In consequence, there were some of the winners that possessed faces distinctly "off." I recollect I showed a splendid-headed dog that did not possess the necessary substance, and felt at the time very disappointed as I walked round the benches and compared his head with some of the winners; but the judging at this show, in my opinion, had a big influence on the breed, and although it was a very drastic proceeding, it may have been that at that period the end justified the means. We have at the present time to a large extent assimilated the two types, and there is no necessity to judge on these drastic lines; but things were different then. Besides, it was pretty certain that the adherents of the perfect head at any price would have their innings at some future show.

Questions for Consideration

1. Should a judge worry about possible criticism when making his/her decisions?

2. What is the role of the judge when faced with dogs possessing desirable qualities but divergence in type?

3. Under the circumstances, can Mr. Richard's judging be justified? Does it appear he was fault judging?

4. On any given day does your judging have an influence on the breed you are evaluating?

The Greed of Gold
"Britisher"

"Field and Fancy"
1905

Disgraceful Scenes at the London Bulldog Society's Show

Referring to the unseemly conduct of an old Bulldog exhibitor and judge at the above show, as the names have now been made public property there can be no objection to my handling the matter openly. The offending party is Mr. W. H. Ford, who, in whatever branch of life

Champion Woodcote Sally Lunn over Mr. Ford's Champion Lady Paget.

In parenthesis I may remark that they are a couple of *pretty* champions to make a fuss over. There were over half a dozen bitches in the show which could give them many points and a beating, and the general opinion of fanciers is that both bitches have been more than lucky in being

George W. Richards, the judge mentioned in both this and the previous article, was one of the earliest Bulldog fanciers, actively involved in the development of the breed. He was imprinted at an early age by what he felt was the greatest Bulldog that ever lived, Ch. Crib, sometimes referred to as "Sheffield Crib," the "father" of the modern Bulldog. Richards admittedly compared every Bulldog he ever saw or judged to this exemplary animal. This fixed vision of what he determined was the ideal Bulldog allowed him to be uncompromisingly consistent in his judging. He demanded that his winners have substance and also be vigorous, strong and active. Although many people did not always agree with his choices, he was, nevertheless, highly respected and a frequent judge.

In his reminiscences of over forty years, Richards felt that excepting certain remarkable individuals, the modern Bulldogs were, as a whole, greatly improved over those of an earlier day. He attributed this improvement to superior nutrition, emphasis in the judging ring on soundness and activity and to the fact that every Bulldog in England, for many generations, was a direct descendent of Ch. Sheffield Crib.

his want of education might excuse him, cannot certainly bring this forward as an excuse for misbehavior in Bulldog matters. Mr. Ford has been judging Bulldogs for years; has been a committee man of the Bulldog Club for years, and his show experience must extend for fully twenty or twenty-five years. Surely long enough to teach any man how to behave! The trouble arose through Mr. Richards placing Mr. Pegg's

made champions. Woodcote Sally Lunn is absolutely devoid of turn-up, her underjaw being quite straight. Her face is somewhat wry and she has one of the worst swamp backs one ever saw. Behind her shoulders she dips into almost a semicircle. She is through these defects certainly not a show bitch in any sense of the word. She might possibly breed some good puppies, but I doubt if the tendency that must exist to reproduce such

Judging Pictures

In an extraordinary article in H. St. John Cooper's book, "Bulldogs and Bulldog Men," G. W. Richards clearly points out the error of coming to conclusions about any dogs of a previous age based only upon a photograph or work of art. The engraving of Crib (see page 5) was created from a photograph about which Richards says, "The best known portrait of him is that in which he was photographed lying on a small table with his head between his paws, but this picture really gives no idea of what the dog was really like, as my readers will understand when I tell them that it was taken only a few hours before he was destroyed after a long and wasting illness."

Although we might find the practice morbid, it was not uncommon in the Victorian era to keep either the skeletons or stuffed remains of famous dogs for display and study. After viewing the taxidermist's disappointing interpretation of his beloved favorite, Richards said, "I am fully aware that many present day Bulldog men who never saw the old dog are inclined to regard these poor remains with a certain amount of contempt. Even less than the portrait I have previously alluded to does this stuffed specimen convey an idea of what the dog was like...Unfortunately, the modern Bulldog man cannot, and will never, know what a really wonderful dog old "Sheffield Crib" was...It sometimes amuses me to hear the modern Bulldog man speak with almost bated breath of an old-time Champion whose qualities he has judged only from engravings, or possibly oil paintings. Photography in those days was, of course, not practised as it is now—it was in the early "wet-plate" stage of its existence, which meant extremely slow exposures, and therefore unsuitability for making portraits of dogs. So, the only pictorial records of some of these Champions are those of the artist or engraver, who usually grossly exaggerated his subject and produced a dog as unlike the original as cheese is unlike chalk."

The problem of slow camera exposures leaves us with a lot of photographs which were taken of dogs half-asleep on their benches and others which were heavily retouched to correct a blurry image. Certainly, while some pictorial record is better than none, it is difficult to form conclusions regarding a particular dog's true quality and character from such scant evidence. This is the case in the photo below of the Bulldog, Ch. Bedgebury Lion. Fortunately, because there were many sketch artists at the shows, some of their original drawings still exist. The charming pencil sketch of Lion was created by Richard H. Voss. Only 11 years old at the time, his shortcomings in draftsmanship can be readily forgiven. Nevertheless, this is clearly the same dog. We can better evaluate his overall head properties and, obviously, see at least one interpretation of the complete dog, something not visible in the photograph.

Bedgebury Lion.
The property of Mr. P. Beresford Hope.

In combination with photography, the advent of dog shows and field trials as popular pastimes led to one of the biggest changes in depicting the canine image—the "invention" of the posed, or static, dog. The photograph of the English Setter, Breeze Gladstone, appeared in "The American Field" in 1893. This weekly paper was one of the few which could afford to print half-tone images on a regular basis. However, for those wishing to showcase their dogs in other magazines, drawings or engravings had to be commissioned. The ink drawing on the right above is of the same dog and it was obviously traced from the original photograph. But, the unknown artist, in changing the vantage point, had to shorten the dog's legs and neck to do so, making the rendering an even more lifeless version than the photograph which shows the dog, not in the fever-pitch of hunting, but probably simply put on a stay command in the field, to pose for the camera. The accuracy of any artistic depiction is completely dependent on the skill and vision of the artist. Thus, in formulating conclusions, one must remember that artists have a tendency to draw what they see—not necessarily what is there. An unknown artist drew the Pointer, Earl of Kent, on the lower left, and G. Muss-Arnolt rendered the older dog, Lad of Kent, on the right, in 1892. Muss-Arnolt's drawing has the notation, "from life" written on it and he probably made many such sketches of dogs in the ring or in the field, adding the ink back in his studio.

While Muss-Arnolt was criticized by many sportsmen for "glamorizing" his field dogs, he consistently tried to show specific dogs at their best but never eliminated any of their faults. By comparison, the primitive quality of the Earl of Kent drawing gives only a general idea of the dog's conformation and it is doubtful he had a triple-jointed pastern as shown. The knowledge of correct canine anatomy, the understanding of the various breed standards and technical mastery as artists put such people as G. Muss-Arnolt and R. H. Moore in a class by themselves when it came to accurately depicting the dogs of their day.

Judging Pictures—Judging Words

Compare the illustrations and photograph to the written critiques of each dog. Are they in agreement? Are some artists more accurate than others? Conversely, assuming the artwork or the photo to be correct depictions, are some written evaluations more useful than others? Keeping in mind that those who wrote the critiques actually saw the live dogs, how would you critique these dogs based only upon what you can determine from the static image? Is it possible to correctly evaluate a dog based only upon a picture?

ORMSKIRK AMAZEMENT *has wonderful quality, combined with good bone and substance, being built more on the lines of a workman than of a show dog. He is slightly pig-jawed, which probably handicaps him somewhat under some judges, although the Collie Club has never declared this to be a fault. He stands 24 inches at the shoulder, and his head, which measures 10.5 inches in length, is beautifully modeled. He has a nice eye, and ears as perfect as need be, a capital body, good legs and feet, and a splendid coat of the correct texture.*

"Canine World"
1890

MERLIN *(Irish Wolfhound). The competition in the Dog Class lay entirely between Capt. Graham's Dhulart and Col. Arnier's puppy, Merlin, the latter is by far the larger of the pair, and stands, I should say, fully three inches higher. Some people thought he should have won outright instead of being second, and, no doubt, it is fairly a matter of opinion. That he will beat the winner in six months' time should they meet again is I think certain provided of course he goes on all right in the interval. He is a very fine puppy of the Deerhound type, with good shoulders,*

legs and feet. Like so many big dogs he is rather cow-hocked, and wants making up in body, and I should like him with more bone, in this respect Dhulart beats him very easily and has also the better head.

Report of The Kennel Club Show—Islington
"The Kennel Gazette"
1888

Judging Pictures—Judging Words

KRILUTT was alone in the Challenge Class. The best of the breed I have seen, and I have critically examined all, or very nearly every Borzoi that has ever been exhibited in England. I consider him almost perfection of combined grace and power. He measures well in height, breadth, and girth, making a compact whole, much bigger than he looks. The head is perfection. I understand Russian gentlemen prefer a dog narrower at the base of the skull but a dog narrow there must be weak in head physically and lacking in neck. Krilutt's neck is long and flexible; the shoulders well placed,

legs clean, stifles fairly bent, and short from the back, with very good feet, compact, although not so sound or with the toes so well sprung as in our English Greyhounds. His back is beautifully arched, the loins strong, and the sloping quarters hard and powerful. The deep brisket "sided like a bream" moving upward from its lowest point toward the loin, gives finish to a beautiful shape. If he is at all out at elbows, it is but a trifle, and I could not detect it in his movements. He is very taking in color and I see nothing wrong with his coat and feather, which the latter at least is, after all, a comparatively trifling accessory. Krilutt was shown in splendid condition, the muscles standing out, and hard and firm to the touch.

Hugh Dalziel
"Canine World"
1890

DUKE WADSWORTH, (St. Bernard), first, is a fine, upstanding dog with a good skull, eye and expression, excellent front legs and feet, a lengthy body, which should be better sprung in rib, and good action; he might have a little more depth and substance before the eye and could be shown to advantage with more flesh.

Report of the Chicago Show
"The American Field"
1897

Judge for Yourself

Before Mr. Pegg dispersed his kennels in 1906, subsequently offering his homebred Ch. Woodcote Sally Lunn for sale at $1,500, she had amassed an impressive show record in Great Britain including eight championships. Not everyone agreed with the scathing critique of her given by "Britisher." One such person who took him to task in print was H. St. John Cooper. As you will discover in another article in this book it appears that Cooper was considerably more gallant in coming to the defense of a maligned Bull bitch than that of a woman judge.

Based upon your observations of this photograph, would you say that her underjaw is "absolutely devoid of turn-up?" Does it appear straight to you? Does her face appear "somewhat wry?" We cannot accurately assess this bitch's topline from the given vantage point. However, from your experience, would you say she has a stance typical of a dog with "one of the worst swamp backs one ever saw?" Although it is impossible for us to have exacting knowledge of all of her contemporary competitors, would you say that this bitch was "more than lucky" in being made a champion? "More than lucky" seems a rather ambiguous term. Do you think the writer was implying the judge was either dishonest or incompetent (or both)? In your opinion, does this bitch have any outstanding features? Write your own critique of Ch. Woodcote Sally Lunn.

The Dogs of the Day
H. St. John Cooper

"Field and Fancy"
1906

Mr. Pegg has undoubtedly the strongest kennel of bitches in England, and at the head and front of it is that grand Swashbuckler-bred bitch, Champion Woodcote Sally Lunn. It is

CH. WOODCOTE SALLY LUNN
1906

not my purpose in this rambling article to run a tilt at any other writer on Bulldogs, but a grave injustice was done to this fine bitch not long ago by a writer who described her as being wry-faced. There is not one grain of truth in this assertion, and in charity I can only suppose that the maker of the statement mistook some other for Woodcote Sally Lunn, or, failing that, he must have regarded the bitch with such a warped mind that she appeared to him to be wry-faced. The illustration of her that appears in these pages is taken from a hand camera snapshot photograph I made on the grounds of the Eastbourne show, and while certainly photography can be made to lie like the truth, there can be no lies about a photograph taken under such circumstances, as this gives a very fair idea of Sally Lunn as she really is—a very representative and typical bitch, good practically all through, the possession of which her breeder, Mr. Pegg, is to be congratulated.

faults would not justify one in discarding such from a kennel of brood bitches. She is not devoid of good qualities, having a nice, long square skull and a well filled up face. She is also low and good fronted. But we do want soundness in our dogs, and can one with such terrible curvature of the spine be considered sound?

Lady Paget is quite another sort. She has a very decent body and front, but her hindquarters are too high and she moves badly behind. She has a small head and a plain face, closely approaching a down face—truly a delightful sort of champion! With all this she is a better one than Woodcote Sally Lunn. At the present moment I will not enter into a description or detail the bitches which can beat the two in question. There were plenty at the show, and there are scores in the country, but time and space will not admit of further reference to them now.

Well, to get back to the disturbance created by Mr. Ford. He firstly abused Mr. Richards, the judge, and to such an extent that Mr. Richards has placed the matter before the Kennel Club. The London Bulldog Society has also taken the matter up. Mr. Ford's next point of effrontery was against Mr. W. Richardson—a man who is highly respected by everyone who knows him. Mr. Ford was raving so much about Lady Paget's being placed second, and Mr. Richardson quietly remarked that, "A man who placed Cambridge Heath Crib over Champion Pressgang should never comment on anything another judge does or may do." (Mr. Ford had previously done this, and Cambridge Heath Crib was not even a good third rater). Mr. Ford, using the most foul language imaginable, not only threatened Mr. Richardson, but assaulted him by tearing open his waistcoat. Mr. Richardson, a very powerful man, refrained from chastising Mr. Ford in the manner he deserved, and Mr. Ford can at least congratulate himself on escaping what would easily have been a terrible mauling.

Questions for Consideration

1. Under what circumstances, if any, should judges ever comment on the decisions of other judges?

2. In the grand scheme of things, how important is a win at a show on any particular day?

3. Although we don't have a picture of Ch. Lady Paget available for comparison, do you think she could possibly have been such a terrible representative of the breed as the reporter asserts? What would be a possible explanation for this type of blistering reportage? Do you feel that the dogs or the judge were the actual target of the writer's criticism in this case?

4. If it is not always possible to come to accurate conclusions based only upon pictorial representations of dogs, should the same be said regarding written descriptions?

5. What is the difference, both in implementation and results, of judging dogs against the concept of the ideal as described in a breed standard or against the qualities of an exemplary representative of the breed, not in the ring, but alive within the mind of the judge? Can an actual dog ever be the embodiment of the ideal in all respects?

6. Despite great technical improvements, how much stock should be put on the determination of quality of today's dogs based only upon their show photographs?

7. Because written critiques are now almost non-existent, and considering most owners only rely on still photography as a record of their dogs, how difficult will it be to accurately assess such animals at a future time based only upon these limited data?

8. What is sportsmanship?

Changing One's Mind in the Ring

"The French Bull Dog"
1913

The Westminster Kennel Club Show—the great national event in American dogdom—is an occasion to which all real doggie people always look forward to with the keenest anticipation, and every minute of its continuation enjoy with an intensity that those who do not share their love of dogs cannot sympathize with, and but faintly understand.

In French Bull Dogs the falling off of entries can mainly be accounted for because of the absence of entries from two of the largest kennels in America, namely the Noswal Kennels and the Never-Never Land Kennels. The reason for the absence of entries from the first named kennel is because its owner has recently disposed of her dogs, and Mrs. Mary Winthrop Turner being the judge this year, of course could not show her dogs. Mrs. Turner's kennels alone would have induced her to have made a larger entry this year than last had she not consented to judge. Her ten dogs entered for exhibition only were not included in the published list of entries. As it was, French Bull Dogs were exceeded by comparatively few other breeds, and in number and quality made an excellent showing.

EXCERPTS FROM THE JUDGE'S REPORT
MRS. MARY WINTHROP TURNER

OPEN DOGS, OVER 22 LBS.—This class brought out Ch. Gamin's Riquet. I know this dog well and outside of appreciating his great quality I am fond of him, for he is the litter brother to my Ch. Hunk's Bequest. If there had been any preference in my heart toward any dogs brought before me it would have been toward Riquet and Parsque, but I was asked to judge the dog not as a pet or with any regard for doggy politics or the owner, and I tried as hard as anyone ever did simply to do justice to the dogs. I did not go over Riquet and Fenway Frenchman so closely in this class, but judged them from a distance. I was greatly taken with Frenchman's general appearance of sturdiness, soundness, bone and muscle, and his alert attitude, being up and doing every minute, and was about to give the blue ribbon to him when Riquet posed finely for quite a few seconds, and from a little distance he can make himself look like a little statue, especially when he is intently looking for someone. At the moment, without again getting the dogs closer together, I awarded the first prize to Riquet and second to Fenway Frenchman. The first and second awards had no sooner been given than I felt I had made a mistake, for the little I had seen of Fenway Frenchman's head in particular, and body, I began to realize I liked him the better of the two. I thought it over carefully and decided that as I had undertaken the task of judging at the biggest, most important show of the year I must judge the dogs entirely as they appeared at the moment apart from my own feelings as regards their qualifications and as nearly as possible to the requirements of the Standard; not as I knew one of them in the home and by past performance and unbiased by opinions of others. I had never seen Fenway Frenchman and if there was any question of personal preference in my mind it was towards Riquet.

FENWAY FRENCHMAN

This photograph was taken at the 1913 Westminster Kennel Club show, when Frenchman was a comparatively young dog. At maturity he was reputed to be the soundest French Bulldog in America, possessing a flawless front and exceptionally short foreface.

CH. GAMIN'S RIQUET

This portrait is from a painting by Marguerite Kirmse. At the time of the 1913 Westminster show, AKC had recently ruled in another case that a judge could not immediately reverse in Winners the awards given in Open. However, the breeder/owner of Riquet, Mr. Grant Notman, was in an awkward position as he had sold a littermate, Ch. Hunk's Bequest, to Mrs. Turner. Consequently, because he did not protest the reversal, the award stood.

Winners Class, with others, brought before me again Fenway Frenchman (winner of the Limit and American-bred classes) and Gamin's Riquet. I had decided in my mind that no matter what opinion the fancy or the world generally might hold toward me, I would use all my care and knowledge in going over both dogs thoroughly a second time and would put the dog I considered the better at that moment, Winner, even if I had to reverse myself. In body both are about equal, Frenchman winning in bone, spring of rib and brisket. Although Frenchman is several pounds heavier than Riquet I feel that in proportion, were they the same weight, Frenchman would still have the advantage in these points. In hindquarters Frenchman is undoubtedly the better. In color, Frenchman is a rich, dark brindle, while Riquet is more of a silvery brindle, a color that I like, but we must remember our standard says regarding color, "dark brindle preferred." In

Mrs. Mary Winthrop Turner

In evaluating Mrs. Turner's performance as a judge at Westminster in 1913, one must take into account that by our qualification standards today she was clearly still a novice in many ways. Mrs. Turner acquired her first Frenchie in 1910 and upon attending her first dog show, Westminster, her pet "Ponto" was awarded a blue ribbon. Immediately thereafter she proceeded to build a modern state of the art kennel on Shelter Island and purchased dozens of winners from breeders in America and England. She made her judging debut in 1912 at the Toy Spaniel Club of America Show (at this time specialty clubs could hold classes for other breeds). She was then invited to judge the French Bulldog Club of England Show in October, 1912, the first woman and first American to do so. By 1913 she had over 90 dogs and 3 full time kennel employees. Her kennel manager's wife raised, what seems to us, an extraordinary amount of puppies, including a total of over 40 in June, 1913 alone. However, we must remember that most successful

breeders were forced to breed enormous quantities of dogs because so many would be lost to distemper before maturity. Mrs. Turner exhibited her dogs herself at practically all the major shows in America at the time. The apparent pressures from this extraordinary undertaking, combined with maintaining another home in New York City brought on a breakdown in April, 1913 from what she herself described as, "physical exhaustion."

Sadly, from that point onward Mrs. Turner's behavior became quite erratic. She would take out full page ads in various magazines to sell many of her dogs yet, at the same time, continue to buy more than she sold. She would also enter large numbers of her dogs at shows and then sell them the night before to people who had no interest in showing. She sold many of her best champions to England including Ch. Hunk's Bequest, a dog she said she would never part with. By 1915 she had completely disbanded her kennels and dropped from the dog scene.

Nevertheless, she did not merely have a large collection of dogs but many of the best the world had to offer and through the fortunate purchase of a prepotent stud dog, Ch. Pourquoi Pas, had great success as a breeder. Money was no object when she backed the publication of the magazine, "The French Bull Dog." The nine issues of this magazine are valuable primary source material for study of the early history and development of the Frenchie. During her brief tenure in the sport she brought positive worldwide attention to her favorite breed and devoted her complete efforts to promoting it.

CH. HUNK'S BEQUEST

shortness and thickness of neck, they are equal. In ears, while Frenchman's ears perhaps round a little too much toward the front, Riquet's ear go out at the side a trifle too much, so in ear carriage both are equal in quality, as both can be faulted. For general appearance I should prefer the ear carriage of Frenchman to Riquet's. Although I examined carefully I could not see in the ring that either of Frenchman's ears drooped and I am positive there was nothing on them to keep them up or any indication that anything had been previously used to make his ears stand erect. No matter how Frenchman stood he had a wide, natural front and straight, sturdy legs and finely cushioned feet. No matter how Riquet stood he was not straight in front, one pastern turning in a little, the other out considerably, and he seemed stiff or lame when in action. Outside of the points enumerated, the two dogs, according to provisions of the Standard, were about equal until it came to the foreface and this is where I think Frenchman excels. Both dogs have flat skulls, but while Riquet's is longer, Frenchman's is wider. Frenchman has the most tremendous amount of wrinkles I ever saw in a French Bull Dog. His whole head is bunched with them, making it seem so very wide that his muzzle and underjaw seem lost. Going over his head carefully I found he had an extremely short nose. He has a fine, dark eye, of good expression and not "pop" eyed. He has very full cheeks and a well-cushioned muzzle, with lots of cushion and quite a good deal of underjaw. He could do with a little more underjaw and layback, but, if he had less wrinkles and width across the cheeks his already good underjaw and layback would look more prominent than they do. He does not show his teeth and when I went over him I did not notice that he showed his tongue when closing his mouth of his own accord. Frenchman's nose lays well back and while his cheeks are full he hasn't the pendulous flews of the puggy dog. The loose skin of his neck forms wrinkles all about his muzzle and this gives the head such a wide appearance that it must naturally detract from the appearance of the

foreface from a little distance. Riquet has a long muzzle from the base of the ear out and while he has more underjaw than Frenchman, Riquet's nose is really longer and from the side he lacks layback most perceptibly. Also from the nose to the underjaw there is no more depth through, if as much, as Frenchman has, for where Riquet excels in underjaw, Frenchman makes up in shortness of nose, well laid back, and fair underjaw. It is odd that from a little distance Riquet seems to have a shorter nose and more layback than he really possesses, looking at him directly from the front. By going closer this effect disappears and his nose and center of the jaw seem to form a sort of triangle which is not so pleasing and his lack of cushion adds to this effect. I have found in breeding that it is easier to get underjaw than a short nose. While we do not want the puggy, froggy type, still to get a really short-nosed dog of good expression, head well wrinkled, well cushioned muzzle, with some underjaw and some layback, is a more difficult thing to get than simply a good underjaw and a longish nose with few wrinkles, no cushion and very little layback. So, carefully considering all the points, I have tried to make plain in this report, and influenced by no consideration save the merits of the dogs as they appeared to me, I awarded the Winners rosette to Fenway Frenchman and Reserve Winners to Ch. Gamin's Riquet, thereby purposefully reversing my placing of these two dogs in the previous Open Class, over 22 pounds.

REVIEW OF THE BREED
CHARLES G. HOPTON

Considering the absence of the noted Noswal Kennels and the Never-Never Lands, the entry of seventy-one dogs, which greeted Mrs. Mary Winthrop Turner, was quite good. Competition was very keen, and the quality seen among the youngsters above the average. Taken as a whole the awards were well received, and with the exception of the Winners Dog, most consistent. In criticizing the reversal in the Winners Class for dogs, one must not overlook the fact that a judge has a perfect right to do so, should the occasion call for it. It is quite possible for a dog to act sulkily in one class, and then in the very next class appear to great advantage. Mrs. Turner was not the only judge at this show to reverse the awards, such "died-in-the-wool" judges as Mr. G. Muss-Arnolt, Mr. William Fraser and Mr. McGough, did the same in their breeds. I recall quite well, judging Irish Terriers in 1898 at Dublin, doing the Puppy and Novice Classes out in the grounds of the Rotunda, during a rainstorm, when a dog afterwards known as Ch. Oxmantou Wonder, acted sulkily and would not raise his ears, or tail, consequently, I placed him second, behind a dog named Ballyhickey, a smart terrier, which showed perfectly, yet was not such a good one. Owning to the continued deluge, we resumed the judging in the ballroom, the change being a most beneficial one for Wonder, who improved to such an extent, that I at once reversed the former award. And so it appears to be at the recent New York show. Fenway

Charles G. Hopton, *was one of the nine founding members of the French Bulldog Club of America and primary author of the first standard of excellence for the breed, written in 1897. Consequently, he was certainly highly qualified to write commentary on Mrs. Turner's French Bulldog judging. An Englishman by birth, Hopton acquired his first Bulldog in 1884. He established a second kennel in New Jersey and probably was the first exhibitor to make frequent and regular trips to all the major shows in both England and the United States. These trans-Atlantic crossings would have been considered a once in a lifetime event for most people (even today), but to Hopton were a regular matter of course. He was a recognized authority on several breeds and besides exhibiting, also judged at most of the major fixtures in England and the United States.*

Instrumental in establishing the Bulldog breed in the United States and active in the early years of the Bulldog Club of America, Hopton was the breeder of Ch. L'Ambassadeur, the first American-bred Bulldog champion. This dog was Hopton's constant companion and "Reilly" was shown numerous times on both sides of the Atlantic. When he died suddenly at a show in America, Hopton never fully recovered from the loss. Hopton's kennel name was "Rodney" and most of his dogs bred in England were rich red brindles, well known for their magnificent headpieces. Quite a few of these dogs were imported to the United States, and, not too surprisingly, in 1905 the Bulldog Standard in the United States was modified to make red brindle the preferred color. Unfortunately for enthusiasts in America, Hopton had to return to England on business for an extended period in 1905 and sold his New Jersey kennel. Up until this time, Hopton was the only person who had produced any American-bred champion Bulldogs and for the betterment of the breed in the United States, he offered these three dogs for sale.

The solid copper Rodney Trophy

Charles Hopton's legacy still lives on in the form of the Rodney Trophy, a unique copper prize which is awarded by the Bulldog Club of America to the national specialty best of breed winner when the requirements of being the breeder, owner and exhibitor of the top winner are fulfilled.

Frenchman, not showing well in the Open, and yet in the Winners appearing to such an advantage, that the judge placed him over Gamin's Riquet, who, as he is apt to at times, assumed a sulky streak, hence the reversal. There is no getting away from the fact that Fenway Frenchman is much the shorter in face, heavier wrinkled and scores decidedly in expression. Personally, with conditions being equal, I think Gamin's Riquet the better all around dog, but he is such a changeable little fellow—one minute looking like a world-beater, then immediately after, develops a sulky mood and appears very indifferent. It is these tantalizing moods which make the showing of animals the exciting pastime it is.

This is a 1913 advertisement of Mrs. Turner's kennel. The dogs pictured in the illustration were a group portrait done by Marguerite Kirmse. Among them, the pied dog on the left is the well known Ch. Charlemagne of Amersham.

Questions for Consideration

1. Mrs. Turner immediately identified Ch. Gamin's Riquet when he entered the ring and said she had never before seen Fenway Frenchman. Do you think this knowledge affected her judgment?

2. What major procedural error did Mrs. Turner make in the Open Class which apparently contributed to her first decision?

3. Mrs. Turner, in making her initial decision, mentioned that Ch. Gamin's Riquet, "can look like a statue—especially when looking intently for someone." When do you suppose double-handling was invented?

4. How important is individual showmanship of the dog when one is making close decisions?

5. In his review, Mr. Hopton supported Mrs. Turner's reversal but stated he felt that Ch. Gamin's Riquet was the better dog, nevertheless. Does judging from a distance necessarily produce the same results as judging up close?

6. Our system no longer allows a judge to reverse a decision (unless both dogs happened to be entered in several classes). Can you see any merit in allowing reversals, or does this practice just make the judge look foolish?

7. Are there any decisions you have ever made as a judge which you immediately (or later) wished you could reverse? Elaborate.

Lady Judges
H. St. John Cooper

"Field and Fancy"
1906

Now, no one will question the fact that Mrs. Evans knows a Bulldog. She has bred some of the best, including, of course, the far famed Champion Ivel Doctor, and certainly if there is one woman in the Bulldog world who might be expected to give a good account of herself as a Bulldog judge, that woman is Mrs. Evans.

But Mrs. Evans in the ring certainly proved herself to be far inferior as a judge of a Bulldog to Mrs. Evans out of the ring. She did not satisfy even herself, for she reversed her awards, and in one case had an entire class called back and rejudged it, with a very different result to that which she first arrived at. For this, however, I am more inclined to honor than blame her,

for it proves that she made an honest endeavor to do her best, and feeling that she had not judged wisely in the first instance she had the pluck to admit her fault and have the dogs recalled.

Still, taking it from first to last, it was not a brilliant exhibition, and I dare say that Mrs. Evans herself must now feel as dissatisfied as a good many others did. At one part of the performance the unfortunate judge was in tears, the result of an altercation with a dissatisfied exhibitor who should certainly have known better than to express her dissatisfaction, but it is a fact that while women do not make the best of judges, a great many of them are equally unfitted for the role of exhibitor.

Mrs. Horsfall judging Great Danes at the Hastings Show, 1903

Mrs. Tottie judging Basset Hounds at Birkenhead Show, 1903

ment is likewise to be a bit faulty! However, there it is; the first lady elected on the list of the Bulldog Club, Incorporated had made a fiasco of her first judging appointment as a club judge, so let us hope that after this we shall hear less of ladies being appointed to judge Bulldogs, at any rate.

There are exceptions, however, to every rule, and even the most prejudiced must confess, while watching Mrs. Carlo F. C. Clarke at work, that here is a lady who can keep her head in the ring and, what is more, judge the dogs fairly without paying any heed to the other end of the string. Mrs. Clarke is a sportswoman of the best type that we have in England. She knows dogs thoroughly and can judge a breed without fear or favor, and as an exhibitor she can take a reverse of fortune with a smiling face and think not one whit the worse of a judge because he has put her dog down. If all lady owners were Mrs. Clarkes, then there could be little objection to lady judges, but they are not, and so the objection, and a very strong one at that, must stand good.

The position of a judge is a trying one, even to a man, and one can well understand a lady losing her head when she finds herself called upon to decide upon the qualities of the various animals that are brought before her. In the privacy of her own home, or, in fact, anywhere but in a show ring, she would no doubt be able to make a fair selection, but in the ring she is apt to lose her head, and when one loses one's head one's judg-

---

Report of the Ladies Kennel Association Show (England) — "The American Field" — 1903
Theo Marples

CH. SPARKLETS
Owner, Miss A. Johnson
1910

Probably all the Griffon Bruxellois in the country assembled to receive the "hallmark" of a native judge in Madame Oban, who, accompanied by her portly husband, had come over from Brussels specially to judge them. These grotesque little ragged-looking toys have "caught on" immensely with the English aristocracy—the ladies, I mean—good specimens commanding big prices. At one time rivalry in the breed was so keen that scarcely an important show passed without a "scene" of some sort in the ring. Happily, more harmony now prevails in the Griffon ranks. The fair Belgian judge seems to have given satisfaction in her awards, but if there were any epithets flying about she was oblivious to them, since she did not understand English. Mrs. Pearce, an enthusiast in this breed and Dachshunds, who speaks German and French fluently, kindly acted as judicial interpreter, and probably prevented any breezy language reaching the judge's ears, unless it was conveyed in other than the "mother tongue."

Women in the Sport

Miss Anna H. Whitney

Almost since the inception of organized dog shows, women have successfully participated as active breeders, exhibitors and judges. Until this time the majority of other sporting activities were traditionally limited to men only. Several historic factors contributed to this relative equality. By the middle of the 19th Century, Great Britain was the richest country in the world. The positive effects of the Industrial Revolution and improvements in farming methods helped create a substantial middle class in England. The actual definition of the middle class encompassed keeping at least one domestic servant, providing the essential luxury necessary for the success of dog shows—leisure time. However, the most significant reason for involvement by women was due the patronage by Queen Victoria. Her Majesty set the example, maintaining large kennels at both Windsor Castle and Balmoral, becoming a prominent fancier in numerous breeds. It is hard for us to imagine the excitement her participation at dog shows engendered, for it was the one arena where the commoner could compete for judgment against sovereignty and, if owning the better dog, actually win—without fear of royal reprisal!

Several other sports were developed during the Victorian era in which women could compete, principally croquet, lawn tennis, golf, archery and, if really daring and risqué, bicycling. However, dog breeding was clearly a more complex and challenging undertaking for people of all ages, providing many additional social activities which were not necessarily limited to those with athletic skills. This is not to say that there were not raised eyebrows at full participation by women. While for many years it was accepted that women could shoot and ride to hounds (albeit sidesaddle), society had decided ideas regarding which breeds were either "feminine" or "masculine." Thus, initially, toy and miniature breeds and the specialist clubs which monitored them were almost the complete province of women.

Before the establishment of formalized dog shows, women evaluated their dogs at friendly competitions in their parlors while the men judged their dogs in the pubs. In November, 1886, two women made a public judging debut at Maidstone show in England. Miss Holdsworth adjudicated Pugs and Mrs. Jenkins, Toy Spaniels. But, perhaps, because this was a regional show with little over 500 entries, neither woman is credited with being the first of her sex to judge. In 1888, Miss Anna H. Whitney, a St. Bernard breeder, drew an entry of 118 at Westminster Kennel Club. For her efforts the club presented her with a bouquet of flowers. The next year Mrs. M. A. Foster judged Pugs, Yorkshire Terriers and Schipperkes at Manchester, England. The big city press thought this a sensational story and thus, Foster is given the credit for being the first woman judge in

Mrs. M. A. Foster

England. A highly respected authority on Toy dogs, she had exhibited Pugs and "Huddersfield Ben," the "father" of the modern Yorkshire Terrier. Success as a breeder of quality animals was the principal criterion for judging invitations. Consequently, many women were given the opportunity. In the United States a very real obstacle against extending judging invitations to women was the tremendous size of the country. It simply was not considered either proper or safe for a woman to traverse the country unaccompanied. Dining out in restaurants in America at the turn of the last century was strictly a male activity and no gentlewoman would have even considered subjecting herself to the humiliation and scandal of dining alone. Therefore, unless one was a woman of means or had relatives in a distant city, judging opportunities were restricted to local shows.

Women in the Sport

The Kennel Club, based upon individual membership, was initially limited to men only. Women did not attain full membership status until 1978. However, cognizant of the great contributions of numerous women dog breeders and influenced by the patronage of the Queen, Edgar Farman adamantly pressed, as early as 1896, for the establishment of a Ladies' Branch of The Kennel Club. This was finally accomplished in 1899. The first Chairwoman was the Duchess of Newcastle. Living at historic Clumber Park, she was obviously associated with the numerous Clumber Spaniel winners produced there. However, her personal choice of breeds to patronize were the Borzoi and Fox Terrier. She bred and owned many champions and also judged both breeds on several occasions.

The Duchess of
Newcastle

The canine political climate in the United States has never been remotely comparable, due in large part to the structure of the American Kennel Club. Although many groups initially wanted to follow the British model and establish AKC as a club based upon individual membership, the Westminster Kennel Club won with their plan to have the organization be a "club of clubs," with Delegate representation limited to men. In 1888, a large group of breeders, dissatisfied with the method of representation offered by AKC established the National Kennel Club of America and Anna H. Whitney was elected Vice-President. Within a short period of time it had gained wide acceptance as a registry and show giving body, rapidly growing in membership. However, in 1889, in what was initially presented by AKC as a move to unify the interests of the dog fancy, the National Kennel Club of America agreed to amalgamate, with the promise that all their members were to automatically become part of the newly formed Associate Members of AKC. But, AKC refused to allow Whitney and the other women members of that organization to either be Delegates or run for office, thus, disenfranchising women from any significant participation in the canine political process for decades.

In an attempt to placate Miss Whitney, she was extended what would have to be considered a permanent judging invitation at Westminster Kennel Club for the next fifteen years. In a pervasive atmosphere of manipulated awards at many shows, she consistently received rave reviews in the press for her fairness, honesty and judicial abilities. Overseas, "The Stock-keeper" wryly referred to her as, "the _only_ American judge." The correspondents to the various papers showed no mercy on judges of either sex with whose choices they did not agree. However, if a man was accused of bad judging he was labeled incompetent—or worse. Poor performance by women was always attributed to the Victorian definition of the fairer sex as being overly-emotional, irrational and not able to make logical decisions in public.

"Men only" became entrenched AKC policy for years. For example, one of the oldest clubs, the Ladies' Kennel Association of America, was required to have a male Delegate. Some sources indicate that this was not a concern for women of the time, but most of the Ladies' KA officers were the wives of prominent members of either AKC, WKC, or both—hardly a formula for progressive change. In 1951, James Austin, who had owned the famous Smooth Fox Terrier, Ch. Nornay Saddler, proposed allowing women Delegates, but was unsuccessful each time he brought this motion to the floor. In fact, there were no women Delegates at AKC until 1974, and no women elected to AKC's Board of Directors until 1985. Nevertheless, as we approach the 21st Century the accomplishments of women fanciers are legion. Yet, several AKC Member Clubs, including the Westminster Kennel Club, which is perceived by many as holding the most prestigious dog show in the country, are still permitted by AKC to function as 19th Century men's clubs, refusing membership to women in the sport.

Judging and Exhibiting
Mrs. Neville Lytton
"Toy Dogs and Their Ancestors"
1911

I am afraid that a great number of judges will never be able to resist putting up their friends' dogs, the temptation is so subtle and nothing can possibly happen to them in consequence. The contempt of the people who know a good dog from a bad one is all that they have to fear, and the material advantages of being on delightfully cordial terms with their friends is generally more important to them than a reputation of uncompromising rectitude and perfect judgment. I have long studied the methods of women judges compared to men judges, and I have come to the conclusion that they are just about equal in every respect. On the whole, I think the women judges know the points of the Toy dogs better than the men. The only thing I have noticed is that in cases of unfairness, the unfairness takes a slightly different form. A man judge, who wishes to take it out on an exhibitor, puts that exhibitor's best dog right back, and with Machiavellian artfulness puts his worst exhibit first in another class. This removes the imputation of personal dislike and leaves his enemy helpless and fuming. A woman, with few exceptions, goes for her enemy wholeheartedly and puts down all that enemy's exhibits to Reserve and VHC, knowing that these barren honors will produce a far more exasperating effect than being passed over altogether, as the dog then appears in the newspaper reports with disparaging remarks attached and everybody knows he has been beaten. A man, however, does not often put a dog down out of pure spite, though some will do so. It is generally only because he has a friend he wants to help, and, having given his friend a "leg up," he is satisfied and tries to make it up to the other owner by giving him a "special." Things have come to such a pass that he is usually only too thankful for such small mercies.

A woman, too, will sometimes delude her enemy into showing under her by deliberately asking her to show and enthusiastically admiring her dogs in her hearing, so that when the day comes the blow is delivered with all the more effect. I have only once known a man to do this. Nor will a man usually favor dogs of his own breeding with the unblushing publicity exhibited by ladies. On the other hand, a man will very often grossly favor ladies to whom he is partial. Considering the ferocious temper of some ladies in the ring, I must say I am sorry for a man who is confronted with the problem of publicly offending a lady he may be privately courting, by giving the coveted prize to her most hated rival.

I have also been immensely entertained by the violent language of the exhibitors behind each others backs. One lady will talk of another as a swindler of the blackest kind, and the next thing one sees is the two ladies walking arm in arm like two love birds. The following week they are openly fighting like wild cats because one has induced the other to show under her and has given her VHC. They are like the lady who, in speaking rapturously of a friendship, exclaimed: "Oh! we have such quarrels—but *such* reconciliations!"

The Gentile Woman

While we tend to harbor the notion that all Victorian/Edwardian women were staid, prim and proper ladies who never raised their voices or lost their tempers, social customs of any age do not make one any less human in one's responses. These cartoons from 1910 clearly show that dogs are much easier to modify over time than people.

THE "HAPPY FAMILY"

DOG SHOWS AS THEY WOULD BE IN AN ANARCHICAL STATE

A JUDGE'S LIFE IS NOT A HAPPY ONE

EXTRACT FROM REPORTER'S DESCRIPTION - "THE JUDGING GAVE UNIVERSAL SATISFACTION"

AFTER THE JUDGING

A Women's Portfolio

Societal restrictions existed initially, but women have always been at the forefront of the dog sport since its inception. Many have made exceptional contributions. Although the images in this picture gallery display the effects of time, they most clearly show the timeless bond between these women and their dogs.

1. Mrs. Pulsifer and her team of French Bulldogs, Musette, Mimouche, Marguerite de Valois and Ch. Maurice, the first American-bred French Bulldog champion, 1903.

2. Mrs. Jack Brazier, one of the founders of the Scottish Terrier Club of America with her Scottish Terriers, Ch. Silverdale Queen and Ch. The Laird and an unidentified Greyhound, 1903.

3. Lady Lacon and two Borzoi she bred, Stone Hill Valda and Stone Hill Zarina, 1911.

4. Mrs. Garnett-Botsfield and her team of champion Chow Chows, 1905.

5. Mrs. Smyth and her Swiss Mountain Kennels Saint Bernards, Lady Castlereagh, King Regent, Dart, Sunray, Harmony, Geraldine, Florette, Lady Blanca, King Ormonde and Princess Hepsey, 1892.

A Women's Portfolio

Organized dog shows provided the first public forum where men and women could compete against each other on an equal basis. They were among the first activities in which husbands and wives participated in the same hobby.

6. Capt. and Mrs. Charles Chapman and their Bloodhounds, Scarthro Hebe, Critic, Kentish Rightaway and Sultan, 1904. Mrs. Chapman was the second person to serve as Chairwoman of the Ladies' Branch of the Kennel Club.
7. Miss Winifred Davie, a Canadian judge of both Pointers and English Setters at field trials and dog shows, pictured with her English Setter, 1906.
8. Mrs. Borman and her Borzoi, Ch. Piostri, 1903.
9. Mrs. E. D. Roberts and Tatcho, winner of the Pomeranian Club's 100 Guinea Challenge Cup at the Crystal Palace show, 1902.

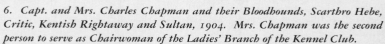

10. Mrs. Lillian Raymond-Mallock, founder of the Toy Spaniel Club of America and her Toy Spaniel, Gaetmore Rollo, 1905.
11. Mrs. Carlo F. C. Clarke and her Maltese Terriers, 1911.

A Men's Portfolio

This masculine montage is presented for both your viewing pleasure and to give a balanced overview. Although men exclusively controlled the political affairs of canine clubs for many years, the sport would not have long continued if a genuine love of dogs was not the main motivational force for involvement by most participants. While it is relatively easy to locate pictures of men with their hunting dogs afield (or holding up a trophy fish), they were not as unabashedly demonstrative as women in posing with a cherished pet for the camera. Thus, such images are comparatively rare.

1. Mr. George Murrell and the famous Bulldog, Ch. King Orry, c. 1891.
2. Professional handler Joe Lewis demonstrates the correct way to show a Beagle, 1904.
3. Mr. G. W. Schenck and his Great Dane, Emin Pasha, 1903.
4. Mr. James B. Scott and his St. Bernards, The Viking and Judith Inman. Judith was said to be the best rough coated St. Bernard in England at the time and Viking was considered by many to have the best head, 1903.
5. Mr. Francis Redmond and his famous Smooth Fox Terrier, Ch. Dame Fortune, c. 1895.
(n.b.—compare this photo of the dog with Wardle's painting on page 38. Observe and elaborate upon the differences and similarities).

6. Mr. James Watson and the imported Collies, Verona Selection, Heather Mint and Old Hall Admiral, c. 1904.

7. Mr. Artem Boldareff and his gold medal winners at the Moscow show, Karatai, Zaviadai and Kassatka, 1904. Karatai was purchased by the Grand Duke Nicholas for 1,000 roubles.

8. Mr. George "Pop" Dunn, a Canadian breeder of Cocker Spaniels, 1902.

9. Dr. J. Varnum Mott, an early member and promoter of the Boston Terrier Club of America, with his Ch. Lord Derby, c. 1900.

(n.b. — while men were frequently photographed holding puppies, the Boston Terrier is the first breed which was apparently masculine enough to routinely be pictured as a man's lap dog).

10. Mr. D. W. Godard and his Bull Terriers, 1905. His postscript captures the true essence of the breed: "Anyone who has ever tried to get a picture of a bunch of Bull Terriers will appreciate this photograph. To keep the two stud dogs, **Joe Wonder** and **Bobby Buster**, from getting together in a hot contest over their female friends, and have them appear pleasant, is a task the owners of the dogs will not attempt again for some time to come."

11. **King Edward VII and his French Bulldog, Peter, at Balmoral, 1899.**

(n. b. — at that time Prince of Wales).

Lady Exhibitors

"Field and Fancy"
1905

Mrs. Waterlow exhibiting
CH. NUTHURST DOCTOR
at Eastbourne show in 1902

Anyone who watched the course of events this week at the show of the Ladies' Kennel Association of America could only have been struck with the mighty advances made by women in the ownership of full-blooded and good looking dogs, and that during the last decade. The time was that to exhibit dogs was looked upon more or less as an outrage on the part of a society dame or young lady, while to lead a dog into a ring was deemed decidedly "fast." Thank goodness, all that nonsense has passed away, and the innocent and engaging cult of having good appearing animals for companionship and exhibition has grown with a will.

Boston, it is believed, was the first place where ladies were prevailed upon to lead into the rings their own dogs. And for that innovation the Ladies' Kennel Association of Massachusetts has to be thanked. Now the custom is general, and there are several women of position and fortune who can today "handle" a dog in the ring with all the ease and finish of the professional man who studies a dog's pose and watches the judge's eye. But to return to ladies as leaders: What Boston promoted was soon backed by the other great cities of this country, with the result that in America today we have some of the leading fanciers of the world, and, what is more, fanciers who can afford to pay for their estimable hobbies in the way of the furtherance of the interests and good looks of the greatest friend of the human race.

Not so many years ago there was the very same objection to ladies leading their dogs into the judging ring in England. And there must have been reasons for that feeling. Rules and regulations were then extremely loose, and we do not think we may be accused of sitting in judgment of others when we advance that the country shows of those days were often conducted by persons who were ill at ease in the company of persons of gentility. They were rough in their manners and uncouth in their actions. Thus it was—knowing all this—that gentlemen would not allow their wives, daughters and sisters to take the risk of being placed in a position in which they might lay themselves out to the rudeness of some official. Then again, some blustering judge of the almost illiterate type might be more than uncomplimentary to a dog about which its fair owner had asked an opinion from the rosetted bully. This has happened over and over again, and to come to days that may not be reckoned in months, we heard of a lady of great social prominence in the East being almost called storyteller to her face by a high official of a kennel club of prominence in America. But God be praised, such an incident nowadays is as remarkable as it is regrettable. Luckily, it is now an unforgotten, unwholesome drop in the enjoyable ocean of dog exhibiting.

Mrs. Carlo F. C. Clarke was exactly as H. St. John Cooper described her, a highly respected sportswoman of her day. She exhibited her first Bulldog in 1894 and had several winners under the kennel name, "Mersham." However, she had a great deal of bad luck with the breed and switched her attentions to both Miniature Bulldogs and Maltese. Even though she produced quite a few Miniature champions of exceptional type, they were all bitches. In fact, because the weight limit for the Miniatures was set at 22 pounds, very few people produced any male champions in the breed as most were not within weight at a year of age. These impossibilities led Mrs. Clarke to eventually enter the masculine domain of Greyhound exhibiting and coursing. She wrote that as she enjoyed being active outdoors it was her intention to stay involved in the dog sport.

Carlo Clarke officiated as judge for the first time in 1906 and she was one of the original members of the Ladies' Branch of the Kennel Club. Active in several other kennel associations and specialty clubs she was also associated with both the South Oxfordshire and Old Berkeley Hunts and rode to the hounds four days a week for twenty-five years.

Mrs. Clarke also wrote quite extensively and in 1912 was the first women ever asked to pen a monthly column on Bulldogs in a popular periodical, "The Kennel," edited by A. Croxton Smith. While many men strenuously

*Mrs. C. F. C. Clarke
and her Greyhounds,
RABY ODINE and ROE
1913*

objected to having a women discuss the "National Breed," they all admitted that her columns were lucid and informative. Today, they are considered excellent primary source material on Bulldogs.

Questions for Consideration

1. Is reversing oneself on an individual award the same thing as calling an entire class back into the ring and arriving at an entirely different result?

2. If it is true that some people are not suited to the role of judge, is it equally as true that some are not suited to the role of exhibitor?

3. Do women have more difficulty making decisions in the ring than do men? (*n.b.*—approximately 50% of the population should carefully consider their choice of words when answering this question in the presence of a member of the other portion of the population).

4. As we approach the twenty-first century, can kennel clubs which limit their membership to men only be justified? As a not-for-profit organization, which is incorporated, shouldn't AKC be required to demand all clubs be non-discriminatory in their membership practices?

Ringside Judging

Laurence Alden Horswell

"The American Dachshund"
1964

I sat at the juncture of two rings where regular classes were judged, with unobstructed views either way, from the first puppies to the final best of opposite sex decision.

When small entries are reported, there is an oft-repeated cliché to the effect that "although the entry was small, the quality was high." Such comment frequently is justified, because only dogs with some show momentum have been interested enough to enter. And the converse also often is justified, that for large entries, diligent club workers have sought out entries from owners who did not specify or pay for show quality when they bought their puppies.

The following comments are not meant to challenge the decisions of the judges—with which, on the whole I concurred—but to discuss the general validity of ringside perceptions by competent, objective witnesses.

Ringside Judging

More than once, I have referred to the fact that at most shows, there are more qualified judges at ringside, than are actually officiating one by one on the day. The usual offset is to ascribe to the officiating judge a peculiarly advantageous, in the ring perspective.

Of course, the judge in the ring can examine the fit of teeth and eye color better than

Illustration from the Horswells' book, "Pet Dachshund." Artist, Lawrence Megargee, 1954

a ringsider, but how many important decisions hinge on these factors? The judge can use hands to establish the shoulder proportions and angulation, rib spring, length of after keel, closeness and strength of loin, muscle quality, coat texture and complement of orchids. But judges at ringside also have advantages.

In an average class of six, while the judge takes each Dachshund over the table and sends it for the AKC prescribed individual demonstration of sound gait, the other five are usually standing at ease and their handlers are not tinkering with their stance, to cover up or distract from imperfections. While the officiating judge waits for compliance with directions, the ringside judge can watch around the whole ring; he often can form a more accurate opinion than can the officiating judge, of a dog as he lives his life and as he or she is likely to pass his or her qualities on to the next generation, which is the AKC's stated objective of encouraging dog shows. Meanwhile, the badge wearing judge is seeing the artfully posed dogs in a concentrated sequence of fractions of minutes.

Posing Poses Problems

Many dogs are gifted, or are trained, to

Laurence Alden Horswell was given his first Dachshund as a child in 1895 and although he never purchased a Dachshund until years later, for the rest of his life he was devoted to the breed. In 1930 he became a member of the Dachshund Club of America and served as secretary, then president and for many years was a director of the parent club. Fifteen regional Dachshund clubs also made Horswell an honorary member. Horswell believed that no specialty club had inexhaustible sources of either man-power or revenue and felt volunteer service by the membership benefited not only the breed but the fancy as a whole. In that regard he completely absorbed all his costs of holding office, including transportation, postage and telephone bills. However, his most important appointment by the parent club was in 1933 when he was named chairman of the club's Information Committee which was charged with publicity, promotion of the breed and public relations. Horswell was a natural choice for this position as he was employed in the advertising industry as a scientific researcher. He made it his mission to increase entries at the specialties and supported shows and made sure the Dachshund was seen by the public in a positive light. Horswell and many others remembered the adverse effects of World War I on the popularity of all breeds of German origin. One of his successful campaigns before the outbreak of WWII was to convince the AKC and breeders to drop the German plural 'e' (Dachshunde) and convert the nomenclature to the Anglicized plural 's' (Dachshunds).

Horswell is pictured judging in 1946 while wearing his trademark pith helmet. In the foreground is one of the commemorative plaques which were commissioned to celebrate the 50th anniversary of the Dachshund Club of America.

Horswell had an analytical mind and incisive wit and was a prolific, erudite writer contributing hundreds of articles to magazines for over 30 years, in particular, "The American Dachshund" and "Dog World." One of his most successful ventures was a small book published in 1954 entitled, "Pet Dachshund," which he wrote with his wife, Dorothy Allison Horswell. During his lifetime he amassed the largest personal library in the world on the Dachshund with important works from 1561 onward, including one of the three complete sets of the German stud book, the only one ever to leave that country. In 1945 he was the first person honored with the Gaines "Fido" award as "Man of the Year."

As a breeder he owned all three Dachshund varieties. He won the first class for Miniatures offered at Westminster in 1935 and also finished the first Miniature champion. One of his show champion bitches placed at the first 12 Dachshund Club of America Field Trials. Horswell was approved to judge Dachshunds in 1934 and all Hounds in 1953. His personal policy was not to judge more than one show a year in his home territory. Many times he refused assignments to do specialty shows because he felt he could do the clubs more service by helping them round up entries. However, the Dachshund Club of America unanimously insisted that he be the judge for their Golden Anniversary show in 1945. Previously, he had judged the Golden Anniversary show of the Dachshund Club of Germany in Cologne in 1938. At the time, he was the only American who had fulfilled the German club's stringent requirements to adjudicate. During the dinner which followed, G. F. Müller, owner of the well-known Flottenburg Kennels, Secretary of the German Dachsund Club and editor of their magazine, "Teckelweld," offered high praise by stating that Horswell's questions on the breed began where their knowledge left off.

walk into a proper show stance, with forepaws even, head forward, back level and hindpaws suitably extended. Less fortunate dogs may have everted forepaws or may stand too wide, and handlers can call attention to these shortcomings by continually 'teasing' the paws into prescribed position. Tendencies of the hind legs to toe in or out, or to crouch under the body, or to hike up the croup, can be corrected manually; but the observant judge must then consider whether this is a

tions, a hot-weather expedient which might well be recommended to other summer shows.

However, it is not necessary for a Dachshund to be 'puttied' into show pose for table examination. Teeth, eyes and expression are not dependent on posture. Arch of feet (if any) can be observed if the dog is standing on all four legs. So can the axis and length of shoulder blade and upper arm be determined, and angulation observed without 'stacking' the dog. The way

---

Politically Correct

Because the most universally ascribed canine character trait is loyalty, throughout history ownership of certain breeds of dogs has always implied political leanings of the owner by association, especially during war. Consequently, the popularity of many dogs has been determined by the winners in any particular conflict. In that regard, the Dachshund has always been associated with Germany. To diffuse this association at the dawn of World War II, this drawing was widely distributed in 1940-1941 to emphasize that an "American" Dachshund had no more use for a plural with a final 'e' than it had for two tails.

---

class for conformation and performance of the dog as such, or whether this is a contest in children's' or adult, or even professional handling.

Particularly does this apply to the examination of the dog on the table. Not all dogs feel equally at home on a table. House dogs are usually not encouraged to explore tables, and know full well that they are out of order when so occupied. Many dogs associate being placed on a table in the presence of a stranger (with or without a white smock) with veterinary attention, including encounters with a hypodermic needle. Also, at many shows, the inspection table leaves much to be desired in the way of stability and footing.

Table Firm, Footing Cool

Let me digress a moment to say that at the show at which I spectated, the tables were firm, and covered with mats on which footing was secure, and which did not hold heat from the sun, as black rubber matting often does. And at around noon, a garden-sized umbrella was moved to the end of the inspection table, where it cast a cooling shade over the site of individual examina-

many judges' hands flutter over a dog's shoulder, it is patent that they are going through gestures which are Greek to them, but they have watched other judges apply their hands to these parts.

Proof is in the Gait

Proof of running gear structure is in gait. The officiating judge has an advantage in watching the dog trot away, across and back, to observe rear, side and front gait. But experienced judges know that many exhibitors do not take a dog as directly away or back as would be desirable. They also know that when dogs move in a circle, it is possible to appraise the gait from these three 'angles' to compare the correctness of tracking, the reach and thrust under the shoulder and pelvic joints; whether the foreleg works under the chest or under the chin, whether the hindleg pushes out behind the croup, or works only 'under cover' of the belly. And the ringside judge has an equally good opportunity to view the circling gait.

Advantages of Being Seated

In another respect, the ringside judge has

an advantage. We have few judges whose eyes are less than five feet from the ground. Army statistics show that the differences in peoples' heights are almost entirely in the lengths of their hindlegs, so when ringside judges are sitting on chairs of uniform height, their eyes are less than four feet from the ground.

How many times have you seen a judge squat in the ring to get a more nearly level view of the dogs? Or put several of them on the table to bring them nearer to the judge's eye level? When a judge's eye is five feet from the ground, and the dog is five feet in front of him, his angle of vision is 45 degrees. He squats to bring the angle down to nearer half of this. The ringsider has the advantage of lower perspective all of the time, helped by the fact that usually the dog is at some greater distance than from the judge. Yet in circling with which classes usually begin and end, each dog comes close enough for detailed ringside observation more than once.

Illustration of three varieties of Dachshund puppies from the Horswells' book, "Pet Dachshund." Artist, Edwin Megargee, 1954

Questions for Consideration

1. If one is truly qualified to pass judgment on a particular breed, does it make any difference whether or not that person is actually in the ring? Whom do you feel is in the most advantageous position to properly evaluate a class of dogs—the official (in-ring) judge or the ringside judge? Elaborate.

2. Can ringside observers or "judges" be counted on to be competent, objective witnesses? Who has to deal with the most distractions during judging—the official judge or the ringside judges?

3. Is it necessary for the handlers to pose or stack the dogs to enable the judge to evaluate them properly? Is it necessary to stack dogs on the table? Can a dog that is posed be properly evaluated?

4. Horswell ascribes to the ringside judge the advantages of a lower perspective and the chance to evaluate the dogs when they are standing naturally. He states that even though the officiating judge has the advantage of examining details up close, such as eye color and bite, very few close decisions are based upon such factors. Do you agree or disagree?

5. In reference to the article, "Changing One's Mind in the Ring," and Horswell's contention that many times there are judges at ringside who are more qualified than the official adjudicator, does it appear that Mr. Hopton was more qualified than Mrs. Turner in the assessment of the French Bulldogs in competition on the day?

6. Horswell stated, "The way many judges' hands flutter over a dog's shoulder, it is patent that they are going through gestures which are Greek to them, but they have watched other judges apply their hands to these parts." Would this seem to indicate that he feels all official judges are equally competent in their abilities to properly adjudicate?

7. From reading this article are you able to determine Horswell's priorities in judging Dachshunds?

What is a Breed?

from the Minutes of the Quarterly Delegates Meeting

"American Kennel Gazette"
1902

Under the head of General Business the protest from Philip W. Moen against the action of Secretary Vrendenburgh was taken up.

Mr. Muss-Arnolt: May I ask if there has been a protest lodged against the win of that bitch?

Mr. Vredenburgh: No. The breed of dog was not stated.

Mr. Muss-Arnolt: It is stated as an "Old Fashioned Scotch Collie." I think it is beyond the scope of this office—that it is a revolutionary proceeding on the part of this office when it undertakes to define breeds. I think I am one of the oldest Delegates here. I do not think that it lies with this office to say that this is not a breed. Without attempting to detract from our Secretary's knowledge of dogs, I never knew yet that he was an authority on breeds, and that he could say a Smooth-Coated Collie was a Rough-Coated Collie when he was not there. I think it ought to be left to the officiating Judge. If there is no protest lodged I do not think that the Secretary has the right to say that it is a Rough-Coated Collie when it is not. This dog was as far from being a Rough-Coated Collie as is a Smooth-Coated Collie, and he is an acknowledged breed of Bearded Collie. I move that the protest of Mr. Moen be allowed and the cancellation of the Old Fashioned Scotch Collie may be and is hereby annulled.

Motion seconded.

Mr. Vredenburgh: The rules say that the Miscellaneous Class shall be open to all dogs of established breeds for which no regular class has been provided in the premium list. Mr. Muss-Arnolt says that the Judge who judged the regular class of Rough-Coated Collies also judged the Miscellaneous Class. I would like to ask how that Judge knew that this dog was entered as an Old Fashioned Scotch Collie?

Mr. Muss-Arnolt: Because there was no Judges'

> "It is rather silly to make a class for every breed of a species known only to its owners. Some of the curios thus provided for were an "Italian Bull Terrier," an "Irish Bull Terrier," an "Irish Rat Terrier," a plain "Rat Terrier," a "Blue-Tan" (whatever that may be), an "Italian Beagle," a "Border Collie," a "Hare Beagle," a "Whipcorded Poodle," and a "Hungarian Beagle." Each had a class to itself. There was some confusion, too, among the breeds of Bull blood. Thus, there were classes for "Bull Terriers," "Boston Terriers," "Boston Bull Terriers," "English Bulldogs" and plain "Bulls," and they were more or less tangled up in the prize list."
>
> *Report of the Springfield Show*
> *"The American Field"*
> *1897*

Book and he had to go by the Entry Book, and it was shown to him what it was, and it was entered in the Miscellaneous Class: "Philip W. Moen, Old Fashioned Scotch Collie—Lady Mabel." Our rules demand that the breed be given, and that covers everything. We have not any established number of breeds here. I know a number of breeds well, forty or fifty breeds in England and

The Miscellaneous Class

Bearded Collie
THE LAIRD OF DUMBIEDYKES
owner, Mr. R. Gordon
1912

The Miscellaneous Class was officially established to serve as a place to exhibit any breed which did not have regular classes provided for it at a show. But, kennel clubs were not required to have classes for any particular breed and generally did not unless substantial prizes had been secured first. Thus, if prizes and separate classes were offered at one show in Dachshunds, for example, their awards would be officially recorded. But, at the next show the same breed might have to be shown in the Miscellaneous Class if no premiums were given. However, it was general practice for most clubs to make separate classifications if, after entries closed, there were at least five of any given breed entered. Exhibitors of the less popular or new breeds were aware of this and until the advent of the so-called "ribbon shows," this situation made it extremely difficult for new breeds to become established in the United States unless they were aggressively backed by fanciers who made the financial commitment to support selected shows with expensive trophies, special awards and entries. Nevertheless, the owners of these "new" breeds did take the time to exhibit as most shows were benched and over the course of four days they could be assured of positive public exposure.

Eventually, AKC did finally establish a list of "recognized breeds" which were all eligible for championship points. The Miscellaneous Class evolved into a place for those breeds seeking full recognition to gain exposure at AKC shows. Unfortunately, the Miscellaneous Class, by being limited to only breeds approved by AKC's Board of Directors is little utilized at today's shows for much the same reason as in the past—the entry fee is the same as that for breeds which are eligible to earn championships. Further, because almost all shows are now unbenched, the ability to expose a new breed to the public through this forum is negligible.

As discussed in the article, the AKC Secretary had sweeping powers to determine if any particular animal listed was indeed a "breed." And that particular Secretary, Alfred Vredenburgh, had absolutely no real knowledge of dogs, having never bred or exhibited any. Certainly, the utter lack of foresight and wisdom of any corporate decision to put those with no intimate knowledge of the subject in charge of making critical decisions has to be seriously questioned and criticized. And, perhaps as a direct consequence, Bearded Collies stayed away for a long time afterward, not becoming officially recognized by AKC until 1977.

possibly forty or fifty on the Continent, but I would not have the courage just from reading a thing like that to say that it is a Rough-Coated Collie. Under what precedent, under what rule? **Mr. Vredenburgh:** I bow with all humility to Mr. Arnolt as the Judge and to Mr. Arnolt's knowledge of the different breeds of dogs throughout England. I do not pretend to have any such knowledge. I did not see the dog. I know nothing about the dog. I have to go by the records. The claim has been made by Mr. Arnolt

that the Secretary has nothing to do with it. Before he can say that he has got to have these rules amended. Here is a rule which says that the Secretary of the American Kennel Club must cancel all wins when he has satisfied himself that these rules have been violated in the following instances, and one of the instances is when a dog is entered in the Miscellaneous Class and the breed is not specified or recognized. If the breed is not recognized he certainly has got to know whether he can recognize that breed, and I claim

What is a Bloodhound?

BRUNO, a so-called, "Siberian Bloodhound," was exhibited at the first Westminster Kennel Club show in 1877. This dog was nothing more than a blue merle Great Dane, a color which has never been permitted in that breed for either show or breeding purposes. This name choice caused a great deal of confusion, both with Great Dane breeders and those wishing to purchase Bloodhounds. Consequently, a few American breeders started referring to their dogs as "English Bloodhounds." Numerous letters appeared in "The American Field" warning those interested in buying a Bloodhound to be sure they were acquiring the bona fide article, a true, "English Bloodhound."

Nevertheless, this additional adjective was not entirely satisfactory, principally because pedigrees on many dogs were not readily available and most people wishing to purchase Bloodhounds knew nothing about them; simply wanting one because they had been captivated by the stories of their marvelous scenting abilities. As late as 1907 this public ignorance still persisted as witnessed by the copy from the following kennel advertisement:

FACTS THAT BLOODHOUND PURCHASERS SHOULD KNOW

"All Bloodhound breeders in Europe or America register their hounds with the English or American Kennel Club. A hound must have certain characteristics to be a Bloodhound; without those characteristics no hound is or can be a Bloodhound. The names English, American, Cuban, Siberian, etc., exist only as words or phrases, to deceive the public, or to swindle a purchaser. Never buy without obtaining a certified pedigree, registration receipt and number of the hound from one or both clubs, as nine out of ten buyers would not know a Bloodhound when they saw one..."

Dr. Knox
Master of the Imperial Bloodhound Kennels
Danbury, Connecticut

Caveat emptor

here that the wording, "Old Fashioned" is not a breed. They had Collies; they had Collie classes; there were Rough-Coated Collies. Here is a Rough-Coated Collie and it is designated as an "Old Fashioned Scotch Collie." They might just as well have said, "A New Fashioned Yellow Dog," but if they had said "Bearded Collie," it would have been a different thing, and in order to be absolutely certain that he did not say that, I sent for the original entry blank, and there is nothing said on that about the dog being a Bearded Collie. It simply said, "Old Fashioned Scotch Collie." I claim I did perfectly right and acted within the rules when I canceled the win of that dog. It is immaterial what that dog was; I go by the record. The rule says that an exhibitor must be responsible for his own errors, and Mr. Moen made an error in designating that breed as an "Old Fashioned" breed and not as a Bearded Collie.

What is a Boston Terrier?

It is very difficult for us to understand the concept that various "breeds," at least identified as such by their owners, could be exhibited at dog shows in separate classes, yet not be eligible for registration. And, if confusion existed regarding breed identification, not only with the general public but also with most AKC officials, there was no confusion as to which dogs could be registered — only those of long established, "traditional" heritage. Most known 19th Century breeds had existed hundreds of years before the Victorian era and were further documented through numerous paintings and artifacts. Though many breeds changed radically in appearance after the advent of dog shows, they could all trace their roots back to ancient sources.

BANKER, an early Boston Terrier very much ahead of his time in conformation. However, after 1896, when brindle with white markings became the preferred color, fawn and white specimens virtually disappeared.

The Boston Terrier holds the grand distinction of not only being the first American breed but the first "modern" breed, as well. It has been established that small Bulldog/terrier crosses existed in the Boston, Massachusetts area at least twenty five years prior to the formation of a specialist club and its subsequent application in 1891 for AKC breed recognition. In fact, the New England Kennel Club offered separate classes for the "Round-Headed Bull and Terrier" in 1888. However, when the AKC Stud Book Committee was presented foundation pedigrees which indicated a purebred Bulldog three generations back, the minutes indicate most members became almost apoplectic at the thought of an "invented" breed. Despite the fact that pictures showing uniformity of type were displayed and consistently large entries were seen at dog shows, the reaction against recognition bordered on violent. This had already been fueled by protests lodged by both the Bull Terrier and Bulldog Clubs against suggested names as the "American Bull Terrier," and the "Boston Bulldog." Thus, the Boston Terrier was denied full recognition in 1891 but was eventually approved, under duress, in 1893. However, this did not end the trouble. As late as 1906 dogs were being registered as Boston Terriers which were the product of crosses back to White English Terriers or Bulldogs and, additionally, to a few French Bulldogs. AKC's consternation was complete upon discovering the Boston Terrier Club approved these breedings to retain and infuse certain selected characteristics into their relatively small gene pool.

While Boston Terriers had initial trouble gaining acceptance with AKC, the public fell in love with the breed immediately. At the time, Americans were caught up in a craze for French Bulldogs — a society dog few working people could afford. It took little imagination to realize that the Boston Terrier was a very similar dog, besides being home-grown. When the dapper brindle and white markings now traditionally associated with the breed became the dominant color pattern, literally everyone wanted to own one of these smart looking dogs. And, within the next 50 years, it seemed as if every American did own a Boston Terrier.

Ironically, the stubborn objections by AKC were against the breed which single-handedly put the company on a secure financial footing. In 1903, ten years after recognition, Boston Terriers posted the largest specialty show in America for any breed at 370 entries. The only specialty in the world which was larger was the Fox Terrier Club show in England. Boston Terriers were the first breed to register 5,000 dogs per year and then the first to top 10,000 registrations. In fact, the Boston Terrier soon led all breeds in registrations and held that position for decades. Indeed, what is the Boston Terrier? A marvelous case study clearly explaining the process of selective breeding and documenting how most canine varieties came into being.

The Origin and Preservation of Breeds

Although breed standards describe the ideal and prioritize traits, the written word is static, while living dogs and the human beings which create each new canine generation are not. Thus, the dynamic evolutionary process of "unconscious selection," as described by Darwin in reference to domestic animals, continues today in dog breeding. "Origin of Species" was published in 1859 and despite the fact that Darwin did a great deal of study of domestic dogs, his work's impact was largely ignored by the kennel community until the early 20th Century. The first prominent dog person to publicly acknowledge its importance, though minimally, was James Watson in, "The Dog Book," published in 1905. To understand, in depth, the issues in dog breeding today, we must start with Darwin's succinct observations on what we choose to identify as "breeds."

"A breed, like a dialect of a language, can hardly be said to have a distinct origin. A man preserves and breeds from an individual with some slight deviation of structure, or takes more care than is usual in mating his best animals, and thus improves them, and the improved animals slowly spread in the immediate neighborhood. But they will as yet hardly have a distinct name, and from being slightly valued their history will have been disregarded. When further improved by the same slow and gradual process they will spread more widely and will be recognised as something distinct and valuable, and will then probably first receive a provincial name. In semi-civilised countries, with little free communication, the spreading of a new sub-breed would be a slow process. As soon as the points of value are once acknowledged, the principle, as I have called it, of unconscious selection will always tend—perhaps more at one period than at another, according to the state of civilisation of the inhabitants—slowly to add to the characteristic features of the breed, whatever it may be. But the chances will be infinitely small of any record having been preserved of such slow, varying, and insensible changes."

While there are some gray areas in the early history and development of the Boston Terrier, this breed represents an exciting departure from the normal method of domestic canine evolution in that its existence was based upon a collective conscious decision to create something new. Generally, as Darwin stated, the intermediate variations in the development process are so slight as to not receive much notice until the animals begin to display such a semblance of uniform "type" as to be more clearly recognizable as a distinct entity or "breed." But, the Boston Terrier was specifically developed at a time when photography was also advancing rapidly and becoming publicly available. Consequently, it seems as if every Boston Terrier ever born had its picture taken, giving the student of canine history ample evidence of the many possible forms and variations in phenotype which occurred before show type was "set." Darwin had also postulated that it is impossible to create a truly intermediate breed from two distinct varieties. Though early Boston Terrier breeders claimed that this is what they had accomplished, the photographic record

76

The Origin and Preservation of Breeds

clearly indicates otherwise. The Boston Terrier has come down to us today as more terrier than Bulldog-like and while there clearly exists a more uniform group of dogs at present, the hundreds of old pictures show infinite combinations and permutations of form, structure and color which not only still lurk within, but are still produced. Our designation of certain characteristics within a written breed standard as faults does not necessarily lead to their elimination from the gene pool.

It is indeed very rare for someone or some group to specifically set out to create a new breed, although this was Louis Dobermann's goal in the manufacture of his Doberman Pinscher. Unlike the Boston Terrier whose raison d'etre was to be a spirited, good-looking companion, the Doberman Pinscher was designed for optimum function as a working guard dog, focusing on yet another set of malleable variations present within the canine. No doubt, man will continue to invent new breeds, despite the fact that hundreds already exist and the market might seem saturated. One hardly thinks that any new breed could be created to out-perform certain breeds extant in their areas of endeavor, such as the Border Collie or the Labrador Retriever. That leaves the modern dog breeder with only a few choices: (1) create another combination of traits for a new breed of pet dog to serve personal vanity; (2) continue to make infinitely minor changes to existing breed standards in an attempt to "improve" phenotype; or, most importantly, (3) diligently work to increase the viability of breeds already in existence.

We know that even conscientious breeders working from the same original foundation stock and adhering to the same breed standard will, in time, produce dogs which are obviously different in emphasis of certain features. The countervailing force of the organized dog show and its impact on the selection process cannot be overemphasized as it tends to radically speed up the breed development process which Darwin outlined. Positively, it keeps breeders from too much variation within a breed. Negatively, as the dog show itself has evolved, it has shifted much of the selection process to highly artificial criteria — show wins — hardly an accurate indicator of hidden deleterious traits.

Although all dog breeding is, in actuality, artificial, as the stewards of living animals, dog breeders have the added responsibility to select for temperament, health and longevity, especially when they have the tools and testing procedures available which allow them to do so. As we approach the 21st Century, Darwin remains the primary 19th Century biologist whose work is not only still relevant, but the direct basis for genetic research. Each generation of dogs collectively creates a new direction for its breed. Hopefully, our cherished companions can continue to be perpetuated in a positive, healthy and beautiful form and not be bred into extinction because we callously or carelessly select their mates based only upon the color of a ribbon.

Mr. Muss-Arnolt: By what proof does the Secretary make the claim that the breed is not known?

Mr. Vredenburgh: The breeds are in the American Kennel Stud Book, and there is no such thing of any breed at all on the records of the American Kennel Club is an establishment of a breed. If that is so, and the name "Bearded Collie" has never been put upon that list, then that is not an established breed.

> *"In the heavy Miscellaneous Class, Jack the Ripper was absent. First prize was awarded to Bertrand, the well-known Basset Hound, and second to Jumbo, a large-sized Mexican Hairless Dog. Ajax, a rather coarse Airedale Terrier, might have been noticed, but that honor was reserved for Cocoa, said to be an "Indian Hunting Dog," but looking very like a bad Collie. In the light division, first prize was given to Floss, a pretty little Maltese Terrier, transferred from the Poodle class. Second to Bluebell, a Bedlington. There were also in this class two Dachshunde and a Toy Bull Terrier, weighing about 5 pounds — a genuine curiosity."*
>
> Report of the Boston Show
> "The American Field"
> 1891

thing in that book as Old Fashioned Scotch Collie. I took the trouble to look through the English Stud Book, and I did not see any classification for "Old Fashioned" dogs of any breed. The Secretary is directed to act under certain contingencies. The only thing he can act upon are certain records. I want to call your attention to a case that was decided where a puppy was entered at one of the Milwaukee shows. I canceled the win of the puppy and fined the club five dollars for entering a dog under age. It was proven conclusively that the man making that entry had made a mistake of about two or three months; that the dog was fully within the age at which he could be shown; but as we had the original entry blank that said the dog was under age, the American Kennel Club ruled that it did not make any difference what the facts were as to the age of the dog. I have not disputed the question at any time that it was a Bearded Collie, but I do dispute that there was any breed of dog known in the world as an Old Fashioned Fox Terrier or Old Fashioned Pointer.

Mr. Viti: It seems to me that the matter narrows down to a definition of the Miscellaneous Class. It seems to me that it is a question of how breeds are established; whether the writing of the name

Dr. Foote: I have had the pleasure of showing in the Miscellaneous Class for a number of years, and if we are going to hold any hard and fast rule on that class, the class might just as well be cut out. We find all sorts of things put down there: Fiji Island Terriers and South American Dogs, Siberian Bloodhounds and the like. It seems to me that the judge ought to be allowed a little liberty, and that the Secretary's duties ought to be somewhat curtailed so far as cutting out wins in that class is concerned.

Mr. Carnochan: I would like to ask the Secretary one question, which may perhaps solve the difficulty: Suppose a dog was entered in the Miscellaneous Class and he was called an "Old Fashioned English Terrier," would he allow that dog first if it won first?

Mr. Vredenburgh: It is all owning to whether or not there was a classification for English Terriers.

Mr. Carnochan: Suppose the dog was entered under the title "Old English Terrier"—would he allow that?

Mr. Vredenburgh: What is an Old English Terrier?

Mr. Carnochan: Will you tell me what is an Old English Terrier?

Mr. Vredenburgh: I don't know.

Mr. Carnochan: I picked up a Stud Book of 1890, and saw that at one time there was some difficulty among the Welsh Terrier exhibitors, and they did not like the type, and they formed another club and called themselves, "Old English Terrier Club," and in this old Stud Book I found Old English Terriers with pedigrees. They are now all merged back into Welsh Terriers again. I ask the question for the reason that I think if a man who had entered an Old English Terrier as a Welshman, for instance, you would order him back to the Welsh Terrier class, yet at the same time he might be eligible for the Old English Terrier class.

Mr. Vredenburgh: It is for this meeting to decide whether the two words "Old Fashioned" constitute a breed in any dog.

Mr. Mortimer: "Old Fashioned" does not designate a breed, but when the words "Old Fashioned" are used in connection with a breed, then it does designate a certain breed. It is a well-known fact that throughout the British Islands an Old Fashioned Scotch Collie is a Bearded Collie. That has been recognized. I do not mean to say it is in the Stud Book or anything of that sort, but it is generally known as such.

Mr. Rodman: Is not the Secretary correct in what he has done, at least to this extent: the Miscellaneous Class is for dogs that have no class provided for them? It does not make any difference whether a dog is a Bald-Headed Collie or a Bearded Collie; there was a class established for Collies; why wasn't Mr. Moen's dog put in the Collie class?

The Chairman: Under the present rule of the American Kennel Club Mr. Vredenburgh has a right to decide whether it is a recognized breed or whether it is not.

Mr. Carnochan: I move as an amendment to the motion already before the house that the matter be referred to the Stud Book Committee until it finds out whether the Old Fashioned Scotch Collie is a recognized breed or not. My reason for referring it to the Stud Book Committee is that a great many of us have never even heard of a Bearded Collie. Some of us know nothing about Collies at all and it seems to be a very easy matter for the Stud Book Committee to find out whether those two terms are used for that breed. If they are used, then the Stud Book Committee will report at the next meeting and we will annul the decision.

Mr. Arnolt: I accept the amendment.

The motion as amended was seconded and carried.

Questions for Consideration

1. What is the definition of a breed?
2. As it stands now, the Miscellaneous Class is for dogs with an approved registry which are working toward full recognition. Should there be any restrictions on breeds allowed to compete in the Miscellaneous Class?
3. Mr. Viti brings up several interesting points. How are breeds established? Does the mere act of writing a breed name on the record books constitute the establishment of a breed?
4. Given the extraordinary capacity for variation within the canine, how difficult is it to create a new breed?
5. How many breeds should be recognized for show purposes? How many breeds does the public want—or need?
6. Should those animals which possess breed standard disqualifications be recognized as breeds under separate names, e.g., White German Shepherd Dogs, Blue Merle Great Danes, Fluffy Corgis, Parti-colored Poodles, and so on?

Keeping the Books

The Libel Trial of Charles J. Peshall

1891

From Across the Sea
Action for Libel
*The Secretary of the American Kennel Club
Prosecutes an Ex-Member of the Club*

From copies of numerous American journals to hand, we see that Mr. Peshall has at last succeeded in forcing the prosecution to bring their case into court. Mr. Peshall is a lawyer and a dog-lover; he was formerly a Delegate to the American Kennel Club, representing one of the numerous canine territorial societies which are dotted all over the United States. He fell out with the club and commenced a course of vigourous attacks on that body's financial arrangements. Finally, he was arrested last September for publishing in *Forest and Stream* a charge against Mr. Vredenburgh, the club's Secretary and Treasurer, of having falsified and juggled the annual report. The Court of General Sessions was well filled with men interested in dogs when the case of Charles J. Peshall, President of the New Jersey Kennel Club, charged with libeling A. P. Vredenburgh, Secretary and Treasurer of the American Kennel Club, was called for trial.

Mr. Assistant District Attorney McIntyre appeared for the prosecution, and Mr. Peshall defended himself. Mr. A. P. Vredenburgh, the plaintiff, was the first to give evidence, his examination and cross-examination lasting three days.

"He winks the other eye"
CHARLES PESHALL

From the dry character of the inquiry and the innumerable objections interpolated by the defendant it is almost impossible to grasp the subject. Mr. Vredenburgh, although he looks a cool enough member of the dude order, must have been well worried before it was over. We should think he earned all his £360 ($1,800) a year in mental distress. Mr. Peshall was very impatient to get at the witness and cross-examine him. This was the treat he had been waiting for, and at last the court had delivered him into his hands, and bang! went the first blow straight from the shoulder when the defendant asked the plaintiff, "Who got you your situation?" and, "I think you did," was the feeble reply. *The World* (USA) remarks on a very effective habit peculiar to Mr. Peshall. When he asked a question he considered important he closed his right eye till the answer came and then it opened wide on the witness and the jury. One of the little sketches which we reproduce from our contemporary shows the defendant in the act of winking the other eye.

"Don't you know that Mr. Watson styled you as the 'Bonanza Boom' in the *Philadelphia Press?*" asked Mr. Peshall, pointing to Mr. James Watson, who sat in the court room and whose likeness we also give. We should like to know what the Watsonian epithet means; it sounds like silvery speech. *Forest and Stream* states that Mr. Peshall has converted the trial into a "fishing

Charles J. Peshall became active in the American Kennel Club in 1885 as Delegate for the New Jersey Kennel Club. A Pointer breeder, Peshall was soon put in charge of the Stud Book Committee and in 1886 he recommended Alfred Purdy Vredenburgh for the position of AKC Secretary and Treasurer. Although the AKC Constitution stated that the Executive Committee was to be in charge of the affairs of the organization, in reality, the day to day management and all decision making was done by the only person who had an office, A. P. Vredenburgh. This changed quite dramatically when August Belmont, Jr. became President in 1888 and began to instruct Vredenburgh on how the books were to be managed. When flagrant book-keeping irregularities came to Peshall's attention he initiated correspondence with  *Belmont and Vredenburgh and then presented an eight page report to be read into the minutes of the next Delegates' Meeting. Vredenburgh not only refused to have the report put into the minutes, but in front of the entire body ripped up the document because it was critical of management procedures. Shocked at this behavior several Delegates demanded an explanation and Vredenburgh responded by sending a letter to "Forest and Stream." Peshall then wrote to the magazine to give his version of events, clearly documenting how the books had been manipulated. (This incident, by the way, was the impetus for Belmont to suggest that the AKC publish its own "Gazette," so that the Club's business did not have to be explained in a public forum).*

In an attempt to silence Peshall, AKC found someone to bring trumped-up charges against him in regard to a supposedly improper transfer of a dog. On the day Peshall was to come to the office to defend himself in a hearing, AKC had him arrested for libel. This was calculated to be done during the lunch hour, knowing that Peshall would not be able to be released from jail until the judge returned from the noon recess. Without being present to defend himself, AKC disqualified Peshall from membership which meant that he not only was immediately removed as a Delegate but could no longer register any dogs. After posting his bond and asking AKC for an explanation, Peshall was told that if he would apologize the charges would be dropped and he would be reinstated.

But, Charles J. Peshall was a lawyer. Believing himself in the right he relished the idea of proving the matter on his own turf. Finally, two years later, the case came to trial and Peshall represented himself, clearly proving that AKC had, without question, juggled the books. Nevertheless, it was a Pyrrhic victory. AKC refused to seat him when his club re-elected him Delegate. They then proceeded to expel the New Jersey Kennel Club from membership for electing him. Peshall was never reinstated and without being able to register his dogs was effectively driven out of the "sport."

excursion." He fished for and hooked information which he could not have obtained in any other way or place. Mr. James L. Anthony, for instance, was forced to disclose that at a secret meeting of the American Kennel Club he voted to suspend the defendant.

The Stock-keeper

Excerpts from Mr. Peshall's closing remarks: Mr. Peshall: Gentlemen of the Jury, this was a controversy in a club; when I say in a club, that means it was a controversy in a family, a contro-versy where each man brought himself into the others' society, and together they agreed to say, we will go along, our interests being identical, and build up this club, do what we can to build up this club, or the interests that we intend to foster. Such a state of facts existed until December, 1888, dawned upon the kennel world. Yes, I will go further, until after or until the *American Kennel Gazette* appeared. I opposed it. From that time on not only myself, because it has appeared here in the evidence from the very beginning that member after member—and when I say a member I do not mean a member as these men would designate him, one of the tools, that came in and that they recognized; when I say member I mean every man that belongs to the American Kennel Club, every man that has got an interest there, every man they have appealed to for his money, every man they have asked for his contribution; when I say a member I say that man is a member. These men came there and thought they would get their information likely, and they had a right to it. But when the spring of 1888 dawned, and this man Belmont, who was the for California. They are right here, and they can whistle him up; he is a good man, too, by the way. They can go down here and whistle up a Delegate for St. Paul—never had lived there and never had been there, never knew anything about it; they gather them for everywhere. You have got the ring, you have got the club, and you have got everything except the money. That comes from these men who send it to them, that they may insult those that give it to them, and then they go around and say I want to break them up. There is not one line in all my writings that will show a

> *"The evidence is complete, is absolute; it is convincing that they have lied about these accounts, and I am going to ask that you take the books with you— I would like to give you all we have got; if you can make anything more out of them you would be a great deal smarter than anybody else."*

President, and his Rodomonti of the club, Anthony, and their willing tool Vredenburgh, got themselves together, with one or two others, they drew down a circle around, and instead of a club it became a ring; and if there was any club it existed only inside that ring. There was no rabble in it. They didn't want the rabble. No, they had no use for the rabble; the only use they had for the rabble is this: If the rabble, the ones outside this ring, will come and just pour the money in it, we will take it; that is the only use we have got for them. And gentlemen, I will say this, that history has taught us that no good government can ever be extracted out of a clique, but it can and does often come out of the actions of a rabble.

There is one way to get rid of a clique, and there is one way to get rid of a ring. You citizens have had an experience with it; to go in and break it and get rid of it; and as long as that ring exists, as long as that Rodomonti of the club, as long as this man Belmont is in control of it, as long as Alfred Purdy Vredenburgh, from Bergen Point, is Secretary and Treasurer, they will have a ring there. They will gather the Delegate

word said against the American Kennel Club, not one line. I have insisted again and again that it is a necessity in this country if you want to encourage and improve the breeding of dogs, and that is what this club was organized for, and not for the purpose to which it has descended at this day. It was organized by those who loved the dog, not for the dollar they could get out of the dog, but for the dog himself. It was organized by men who recognized the dog, the animal, gentlemen, above all others.

Those were the men that started this club, and wanted to bring it to a good use. Those are the men that had worked for it; not dog traders, men who had this in view; and when I say this I count myself among them, for I have labored years here, I have spent hundreds of dollars in dogs, when, in fact, I could not afford it, always doing my best, never a penny coming back to me in any way or shape, or any expectation of any; and yet, when I go there and say, taking Vredenburgh to lunch with me, without ill-feeling whatever, giving him good advice: "Make your statements, make your report, do what you want to do. No one is asking you to do anything wrong." No sir; the master is behind him, the fine hand of him who ruled the club was there, and the Rodomonti was there to aid him in it.

Now gentleman, when a man is a public treasurer of an institution that depends upon charity for its support, and there comes up a dispute about it, it is his duty, if he can settle it, to do so then and there. And after all the arguments, after the cross-examination of that man for two days and a half here, after I had dragged at him and talked with him, there is not one of you could today tell the condition of the American Kennel Club upon the 31st day of December, 1888. The experts couldn't do it. Brought in here and they sat thirty-three hours, thirty-three hours going over them to give us nothing—a general statement—that is all there is in it. Here are the books. Ask him about that book: "Well, I never saw that book." Here are the accounts, a book, gentlemen, is supposed to have sanctity.

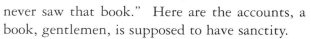
ALFRED VREDENBURGH

Well, we saw this man's books were here. He says no one could see them. Propositions were made in the sporting papers about your committee, let us examine, oh, no, that would insult this auditing committee, that had gone down here and taken this man's figures and, as one said, in two or three hours had audited those accounts. Now, do you think that I believe that there is any juryman in this box who is so thickheaded, as to for one moment believe, that can be ever made to believe, that they could go over those accounts in three hours? We know it is not so. Alfred Purdy Vredenburgh cannot tell you himself what those accounts are, and nobody else. It was his duty to simply take those books and show them.

This very man stands up in the Club in December, 1888, just a short time before this sum of $1,228.28 appears, and offers a resolution to increase the registration fee from fifty cents to one dollar. What for? To put more money into the coffers of their club; and gives as a reason that it costs more than they get in. Then when his February meeting comes and I have attacked their *Gazette*, and in a letter I have written to the press, they make this statement then they have $1,228.28; and on that December, when this man wanted this fee increased they had $5.39, and when these members ask for an explanation, just as the Rodomonti of the Club said, as you will see in their published proceedings there, said, "Go to the Devil." That is exactly how they work you. You have got no rights unless you do as they say. Come in and apologize, change your opinions as Mr. Vredenburgh writes—change your opinions; and when I change my opinion there in that ring, at the feet of the Rodomonti of the club, pursuant to the call of the master—if they wait for me to do this, this country and the one to come will both have passed away.

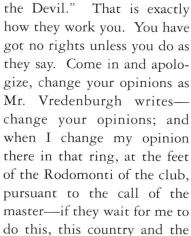

The evidence is complete, is absolute; it is convincing that they have lied about these accounts, and I am going to ask that you take the books with you—I would like to give you all we have got; if you can make anything more out of them you would be a great deal smarter than anybody else.

I will say this, and I can conclude this case very quickly, because I am satisfied and believe that you will come to the very same conclusion that I have and by your verdict you will forever stamp these clubs with rings formed within them, and will declare that they ought to give an honest and fair statement.

Again, I have a right to so publish all these articles that I have been charged with publishing by this party, by the very same man that I was charged with writing hypocritical letters, writing letters to the press, misstating these matters, when all the time I was saying, "You have got the books, give us the items," and that was

Alfred Purdy Vredenburgh was born and reared in New York City. He was a member of the Thirty-seventh Regiment of the National Guard of the State of New York where he became a captain. Known as an amateur actor, Vredenburgh secured small parts in numerous plays over the years in both New York and Brooklyn. In 1871 he moved to Bayonne, New Jersey where he became prominent in community politics. Besides becoming president of the local Board of Education and a trustee of the Bayonne Free Library, he was a delegate to the New Jersey State Democratic Convention and represented his state at the National Convention in St. Louis in 1904. Not known to be listed among any of his hobbies or interests, however, was anything to do with dogs. He did own at least one English Setter, but was neither a breeder nor exhibitor at either dog shows or field trials, limiting his participation to an occasional afternoon of shooting.

The significance of Vredenburgh's utter lack of interest in dogs is that during the formative years of the dog show sport in this country, he was the only employee in the AKC offices. Although authority for running the business of the club was technically vested in the Executive Committee, in actuality, Vredenburgh made all day to day decisions regarding registration, awards, dogs in general and company policy. Thus, a tone was set for unilateral decisions based upon personal convenience rather than seriously entering into discussion and debate on the the real concerns of the experts within the dog fancy.

Vredenburgh served as both Secretary and Treasurer of the American Kennel Club for 35 years, from June, 1886 until December, 1919. In reading through the entire libel trial transcript it is clearly evident that the books were "juggled," just as Peshall had claimed. When one considers the public nature of this case and the resulting verdict, it is rather inconceivable to realize that such dereliction did not result in the immediate dismissal of Vredenburgh, and with him the mastermind of this unique form of bookkeeping, August Belmont, Jr. But, at the time the AKC truly was a "club" and not incorporated. Thus, accountability was limited to any demands which might be put forward by the Delegates, who for whatever reasons, chose to do nothing. When Belmont claimed at the Delegate's Meeting of May, 1891 that the legal proceedings had been instituted by Vredenburgh as an individual and not as an employee of AKC, this simply wasn't true. The total legal bill of $5,000 to prosecute Peshall was, in fact, paid by the AKC.

When the "Gazette" was created, overseeing its production was added to Vredenburgh's responsibilities. For many years, the magazine contained little of interest in the way of informative articles. Most of those which appeared were penned by James Watson. Until the birth of this magazine, other sporting papers routinely sent stenographers and printed verbatim minutes of the Delegates' Meetings. If one compares their notes of the proceedings to those selected by Vredenburgh to be published as "official" within the "Gazette," discrepancies in reportage become evident. Vredenburgh made it a habit not to publish anything said which he felt was negative. Until all outside reporters were finally banished from the proceedings by Belmont, the fancy still had some idea of what really transpired at the Delegates' Meetings — if they read the reports published in other journals.

Despite all this, Vredenburgh can be officially credited with one significant accomplishment in dogs. When the heated debate raged about recognizing a breed with no universal name, the proferred choices of "American Bull Terrier" or "Boston Bulldog," met with strenuous proprietary objections from both the Bull Terrier and Bulldog clubs, respectively. In the midst of the angry shouting, it was Vredenburgh who was quoted as saying, "Why not call them Boston Terriers?"

done for a good purpose and with a good motive. The object was to compel them to do their duty and to break up the ring and release the dogs from the infamous ring that was attempting to and was at this time controlling them.

Now, then, there was another thing, the Delegates, they must control the Delegates. If a man got down there that is opposed to them, they do not let him in. That settles it. If they do he is a stool-pigeon, as they say, they claim in the evidence here. Mr. Anthony, another witness in this case, goes upon the stand—I intended to give him quite a long examination, but he didn't go far before he absolutely stated a lie here, which I will show you by his own testimony. Didn't know I was arrested? No, not until after the meeting was over. Didn't go but hardly three sentences, three questions more were asked him and what did he say: "I sent the boy down myself to point you out to the officer." Now, think of it, think of it. You remember the testimony? I will read it to you. Then what wonder that I opposed them? I am to be still and allow them to do what they please, or else go out and let the dog world go alone. Drive him out, "down him," that is their word, "down him," that is the great word among them.

Now, then, another question is, were those men competent for the positions which they occupied? Were they not a disgrace to have the management of a noble animal, the dog, in this country? Men who cannot give natural justice to their fellow men are unfit to have the jurisdiction of this noble animal—the dog in this country; a man who will go and deprive another or hurt another or strike another when he is down, is unfit to assume jurisdiction over any such animal as a dog; and these men come in here and state themselves that when I was under arrest at their own instance, they did not know I was being arrested. One said, "I knew you were going to be," and another said, "I was sending the boy there to point you out;" while they charged me

> "Now then, another question is, were those men competent for the positions which they occupied?"

with the offense and called a meeting to try me, to have the officer to come to that meeting, clothed with the power of the State and with a mandate of this Court to take me away, and so they sent the boy down to that café to point me out and when that boy comes back and reports to them, with a disregard for natural justice, they then sit upon my case. Why, we have got him before the Court. We will dispose of him here and find him guilty of what we have got him indicted for. I say a man who will do that is unfit to have charge or control of a cat club, let alone a dog club, a rat club, or any other club; a man who will rob another of his rights or that will put him down, is not fit to be called a man. There is only one way you can designate him, and that is, he is a most consummate coward. The brave man will stand up, and he will always give the other man a chance. The coward always attacks in secret, in star chamber proceedings. This is the rule.

These are the gang I am working with here. What do you think of that? What would you think of yourselves if you jurymen should go tomorrow and swear out an affidavit and say John Smith was guilty of such an offense and then come here next week and sit on the case and try him. Do you think you would do it? No, no other man would do that that was a man. Sportsmen do that? No sportsman ever did it. A sportsman that would do that, the next game that ran would drive him from the field. No sportsman ever did that, no man would think of doing it. It was outrageous, it was infamous.

Then again, I was to apologize. Another one of the men comes to me. The object is to get this indictment and not try it. He won't try it. He won't fight. They made a mistake. I will fight, that is, not personally; what I mean is I will fight this way. They were mistaken. I would and I have, and then they want to see it settled. Mr. Schellhass writes to me; now he takes it up: "You apologize, then you won't be sent to jail." Then

85

you twelve men would be deprived of sending me to jail, if I had gone and apologized. His Honor will give you the law in this case, and I think, gentlemen, I should be blamed for detaining you any longer than the other side, because I do not think that I have really occupied much more time than they have or will."

The American Field

The jury left the court room, to consider their verdict, at 1:40 p.m. After they had been in the jury room fifteen minutes, the foreman sent a communication to Judge Martine, asking that the jury be permitted to have the two cash books, the ledger and the stubs of the check books of the AKC. By consent of counsel, these exhibits in the case were sent to the jury room. At 4:35 the jury returned to the court room.

JAMES ANTHONY

"How say you, gentlemen of the jury?" said Clerk Hall. "Do you find the defendant, Charles J. Peshall, guilty or not guilty?"

"Not guilty," replied the foreman.

Mr. Peshall thanked the jury, and his friends crowded about him, shaking his hand warmly.

"Is there any other charge against the defendant, Mr. McIntyre?" asked Judge Martine.

"No, sir," replied Mr. McIntyre.

"Then the defendant is discharged," said Judge Martine.

The American Field

The evidence was summed up on Thursday afternoon. Judge Martine concluded his charge shortly after one o'clock on Friday, and the jury retired. They were an intelligent set of men, "a jury of business men," as the Court had characterized them, and among the twelve were three practical bookkeepers. Their first ballot showed seven for acquittal and five for conviction;

the second eight for acquittal; the third nine. There it stood, and so determined were the three for conviction that in the jury room a disagreement was thought inevitable. Then they sent for Mr. Vredenburgh's books. It was discovered that, although these were a part of the evidence in the case, they had already been taken back to the AKC office, but after an hour's delay they were brought into court, and by consent of counsel on both sides were delivered to the jury. The three jurors who had all this time been standing out for conviction took a look at the books. There was no further argument nor delay. The jury returned to the court room and Foreman Samuel Levon announced the verdict, "Not guilty."

Forest and Stream

From Over the Sea

"The gang" is not in a happy frame of mind by any means. Mr. Vredenburgh is no longer visible to the vulgar eye. He is now safely ensconced in a "private office" where none can approach him until "your card, sir!" has been complied with, and then, if his majesty (!) will receive you, you may enter the *sanctum sanctorum* and listen to him talk of everything else except the trial, which resulted so disastrously to his end of the rope.

It seems that Mr. Peshall, in calling the AKC President "this man Belmont," has injured and greatly wounded that gentleman's sensitive and very high-toned feelings, and I also heard the other day that his brother, Perry Belmont, the Democratic Congressman, a man highly respected by both political factions, is exceedingly desirous that his younger brother should withdraw from the kennel world after the "exhibition" he has made of himself. Some of our brilliant writers for the sporting papers are making a terrible mess of it trying to support the AKC and its Secretary's accounts, claiming Mr. Peshall so befuddled the jury with figures that they were obliged to render a verdict of "not guilty." Mr. P. in addressing them told them to take Mr. Vredenburgh's books, and if they could make head or tail of them it was more than any member of the kennel world could do, and it was true. They (the upholders of this peculiar bookkeeping) may talk till the crack of doom, but they will never be able to convince anybody but a fool that when Mr. Vredenburgh rendered an account of five dollars and thirty nine cents being in the treasury, while the bank book showed $750 to the credit of the club, that the report was correct. Nor later on, when he showed the great success of the new system, by giving the balance on hand as $942, when really it should have been $155; the burden of it all lies in the fact that the accounts were "juggled," just as Mr. Peshall said they were. The fact that certain moneys paid to the treasury belonged to certain accounts is no earthly reason why he should not acknowledge receipt of them. Thousands did think the balances reported were false, and they were, and he may wriggle and twist and squirm as much as he will, he can never blot out his evidence on the witness stand, which convicts him as "forcing the balance," as it is called by accountants. If he had one particle of delicacy about him he would resign, but he will never let go of the 1,800 "shekels" till he is compelled to, nor get out till he is "bounced."

The end is not yet. The Albany Club are all afire, and already suits have been instituted against prominent members of the AKC. Mr. Peshall has got a pickle in for everyone who voted for his disqualification, and all I hope is it will result in the AKC being relieved of "the gang" that rules it now with an iron rod, and men put in their places who have the moral courage to follow out a course that will cast credit upon the club, and not make it a bye-word and a subject of ridicule, on all occasions.

The brilliant journalist(!) Mr. R. F. Mayhew, was at the trial in sweetest flesh and purest blood. He made two reports of it in the

> "Will AKC call him a persona non grata?
> Will they dare to refuse the credentials of a man they tried and convicted without a hearing?"

Philadelphia Fanciers' Journal, and one has but to read them to be wholly disenchanted of the idea that he is either "to the manor born," or a humorist. His attempts to be funny at Mr. Peshall's expense are like the reverting boomerang, and show him in a coarser light than ever before. I see by the last issue of the *American Kennel Gazette* it omits the names of the disqualified members, and I'm also informed the reason of it is that Mr. Vredenburgh considers it has been published sufficiently often now to answer the purpose intended! This is not only rich but truly rare. The question at once presents itself, "Would those names have been withdrawn if the Albany suits had not been instituted?" Methinks not.

One of the events of the season was the meeting of the New Jersey Kennel Club on the 11th. I have it on good authority that never before in the history of the club has so large an attendance been held, all excepting two being present. Mr. C. J. Peshall was elected President for the ensuing year! After this came the sensation of the evening, the vote for Delegate to the AKC being next in order. This resulted in the selection of Mr. Peshall! Will AKC call him a *persona non grata*? Will they dare to refuse the credentials of a man they tried and convicted without a hearing, and if they do accept him, what will be the feelings of the sweet trio—Messrs. Vredenburgh, Anthony and Belmont? One thing is certain, and that if he "qualifies," he should at once ascertain the names of the Delegates who voted against him, and have them disciplined by their respective clubs, just as the AKC "gang" disciplines it members that are prone to kick over the traces. It is greatly to be regretted Mr.

Peshall is not of a calmer mood at all times—one who could hold his cutting sarcasm in better control. He would then be a leader who could bring the club out of its present unsavory position, and elevate it to the place where he and the minority would have it. With gentlemen such as Messrs. Donner, Winslow, Child, Thayer, Perry, Cryer, Huntington and Fay at its head, and Messrs. Vredenburgh, Anthony, Belmont & Co. out, a vast amount of good would be done, and the mismanagement of the past be supplemented by proper proceedings.

> "We have always foreseen that the lack of dignified repose which has demeaned the meetings of the American Kennel Club, and the active personal partisanship of its leaders, would endanger its authority; and this has come to pass."

Word has just reached me that when Mr. Peshall presented his credentials as Delegate of the New Jersey Kennel Club at the AKC meeting of May 21, they were rejected by a vote of twelve to three. Mr. August Belmont presided, the great Secretary, Mr. Vredenburgh, was on hand, as fresh as a new laid egg, while "out only" Mr. Anthony made a trio of great men complete. A very Wise man addressed the meeting by saying that as Mr. P. was a disqualified subject he would move to have his credentials rejected. He said the law was that where a man was rejected he could not be returned by his constituents. This Wise specimen evidently has forgotten what little law he knew when he lived elsewhere, for, if I remember rightly, Mr. Bradlaugh, M. P., was rejected, yet when his constituents re-elected him and sent him back, the House of Commons was obliged to accept him and it did. This Wise man in making this statement misled the Delegates. For there is not the first word in the constitution touching upon the acceptance or rejection of a Delegate. The Delegates, twelve of them, accepting his erroneous statement as true, voted against the admission of Mr. Peshall as Delegate, while the Philadelphia, Lynn, and National Greyhound Clubs voted for his admission. How was this all done, and why? Here goes! Mr. Watson was recalled by the Spaniel Club as its Delegate, but influence was brought to bear on the California KC who threw over Mr. Wenzel and substituted Mr. Watson. Mr. E. H. Oldham succeeds Mr. Watson. The Mascoutah KC, of Chicago, had as its Delegate Mr. Mortimer, the WKC's superintendent and kennelman. Word was sent that he was supplanted, but the mighty Vredenburgh jumped from his chair and stated as his (Mr. M.'s) credentials were still in his possession, he was still the Delegate of the Mascoutah Club. You see it was of vital importance that the gang should hold all its followers as long as possible. The plot thickens! The gang have now given it out that the books on the basis of which they claim the verdict was given were not the right books. "Alfred P. Vredenburgh of Bergen Point," swore on the witness stand that the books offered in evidence were the only books the AKC had. Will he now explain? Look out, Allie! They're after you.

The Stock-keeper

The American Kennel Club's Meeting
May 21, 1891
Mr. August Belmont presiding

The President: I notice the presence of a stenographer here other than our official stenographer, who, in reply to my question as to whom he represents, says one of the sporting papers, and as this is not a public meeting of the American Kennel Club, I have requested him to retire from the room from which he has not done. Therefore, I ask the vote of the members on the subject. We have our own stenographer here to take the minutes of our meeting which are naturally the property of the American Kennel Club and its members.

Mr. Whiton suggested that it would be better to call the meeting to order, and then if the members desired to go into executive session they could do so.

Dr. Cryer: I move that this meeting be called to order.

Motion carried, and the meeting called to order. (Roll called).

The Secretary: Are there any members present representing any club whom I have omitted?

Mr. C. J. Peshall: I have not heard the New Jersey Kennel Club called. I believe the New Jersey Kennel Club is a member.

The Secretary: I have called the names of the Delegates whose credentials are on file here.

Mr. Peshall: I present my credentials now.

The Secretary: I have three credentials now.

The President: The Secretary will please announce the credentials.

The Secretary then read the credentials of James Watson to represent the Southern California Kennel Club, which were, on motion, accepted.

Mr. Richards: I now move that all persons other than the duly qualified Delegates to the Club, or the members of the press authorized to represent some recognized paper, be excluded from the room.

Motion seconded by Mr. Schellhass. Carried.

The stenographer referred to by the President retired.

Mr. Peshall: I represent a club here rem—

Mr. Richards: I rise to a point of order, whether Mr. Peshall's name has appeared as a Delegate, and if his credentials have been recognized.

The President: Mr. Peshall, you will not interfere with the business of this meeting until you are properly authorized to do so. I believe under the resolution just adopted your presence is not admissible in this room.

Mr. Peshall: I am here representing the New Jersey Kennel Club.

The President: You cannot vote on your own credentials, and you cannot take any part in the meeting.

Mr. Peshall: Mr. President, I can presume that my credentials are passed upon. We can test this matter very easily.

Mr. Richards: I move not as a matter of right but as a matter of courtesy, whoever presents colorable credentials as Delegate of some club which is a member of the American Kennel Club be permitted to remain until the credentials are taken up and passed upon, and I move that the unanimous consent of the members be given to the taking up of the credentials.

Motion seconded and carried.

The Secretary then read the credentials of E. B. Sears, as representing the Massachusetts Kennel Club.

On motion of Mr. Whiton, the credentials of Mr. Sears were accepted.

The President: Mr. Morris, may I ask you whether you represent a paper here?

Mr. Morris: Yes, I represent the *Forest and Stream.*

The Secretary then read the credentials of C. J. Peshall, as representing the New Jersey Kennel Club.

The President: What is your pleasure as to the credentials of the New Jersey Kennel Club?

Mr. Richards: I move that the credentials be rejected and that the Secretary be directed to inform the New Jersey Kennel Club of the rejection, and also request the Club to communicate with the American Kennel Club any excuse which the New Jersey Kennel Club has to offer for presenting the name of Mr. Peshall as Delegate. I suppose properly that might come in

> *"The AKC must put their house in order now, and also set about regaining the esteem of the best men in the kennel world; they cannot exist on the rickety support of a few fawning lickspittles who truckle to their masters for clerk work, judgeships, reporting, managing, and so on."*

the form of some charge against the New Jersey Kennel Club, and they may plead ignorance of Mr. Peshall's status.

Motion seconded.

Mr. Wise: I presume the motion is debatable. I should certainly vote to reject Mr. Peshall, but I do object to the New Jersey Kennel Club presenting any excuse. I don't know that they have any to make, or that they propose to make any. They may send whom they please and we may accept whom we please, or we may reject whom we please. If it is necessary to embody in the resolution a statement of the reasons why we object to him and reject him that is a different matter. The reason why I shall vote to reject Mr. Peshall is this: Mr. Peshall stands disqualified by this Club. This New Jersey Kennel Club, was fully aware of that. Sending him here as a Delegate was not a proper course for the New Jersey Kennel Club to pursue. That club must be aware of the fact that a judgment of expulsion stands upon this record against Mr. Peshall. They cannot attack that judgment in this collateral way any more than a man who had brought suit and had judgment rendered against him would be allowed to bring another suit without opening the old judgment or appealing from it, or having it reviewed. It would be a very different question if the New Jersey Kennel Club presented itself here in an aspect which did not ignore our past action. It has chosen with its eyes open to come here to offer to the American Kennel Club as a Delegate one who has been disqualified, and I do not see how it can continue to do it. It is the old case; it is found in the British Parliament and other bodies, of a man rejected by the body to which he was sent, being re-elected. That course carries with it its own gratification, no doubt, but it carries with it its own redress by leaving the body which it would otherwise have.

James Watson

Mr. Peshall: Will you allow me to ask you a question?

The President: There must be some limit to this. I desire that this meeting shall be in order. Mr. Peshall insists upon these interruptions. The discourtesy of such an act would be very summarily dealt with by this meeting, if it were not for Mr. Peshall's popular position, and I should think that common decency would compel him to keep quiet until he has really a right to speak. I desire only that order shall be preserved at this meeting.

Mr. Wise: I was going on to say that I suppose there is no man in this Club who really has so little feeling about Mr. Peshall as myself, and the multifarious proceedings that have occurred I have fortunately, or unfortunately, escaped. In a proper proceeding my mind is in a condition of not only not knowing the real details of what has occurred but of an utter lack of impression as to recent events. I should be inclined to deal with the matter in the broadest way, and handle it so as to put aside all implication of passion or prejudice, but I do not consent, and will not agree that the New Jersey Kennel Club or Mr. Peshall can ever come back into this Club by any such indirection as this, or that that judgment shall be annulled, and this Club stultified by permitting a man to come back here as its representative when our judgment of exclusion stands against him. For that reason I move as an amendment to the resolution offered by Mr. Richards that this Club respectfully decline to receive Mr. Peshall as a Delegate of the New Jersey Kennel Club.

Mr. Richards: I accept the amendment.

Mr. Peshall: I should now like to address this meeting.

The President: I cannot allow you to take the floor.

Mr. Anthony: I should like after this vote is

taken to ask the consent of the Club to give Mr. Peshall an opportunity to be heard.

Mr. Whiton: I second the motion.

The President: Mr. Anthony's motion is not in order.

Mr. Wise: I do not desire to be placed in the attitude of refusing to give Mr. Peshall an opportunity to be heard; although I do not think anything he can say would alter my judgment, I am not prepared to press the resolution I have offered without debate. A debate upon that resolution is proper certainly by every member of the Association and I understand that it is in order during the period that the debate is open before any motion has been made to close it—a motion which permits the opponents of their resolution to be heard is not out of order; in other words, that a vote upon the resolution is not forced before the resolution of Mr. Anthony could be passed if it be the sense of the meeting to hear Mr. Peshall. For my part, I do not desire to be put in that attitude of cutting off the presentation of whatever he has to say in regard to his right to come here with these credentials, and I trust that the Chair will not rule that it cannot entertain the motion to suspend the rules and hear Mr. Peshall while debate is pending upon the resolution.

The President: I should like the privilege of saying a few words before I announce any ruling upon that point. It has been my object as your executive officer to exclude from the business of the American Kennel Club and its affairs in every way possible everything of a personal character involved in this case of Mr. Peshall, and see to it that the time of the meeting should be devoted to the interests of the Club and not wasted in wrangling or in interference when you are here assembled. The suit which has just terminated and which is entirely a private matter, one conducted by the district attorney for the benefit of an individual, not as your Secretary, but a private individual, and in which the American Kennel Club has taken no part notwithstanding the fact that it has been attempted to drag it in through the newspapers, I distinctly say that it was with that object always that I have endeavored to prevent Mr. Peshall coming here unless he had a right to do so, and taking part in your debates, because it has never transpired that when we have been here for business other than that of Mr. Peshall, when he was present, that we have been able to transact our business because all sorts of outside questions are dragged in and stump speeches are made, and our whole time is wasted. The interests of the Club require attention to business, and while if it is your wish to open the debate so that Mr. Peshall shall be heard I naturally shall rule if there is no objection to permit that if I think that is the general sentiment. Personally, I have no feeling on the subject at all. My duties as President of this Club have been simply to endeavor to have its business transacted properly, and what has come in its way I have tried in the best manner to brush aside. I fear that by opening the debate to Mr. Peshall, we will transact no other business here this afternoon. I cannot think that he is sent here for personal justification. The fact simply arises that Mr. Peshall comes here as a Delegate, and under his disqualification it does not seem possible for him to act. Therefore, all you will listen to will be the pros and cons of the back history of all this trouble with which the American Kennel Club has nothing to do whatsoever. If there is no objection made I shall recognize Mr. Peshall.

Mr. Richards: I move an amendment to the motion to suspend the rules to admit Mr. Peshall to be heard, that all debate upon this principal motion be limited to ten minutes.

The President: I think you will have to pass the first amendment.

Mr. Whiton: I was going to suggest that Mr. Peshall be allowed to be heard if the time is limited to ten minutes.

Mr. Anthony withdrew his amendment.

Mr. Whiton: I move that the rules be suspended, and that Mr. Peshall be allowed to speak ten minutes.

Mr. Watson: I understand this must be by unanimous consent?

91

The President: Yes.

Mr. Watson: I shall decline to give my consent. Mr. Peshall should come here at the proper time with measures toward the removal of his suspension and disqualification. I call for the question upon Mr. Wise's amendment.

The ayes and nays being called resulted in the following vote: Ayes 12, Nays, 3.

The President: The amendment is carried.

Mr. Richards: I withdraw the original motion. I understood the amendment to be offered as a substitute.

The President: Under the original resolution I think Mr. Peshall should retire from the room, but I do not need ask him unless it is your wish.

Mr. Peshall: I shall leave.

(At this point Mr. Peshall retires).

The American Field

The first act in the Peshall play is over, and now perhaps the trans-Atlantic Press will give the subject a rest for a while. We must compliment *The American Field* upon having outdistanced its contemporaries in fullness of reports. One issue alone of the journal named contained fifty-four columns of reporter's notes! As our readers know, all this trouble has arisen out of the American Kennel Club's way of keeping their accounts. A letter appeared in *Forest and Stream* signed by Mr. Peshall, charging Mr. Vredenburgh, the Secretary, with having "juggled" the club's accounts, and hereupon Mr. Anthony and other members of the committee had Mr. Peshall arrested for criminal libel. This act was considered rather too extreme for the offense, and sympathy settled on Mr. Peshall, who hotly denounced the high-handed procedure of the club tyrants.

Nobody thought Mr. Vredenburgh had falsified accounts for his own ends, and nobody seems to deny that the club's supporters, chief among them Mr. August Belmont, have rendered valuable services to the kennel community, but your American citizen is so uncomfortably independent that he wants to see for himself how things are being done, and will allow nobody to come the "superior" in business over him. Mr. Peshall is one of that ilk. It was no use Mr. Vredenburgh trying any hanky-Yankee on him, if Mr. Peshall was to be doodled, it was not by sticking a feather in his cap and calling it macaroni. He wanted to see the feathers the club was flying with, and not where they borrowed their plumes; he did not want the Italian comestible, "cooked," or otherwise. Well, however the club came into this case, Mr. Vredenburgh has trotted out of it with his face to the pony's hindquarters.

Nobody who reads the reports of this case will deny Mr. Peshall's legal ability, or his ingenuity in cross-examination. He wearied the Court a good deal with figures, but that appeared inevitable. It seemed any odds in the defendant's favor from the beginning. As he was conducting his own case the judge allowed him a remarkable amount of latitude, so much, indeed, that one might imagine the fact of Mr. Peshall's being himself a lawyer was now and then forgotten. Mr. Peshall several times took undue advantage of this indulgence, as when he told the Court he would show that Mr. Anthony lied from the time he got into the witness box until he left it. This witness, in one of his replies, used an expression we have never met before, when he told Mr. Peshall that he had in the person of Mr. Leslie a "stool-pigeon" at one of the club meetings. We do not find the word in our Slang Dictionary, perhaps one of our friends in another department can explain. It could not have been complimentary to Mr. Leslie, because the judge ordered the word to be struck out.

Then he called Mr. Vredenburgh an "amateur actor," but Mr. Peshall's most offensive and pet form of insulting a witness was to ask when he had received a reply: "And that is what you want the jury to believe?" And on the witness rejoining it was the truth, his unrestrained questioner would retort with the sneer: "And as truthful as any other of your answers today?"

A smile must have encircled the Court when the Secretary disclaimed Mr. Wade, Mr. Peshall asking:

James Watson *was an early pillar in the American dog community. As a promoter of the then faddish black Field Spaniel, he was active in the formation of The American Spaniel Club, the first specialist club in the United States (1881). Originally from Scotland, he brought along the love for his native breed, the Collie, and was a charter member of the Collie Club of America. Watson was a journalist by trade and for many years wrote sporting and kennel pieces for such newspapers as "The New York Herald," "The Philadelphia Press," "Forest and Stream" and numerous others.*

Although one of the original founders of the AKC, Watson had come down very hard in print against the Westminster Kennel Club/American Kennel Club clique and the AKC's questionable management practices. Appropriately known for his caustic writings under the pen name, "Porcupine," even a cursory reading of his letters and editorials reveals a man who could be venomous and vicious in his attacks. Still, his outspoken honesty and canine expertise had earned him a strong following. But, if it is true that every man is said to have his price, then that price was found in the calculated move of offering Watson the editor's position of the fledgling "American Kennel Gazette" in 1889. Subsequent publicity surrounding the Peshall case necessitated A. P. Vredenburgh being listed in charge of the magazine and Watson never officially appeared on the masthead until 1898. But, much of the editorial writing, some of it signed, was done by Watson. Whatever deal was proferred, it successfully silenced Watson's attacks against the AKC. Almost overnight he became a staunch supporter of the status quo and was appointed to the Stud Book Committee to replace his former friend, Peshall. By the time the libel case went to trial, Watson seems to have completely forgotten that it was he who had made sure Peshall's letter was published in "Forest and Stream."

It is extremely difficult to explain this major lapse in both memory and character for when it came to dogs, Watson could not be compromised or convinced to do anything other than judge them solely on their merits. His major work, "The Dog Book," published in 1905, is a brilliantly researched piece containing numerous first person accounts tracing the development of many breeds. However, the real charm of the book is the further revelation of Watson's personality. In many breeds, including the spaniels, Pointers, Collies and most of the terriers, he is truly expert. In others, such as some hounds and most of the toys, he substitutes a great deal of opinion for actual experience. One of the unique features of the book is that it ostensibly included all the official breed standards, but these should be viewed with a caveat. In certain breed standards with which Watson disagreed he substituted his own opinions on the correct interpretation of type under the heading, "Descriptive Particulars."

Nevertheless, as stubborn and opinionated as he was, he could change his mind regarding dogs if compelling evidence was presented. Watson was the person on the Stud Book Committee most adamantly opposed to the recognition of the Boston Terrier. In his book, however, he actually acknowledged that they were indeed a breed. In relating the events he discussed the question of allowing back crosses to foundation breeds, to which he had violently objected. But in proper third person journalese he concedes, "We can recall that at the meeting at which this solution of the difficulty was accepted, February, 1895, we unconditionally surrendered and stated that in no breed then being shown was there more uniformity of type or such an advance in that direction within two years, and that the Boston Terrier deserved all the encouragement the American Kennel Club could give it." From that point on, Watson became one of the most public supporters of this new breed of dog.

Q. Do you mean to tell me that you do not read Mr. Wade's letters?

A. I mean to state that whenever I see the signature of Mr. Wade to a letter I do not read the letter.

The Stock-keeper

By their verdict the jury have absolved Mr. Peshall from criminal consequences for saying that the American Kennel Club, "cooked," "juggled," and "monkeyed" their accounts. We are sorry for the whole business, as the bitterness engendered by this trial, and the splits it will lead to, must shake the American kennel world to its very foundations. Authority has badly used its power, and the individual has publicly derided it. The effect will be felt in the growth of a spirit of mutinous resistance to kennel government. We have always foreseen that the lack of dignified repose which demeaned the meetings of the American Kennel Club, and the active personal partisanship of its leaders, would endanger its authority; and this has come to pass. They must put their house in order now, and also set about regaining the esteem of the best men in the kennel world; they cannot exist on the rickety support of a few fawning lickspittles who truckle to their masters for clerk work, judgeships, reporting, managing, and so on.

Forest and Stream

We have perused the judge's summing up, and must characterize it as masterly, impartial, and a credit to a judge in any land. We see that Mr. Peshall now intends to bring the American Kennel Club to court for expelling him.

The Stock-keeper

Questions for Consideration

1. Should the American Kennel Club have any secret meetings?

2. Who should run the business of the AKC? What exactly is the business of the AKC? With what particular business should AKC be involved—now and in the future?

3. Should reporters be allowed to attend the Delegates' Meetings? Should any member of a Member Club be allowed to attend these same meetings? Why or why not?

4. As a non-for-profit corporation (today), how detailed should the AKC's Annual Report be? As a virtual monopoly in the dog registration field with no major competitors, shouldn't the AKC and its finances be completely accountable to the Delegates?

5. Is it possible to insist on accountability with the present corporate structure being that of a club of clubs? Doesn't each Delegate have a right to demand a complete accounting on all corporate decisions such as spending?

6. Apart from employee records which are required by law to be kept confidential, what logical reasons could there be for the Board of Directors to hold any secret meetings? Shouldn't the Delegates receive complete, accurate and exact minutes of all proceedings, as they do in their individual clubs, rather than abbreviated and generalized reports?

7. What could or should be done by the Delegates to secure and demand accountability from the Board of Directors of the AKC?

8. When abuse of power and malfeasance are clearly proven, should the guilty parties be allowed to remain in office and in control of the sport of dogs? Can you think of any other business or sport where this would be allowed or tolerated?

9. Would you characterize most Delegate commentary as elucidating, meaningful or contributing significantly to the advancement of purebred dogs?

Canine Progression

"The Kennel Gazette"
1894

In this progressive age it cannot be a matter of surprise that dogs come in for their share of attention, notwithstanding that there are old fogies—adherents of the good old times—ever ready to decry any improvement that has been brought about. Fashions change as years roll on. The old-fashioned throaty Foxhound, with his line hunting propensities of a generation ago, has

As with the style of hunting, so in almost every breed of dogs that has been admitted to the Stud Book, some change has been effected with a view to improvement. The fact that it has obtained official recognition has given it a status, and in most cases a specialist club has been formed to look after its interest. In this connection it must be admitted, however, that specialist

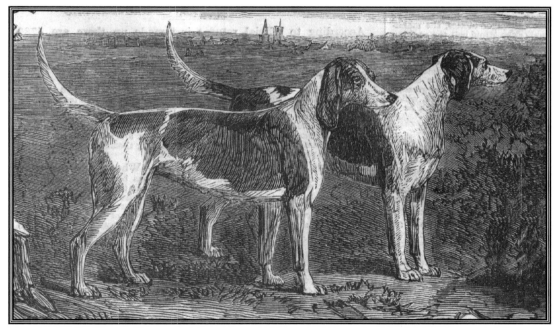

Foxhounds from 1861

been supplanted by a more racing-like animal. The foxhunter of half a century ago will tell you that the sport is spoilt; that the science of hunting is in seeing hounds work out the line of their fox, and cast themselves when at fault; and that a hunting run of two hours is preferable to a quick burst of thirty-five minutes without a check.

clubs are not altogether unmixed blessings. It is an open question whether in some cases the dogs would not have got on quite as well, if not better, without the special care that has been bestowed upon them. This does not, however, apply to some clubs that could be mentioned, which are conducted by those whose sole desire is the benefit of the dog; but in

95

too many instances personal interests and petty jealousies are very much in evidence.

The subject is not, however, specialist clubs, but the improvement or otherwise of the various breeds of dogs. To commence with, it must be admitted that, through the advantages offered by registration and competitive shows, a greater regularity of type has been obtained, objectionable features have been eliminated, and each race has become more defined, although there may be no individual specimens superior in character to what may have been seen a few years ago. This does not, however, alter the fact that fashion has exerted its influence in dog breeding as in all other matters, and changes for the better have been made in almost every breed.

The most important matters under consideration just now are in connection with the size of Fox Terriers and the capacity of Field Spaniels for work. Before, however, touching upon these, it may not be out of place to observe that had breeders kept to the type as handed down to them one hundred years ago, very few of the handsome races of dogs, of which England has so much reason to be proud, would ever have been in existence. Take, for instance, the Mastiff as it is portrayed by old artists. Then, with regard to the St. Bernard, it is admitted on all sides that the most perfect animals that have been bred in this country are quite unlike the St. Bernards that in former times were used at the Hospice for work in the snow; in fact, that the finest specimens of the rough-coated variety would be entirely unfitted

The Greyhound FULLERTON, winner of the Waterloo Cup 1890-1893. Some breeds change little over centuries while others are radically altered within a short period of time. Artist, R. H. Moore

for the purpose.

Bulldogs, again, could not do the work that their ancestors were required to perform, and the wide-ranging Pointers of today are distinctly different from the pottering dogs from which they are descended. The same may be said of almost every breed that has gained any popularity, which goes to show that in striving for the ideal it has been found impossible to keep to the old beaten track.

Those who are so ready to condemn show dogs as being useless for any purpose except winning prizes should remember that show condition is not working condition. No one would think of exhibiting a hunter directly after a hard season.

An animal has to be prepared for the show ring, and in the short-legged dogs, such as Field Spaniels, in which abundance of coat and feather with closeness to the ground are important factors to success, working properties are lost in the preparation. It does not, however follow that they could not work under other conditions, nor that the fashionable black Field Spaniel, with his long, low body, cannot do as much work as is to be expected from any spaniel. In dealing with the subject at issue neither the advocates of the small nor those of large appear to be very clear as to the original use of the Fox Terrier. The nine inch drain is as much a fallacy as the idea that any Fox Terrier that ever was bred could live with a pack of hounds running breast high with a burning scent, whereas, whether large or small, it would be at the end of any run by the time it was

Dr. Nicholas Rowe *was the son of an English Episcopal missionary and spent his childhood in Barbados. He studied medicine in New York City but soon discovered a stronger passion for gambling, horse racing, hunting and fishing. Thus, he gave up his medical career to become a sporting journalist. He initially worked as a reporter for the "Turf, Farm and Field," "Wilkes' Spirit of the Times" and "Rod and Gun" under the nom de plume, "Mohawk." Negative reports described him as a wild and shady man in business who let his wife support him with her wealth, but in 1876, Rowe took the opportunity to move west and became editor of the then, "Chicago Field." A champion of American sportsmen and one of the earliest environmentalists, he quickly built the weekly into the most widely read sporting journal in the United States. With this change from a regional to a national scope the paper became "The American Field" in 1881.*

Rowe was long associated with sporting dogs, particularly English Setters, and was the principal financial backer of the first successful dog show held in the United States at Mineola, New York in 1874. Although Arnold Burges is called the "father of the stud book," his 1876 work, "The American Kennel and Sporting Field," did not initially serve as a basis for a registry but was actually more of a narrative compilation of dogs owned by various American kennels. In 1876, Rowe founded and was the first president of the National American Kennel Club, whose mission was to establish a stud book and registry for field and bench dogs, support the formation of kennel organizations and establish uniform rules for the running of field trials and dog shows. A firm believer that it was necessary to know a dog's background in order to make improvements, he created and published the NAKC's first stud book in 1879. When the American Kennel Club was founded in 1884, their initial intent was to be an organization to promote bench shows. However, Rowe convinced them of the necessity of having an official stud book and registry, turning over his plates and publishing rights for the stud books at no charge. This fortuitous gift immediately put the fledgling American Kennel Club in the black and gave it automatic status as an official governing body in the dog show world.

Nicholas Rowe died on his birthday in 1896 at the age of 54 from Bright's disease, a complication from his long battle with "locomotor ataxia," as it was called then (tabes dorsalis), an excruciatingly painful and debilitating syphilitic condition. Upon his death his wife assumed the duties as editor of "The American Field" and it continued in the same direction for many years. With the establishment of the Field Dog Stud Book in 1900, "The American Field" devoted itself more and more to field trial dogs, focusing on Pointers and Setters. But, until World War I, anything pertaining to the advancement of purebred dogs could find its way into print. After the war, bench show news gradually disappeared. While Rowe is remembered for the stud books, "The American Field," still in publication today, is truly the legacy to which the complete dog fancy must be indebted. Without this journal we would have very little accurate chronological history of the development of dog shows and most canine breeds within this country. Of exceptional value is the fact that letters from just about anybody who took the time to write would be published, unedited, and could even be libelous, as long as they were signed. Thus, we have the opportunity to observe the discussions on critical issues in all aspects of the dog sport during its formative years, set within the context of other 19th Century sporting interests.

Canine Progression—Full Circle

The advent of competitive dog shows focused attention on "improving" breeds, in many cases to suit the demands of fashion. Several changed so dramatically from the foundation stock that all are now recognized as separate breeds in their own right. Because each new generation of dog fanciers has its own definition of canine improvement, it will always be difficult to maintain original conformation, even with breed specific gene pools.

1881

1929

1845

The King Charles Spaniel, a royal pet for centuries, fell from grace with the beheading of its namesake, consequently being viewed as the symbol of Catholicism in England. Not considered a proper Anglican dog, the breed languished. With the opening of Japan and the Orient in the 19th Century, the importation of many new canine varieties, in particular, the Japanese Spaniel, provided the necessary tools to make the King Charles a more "modern," if not more politically correct, breed. Very few breeds changed as radically in head type and the new version, called the English Toy Spaniel in the USA, became so universally popular that the older style disappeared. But in 1926, an American, Roswell Eldridge, offered prizes at Crufts for anyone who could reproduce the old type. Using the same blood stock, the present day Cavalier King Charles Spaniel was reborn, in surprisingly pristine condition. Dog shows have always provided the impetus for change. The original Fox Terriers became sleeker, more refined and taller. The Collie, via the Borzoi, developed a new head shape with considerably more coat than the original Scotch Sheepdog. Today, fashion has gone full circle. In a remarkable revival, the old forms, under the names Cavalier King Charles Spaniel, Border Collie and Parson Jack Russell Terrier have all returned among the most popular breeds worldwide.

1890

1884

1908

From top, clockwise: King Charles Spaniel, Scotch Sheepdog, "Early" Smooth Fox Terrier, English Toy Spaniel, Collie, "Modern" Smooth Fox Terrier.

Spaniel Progression

By the time this article was published in 1894, the black Field Spaniel had become a fashionable show dog, already displaying distinctive divergence from original type, particularly in the United States. In 1892, when a Mr. G. Bell wrote and questioned previous remarks of a judge, Mr. Otis Fellows, "The American Field" commissioned G. Muss-Arnolt to depict these two contemporaries, the Field Spaniel, Beverley Negus, on the left, and the Cocker Spaniel, I Guess, on the right. Judge Fellows had awarded both spaniels first prizes in Toronto. He stated that Beverley was a true type of Field Spaniel, contending there was as much difference between the head of a Field Spaniel and that of a Cocker as between the head of a Greyhound and a Beagle. Mr. Bell did not agree. Can you identify any pronounced differences?

wanted in the event a fox having been marked to ground, whether it be over the pastures of Leicestershire, or in the most cramped country that is known. A Fox Terrier should not be powerful enough to kill a fox in its earth, but sufficiently plucky to go to the fox, and if not able to bolt it, to worry it so that the workmen may hear to what point they are to dig.

There appears to be more reason in the discussion that is going on about the size of the present day Fox Terrier, which is not improved for show purposes by being shown fat. Before, however, expressing an opinion as to the justness of the accusation that some prominent breeders are ruining the Fox Terrier by breeding it too large, it must be admitted that, considering the short space of time that the modern Fox Terrier has been acknowledged as a breed, unbounded credit is due to those who have raised him to the position that he now holds as the most popular dog in England, and in having produced, out of the material that was to be obtained, so much fixity of type in little more than a score of years.

Questions for Consideration

1. The writer contends that because petty jealousies and personalities interject themselves into the running of clubs, many breeds would be better off without any "special care." What role, if any, should specialty clubs play in the development, maintenance, improvement and protection of a particular breed?

2. Is it not only unreasonable, but impossible as well, to expect breeds to be perpetuated in their original form over many years? Elaborate upon your reasons.

3. The assertion is made in this article that registration and competitive shows have been responsible for bringing about more uniformity in type among the various breeds. Can this be verified? If so, is this uniformity necessarily good if the breed has been radically changed from the original specimens of the breed?

Is the Pug a Toy?

"The Stock-keeper"
1905

Is the Pug a Toy dog? This is a question which is promptly answered by everyone. Yes! Why, then, do we see the huge dogs that are benched today winning at the shows? It is true that the larger dog, as a rule, has better type, his skull is wider, his wrinkle heavier and in body he is thicker, but surely his size should handicap him somewhat. A Pug has from its earliest days, which can date back some four or five hundred years ago, been looked upon as a ladies' lap dog, but I fancy there are few ladies who would care to nurse for long some of the present day champions! That there are some breeders who strive hard to breed small Pugs cannot be gainsaid, and there are a good few fanciers who have them both small and typical; but, alas! when these small specimens are exhibited they are usually passed over for the larger animals. It is true Pugs are not so popular among ladies as pets as formerly, other breeds having pushed their way in being partly the cause, but to a great extent the large size so many of them attain is the chief reason for their wane in popularity. The Pug of medium size is to be preferred to the larger one or the very small, where type and quality can be obtained, and yet at the same time an animal which will be useful for breeding purposes.

BLACK FAIRY
1903

Questions for Consideration

1. In general, are dogs larger today than in years past? If so, to what causes can this be attributed?
2. If dogs are larger today because of better nutrition, what would have caused the proliferation of larger specimens in and around the year 1905?
3. What is the purpose of breeding Toy dogs? Is it possible to breed Toy dogs of both correct type and size?
4. Is size an element of type in Toy dogs? In other breeds?
5. How big should a Toy dog be? How seriously should oversized Toy dogs be penalized?

The Scottish Terrier: Size & Type

W. L. McCandlish

"The Kennel"
1912

The effect on a breed of breeding for show success is commonly regarded as the production of abnormal qualities, or, in other words, of fancy points. It cannot be denied that abnormal features are produced, are exhibited, and are bred from. But the breeder who endeavours to produce the abnormal has not, as a rule, continued success in breeding, and in most breeds judges do not favour such creations. The adverse effect of show breeding is caused more by breeders pursuing a stamp of animal that conforms in detail to the perfect form, and that is comparatively easy to perpetuate. It is for this reason that correct type is usually lost. "Correct type" is an unsatisfactory definition, because few people have a similar conception of its meaning; but in a general way type is understood to imply the general appearance of a dog as seen from some distance, and correctly, type is that general appearance which each deponent fancies. One thing type has no connection with, namely, points. If the desired features, for example, consist of a long head and a short back, one animal with a short head and a long back may be of the correct type, whereas another animal with the desired length of head and body may be absolutely wrong in type.

Now in Scottish Terriers the original framers of the standard stated that the skull should be proportionately long and the body should be of moderate length, and that is absolutely every word that is said about the length either of head or body. It is to be presumed that those who framed the original—and existing—standard based it upon the dogs of that time, dogs which had not been influenced by breeding for show competition. I take it that the aim of a breeder should be to improve the existing animal, but not to alter what we call its type. He should retain the dog, but improve the details. Have we done so? I have heard some declare from a pedestal they erected for themselves that they have no patience with what they call an antiquated animal, and that they want an improved animal. Their improved animal is probably quite a different one from the original, but that is only a sign of their superior and progressive minds. I trust I am no pessimist, but I have grave doubts about the form of improvement we have made on the breed. Many of the dogs I see winning, and owned, among others, by myself, are not my conception of what a Scottish Terrier ought to be, and it is well occasionally to have a day of humiliation and examine our sin and the cause of our sin. As a struggler among the many difficulties of breeding, it seems

CH. NOSEGAY FORGET-ME-NOT
The first American-bred Scottish Terrier champion whelped, 1900

The methods of the morally defective to entice judges from the path of rectitude are many, and, even in this unsavory business, there is room for comedy. In these days of little cash and high-priced food, the arrival at the house of a judge, prior to his leaving for a show, of a beautiful, spicy, cured ham must send him to the show glowing with gratitude towards the donor, and as he looks at the donor's dog the saliva of expectation must produce a film over the eyes which prevents sight of its defects. It may be well for the morality of dog shows that none were held at the time when, for the ordinary mortal, whisky was unattainable. Had shows been held, all prizes would have gone to those who had access to a supply, unless a special rule had been passed that only teetotalers were to judge. Every man is said to have his

price, but what astonishes is the poor value some people place upon their honor, and the wretched poverty of the bait which has ruined the prospects of men who have aspired to be all-round judges.

Popular Dog Show Maxims:
Judges, Judged and Judging
c. 1925

to me that the easiest type of dog to breed in order to secure show success is the stamp of dog which possesses a head of considerable length, a body that is short, and a pair of fairly straight legs, and of a weight, in rather full condition, of about 20 pounds; or if run off its legs by hunting, of from 15 to 17 pounds. Many terriers can be shown, in appearance not over fat, fully 5 pounds heavier than in hard herring-gutted condition. I am not saying that either the fleshy or the rakish state is the correct one, I am merely making the distinction so that weight may be an indication of size. The ordinary faults of this sort of dog are that it is too straight at the shoulder and at the stifle, the thighs are thin, the bone is often light, the ribs are too flat, and the lower ribs are not carried far enough back, the front action is stiff, and the hindquarters have not the power nor the formation for jumping. Such faults however are not prominent, the dog looks smart, and so he is preferred to the dog more correct in structure, but with one or two failings which everyone can detect at once. The consequence is that breeders see such dogs winning, and realise that to try to

breed such dogs is the easiest road to success.

The good dog of good type does not differ much in points from the good dog of the type I have tried to describe, but he is very much more difficult to breed and also to rear to perfection. The question I wish to put is, how can we encourage breeders to try for the best type? We can possibly answer this by seeing how the other type came into prominence. Personally, I regard the prevalence of the small, often rather weedy, straight shouldered, poor thighed terrier as due to handicapping length of body too much, and I think we have arrived at a stage where length of body, as length and nothing more, should be ignored within reason, provided that, with the more lengthy body, we have big quarters, well bent stifles, and big muscular thighs, from whatever point they are looked at. Provided also that the shoulder is well laid, and that the body appears hung by springs upon the legs and not placed upon them, and that the loin, even if it is lower than is what we aim at, is muscular. If we can get more of this type of body by preferring it in competition to the straight-topped, short stilty

102

Type—Old and New
Harding Cox
"Dogs and I"
1924

I must say a few words about a controversy which arose in the "twenties" of this century. Some of those who had taken up the breed, professed to be much exercised in their minds as to the correct type which the Labrador Retriever should display. These quoted the fact that, in dealing with the leading show dogs of the day, different judges frequently reversed one another's decisions; whereby those who were thirsting for information and knowledge of the breed were left guessing. I cannot help thinking that a mistake was made; that the true interpretation of the term "type" was missed and that the complainants had confused the issue with a question of a different assessment of "points," for, personally, I could not see any appreciable variation in type of the half dozen dogs which were quoted. At the time of which I speak H. M. King George the Fifth was exhibiting some very fine specimens, but there were those who averred that they were not of the correct type, and pointed to a very striking dog belonging to a certain enthusiast, as being of an altogether different type, and that the true one. I had judged both of the Royal dogs and the other in question on several occasions. The latter was the most splendidly ribbed and quartered dog that could be desired, and he had a fairly typical head; but he had not the quality of either of His Majesty's representatives, being throaty and a bit short in the neck. This throatiness suggested a reversion to a fault possessed by almost every one of the original imported dogs, and that is why the dog which I write of was, I suppose, picked out as a closer representative of the "true type" than others which had had the fault eliminated by careful breeding.

Verily it is a fine thing to keep to an ideal type, when it has been attained; but to foster pristine faults because they were typical of uncouth forebears, is fatuous in the extreme. Evolution goes forward and quality must be sought for, as long as it does not lead to physical or mental degeneration. The development of the Lab has been extremely rapid. When the mind's eye reverts to the three-cornered, yellow-eyed monstrosities that were exhibited as Labradors but a few years back one wonders at the celerity with which a very fairly level type has been established. In a great many breeds of longer standing in public favour, the dissimilarity of type is far more noticeable.

CH. BLACK DRAKE
Flat-Coated Retriever
Breeder/Owner, Harding Cox
1898

Cox was one of the earliest promoters of the Flat-Coated Retriever, finishing numerous champions. Considered the "original" retriever, within a period of thirty years the breed virtually disappeared into obscurity in direct correlation to the rising popularity of the faster, more versatile Labrador Retriever.

W. L. McCandlish served as the Honorary Secretary of the Scottish Terrier Club (England) and was elected to membership in the Kennel Club in 1902, eventually becoming Chairman from 1925-1935. Unlike many of his contemporaries who owned and raised many breeds, McCandlish had a passion for only one—the Scottish Terrier. An author of several books, McCandlish had no tolerance for dishonesty or unethical behavior, especially involving those who judged dog shows. He was a true dog breeder and had nothing but contempt for those who merely raised dogs for fashion. A preservationist, he believed that "true type" meant nothing less than original breed type. In his book, "The Scottish Terrier," he made this particularly clear. "One thing I would ask for...would be the means of preserving the individual character, appearance, and idiosyncrasies of the Scottish Terrier. The breed is often judged by persons better acquainted with longer-legged Terriers, who naturally lay stress in their judgments on points which are of importance in the breed they know best, that the lame, the halt, and the blind are led to believe that such points are also required in a Scottish Terrier. These judges are doing their best, and I have no intention of firing at them, but I should like to shoot all breeders of Scottish Terriers who breed dogs to suit judges, those who tell you, for instance, that they must breed for straight fronts and short backs, because such judges insist on these two catch-penny phrases, even though they are fully aware that to obtain these two subsidiary features they must ignore expression and intelligence, type of body, and true activity...All breeders should breed to establish and preserve the true type and expression—the low set, muscular, active dog with the intelligent searching expression, and pay but secondary attention to points, and I would ask all who have to judge to make working qualities their chief consideration, and to do all they can to preserve the breed from becoming the tool of that terrible nightmare—the fancier."

kind, we shall be able by selection to retain the type and shorten up the body.

Another reason for the prevalence of the present day type is size. We have been so set on getting our terriers small that we have been afraid to breed from big terriers possessing the power and substance demanded in almost every sentence of the standard. We have used small dogs, regardless of their want of this desired power, and once we commence to travel along the path of want of power the decline becomes rapid. We have got much smaller dogs today in the front rank than we ever had before, but have we gained by it, and have we retained type? I think not. We all want a small sized terrier if he is a big one in little, but no one can hurry change in size, so let us not be afraid of using the big dog if he is right in type. If we are to get the right type of dog of the right size, we must get back to the right type, whatever the size, and then reduce by selection, retaining the type. Let us not, however, rush blindfolded to the big dogs. There is no object in reverting to big dogs without making a gain; so the big dog, to be pardoned his excesses must possess the same qualities as the over-long terrier.

Lastly, let me plead for quality. We want our show dogs to be distinctive from street dogs. The smart little short backed dog is to be found in almost every street in the country. Most of them, even the winners, are common in appearance. The quality we should aim at is not delicacy or fineness; it is what was meant by the old expression, "The Quality." What is wanted is aristocratic bearing. This implies good carriage, and this the short backed square built dog has not. The light motion which comes from clean well laid shoulders, from muscular quarters, and well bent stifles gives an air. Many poor creatures are purebred, but in our winning terriers we want the look of "blood."

LOYNE RUFFIAN and LOYNE GINGER
Owner, Nosegay Kennels (Dr. Fayette Ewing)
Artists, R. H. Moore and G. Muss-Arnolt
1899

Questions for Consideration

1. McCandlish clearly believes that purebred dog breeding should strictly adhere to the type as set down by the original framers of the standard of any particular breed. Do you agree or disagree?

2. McCandlish also feels that many so-called "improvements" are blatant alterations of type. Give examples to either defend or refute this position.

3. Is it more difficult to breed to the same level of type as the original dog than to change and "improve" it? Is it easier to breed a current style which is winning in the ring than to breed to "original" type?

4. Are the original dogs in any breed necessarily the ideal representatives or should they more accurately be considered a starting point for improvement? Cox maintains that the object is to keep the general stamp of original type yet still improve the breed as a whole without perpetuating original faults. Is this possible?

5. In a letter in, "Great Dane Type & Theories," A. H. Heppner stated he maintained two types of Great Danes in his kennel, heavy and light, for the sole purpose of allowing the judges to determine which should be considered the correct type, a practice McCandlish clearly finds offensive. Whose responsibility is it to determine correct type within a particular breed—the judges, breeders or exhibitors?

6. In the article, "Criticism," a distinction is made between a "dog lover" and a "dog fancier." McCandlish makes a further distinction between a "fancier" and a "breeder." How would you define these terms?

7. Is the problem of assuming that priorities of type are the same from one breed to another widespread? Does this contribute to the development of the so-called, "generic" show dog? If so, what should be done to correct this problem?

8. What has size to do with type in Scottish Terriers? In other breeds?

9. Can you determine McCandlish's priorities in judging Scottish Terriers from this article?

10. The various parent clubs are empowered to define the "true type." What is true type?

Soundness in the Pekingese

Opinions of Judges

"The Kennel"
1913

The question of "soundness" is one of such vital importance to every breed that the endeavour of the Committee of the Pekin Palace Dog Association to obtain judges' opinions on this matter will be followed with keen interest. The definitions sent in by the Association's judges are, therefore, valuable, not only as individual expressions of opinion, but as helping to make clear the various points to which exhibitors as well as judges should pay attention. It is not to be expected that judges should possess the knowledge of a veterinary surgeon; it is visible defects, of course, and practical tests to discover weakness which are within the power of everyone to apply, which are the basis of all these opinions upon what constitutes soundness or unsoundness in the Pekingese.

Mrs. Browning writes, "Whether a dog is organically unsound or internally wrong can only be discovered by a veterinary surgeon, after a thorough examination. So the question of unsoundness from a judge's point of view seems more or less a matter of legs. A judge should ascertain by feeling whether the limbs are properly jointed, and should endeavour to observe the dog's action in walking and running, and note whether it stands firmly and well up on its feet. The front of a dog is easily seen, but it is sometimes difficult to get a good view of the hind legs when on the move owing to profuse featherings. A judge when standing in a small ring, with the dogs all crowded close round, is much handicapped. Some exhibits are dragged along, half sitting down, so that should unsoundness exist, it is not easy to perceive it. Some Pekingese run the risk of being unjustly voted unsound owing to excessively bowed front legs; but I think a rickety or really unsound dog should be at once evident to a good judge, providing a fair view can be obtained of it."

Mrs. Hugh Andrews, "Some judges appear to consider a dog very much out at elbows a malformation, and consequently unsound, whereas I would call it simply an exaggeration of true type of legs; and I wish we had more that make of dog to counteract the straight legged dogs that are now coming before us at every show. Some of these dogs have faulty hind action, the kind of action we often see in Japanese imported dogs. A really typical Pekingese, to my mind, is heavy in movement, with a rolling laboured action owing to the short bowed-out legs. As a judge I should never pass over any actual or perceptible lameness but I could not honestly and without tangible evidence, pronounce any dog as actually 'unsound' without the technical knowledge of a veterinary surgeon."

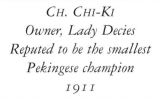

CH. CHI-KI
Owner, Lady Decies
Reputed to be the smallest
Pekingese champion
1911

106

Lady Evelyn Cotterell says, "Soundness, in my opinion, is when a dog shows no sign of lameness, and stands properly on his feet, without knuckling over or dropping at the shoulder."

Major Becher, "A dog is unsound if he does not stand up firmly on his feet, or if he turns in or out one foot to a greater extent than the other in standing or moving; if he were loose or out at the shoulder joints, or cowhocked, or had any weakness that interfered with his free action and movement."

Mrs. Becher, "I should consider a dog unsound who did not stand quite evenly and firmly on his feet; if he were cowhocked, out at shoulder (to the extent of being loose in shoulder joint), or, indeed, showing any weakness in joints and not using his legs evenly and freely."

It will be noticed that both the two last judges consider a Pekingese that is cowhocked as unsound; and a similar view is also held by **Dr. J. Sidney Turner,** who says, "I should say that a Pekingese which is correctly made and able to walk and run in the natural and proper manner (that characteristic of the breed) is perfectly sound. However, a Pekingese which is not correctly made may be quite sound in movement, but if he be much misshapen in limb, such as turning in of the forefeet, or straight in hock (like a Chow), I should certainly say he is not sound in limb. To sum up, I would say, soundness of limbs is present in a Pekingese when the animal can walk and run in the natural and normal manner, characteristic of

that particular breed; and when there is no disease of, nor anatomical formation of any of the limbs, which would be likely or liable to produce or lead to inability to make such movements."

This would appear to indicate that, as the characteristic rolling movement is due to the short bowed forelegs, that absence of that movement, due to the anatomical formation of straight forelegs, might be regarded as unsoundness in that point.

Mrs. Douglas Murray, "Unsoundness is, looseness of limbs, faulty joints, feet turning in, a roach back, and general want of firmness in body, muscles and joints. A Pekingese must stand well up on his feet. In most terriers bent legs are unsound, therefore I do not see why straight legs in the Pekingese should not be regarded as unsound."

Mr. Sydney Spencer, "I think the whole question of unsoundness is, in a nutshell, that it consists simply of joints, which are not properly or firmly knitted in their sockets. A certain kind of malformation is natural in the Pekingese, but there is one species of deformity which is not right, and which tends to produce the effect of unsoundness as far as action goes, by which I mean dogs standing too much down on their ankles and not properly on their feet."

Miss Keith Wright, "I should call a dog unsound who showed any weakness in the joints, and who, instead of standing up upon his feet, stood on his elbows in the case of the forepaws, and his hocks in the case of the hinder ones. This, of course, would be the natural result of the weak-

Three generations of typical Pekingese
CH. CHU-ERH OF ALDERBOURNE, *his son,*
CHU-TY OF ALDERBOURNE, *and grandson,*
CH. CHOO-TAI OF EGHAM
1913

Gaiting the Dogs

Anyone attending a dog show would never question that the procedure of individually gaiting the exhibits is an integral part in analyzing which dog is "best" on the day. Much of what we take for granted became part of the system only after a long period of trial and error. Further, before the advent of dog shows, it was logically presumed all dogs could move in a manner appropriate for the work for which they were bred. A Pointer unable to go all day in the field, a hound which could not keep up with the pack, or a terrier which was too big to go to ground, could not justify its expense and would have been destroyed. Apart from royalty, the concept of the dog as a pet and companion for the average person was unheard of and only developed concurrently with the increase in dog shows during the Victorian era.

Miss Owen takes her
Pekingese for a walk
1913

Many of the earliest dog shows in England were run along the same lines as agricultural fairs. This meant that judging was done behind closed doors and the owners were not present. As dog shows advanced and became public events the judges started evaluating entries on their benches. Again, owners were not permitted in the aisles during the judging of their breed. Thus, one could only hope one's dog would be awake and alert when the judge walked by. But, this method brought forth many complaints. Often, the judges simply awarded prizes to well-known winners, regardless of their condition or the quality of the other dogs in competition.

Edwin Brough, G. Muss-Arnolt and Harding Cox were among the first to insist all dogs be gaited as part of the evaluation process. Brough created quite a stir when he advised the Bloodhound exhibitors that he not only wanted to see the dogs "in the round," but have them individually gaited as well, a previously unheard of judicial request. One journal thought it outrageous that the dogs had to be "lugged about the ring," and referred to gaiting Bloodhounds as "circus work." However, Brough's written show reports are worthwhile reading for anyone who wants insight into how judges must weigh faults, virtues and individual breed priorities when making their awards. "I eventually gave first prize to Cromwell, although he is a very bad mover, and seems to be getting even worse in this respect. I have no doubt that some judges would reverse this order, but I cannot forget that Cromwell is very exceptional in head properties, and I know the difficulty in breeding hounds of this character."

It did not take show committees long to realize that having the dogs paraded in a ring would create more spectator interest and by 1897 the practice became customary at all shows in England and elsewhere. In fact, if entered dogs were not in the ring when their classes were called the judge could authorize "runners" to take the dogs off the bench and serve as their handlers. This was not such a problem in England because most people exhibited their own dogs. But in the United States, many owners never attended a show, instead shipping their dogs off to distant cities by train where they would be in the complete charge of the show superintendent upon arrival. Unless one was an owner/handler the exhibits were generally led into the ring by complete strangers who were under no obligation to present the dogs at their best. As a result, the judging "ring" further contributed to the establishment of the professional handler as an integral part of the American dog show. Nevertheless, the majority of judges still did not gait the animals, simply having them brought into the ring to be evaluated in a stationary position. To counteract this lapse, certain breed standards, such as that of the French Bulldog, added directives for judges to gait the dogs before making their awards. But, despite such explicit instructions, to gait or not to gait was solely the judge's discretion. Consequently, many decades passed before official requirements demanded all dogs be gaited as part of the judging procedure.

ness of the joints. Any malformation of the legs which cased lameness would also render a dog unsound in my opinion."

Mrs. Kennedy, "I consider a Pekingese to be unsound should he be loose in joints, walk lame, or have any structural malformation."

Lady Sutton, "In the first place I should judge unsoundness by the dog's action. If its movements were not free, and its legs, instead of being well thrown out, seemed, so to speak, tied, I should then expect to find the toes turning in, and that this was caused by its being out at elbows. By this I do not mean bowed, but the elbow standing out too far from the body and too loosely knit—a fault which a large coat might hide, but which I should consider a sign of rickets. Of course if a dog's knees and hocks are enlarged, I should not consider it sound, even if it moved all right; and I think loose joints, and being able to turn the foot below the pastern, up and to one side, is a sign of unsoundness. I should also suspect unsoundness in any dog who stood perceptibly lower on its front than its hind feet; and if a dog does not stand properly on the balls of its feet, I should not consider it sound."

Mr. Hubert D. Astley, "Unsoundness in Pekingese: (1) If a dog does not walk firmly on its forefeet, but at all uses its pastern joints for progression, which may, at the same time bring about a lack of straightness in the correct level of the back; (2) If a dog's elbows are so loosely bowed out as to cause its front feet to turn inwards; (3) If a dog is at all down on the hindquarters, owing to its not being able to stand up well on its hind feet."

Mrs. Goddard, "A Pekingese, to be sound, should have the actual shoulders close to his sides, and that he should throw the front feet out in walking, and stand firm upon them—in fact, he should 'dish' when he walks. I love to see a dog move freely and yet have the roll peculiar to the breed."

Mrs. Weaver and one of her sleeve dogs, weight under 5 pounds
1913

Mrs. F. M. Weaver, "Soundness in a Pekingese I understand to mean the possession of the following qualities: (1) That the joints should be firmly and closely knit together, so that when pressed by thumb and finger they do not move or feel double-jointed; (2) That the dog stands firm and erect when 'at attention,' whereas an unsound dog shows quivering legs and a tendency to change his stance frequently; (3) That the back should be level, the forelegs not unduly shortened or the shoulders unduly down, as the last two defects are nearly always the evidence of rickets in puppyhood."

Mrs. Peel, "A sound dog ought to stand with all four feet firmly planted on the ground, with even pressure on all pads. The forelegs ought not to 'waggle' loosely when standing or moving; and a Pekingese should not be cowhocked. The latter fault seems to be too frequently overlooked by judges. Personally, I always watch a dog's action when it is being turned from or towards me, when any weakness of its hindquarters can be easily detected."

Mrs. Bertram Corbet, "I hold that limping from any cause, even be it only a temporary injury, is unsoundness, and should heavily penalise a dog, as if he is good enough to win, he

No Dog Should be Called a Toy

Harding Cox
"Dogs and I"
1924

Among some breeders of "Pet" dogs, there seems to exist an idea that it does not in the least matter how decrepit, obese or inert they may be. I remember on one occasion I was judging Pugs—a class of "Pet" dogs for which I have a sneaking fancy. As soon as they and their fair handlers had assembled in the ring I invited the latter to "circle round" with their charges.

I could not help overhearing a remark from a bystander at the ring side. It was uttered in tones of sarcasm and was to this effect: "Look at him making the Puggies move round! I suppose he thinks he is judging Fox Terriers!"

Not only do I make "Pet" dogs "move round" for preliminary inspection, but when it comes to serious competition, I always make each one show its paces. I would no more give a prize to a lame or unsound "Pet" than I would to a Gun dog similarly afflicted. And why? Because I figure that a "Pet" dog,

Beau and Little Gypsy Queen
1886

no matter what its breed or size, should be a pal to its beloved and loving lord or lady and able and willing to accompany him or her in a long tramp, even where the going is a bit rough. There are judges who make their awards simply and solely on the points of a stationary competitor. Such never think of seeing if the little creatures are sound and active movers. I am not one of these. Apart from the question of their adaptability as workaday pals and domestic pets, there is that of character and expression. There is no breed of dog, "Pet" or otherwise, that should not possess these distinctive hallmarks; nor is there any way of assessing such, except by trotting them around and giving them the opportunity to "show off!"

will be better withdrawn from the show ring until sound again. The matter of unsoundness from weakness or malformation is, of course, a much more serious and difficult question. When judging I personally look for weakness in the pastern joint, which is apparent by the dog 'knuckling over' and walking on the side of the foot. Also in walking on the pastern and not on the ball of the foot (this in a horse would be called 'broken down'); also, when handling the dog's foot it can be felt to be feeble and weak and too supple. Another unsoundness is weakness in the shoulder, causing a dog to be 'out at the elbow' instead of only bowed as a Pekingese should be. A dog with this weakness does not stand firm and strong on his forelegs—if the hind legs are lifted up, compelling him to bear all his weight on the forelegs, or you press heavily on his back at the

top of the shoulder, he can be felt to 'give way,' and the elbows sag out weakly. Another unsoundness, which I consider a very bad one, is that in the hock joint; when moving, the hindlegs, instead of bending well under the dog, feebly bend outwards at the hock joint, and cause an unsound gait. That formation I consider distinct unsoundness, although it is difficult in a Pekingese to draw the line between the grotesque, which is their charm, and malformation, which is a grave defect. I think the nearest one can get to a definite decision is that malformation which develops any sign of weakness, and evidently arises from weakness is an unsoundness which should be well considered by the judges and heavily penalised. But the grotesque is sadly wanting in the exhibits at present; and it would be a sad pity if in ruling out unsoundness, the grotesque were ruled out with it."

Mrs. Sealy Clarke writes, "A definition of soundness in a Pekingese is at present an elusive term, for few agree as to what soundness is.

Some hold the opinion that a very much bowed Pekingese is unsound; others that unsoundness is constituted by a weakness at the joints, and I must say that I entirely agree with this opinion. In judging I have handled a great many unsound dogs, and a great many who may have been so before they came under me, but who were perfectly sound when I judged them, though their action, being very exaggerated gave rise to the idea that they were not quite sound then. I had a very pronounced case recently. On first seeing the dog I had my doubts, though he had no lameness and only an exaggerated roll; but I found him to be perfectly sound, although I subjected him to every test I knew several times. I was, I believe, blamed for putting up an unsound dog. It was impossible for anyone to pass a decided opinion on that dog but myself as judge, and I realised then how hardly treated a dog might be by a judge who did not thoroughly examine a doubtful exhibit. We all who have bred Pekingese know how liable we are to get a rickety pup in a litter, and what care and attention such a one requires. I have known many who have perhaps not had the right treatment at first eventually get quite well of any ricketiness, but it has left the legs permanently bent, though quite sound. In my opinion a dog can only be called unsound when he is out at a joint, and this is perfectly easy to detect if the joints be properly examined in a suspicious case. It must always be borne in mind that the rolling action which is so very characteristic makes it almost impossible to tell for certain without a thorough handling, whether a dog is unsound or not."

The lessons to be learned from these judges' opinions are: that unsoundness is a defective condition of the joints; that it is most often found in the forelegs (the pasterns or shoulders), that it is most difficult to detect in the hind legs, and that judges should remember that profuse featherings may screen faulty formation (cowhocks) and action. And that a sound dog stands up firmly and with even pressure on the pads of all four feet, moves freely and easily with the characteristic 'roll' and thrown out feet, and has strongly knitted, firmly set joints.

Questions for Consideration

1. G. Muss-Arnolt stated in "Great Dane Type & Theories," that soundness in Great Danes was his next most important consideration in the breed after correct type. While this can be easily justified in a Working breed, does the Pekingese seem a likely candidate for such a lengthy discussion on soundness? Is soundness an important consideration in Pekingese? In other Toy breeds?

2. If type is the most important consideration in evaluating dogs in competition, is it really necessary to gait dogs in the ring to determine which is the best animal? Is soundness an element of type or a special consideration?

3. Why should soundness be such an important consideration in dogs which seemingly have no functional work to perform other than companionship?

4. Is soundness a functional reflection of correct type? That is, is it a result of the correct formation and effective interaction of the component parts delineated in the breed standard? In evaluating soundness, is it an absolute or relative quality?

5. Some of the judges in this article describe unsoundness as a condition of the joints, others as a temporary change in locomotion, and others as something caused by injury or structural malformation. Is it logical to use such a term which seems attributable to so many varied causes? Does it appear that all judges define the terms "soundness" and "unsoundness" in the same way?

6. Can soundness or unsoundness be determined by the judge in the ring or does this require the expertise of a veterinarian?

7. Mrs. Peel states she always watches a dog's action when it is turning toward her or away from her and claims that weakness in the hindquarters can be evaluated at that time. When gaiting dogs in the ring is the manner in which the dog handles itself when changing direction important for evaluation purposes?

8. What is your definition of soundness?

9. Is soundness breed specific?

10. Cox claims that apart from evaluating soundness, the only way to assess a dog's true character and expression is by gaiting it around the ring. Do you agree or disagree? Elaborate upon you reasons.

Lame Dog Best in OCKC Show

Don Gillies

"Detroit Times"
1957

When Champion Siefenjagenheim Lazy Bones, a Basset Hound owned by Chris Teeter of Detroit, limped into the show ring for the group judging at the Oakland County Kennel Club show

n.b. — *Lazy Bones was photographically neutered, apparently to spare the 1950's sensibilities of the "Detroit Times" readership.*

last night at the Detroit Artillery Armory, few gave the dog a chance to go on to win Best in Show.

Alva Rosenberg of New York, who was judging Hounds at the time, walked over to Teeter and at the moment every indication was that Lazy Bones was about to be excused.

But Teeter, who is president of the Detroit Kennel Club, argued that Lazy Bones' lame condition was only temporary and for that reason he could not be disqualified.

Dog Called Fit

Whereupon Rosenberg ordered a veterinarian to examine the dog. Dr. Fred H. Gasow of Birmingham checked Lazy Bones from head to foot, filled out a medical certificate pronouncing the dog fit and judging continued.

After looking over all the other Hounds, Rosenberg finally selected the sad faced, long eared Lazy Bones as best Hound, thereby qualifying him to advance to the finals.

In the final selections, which found Lazy Bones being judged Best in Show, were such greats as Ch. Grousehaven's Beau Brummel, a German Shorthaired Pointer, owned by pretty teenaged Ora Le Van Tassell of Detroit; Ch. Luxi von Liebestraum, a German Shepherd Dog, owned by Emil Lederer, of Detroit; Ch. Cranbourne Alexandrite, a West Highland White Terrier, owned by Mrs. John T. Marvin of Xenia, Ohio; Ch. St. Aubrey Kailo of Raymede, a Pekingese, owned by Mrs. Nathan S. Wise of Cincinnati and Ch. Pall Mall V, a Boston Terrier, owned by Mr. and Mrs. Ray Perso of Royal Oak.

Questions for Consideration

1. Should dogs be judged solely on their conformation, without regard to soundness?

2. Can anyone, even a veterinarian, make the determination that lameness is only "temporary?"

3. What logical explanation or justification can there be for a judge to award prizes to a dog which is lame?

Introduction to Breed Standards

Laurence Alden Horswell

"Dog World"
1964

Magnetic Pole

If it might be said that each breeder, exhibitor and judge employs his knowledge of a breed as a compass, to point the way to correct breed conformation, performance and temperament, then the force which coordinates these several compasses is the breed standard, serving as the magnetic pole, guiding the individual compass needles toward agreement.

Without this stabilizing influence, the variations from animal to animal, litter to litter, kennel to kennel would operate like compound interest or regenerative electronic circuits to increase, rather than decrease differences.

Before it became so customary for judges to fly from one part of the country to another, and for bitches to be flown cross country for breeding, it was not uncommon to hear references to "eastern" type vs. "western" type, or "northern" type vs. "southern" type. And the influences of dominant strains or prepotent individuals could be seen as distractions from the essential type of a breed. Now, access to transportation by air and turnpike also reduces distances for competition, and large shows or circuits attract entries from every part of the country. In a very real sense, a breed standard is the cohesive magic carpet which unites all three phases of breeding, exhibiting and judging purebred dogs from coast to coast.

CH. YOUNG PHAENOMEN
Owner, Dr. C. Motschenbacher
Artist, G. Muss-Arnolt
1899

Functional Origins of Early Standards

In their descent from some common, prehistoric pre-canine ancestry, early breeds gradually took form as most suitably constructed, for particular functions, in particular areas. Further separations were developed as their functions became more specific. Such divergence on separately advantageous patterns usually were comparatively local. By the time strains were sufficiently differentiated to take on types and names as breeds, their breeders had formulated certain relationships between function, conformation, performance and temperament which could be reduced to words.

Some of these early breeders were more articulate than others, and there is the greatest diversity in the way breed specifications are set forth in breed standards.

In general, it may be said that the original formulators of breed standards "knew what they wanted," and "knew what they meant." With an acceptable animal before them, or with a mental image combining the best features of several animals in their several minds, we can understand such phrases as "head not too long or too short," or "in nice proportion to body," representing cautions not to deviate from the symmetry of the then approved animals. But now, to apply this to each up-coming generation of dogs, whose skeletal development may be influenced by more extensive available breeding potential, and

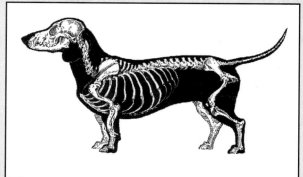

One of the very first illustrated breed standards available in this country was produced by the Dachshund Club of America in 1904. In essence a reprint of the Dachshund Standard of the German Teckel Club, it was translated and edited by Mr. G. Muss-Arnolt and Dr. C. Motshenbacher with the assistance of

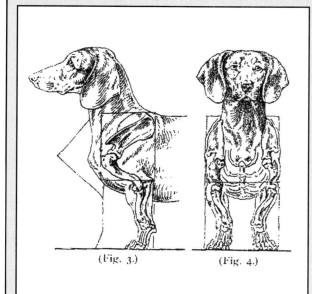

(Fig. 3.)   (Fig. 4.)

Professor D. Willfred Lellmann of the University of New York and the appointed committee of the Dachshund Club. Originally priced at 50 cents, this little pocket-sized book quickly became a handy reference guide for those interested in the finer points of the breed.

Although we accept it as the common format for illustrated guides today, the 26 well-executed drawings depicting coat varieties, anatomically correct skeletal structure and examples of both desirable and undesirable specimens, in combination with the written standard, were unique features of this work. At a time when there were no formal requirements for judging other than to be asked and accept an invitation, this illustrated standard was highly acclaimed as a significant aid to those who wished to properly adjudicate Dachshunds. Other specialist clubs immediately realized the importance and impact of such an educational tool and began producing their own individual guides.

by better understanding and fulfillment of nutritional requirements of optimum growth, has not a standard a greater responsibility for defining desired type?

Stable, but not Stagnant

There also is the aspect of a standard that it is to be hoped that breeds are improving and that a standard which does not encourage improvement may become a handicap at the same time it fulfills its stabilizing function of coordinating the efforts of breeders, exhibitors and judges.

In that respect, each standard must be considered individually. A study of the 114 standards shows the greatest difference in perspective. Some are phrased that an example of the breed "should" appear thus-and-so; others that the "ideal" example appears thus-and-so. Others are expressed that the breed "is" thus-and-so in such a manner that a novice may be led to apply these words to any or every example before him. This form of standard evidently assumes that the reader will take for granted that the description applies to the correct example of the breed, not to the specimen being evaluated with respect to its correctness. Yet, where would a student of the breed locate any example so perfect as to fulfill this form of description?

Cross References

Another aspect of Standards which fortunately applies only to a comparatively few breeds, is derogatory cross-references to other breeds as bad examples. Worse yet, there are instances of disregard of the standards of breeds so disparaged by cross reference. It might be questioned whether a standard should expect knowledge of, or familiarity with, another breed to avoid its pitfalls.

The Constructive Approach

However, these critical observations are akin to that function of dog judging which must appraise a dog's faults. It is true that a fault stated as a disqualification must be so penalized under AKC rules, and lesser faults assessed as weighted in individual standards. But good judging of dogs concentrates on comparison of each animal with the standard and with its immediate competition, to ascertain which animal assembles the most of the desired characteristics in the most advantageous combinations of breed type, soundness, symmetry, performance and temperament.

Applying the same general principle to the standards themselves, they are the most constructive approach we have to appraising the current competition; to breeding out faults—particularly as they are recognized by adverse judicial appraisal; and to breed improvement in two ways; (1) to try to increase the proportion of good quality within the breed population, and (2) to seek for ever closer exemplification of the standard of perfection in the widely accepted prototype of the breed.

Interpretation

Of the 114 standards currently in force, the dates of approval of 96 are available, ranging from 1933 to 1964. It therefore is fair to suggest that interpretation of a standard should undertake to apply whatever aspects of idealism are expressed, rather than to encourage compromises at lower levels of acceptability.

While it is conventional to repeat the comment that the ideal dog of any breed has not yet been achieved, it is the function of a standard to direct favorable attention toward the current animals which most nearly approach the concept of the breed ideal. And beyond the current scene, there should be guide posts toward improvement beyond present examples.

Justifiable Adjustments

Review and revision of breed standards should be approached with utmost conservatism. Only when there is stability in breeding, exhibiting and judging objectives can there be a common denominator for planning or recognizing progress. If a breed's standard lacks definition of desirable characteristics, if it has not kept pace with the progress of the breed it should idealize, if it employs phraseology which obscures, rather than reveals the correct breed image, or if it is not complete in not providing references to important aspects of breed conformation, performance or temperament, a breed may benefit by revision. The ideal standard should closely relate to the function of a breed, should reflect the development of the breed as a foundation for its present appraisal, and leave room for improvement, thus guiding breeders, exhibitors and judges forward, rather than encourage compromise. But to change a standard for the sake of change, or to drift with current trends opens Pandora's box!

The magnetic pole, to which I originally compared the function of the breed standard, is not stationary. But its movement is not erratic or subject to transitory considerations. It sets a high ideal for the idealism of the standards of breed perfection.

Questions for Consideration

1. Horswell maintains that breed standards are not stationary but can be compared to a magnetic pole which coordinates the efforts of breeders, exhibitors and judges toward a common goal. Does this seem reasonable? How would you define the purposes of a breed standard?

2. Horswell claims that without the stabilizing influence of a breed standard, type would quickly be lost, the result being regionalized representatives which are more or less similar. Is a written breed standard necessary to define and maintain a breed?

3. McCandlish believes breeders should strictly adhere to type as set down by the original framers of a standard. Horswell states this is impossible because standards are not stagnent and while standards describe the ideal, the actual dogs then in existence must be evaluated in regard to defining type. Further, he contends that better nutrition and larger breeding populations provide us with many better representatives from which to chose. While this may be true, does it necessarily preclude dogs of original type?

4. What two things does Horswell say must be done to breed out faults? Do you agree or disagree?

5. Before attempting to revise a breed standard what common denominator of stability must exist first?

6. What are the only acceptable reasons to change a breed standard according to Horswell? Are there other reasons which you can enumerate?

7. Does Horswell believe breed standards should be closely related to the function of the particular breed? Can this opinion be justified in those breeds which are no longer required to perform their original function? How should the quality and type of those dogs which no longer perform their original function be evaluated?

8. How would Horswell feel about current AKC policy which allows parent clubs to alter standards as often as every five years? How often, if ever, should breed standards be changed or modified?

9. To the best of your knowledge, are there any recent changes to particular breed standards which have resulted in desirable or undesirable changes in the appearance and/or character or a particular breed? Can you think of any recent changes which have either made it easier or more difficult for judges to evaluate the dogs in the ring? Elaborate and give specific examples.

Are the Standards at Fault?

Kyle Onstatt

"Pure-Bred Dogs—American Kennel Gazette"
1950

Another chore the AKC postponed as long as possible was the licensing of judges. When I first became interested in dog shows and until long afterwards anybody—just anybody—a show giving club chose as its judge, was permitted to hand out its ribbons. There was no obligation to consult the AKC or to obtain its approval. Shows were not numerous and a scant dozen judged most of them—men like Mortimer, Watson, Oldham, Harry Lacy, and a few others, capable and trustworthy. This was all very well until some of the clubs tumbled to the fact that Joe Doaks' awards were just as final as James Mortimer's, and Joe could be trusted to accept the program laid down for him.

Again, the AKC waited in long-suffering indecision, reluctant to impose its authority. For those appointed who really wanted to make correct awards, the process at the time was comparatively easy. Classes were small and all but judged themselves, since they were made up largely of a single rather excellent dog that stood out like a sore thumb, a couple of mediocrities and a ruck of inferior exhibits with ribbons around their necks or at least wide, studded collars to emphasize their importance. One could judge them at a glance when they entered the ring. But shenanigans—unprovable shenanigans—grew until the AKC was forced to take some action.

Thus began the licensing of judges and however long in coming the initial process may have been, the AKC retained the right to cancel a license at any time and for any cause, or none. Almost any person never convicted of a felony could obtain a license, but the license could be forfeited. No AKC approval of a licensed judge for an individual show was required. Simple and informal as the system was, it was salutary.

Nobody will claim that the system of licensing judges even now is perfect but there are few, if any, judges on the roster who deliberately and wilfully misplace the ribbons. To err occasionally is human.

If the AKC can reform the process of registration and can supervise the choice of judges for the betterment of awards (and it has proved its ability to do both), so too it can provide its licensed judges with a series of definite Standards by the employment of which they can make better awards and justify the awards they make. The AKC can complete the cycle.

It is a large order and one that the AKC will not undertake to fill without grave deliberation and without a conviction of the great need that it take the action. However, in my opinion that action is requisite and cannot be long delayed. With valid Standards it will be possible to hold judges to accountability when the tenets of the Standards are habitually violated, whereas, as of today, if some of the Standards are inept, the judges are justified if they disregard the terms of all of them.

> *"Nobody will claim that the system of licensing judges even now is perfect but there are few, if any, judges on the roster who deliberately and willfully misplace the ribbons. To err occasionally is human."*

The Standards are not required to be long (rather, the shorter the better), provided they are definite and fully descriptive. An explanatory glossary may be used to describe and define terms that are repeated in many Standards, such as "scissors bite" and "turn of stifle." The descriptions of the breeds should declare what is demanded, rather than what is to be avoided. This does not apply to disqualifying points, which should be stated forthrightly.

There is no need for explanations within the Standards for the reasons for the various specifications. Many such reasons are specious, at best. For instance, the "width of skull to provide room for the brains." The dog's brain pan is at best rather small and width of skull seems to have nothing to do with intelligence—the Miniature Pinscher with his small, narrow skull does not yield in his intelligence to the Mastiff with his massive, wide one. There exists plenty of scope outside the Standard for the discussion of why breeds should be as they are. Conscientious judges will learn the lore of the breed they judge, the purposes (if any) for which the breeds are used or are designed to serve, and can readily rationalize the reasons for the arbitrary specifications.

Nor should the Standards waste space on the purely mental and temperamental attributes of the breeds, their encomia introduced by the specialty clubs with the purpose of furthering interest in the popularity of their breeds. That a breed is game, intelligent, obedient, that it "loves kids, eats anything," is beside the point, even if true. The Standards should confine themselves to simple and forthright statements of what the breeds should look like and how they should move. They should embody nothing that it is impossible for a judge to evaluate in the show ring after an enforced brief examination.

These should be the AKC Official Judging Standards and so designated. If it is desired to offer a sop to the specialty clubs and to give them scope, they might be permitted to formulate and publish what might be designated as "Breeding Standards," in which they should be permitted to praise the mental attributes of their dogs and to set forth reasons for the various qualifications to their hearts' contents.

There are numerous benefits to be gained from having the Standards compiled by the AKC as well as promulgated by it. The first and most patent is that they would presumably be lucid, literate, and definitive. They would give the judges something to go by, a line to hew.

Moreover, they would be schematically uniform. Compiled by the same committee, all the Standards would be alike in the sequence of the parts of the breeds under discussion, alike in their nomenclatures and styles (a tail would be a tail and not a stern in one, a flag in another, and a tail in the third), alike, it is to be hoped, in their brevity. Best of all, they would be alike in the

Dr. John H. Walsh is called the "father" of the modern dog show. While Walsh may not have been the specific person who originated the idea of formal exhibitions of dogs, he was clearly the one who helped them rapidly develop into a valid, recognizable format. A deep thinker on the subject, he never gave quick answers or offered solutions until he had weighed all the possibilities and their future impact on the sport of dogs. One of the three judges for the first show at Newcastle-on-Tyne in 1859, Walsh was principally responsible for creating a public, if not international, interest in purebred dogs. In his capacity as editor of "The Field" from 1858 until his death in 1888, his comprehensive writings as "Stonehenge" on canine health, kennel management, dog show judging, histories and descriptions of the breeds—in short, on all canine topics—established him as the worldwide authority on dogs.

Walsh was a medical doctor, practicing for twenty years in Worcester, England. During that time he maintained a small kennel of Greyhounds, participating in coursing events. His first step into journalism was writing accounts of these meets for "Bell's Life." He was then asked to edit, "Thacker's Coursers' Annual Remembrancer," which gave yearly coursing reports. He greatly improved upon this work and the result was "Stonehenge's Coursing Calendar," the first compilation of authentic Greyhound pedigrees.

One of Walsh's primary goals in the establishment of formalized dog shows was to make them a forum for those who kept dogs for sport and maintained breeds to improve their qualities, as opposed to those who were dog dealers or whose interests in dogs were strictly pecuniary. Walsh was one of the original sixteen people to found the Kennel Club. Although he later resigned in a dispute between the KC and the fanciers of the Birmingham Committee, whom he supported, he never questioned the importance of an authoritative registry body and neither expressed any animosity nor personally attacked those who differed with him. That this was merely a disagreement between gentlemen is verified by the fact that when the Kennel Club decided to publish its own stud book they immediately sought Walsh's sage advice on the best way to produce it. Further, they followed his recommendation for whom should be selected as best for the job.

Unlike most editors of sporting journals then published, Walsh believed anything worth reading was worth paying for. This policy secured the best writers available for "The Field." Walsh was himself a writer of considerable thought and talent. His compilations in book form, "Dogs of the British Islands," became the first publication with accurate breed descriptions. He also explored, in depth, various systems which could be established to improve dog judging. Walsh was the principal advocate of judging dogs on point scales, as was customary in other livestock adjudication. But, because dog show judging rapidly developed into a system of having generalists process large numbers of dogs, this method proved impractical for show ring application. Despite strong criticisms questioning the validity of assessing dogs "mathematically," point scales are actually a very good way for experts to evaluate breeding stock against the ideal. Regardless, Walsh's ability to stimulate the discussion prompted the specialist clubs to establish breed specific priorities.

Walsh felt exhibitors had the right to know the criteria by which their dogs were being evaluated, insisting each breed have a written standard of excellence. His influence on Harding Cox was significant, for it was Cox who helped initiate both the Bulldog Club in 1875 and the Fox Terrier Club in 1876. These two breeds were among the first to have formalized written standards with point scales appended. Each word within them was carefully chosen and comparative study indicates much of the writing originated with Walsh. Today, these standards are a tremendous tribute to Walsh's forethought, wisdom and vision as evidenced by the fact they have remained relatively unchanged from their first incarnation, yet their clarity in defining the ideal has guided breeders to produce outstanding specimens in both breeds for well over a hundred years.

Personal Opinion vs. Standards
"The American Field"
1907

The spring show circuit is now in full swing, but much of the anticipated enthusiasm has waned, due entirely to injudicious selection of judges—judges who had not heretofore officiated and whose preferences as to type, character and conformation were not known to be based on any published standard of excellence or previous decisions of their own at any show. Without a standard to guide untried judges, exhibitors realize the force of the adage, "Every eye forms its own beauty," is a very poor rule to determine the correct type of any breed. Breeders and fanciers are entitled to something more definite than individual opinion.

Quite a number of exhibitors, more especially old-timers and professionals, are not particularly in favor of a standard of excellence for each breed, some, in fact, decrying in no uncertain terms any rule that would compel the judges to be guided by standards. Exhibitors wonder thereat, because, as they argue, if there is no standard to breed to, how are we to know what points are lacking in our dogs or make them winners? As judging is now conducted it is one man's opinion against another. The reason professionals and old-timers are not advocating from the house tops standards of excellence may be attributed to the fact that they are in the dog show business for profit or emolument of some kind. If handlers of large strings do not depend more on the favor of a judge than they do upon the correct interpretation of a standard, then why is it that managers of dog shows occasionally receive letters from handlers stating that they will not attend the show if certain judges are appointed?

In the early days before professionalism became a factor in dog shows the true amateur fancier exhibited his dogs personally and for the pleasure there was in it. With breed standards, the amateur then had a chance to ascertain why his dog lost. With the growth of shows and growing increase of numbers of judges who thought they knew better than the standard of what a dog should be, the application of the standard diminished proportionately, and finally fell into innocuous desuetude. What has been the result? For years personal preferences have controlled the destinies of dogs in the judicial show ring, and the public and critics alike have had no uniform basis to which they could anchor when it came to differing with the decisions that placed the dogs. In these days of specialty clubs and Twentieth Century enlightenment it should not be a difficult matter to draft standards of excellence for every breed classified at a show, to guide breeders, fanciers and judges alike. The self-styled, self-opinionated judges would thereby have to go or suffer the consequences of misapplying the standards of excellence.

When exhibitors pay entrance fees they are entitled to the same careful consideration. With standards, a judge would have to be a judge in all that the word implies, or have his incompetence proven. At present there are men officiating whose experience is limited and whose knowledge of breed standards is nil. Why should exhibitors be put up against such a condition? A competent judge following the standards would not require much time to weed out the "no chance" dogs. Indeed, finding the winners would not take nearly as much time as is now consumed by those judges who never forget the gallery and try to add effect to their judgment by "posing" and "acting."

THE OFFICIAL ILLUSTRATED STANDARD

OF

THE GREAT DANE CLUB OF AMERICA, INC.

The Great Dane Illustrated Standard

Kyle Onstatt's article specifically mentions the Great Dane Club of America's Illustrated Standard, published in 1945, as a work which all judges should study and all specialty clubs should emulate. Although this guide, illustrated by Donald E. Gauthier, depicts the Great Dane in a highly stylized drawing form typical of its era, it was one of the first interpretations which placed major emphasis on the importance of the underlying musculature to determine correct form. Surprisingly, in contrast to the detailed anatomical drawings, the remaining illustrations are quite schematic, but still effectively convey their intended meaning.

Compare these drawings with those from the early Dachshund guide (page 115), and other illustrated standards with which you are familiar. Do drawings need to be "realistic" to adequately and accurately deliver the correct interpretation of a breed standard?

Is it necessary for a dog show judge to be familiar with canine anatomy in order to properly judge a particular breed, or dogs in general? If so, should judges be required to pass anatomy tests before official approval? Does knowledge of anatomy have any relationship to correct interpretation of a breed standard?

Justify your position.

c1. Nose (no points)

The nose must be large and in the case of brindled and "single-colored" Danes, it must always be black. In harlequins, the nose should be black; a black spotted nose is permitted; a pink colored nose is not desirable.
(See Charts #63-64)

CHART # 64
SPLIT NOSE

c2. Ears (no points)

Ears should be high, set not too far apart, medium in size, of moderate thickness, drooping forward close to the cheek. Top line of folded ear should be about level with the skull. (See Charts #65-66). Faults: hanging on the side as on a foxhound (See Charts #67-68).

Cropped ears: high set, not set too far apart, well pointed but always in proportion to the shape of the head and carried uniformly erect (See Charts #69-70).

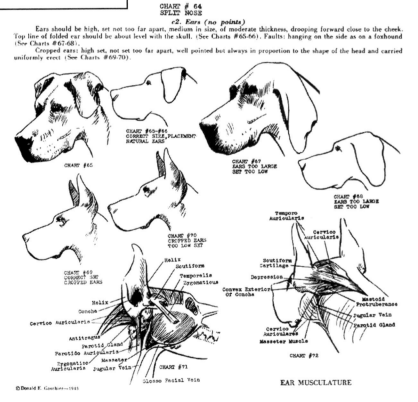

EAR MUSCULATURE

122

Say What You Mean

Early dog breeders were familiar with equine terminology and applied it to written breed standards for dogs. However, extreme variations in canine physical appearance fostered development of breed specific jargon. This was fine for the cognoscenti but created judicial confusion, as universal interpretation or application of terms from one breed of dog to another was non-existent. Nevertheless, many specialty clubs were quite proprietary in the use of terms which applied only to their favorite breed, refusing to give them up. The first serious attempt to bring order to this situation occurred in 1908 with a comprehensive glossary created by Theo Marples and illustrated by Arthur Wardle. While complete uniformity is still unattained, upon reflection, it might not be desirable. When breed specific terms clearly delineate exact shades of meaning, it does not follow that reducing language to the lowest common denominator always provides elucidation.

elimination of meaningless drivel, specious reasoning, the tone of the bark, the descriptions of mental and temperamental idiosyncrasies.

Revisions could be made in all the Standards at once, at intervals of perhaps five years, and no revisions except after such intervals. Judges would know when to expect changes, not a change in one Standard next month and in another next year, and in a third not at all despite the recognition that the breed no longer conforms to it.

And breeds do change and "evolve," despite all that the fancy can do to keep them static. By common consent, they grow larger or smaller, higher or lower in their stations. The tendency is gradual, but at intervals these changes require to be officially recognized and their Standards altered to conform to the facts. This should not be left to the action or inaction of specialty clubs.

In AKC compiled Standards, the public would be assured that they were not framed in favoritism. The Standards would determine the breeds, rather than the dogs in the kennel of some influential member of a specialty club determining or modifying the terms of the Standard. It cannot be proved, perhaps, that specialty club members wrangle descriptions of their own dogs into the Standards, but it is much alleged and the present Standards bear some internal evidence of it. Let them do what they like to the non-official Breeding Standards.

The AKC's Judging Standards would be AKC property and protected by an AKC copyright. The AKC would be free to license, with or without royalty, the reprinting or reproduction of the Standards or of any part or parts of them. As a source of revenue to the governing body, the yield would only be nominal, perhaps, but it would offer a degree of control over the part of the press at which the AKC might be at loggerheads, for instance such publications as print Standards in lieu of fresher news and constructive articles.

If it is possible to obtain adequate drawings to illustrate the ideal type of the respective breeds, it is well that they should be included as integral parts of the Standards, as has been done in the present Standard of the Great Dane. Inadequate illustrations, however, are worse than none.

No Standard should, in my belief, have a "scale of points" appended to it. The score card method of judging dogs has long since proved fallacious. The inclusion of scales of points in the Standards serves only to perpetuate a belief that dogs can be judged by arithmetic. The allotment of a stated number of points to the spotting of the Dalmatian only serves to detract from the emphasis upon structure and makes it possible for a nicely spotted but ill structured dog to defeat a well made dog without perfection of spotting.

Under the scale of points of the present Standard of the Fox Terrier, only fifteen points are allotted to head, skull, muzzle, mouth, eye, ear, and expression. Of those fifteen points for the whole head how many could you subtract for a badly undershot mouth or for a big, light eye? A dog might have both faults in exaggerated degree, and yet win over a well balanced dog with neither fault. I hold no brief for judging only a Fox Terrier's head, but a judge who should apply literally the scale of points of the Fox Terrier Standard would be mobbed by the exhibitors—and rightly.

Questions for Consideration

1. Should anybody be allowed to officiate as a judge without obtaining approval of the governing body? Shouldn't the show giving clubs be permitted to select whomever they choose—without restrictions?

2. Onstatt suggests that because of increased numbers of show dogs and better quality exhibited in the ring the licensing of judges became a necessity. What does official approval have to do with the quality of dogs being exhibited?

3. Should the AKC have the right to cancel approval for judging at any time?

4. Many of the suggestions made by Onstatt regarding breed standards have since become reality, viz., a glossary of terms, a system for logical formatting and a five year moratorium on changes. Have these steps helped to improve overall judging quality?

5. Onstatt states that because many standards are inadequate judges should not be held accountable for their decisions in these breeds. Further, because many standards describe at great length qualities which cannot be accurately assessed in the show ring, Onstatt argues that AKC should formulate Judging Standards, allowing parent clubs to have separate Breeding Standards. Does this seem a reasonable suggestion?

6. If the governing body has the right to establish rules for the running of dog shows and the approval of judges, isn't it logical to assume they have the right to establish standards for dogs being exhibited as opposed to dogs being bred?

7. Can you think of one person or name one committee which could write acceptable Judging Standards for all recognized breeds?

8. Who owns the breed standards and responsibility for any changes? Who should own the breed standards and possess authority to make changes to them?

9. Do most breed standards, as now written, contain a lot of "meaningless drivel?" If you agree, give specific examples.

10. If the original standards were written to incorporate dogs which actually existed, why should it be problematic for specialty clubs to modify their standards to correspond to dogs in existence today? Certainly, in breeds which have been around for hundreds of years, can't it be logically assumed that today's specimens are better representatives of their respective breeds than their ancestors?

11. Does a scale of points necessarily indicate that a judge should use a system of mathematical evaluation, or is it more probably a numerical representation of the specific priorities within a breed? Because the utilization of point scales within the show ring has proven unwieldy does it logically follow that this is an invalid method for evaluating quality?

12. Should representative drawings be included as part of a breed standard or should such illustrated interpretations and guides be considered supplemental educational enhancements to the written standard?

13. Is it possible for any artist to represent the "ideal" of any breed? If so, is it then possible to breed the ideal specimen? Is the concept of the ideal static or dynamic?

14. What is the difference between personal opinion when judging and informed opinion? Can they ever be one in the same?

15. Is it possible to judge dogs properly without having a thorough knowledge of the individual breed standards? Give examples.

Let's Forget the Horse and Buggy

Gerald Taylor White

"American Kennel Gazette"
1946

It sometimes appears that progress has left the dog game flat on its back. By that we mean that dogs are still being judged—providing the Standard is the criterion—on the basis of some duty which it is no longer possible to fulfill. I offer as one example the popular Dalmatian. According to its history it reached great popularity as a dog to accompany a horse drawn rig. The Dal was supposed to have certain attributes that would allow it to trot along between the hind wheels of the vehicle for hours on end.

In a recent conversation about the size of Dals it was pointed out that a dog that was a bit oversize could not fit in under the axle of the buggy! I am not contending that the Standard is worded to call for a dog to trot under a buggy, but people interested in that breed are still thinking in those terms. What they are after, of course, is a dog with stamina. This is a much to be desired virtue, but why should it be coupled with a horse drawn vehicle? Who cares a whoop whether a Dal will fit under a buggy axle? In fact, where will they find the buggy axles to measure?

The Bulldog has certain characteristics to enable it to get a firm hold on the nose of a bull. Or, so I have been told. If it is still being judged according to that specification I fail to understand the reason. Bull baiting is no longer possible. I would even go far enough to say that probably not one Bulldog in a hundred has ever laid eyes on a bull. There is no reason why he should. But should the characteristics—the physical ones I mean—still be considered important enough to turn down an otherwise fine specimen just because it couldn't hang on to the nose of a bull?

The Irish Wolfhound may well have been developed to hunt wolves, the Scottish Deerhound's quarry was deer. The Elkhound was, I assume, used to chase elk and, according to rumor, the Chow Chow often ended his existence as the main course for dinner. Surely the modern judge isn't supposed to look upon the Chow in the light of its suitability when roasted.

I happen to know something about Briards. They were originally used as cattle and sheep herders, especially over rough ground. Early pictures of them show matted coats and a conformation that would not be tolerated in the ring today. The huge pads are intended to keep the big dogs from sinking into the swampy land. Their inordinate love of the water may well go back to the days when they had to cross bogs and even swim after cattle which, in the time-honored fashion of the artists, were standing knee deep in

*"**W**ho cares a whoop whether a Dal will fit under a buggy axle? In fact, where will they find the buggy axles to measure?"*

the streams. Yet, I seriously doubt if any judge looks upon our dogs on the basis of their ability to wallow through the mud.

If we are not actually going to judge on the basis of original intentions, would it not be better all around to judge dogs for what they must do today? Wolves, sheep, cattle, badgers and bears are not chasing around on the loose in the more civilized sections of the country. With few exceptions we have no opportunity to prove that our dogs can perform the same service for which they were originally developed. But our judges are being asked to pass out ribbons on utterly false assumptions. Isn't it hard enough to be a judge without having to try and imagine how the specimen in front of you would react if suddenly faced with a duty known only to the distant ancestors of the dog?

I had heard about the herding instinct of the Briard so I tried some of mine out on my milk goats. As far as any instinctive goat herding is concerned my beloved Briards are wash-outs. I am just as glad, for there is utterly no reason why they should herd goats. Does this mean that my dogs should get turned down at the next show because they failed to live up to something known only to their ancestors in France?

In this particular case, nothing has been done physically to alter the dogs for the job they used to perform. Nature may have altered them, but, thanks be, nobody cuts, clips, disfigures, mutilates, molds, flattens or squeezes the dogs into something else than the natural conformation. Yet, there are breeds where such things go on under the pretense that the result will fit the dog for some service which he will never be called upon to perform.

One hears a lot about temperament, especially the temperament of the purebred as compared with that of the mongrel. Is it not possible that temperament is being harmed by breeding to some set of directions that are outmoded? The modern dog—excepting those that are bred and trained specifically for the various types of hunting—is primarily a friend and guardian of his master and the immediate family. Let's bring the requirements up to date. If we must call for certain virtues beyond friendliness, fidelity, stamina and intelligence, why not modernize the demands?

We can think of a lot of very fine virtues the modern dog might well pick up. Virtues far more important than the ability to fit under a buggy axle or worm his way down a hole after a badger. Perhaps this will initiate a new trend in judging standards. At least they would be easier to prove in the ring than some of the things we are asked to accept nowadays.

Questions for Consideration

1. Horswell contends that written standards must reflect a breed's original function. White maintains this is an unreasonable expectation in those breeds whose function is obsolete. Should we attempt to preserve original breed specific characteristics related to function or are these traits outmoded?

2. Should the ability of a dog to perform its original function be a consideration in the show ring or in selecting breeding stock? How much emphasis should be placed upon these characteristics, including original temperament?

3. Can functional traits be properly evaluated in the show ring? Should all breeds pass tests which exhibit the capacity to do their original work before becoming champions?

Cross Reference in Breed Standards

Laurence Alden Horswell

"Dog World"
1964

When a standard is consulted for specifications of correctness in Breed A, it cannot reasonably be assumed that the reader will have, handily available for reference, the corresponding standard of breed G or Q to which reference may be made for similarity or contrast; or will have first hand correct knowledge of the qualities cited, by reason of close association with worthy examples of breed G or Q. Also, some cross references disparage another breed for faults just as reprehensible in the second breed as in the first, ignorantly assuming their acceptance in the second breed.

With this introduction, let us pursue the cross references in standards of perfection of breeds in Group II, Hounds.

Basenjis

While not a cross reference to another breed of dog, the Basenji standard prescribes a "tireless running gait (resembling a race horse trotting full out)" in complete disregard for so great a difference between running and trotting gaits that jockey-ridden running Thoroughbreds are registered in a separate stud book from sulky-driven Standardbred or trotting horses.

Beagles

Under Forelegs and Feet Defects: "Forelegs crooked like a Dachshund." Crooked forelegs have been disparaged in the Dachshund breed for more than half a century, and now are scarcely more prevalent among show Dachshunds than among Beagles.

The Beagle standard, under General Appearance, states: "A miniature Foxhound, solid and big for his inches" (shades of the measuring stick), "with the wear-and-tear look of the hound that can last in the chase and follow his quarry to the death." During the last ten years, American and English Foxhounds together have averaged competition in regular classes at AKC championship shows from coast to coast of 28 present per annum; if distributed one Foxhound per show, they would have been represented at only about one show in 16—not a very wide sampling of examples for Beagles with an average of 4,640 present per year or 11 per show. How many Beagle fanciers or novice exhibitors or breeders—or Beagle judges for that matter—have fortified themselves for this cross reference by making a detailed study of a Foxhound well authenticated as representing their standard?

Borzois

"Neck...somewhat shorter than the Greyhound." The Greyhound standard says: "long." How long is "shorter than long?" Why not express neck length for each breed in terms of head length, as is done in several other species? Borzoi owners cannot count on always having a proper Greyhound ready at hand for comparison.

128

Dachshunds

In this standard, the coat of Longhaired Dachshunds is likened to that of Irish Setters, and of Wirehaired Dachshunds to that of German Wirehaired Pointers. The same problem of availability of standards and/or authentic examples when wanted for consultation applies to these cross references, plus the fact that the reference to the Wirehaired coat appeared in the Dachshund standard for 33 years before the German Wirehaired Pointer was recognized and its standard published by the AKC as an American breed.

Another reference is among the secondary faults, which in Germany preclude championship, "Excessively drawn-up flanks like those of a Greyhound." By what criterion "excessively drawn-up?" Greyhound or Dachshund?

Scottish Deerhounds

There are no less than six references to Greyhounds in this standard. "A typical Deerhound should resemble a rough-coated Greyhound with larger size and bone...with likeness as to ear set and carriage, although in excitement ears may be raised above the head without losing the fold...length of neck befitting the Greyhound character of the breed, except that they do not stoop to their work like the Greyhound," and for variety, "there should be a slight fringe on the inside of forelegs and hindlegs, but nothing approaching the feather of a Collie." By these specifications, a Scottish Deerhound might about as well be a rough-coated variety of Greyhound, and simplify cross referencing their standards.

English Foxhounds

"Hindquarters...straight stifles are preferred to those much bent, as the Greyhound." Beagle standard students are now referred from Foxhounds to Greyhounds. In other sports this might be a double play—but in a breed standard?

Harriers

"Points very similar to those of the English Foxhound, except smaller." As, by the ten year back sight we used in comparing Beagles with Foxhounds, here we have an average of about one Harrier per 39 dog shows to compare with one English Foxhound per 79 dog shows: of scarcely significant value as cross references.

Irish Wolfhounds

"In general he is a rough-coated Greyhound like breed...Ears Greyhound like in carriage...Hindquarter: muscular thighs and second thighs long and strong as in the Greyhound...Colors...or any other color that appears in the Deerhound."

Otterhounds

"Much resembles the Bloodhound...head broader in proportion than the Bloodhound." Over the past ten years, Bloodhounds in the regular classes have averaged about one per all-breed dog show, and Otterhounds about one for seven shows, so this cross reference would seem to benefit the Otterhound fancier seeking to study the Bloodhound pattern *in vivo*—provided that all Bloodhounds shown were of exemplary quality.

Salukis

While not a cross reference, I wonder how a breeder, fancier or judge is to apply the Saluki standard calling for "deep, faithful, far-seeing eyes"—a phrase more poetic than demonstrable.

That's enough for one report. There are certainly more in that big book!

Questions for Consideration

1. Should breed standards make references to other breeds for descriptive purposes?
2. Should breed standards make references to members of other species such as bears, butterflies, eagles, (even humans beings!) to describe either physical or character traits?
3. Is it necessary to know anything about other breeds in order to judge one breed well? Could such knowledge make one a better judge?

Toy Dog Notes

"The Kennel"
1912

POMERANIANS.

The question of colour in Pomeranians is so wide and so extremely interesting that there is much importance in the matters discussed at the recent meeting of the Kennel Club Committee, as set forth in the current number of the *Kennel Gazette*. In one case, a Pomeranian was registered at the Kennel Club as an orange-shaded sable, and shown in the classes for that colour; as it grew older it lost much of its dark shadings, and became an orange, and, as such, was entered in orange classes, wherein he won, although handicapped by the presence of some black hairs, which the perfect orange should not own. The owner, however, had omitted to re-register the change of colour; and the Kennel Club, in disqualifying the dog, pointed out that, "dogs must be exhibited in classes given for the colour in which they are registered." The extreme difficulty in this definition of colour for owners is well shown by the other cases heard by the KC Committee at the same time. Here one Pomeranian was registered as a "sable," which, it was contended, is the same thing as a "shaded sable," the word shaded being a mere redundancy. And it was argued that as classes for shaded sables were given at the show in question (that of the Pomeranian Club in March), this dog should have been entered in those, and not in the classes for "any other colour" in which it competed. The point raised, as to whether sable or shaded sable means one and the same thing, does not, however, agree with the common sense reading of the standard, as approved and adopted by the Pomeranian Club, North of England Pomeranian Club, and Mid-land Counties Pomeranian Club, which clearly sets out that a "shaded" sable must be shaded throughout with three or more colours, the hair to be as uniformly shaded as possible. The fact of the dog in question having chocolate or brown tips to his coat did not, in the opinion of the Committee of the Pomeranian Club (which was endorsed by the finding of the Kennel Club Committee), constitute it a "shaded sable."

The other case was even more interesting as showing the changes of colour to which a Pomeranian's coat is liable. This had been registered as an orange sable, which, as in the former case, was urged implied an orange-shaded sable, and as such ought to be entered in orange-shaded sable classes, and not in those for "any other colour." Here it was shown that the dog's coat had completely changed in colour. Shown as an orange sable on March 21, and carefully examined on April 10, it was then called a "brown" by one judge, and pronounced by all not an orange-shaded; and at the meeting of the Kennel Club Open

MARCO
Owner, Queen Victoria
Artist, R. H. Moore
1900

The Toy Concept

Diminutive canine specimens have always existed and are well documented in ancient paintings. That these dogs served no useful function, other than companionship, is evidenced by their invariably being found in royal households. The common man could not afford a dog which did nothing productive to earn its keep. Yet, during the Victorian era, numerous societal factors combined to permanently fix the Toy breeds as more than just a passing fad. While detailing these numerous inter-connected principles would require another volume to adequately show their relationships, among them was the Victorian love of the grotesque or fantastic. Thus, canine exaggerations toward either end of the size spectrum came into vogue. The inherent variation available in the dog's genetic make-up permitted countless expressions and it seems as if there were attempts to either miniaturize or enlarge every known breed of dog.

Miss M. A. E. Holdsworth
and a Brussels Griffon

Although Mrs. Jonas Foster is generally credited as the first lady judge in England in 1889, Miss M. A. E. Holdsworth adjudicated Pugs and Mrs. L. E. Jenkins judged Toy Spaniels at Maidstone in 1886. But, not being a large championship show, this groundbreaking event went unnoticed by the canine press and public. Nevertheless, despite the historical oversight regarding which woman was the first to judge, Mrs. Jenkins, a dedicated Toy Spaniel breeder, and Miss Holdsworth made many other significant contributions to the dog sport for which they can be independently remembered.

In particular, Miss Holdsworth was one of the earliest advocates of Toy breeds. At the dawn of organized dog shows, Toy dogs were generally considered a lesser type of canine by many men because they did nothing "useful." Having been relegated to the status of "ladies' pets" they were not initially taken seriously as show dogs. Directing all her energies to obtain proper recognition for Toys, Miss Holdsworth was the first to suggest specialist Toy Clubs and actively assisted in the formation of many. As a dog breeder she confined herself to several Toy breeds, enjoying success in each. Always a champion of the Toy dog, Miss Holdsworth founded the "Pet Dog Journal" in 1886, of which she was editor and sole proprietor. In 1889, this popular magazine expanded as an all-breed periodical, becoming the "Illustrated Kennel Magazine." Due to illness, Miss Holdsworth discontinued publication of the magazine in 1890 but still exhibited and judged on a limited basis. She did continue to write and was long associated with "Our Dogs" and the "Lady Exhibitor."

Mrs. Jenkins and her
Clevedon Toy Spaniels

It is no accident that Toy dogs now comprise some of the toughest competition to be found at any dog show in the world. Freed from having to prove their dogs were "useful" early breeders and advocates of the petite could set their entire focus on issues of type. And because correct size is easily lost, of necessity, Toy dog breeders became extremely diligent and detail oriented in their pursuit of perfection and success. While these many variations could have easily become passing Victorian anachronisms, after World War I the increased urbanization of society, which continued throughout the 20th Century, secured a permanent niche for small dogs which could adapt to any environment. Most importantly, many breeds have come and gone over the centuries but Toys flourish today because they were developed concurrently with a growing belief that companionship and enjoyment were valid reasons to keep a dog.

A Question of Color and Size

Mr. John H. Duckworth and
CH. BRILLIANT
1900

Specific color has always played a major role in the show ring evaluation of Pomeranians. In the late 19th Century, most of the best Poms in England were either solid black or solid white. Vast differences in quality existed between these specimens and dogs of other colors. As a result, classes became divided by color. But color was not the only consideration in the development of the breed as we know it.

In the past, Pomeranians had numerous weight divisions —up to 28 pounds. Nevertheless, there was strong interest in perfecting Toy Poms which would breed true to the desired size of seven pounds and under. At the turn of the century, several orange, fawn and red dogs of correct size and type came to the fore which consistently produced offspring of small stature. Furthermore, these dogs generally possessed excellent coat texture, being less prone to have faulty open coats. For these reasons, the orange Poms became the immediate color of choice. Theo Marples, well-known as the founder and editor of "Our Dogs," is credited as the driving force behind the promotion of the now seemingly pervasive solid orange colored Pomeranians. When orange became the hue of the moment in England, most of the larger white specimens were shipped to the United States. These intelligent dogs did not find favor here as Pomeranians but became popular as circus performers and were eventually the direct ancestors of the American Eskimo Dog.

Today, Pomeranians of all colors can be found of correct size and coat texture, although worldwide the orange dogs still predominate. Because so many Toys, at least those seen at dog shows, are now relatively fixed in terms of size, we sometimes forget that as little as a hundred years ago much larger animals in various breeds were winning, even while attempts were made to attain smaller specimens. The illustrations shown address this question of scale, reminding us of the difficulties that have been overcome through selective breeding. The drawing of Ch. Brilliant by R. H. Moore shows us a dog with no reference to size. Modern viewers usually automatically assume any champion of the breed to be small, relative to today's standard. This fawn dog was said to possess the best coat quality and one of the finest heads of his time. Yet, when seen on the lap of his owner we realize he could never pass muster as a Toy today. We must be cautioned, however, not to fall into the common trap of saying that dogs of the past were not good representatives of their breeds based upon the advances of a hundred years or more. In actuality, most of these animals were not only good, but great dogs, because the vision and persistence of their owners made it possible for us to realize the goals they had in mind when they set out to perfect Toy dogs.

CH. BRILLIANT
Artist, R. H. Moore
1900

Committee on May 29 it was so entirely different that it was called by one, "an orange," and by another, "to all intents and purposes a self-coloured dog."

On the technical point of what is a "sable" or an "orange-sable," the position of the Pomeranian Clubs is that they recognise neither. The recognised varieties are the whole coloured Pomeranians, i.e., white, black, brown (either light or dark), blue (which should be as pale as possible), orange (which should be as deep and even in colour as possible), beaver, and cream (in which black nose and black rims around the eyes are required); parti-colours (in which the colours should be evenly distributed) and shaded-sables, in which the hairs would be of three or more colours evenly shaded. Beyond these recognised divisions lies the limbo of the "any other colours," no matter under what pretty description they are registered.

This opens the question of whether it is logical for the colour of Pomeranians to be registered at all. It is obvious that a judge at any show can only pronounce upon a dog as it is at that show. He cannot know, or if he does know, he cannot judge by, what that dog was as a puppy when it

CH. OFFLEY WEE BLACKIE
This dog, bred by Mrs. Dennis, was exported to America in 1913 for the then record price of £1000.

was registered. An owner cannot, equally obviously, be perpetually registering and re-registering a dog as its colour bleaches in sunlight, or changes with its growth of coat, or the passing of time; it is making a kaleidoscope of the Kennel Club. Further, the payment of perpetual half-crowns for re-registration is not a course of perennial enjoyment to any owner; nor should the most conscientious of exhibitors be constrained by conscience to such a variegated life. It is, of course, well known that if a Pomeranian's coat is washed with ordinary soap and water and dried in the sunlight it becomes lighter; if it is kept in a dark room it becomes darker, and this by the perfectly legitimate action of sunlight or its absence. It was a wise man who, at this Kennel Club Committee, when asked what colour he would call the Pomeranian present, replied, "I do not know!"

The subject which has most completely filled the minds of all owners, and every Pomeranian Club was that of the objection lodged against Mrs. Langton Dennis' dog, on the second day of the Toy Dog Show, because its ears had been trimmed; and the objection came before the Kennel Club Committee on June 18th. The point which gave special interest to the whole thing is, of course, that this trimming is practically universal amongst Pomeranian exhibitors, who prepare their dogs for show with perfect openness by trimming the superfluous hair from the ears, and this has been done by most exhibitors at every show for a considerable number of years without objections being lodged, or action taken under KC Rules. Nevertheless, it is a breach of the KC Regulations for the preparation of dogs for show; and either these regulations would have to be altered, or the Kennel Club would have to institute the necessary machinery for enforcing them. The decision of the Kennel Club in a very difficult matter was naturally very eagerly awaited; for the question touched owners of other breeds than Pomeranians, in which the preparation of dogs for shows is carried on by more or less openly practised trimming. Mrs. Langton Dennis' rejoinder to the objection brought against her dog by the Chairman of the Kennel Club was to lodge an objection against all the other Pomeranians, some eighty dogs, at the same show, as also being trimmed, which was the reductio ad absurdum of the case. And the KC

Committee's decision, that Mrs. Langton Dennis be "cautioned," is as far as matters go at present, and the first step on the way towards clearing up the existing tangles on the Pomeranian path, though this does not go far.

The arguments on both sides, for and against trimming, are these: Against it, is the feeling that dogs should be exhibited in their natural coat; that it would be difficult to permit the use of scissors for ears and deny it for body coat, and that scientific breeding could, in time, regulate coat production so as to preserve the short hair on the ears, and yet encourage the long coat on the body. For trimming, is the argument of breeders that the present day heavy growth of coats on Pomeranians cannot be obtained without, by necessary correlation, increasing the hair on the ears; that trimming does not alter, but only reveals the shape; that if the superfluous hair be left on, it not only hides the shape but misleads as to size and type; and that it is, and has been for years, a recognised practice. Whatever the upshot of the whole affair may be in the immediate future, there will be no finality until either trimming is officially recognised, or until the Kennel Club's regulations are adequately enforced.

Today, most would label these two white Pomeranians as American Eskimo Dogs. VICTORIA REX and LAKEWOOD PRINCE were exhibited at the New Orleans show, 1903. They were typical of the white Poms imported to the United States in the early 20th Century.

Questions for Consideration

1. How many breeds can you think of which are born an entirely different color from what their color may be at maturity?

2. In some of these breeds, does the color listed on the certified pedigree have any relevance? Should colors be registered at birth or at the time of breeding, if bred?

3. Should breeders and exhibitors be expected to pay a fee to change the color classification of a mature dog?

4. What color is "beaver?"

5. How important should color be in the consideration of type of a particular breed?

6. While separate Variety classifications for color might have made sense during the formative years of any breed in the 19th Century, can such examples as three Cocker Spaniels and two Bull Terriers in Group competition be logically justified today?

7. Enumerate and discuss the critical features of type which you believe are essential to all Toy breeds.

8. Who should determine trimming practices in a breed—the parent clubs, the exhibitors or the regulatory body?

134

Faking

E. B. Joachim

"Illustrated Kennel News"
1904

Interview with Mr. J. C. Tinne, Vice-Chairman of the Kennel Club and Hon. Secretary of the Fox Terrier Club

We took advantage of Mr. Tinne's stay in town this week to obtain his opinion on the question of "faking" and over-trimming which, beyond doubt, is becoming more and more acute.

Mr. Tinne readily gave us an appointment at the Kennel Club. Having settled ourselves in a cosy corner of the comfortable smoking room, we entered upon a conversation in which our host betokened the liveliest interest, and, said the subject is "bristling" with difficulties. However, no question can arise about the fraudulent intent of

Dyeing a Dog's Coat

so that was only mentioned *en passant*, and the first point that came under discussion was the

Hardening of Coats.

There might be, said Mr. Tinne, substances where there would be absolutely no doubt that they were employed solely for the purpose of hardening the coat temporarily, and, if evidence of their use could be given, the proper penalty would follow, as a matter of course; but a difficulty arises in the case of remedies, as, for instance, chalk, which is considered excellent for cleaning a dog's coat, and which, with the addition of a little carbolic acid, kills fleas, at the same time avoiding the softening effect of washing; so

J. C. Tinne and two of his Smooth Fox Terriers, CONSTANCE and CH. THE SYLPH 1905

that chalk may have been used for that legitimate purpose, and its hardening effect occurs incidentally. The KC Regulation provides that nothing must remain on the dog's coat. Some of the judges take a very lenient view of this, and Mr. Tinne mentioned an instance where a judge, finding some white dust flying out of the coat on being patted, advised the exhibitor to retire, give the dog a good brushing, and bring him back again.

Then there is sea bathing, which on the authority of the Rev. C. T. Fisher, Mr. Tinne mentioned as having a hardening effect on a terrier's coat. The Kennel Club can naturally not "taboo" seaside residents or prevent their dogs going into the sea, and they would, consequently, have an advantage over inland exhibitors, unless the latter gave the dogs the benefit of an occasional dip in a sea salt bath. Now, would that be a legitimate preparation for an exhibit, and, if not, where is the difference between that and bathing in the sea? These are a few of the difficulties in deciding what is fair or unfair treatment of a dog's coat.

We also asked Mr. Tinne if he had noticed a statement that the horribly cruel operation of

Cutting Toe Nails Down to the Quick

is practised to make dogs look better. Of course, we said in cases where dogs do not get enough exercise on hard ground to wear down their toe nails naturally, it would not only spoil their feet, but be actually cruel not to shorten the nails now and then, because with overgrown nails every time a dog puts his feet to the ground the toes get twisted and the nails are strained from the flesh. "I am very glad you mentioned this," said Mr. Tinne, "because I quite agree with your opinion regarding overgrown nails; and, as to cutting them down to the quick as a practice to induce dogs to show better, to produce the state for a catch-penny sensation, even a tyro knows that a dog in pain becomes dejected and loses half his chances in the show ring. Should some heartless and ignorant person be guilty of such an inhumane act, the most effective and proper place of dealing with him would be in the police court, and the SPCA would certainly give every assistance for that purpose."

And finally we come to that most difficult of all problems—namely, the line of demarcation between

Grooming and Trimming,

which has always puzzled our kennel authorities. Mr. Tinne admitted that trimming was done, not only for the purpose of showing dogs which grow an overprofuse coat in a jacket of the regulation length, but actually to hide imperfections in a dog's conformation, and re-related an instance that came to his knowledge. An expert "artist," after the judging was finished, saw at a show a novice with a Fox Terrier whose legs were not

Above, a "Dangerous" untrimmed Poodle and below, a trimmed dog, at the Birmingham, England show in 1887

straight. The "professor" drew the attention of the owner to the defect, remarking at the same time, "I'll soon put that right for you." In a short time one leg was trimmed to make it look apparently straight, and showing by contrast with the other one how bad it had been. A few minutes later the other leg was done likewise, with the satisfactory result that a pair of crooked legs had become straight.

Notwithstanding the acknowledged difficulty, we thought the specialist clubs could do much to stop the evil.

The Fox Terrier Club, replied Mr. Tinne, has made attempts in that direction—in fact, at one time they appointed a special committee to watch the condition of dogs at shows, but nothing was done.

Perhaps, we suggested, this committee was not suitably selected. There are members of the club who have a thorough knowledge of the malpractice *en rogue*, and who, not being any longer exhibitors, do not lay themselves open to the suspicion that any action of theirs is caused by jealousy. Some of these gentlemen take still sufficient interest to place their services at the disposal of their club for the benefit of the breed. Let the specialist club depute some of them to report on the judging at important shows, and, if they find that a judge gives prizes to overtrimmed dogs, recommend to their committee that such a judge, whether professional or amateur, should in future not be supported by the

Creating A Show Dog — The Wire Fox Terrier

Acquiring his original dog in 1813, the Reverend John Russell is the first recorded breeder of anything specifically called a Fox Terrier. The majority of Russell's terriers possessed dense, short wire coats, which he felt was the appropriate jacket for the breed. Oddly enough, although all the present day Smooth Fox Terriers can trace their lineage back to Russell's dogs, the fountainhead for Wires sprang from a different source, Kendall's Old Tip, whelped in 1866 and bred by Tom M. Kendall, Master of the Sinnington Hounds in Yorkshire from 1860 to 1875. Pictured below are direct line descendants of Old Tip, spanning 50 years.

| OLD JESTER 1875 | MEERSBROOK BRISTLES 1892 | CH. CACKLER OF NOTTS 1898 | CH. CATCH 'EM OF NOTTS 1904 | CH. TALAVERA SIMON 1924 |

Not until the advent of dog shows were attempts made to meld the Smooth and the Wire into one breed with distinct coat varieties. To early Fox Terrier exhibitors the name, "Fox Terrier" was synonymous with a Smooth coat. Wires lagged behind for a good ten years and were usually relegated to the Miscellaneous Class under the general heading of "rough-coated terriers." The shorter-legged Wires were simply not considered as elegant as the Smooths by most fanciers, particularly because they did not possess the long, lean heads of the "modern" Fox Terrier. Furthermore, the wire coat, even when trimmed and shaped close to the body, could not replicate the same flowing, symmetrical outline of a Smooth. When the advocates of Wires began crossing them with Smooths to improve the general conformation their experiments were highly successful and soon Wires appeared which could provide real competition to all comers.

But, the show presentation of Wires involved grooming techniques which were contrary to the Kennel Club rules mandating all breeds be presented in their "natural" state. Since it was impossible to trim a Wire to look like a Smooth, handlers took advantage of the extra coat to create a completely different outline for the variety, covering up faults in the process. No one complained until the Wires started winning and some of their handlers claimed the dogs shown were completely natural in appearance. To prove a point, Francis Redmond, the premier breeder of Smooths, brought out his first Wire for exhibition in 1888. She was shown completely in the rough — long, shaggy and unkempt — but in a "natural" state. Thus, the judge was forced to award Redmond all the prizes for Wires or risk violating the KC rules. For almost twenty years the pot boiled on the trimming controversy until it was agreed that hair could be removed by brush, comb or fingers, but not by any "artificial" means such as knife, scissors or taper (singeing the hair with a candle).

This ruling had a significant impact on the sport and vaulted the Wire Fox Terrier to the top position as a unique and popular show dog. The emphasis on grooming and the difficulty of preparing broken coats to perfection created an elite class known as the terrier handler. The average person could never hope to put the Wires down in the form demanded to win in the ring. Consequently, long-time breeders were replaced by wealthy owners who turned their dogs over to experts to condition and show. Positively, quality increased dramatically as it was senseless to put any time and energy into grooming an average specimen. After World War I there was a decided trend to favor newer breeds and many of the most popular Victorian breeds, including the Smooth Fox Terrier, were deemed old-fashioned. As a result, the Wire Fox Terrier, with its smart, stylish appearance replaced the Smooth as the public's perception of a Fox Terrier and became the undisputed leader worldwide in the number of Best in Show awards won.

137

The Story of Tumuch

Trimming of Wire Fox Terriers was still an issue of concern in 1913 as the cartoon indicates.

1. Mr. Verdant, having shown "Tumuch" on several occasions, with but indifferent luck, decides to send him to Pluckem, the noted handler. He instructs Pluckem to observe the rules of the Kennel Club, and draws his special attention to Appendix II.

2. "Tumuch" as Mr. Verdant showed him.

3. Pluckem, having ideas of his own upon the subject of the preparation of dogs for exhibition, sings: "You takes it all off if you wants to please 'em," as he sends an eighteen-penny telegram to Mr. Verdant, announcing the success of "Tumuch."

4. "Tumuch" as Pluckem put him down.

offer of specials or the guaranteeing of classes, because a competent judge ought to know when a dog is shown simply groomed, to give him a neat appearance, or unnaturally and dishonestly trimmed. After all, the chief purpose of giving specials and other support is to encourage the improvement of the breed. But this is surely not done by aiding or 'winking at' a custom which induces breeders to pay no attention to so important a point as a good coat because exhibitors can insure success in the ring by trimming. We were pleased to hear that Mr. Tinne thought the plan certainly worthy of being submitted to the consideration of his colleagues in the Fox Terrier Club. Something, we said, will have to be done to save certain breeds which are in danger through unnatural trimming. We pointed out that one or two breeds are dying out from that cause, and others will go the same way if it is not stopped.

A Radical Remedy

"Ah!" said Mr. Tinne, with a triumphant glance, as having at last found the key to the enigma:

"Let the Trimmers Have Their Full Swing,
and perhaps that may be the solution of the whole question! Let them trim and barber to their heart's content,

And Work Their Own Undoing,
so that the breeds which give these opportunities for barbering and are dishonestly shown die out, and give place to breeds which can be shown in a fair and natural state."

James Capellene Tinne was educated at Eton and University College, Oxford and while there was pre-eminently known as a rowing man and considered one of the finest oarsmen in his day. But, he was also interested in dogs and became a member of the Kennel Club in 1880 where he continued throughout his life. He was elected a member of the Committee in 1886 and was responsible for inaugurating many reforms in the KC government. In 1900 he was elected to the office of Vice-Chairman of the Committee, a position to which he was continually re-elected.

Tinne was primarily interested in only one breed, the Fox Terrier, which, at the time, meant the Smooth Fox Terrier. He owned and bred many fine specimens, with numerous champions, under the kennel name, "Brockenhurst." He joined the Fox Terrier Club in 1879 and in 1881 was elected Honorary Secretary, a post which he held for over twenty years.

His reputation was that of a forceful but quiet man who had the patience to wait for those who opposed him to either wear down or come around to his way of thinking. It was also said of him that he was living proof that one could be involved in breeding, exhibiting and judging dogs yet still remain a gentleman.

J. C. Tinne judging Smooth Fox Terriers at Birkenhead Show, 1903

Questions for Consideration

1. Of the various presentation techniques under discussion, which do you consider "faking," i.e., unethical and unacceptable?

2. Is preparation for showing breed specific, meaning, are grooming techniques which are acceptable in one breed not legitimate in another?

3. Is the practice of cutting the dog's nails down to the quick "inhumane?"

4. Can you think of any breeds which have lost favor as show dogs because of grooming practices? Can you think of any breeds which have equally lost favor with the public for this same reason?

5. Is it dishonest to groom or trim a dog to disguise its faults? Isn't it the judge's responsibility to be knowledgeable enough to find a dog's faults as well as its virtues, no matter how artfully it is presented?

6. Is it a normal expectation for exhibitors to shoulder the responsibility of policing and reporting the suspicious grooming practices of other exhibitors?

7. If judges insist upon putting up dogs groomed or trimmed contrary to the wishes of the parent clubs, should these clubs be allowed to publish lists of those whom they feel either do or do not adhere to the tenets of the official written standard? Should exhibitors be forced to prepare their dogs in a manner contrary to the written standard just to please the judges who may, or may not, know better?

The Faking Problem

E. B. Joachim

"Illustrated Kennel News"
1904

Mr. Edgar Farman in the Witness Box

The immense interest which our interview with Mr. J. C. Tinne, Vice-Chairman of the Kennel Club, has created, prompted us to seek an interview with Mr. Edgar Farman on the absorbing subject of "faking." We entered the office of this busy lawyer with a certain amount of misgiving, as we overheard him say to the clerk who took our Editor's card, "Oh, Mr. Joachim; show

worthy Vice-Chairman has set the example, and also because I hold equally strong views on the subject."

"Now, Mr. Farman, we particularly desire to elicit your opinion, because the breeds with which you have been closely connected can be shown without artificial preparation. Your mind is, consequently, perfectly unbiased, and you can speak upon the subject as it affects the general

E. B. Joachim *was renowned as the founder, then editor, of "The Illustrated Kennel News." Exhibiting his first Irish Terrier in 1883, he joined the Kennel Club in 1892, remaining a member until 1901. A prominent exhibitor and judge, Joachim owned numerous breeds, among them Dachshunds, Irish Water Spaniels, Dandie Dinmont Terriers and harlequin Great Danes. However, his greatest success came from his involvement with Schipperkes and Beagles, finishing the first champion in both breeds.*

Joachim was a business partner with George R. Krehl of "The Stock-keeper," contributing many articles to that and other publications for over forty years. Though Joachim used a more trenchant pen, he and Krehl possessed the same witty, slightly irreverent, erudite writing style. When Joachim retired and "The Illustrated Kennel News" ceased publication in 1918, it represented the end of an era of intellectual writing on all matters canine.

him in. I want to tackle him for publishing my *Kennel Gazette* news." However, we explained that we had not come to discuss anything else but faking, and to interview him. "Well," replied Mr. Farman, "nothing whatever would induce me to be interviewed, except for the fact that the

public as well as the fancier."

"Well, my view is this," said Mr. Farman. "The Kennel Club is established to promote
The Breeding of Good Dogs,
not artificially preparing them for exhibition. The general public which goes to shows expects

to see dogs in a clean and proper condition, but at the same time in a natural state. The public has hitherto looked upon shows under rules and regulations of the Kennel Club as above suspicion, but if trimming, powdering, weighting, etc., are going to be winked at, the sooner it is publicly stated that these things are allowed, the better. Meantime, it is a fraud on the public to weight a dog's ears, to alter their carriage problem, to artificially curl a coat and glossen it, to trim a dog to make a coat that is too long appear of the correct length, or hide defects of conformation by taking the coat off in certain parts, and this practice of 'legitimate trimming' is simply the

Modern Expression for High-Class Faking."

"But," we observed, "don't you agree with Mr. Tinne that the subject of overtrimming is bristling with difficulties?"

"Not a bit," replied Mr. Farman. "I consider that his attitude toward the subject savors of excusing what goes on at the present day—in fact, it seems to me that the whole trend of that interview is an *apologia* on behalf of the Terrier fancy. It is quite plain that trimming is faking, and faking illegitimate. That 'sea-water' proposition and 'dry white powder cleansing'," continued Mr. Farman, warming up to the subject, "is just the thin edge of the wedge, which gives rise to the possibility of fakers being able to discuss with honest men, and with the calmest assurance possible, whether it is wrong to weight a dog's ears before he goes into the show, or pull out surplus hairs, which are surplus because they would spoil the dog's chance of winning."

CAESAR, King Edward VII's Wire Fox Terrier. Even those in the Royal Kennels did not have the skill to properly groom this dog as he had originally been when first acquired.

"However," we said, "Kennel Club Rules admit certain practices. Look at the *'Regulations for Preparing Dogs for Show'.*"

"As they are," replied Mr. Farman, "one could almost drive a half dozen carriages and pairs through them. For instance, the chalk remedies and the little carbolic acid for killing fleas is simply an excuse for the artistic faker. I see Mr. Tinne refers to the question of powdering dogs, and states some judges take a very lenient view of this, and mentions one who, on finding white dust flying out of the coat on being patted, advised the exhibitor to retire and give the dog a good brushing and bring him back again. In my opinion, that judge and exhibitor should have been brought up under Rule 12. Look here!" cried Mr. Farman, "The Kennel Club was intended to 'promote the general improvement of dogs,' but if the moral standard of the dog world is to be

Levelled down to the Grade of the Faker or

Legitimate Trimmer,

if he is to be called so, all I can say is, the above mentioned Rule should read 'promote the general improvement of dogs by artificial methods or otherwise'."

Referring more particularly to trimming, we drew Mr. Farman's attention to the fact that only last week a well known judge stated in a kennel organ that, "You cannot exhibit a Wire-Haired Fox Terrier with a coat like an unshorn sheep. Nobody will buy or keep such dogs, they are practically valueless."

"Well, there you are," emphatically remarked Mr. Farman, "this just supports what I

The "Faking" Controversy

Harding Cox
"Dogs and I"
1924

One of the most controversial problems in connection with dog shows is that which pertains to what is known as "faking," i.e., the improper preparation of dogs for exhibition—or what the Kennel Club has ruled to be so. During the time I was a member of the Committee, there were constant discussions on the subject, and a decided difference of opinion existed. I then held—and I still maintain—that as long as there is no cutting or maiming of sensitive tissue, and as long as there is no dyeing or alteration of colour of skin or coat by unnatural means—exhibitors should be at liberty to cut, singe, shave, trim or otherwise improve the coat of their dogs, *ad lib*. This seems altogether reasonable, because, in most breeds, the length, breadth, density and texture of the coat is constantly changing, so that it is impossible to keep it in a state of level quality. The idea was that dogs of the long and broken haired varieties should be so bred that there need be no necessity to tamper with their coats, which would then maintain a constant length and texture. Rubbish!

Nature has ordained that hirsute growths on man or beast are continually undergoing change. It is therefore utterly futile to attempt to breed any sort of long haired or broken haired dog with a coat that never changes! When certain breeders of Wire-Haired Fox Terriers declared that they never trimmed their dogs, I formed my own opinion as to the exact value of their veracity; so in order to consolidate the position which I had taken up, I offered to wager any sum in reason that if one of these "untrimmed" (alleged) prize winners was handed over to my care, I would have it most scrupulously fed, tended and regularly brushed and groomed; that nevertheless, in the course of three months at the most, its coat would be long and open, with a considerable undergrowth of soft, linty hair, which would cause the old hard coat to be in strands. None took up my challenge.

Under these circumstances, why on earth should not an exhibitor manipulate his dog's coat in conformity with the fashion of the hour? Do exhibitors of hunters and hackneys bring their horses into the ring with hairy heels and shaggy coats? Do any of the Equine Societies bar the clipping of a horse? Is every mature male of the Human Species clean shaven? Not on your life! By way of compromise, the KC ordained that a comb might be used to remove old hair. Did you ever? The consequence was that some ingenious and enterprising caterer for the needs of exhibitors invented a fearsome implement in the way of a "comb" so contrived that a dog's coat could be torn out, broken or shortened at will, without the Law, as laid down by the Pundits of Piccadilly, being broken. No law is a good law that cannot be reasonably obeyed. The "faking" regulations of the KC are indeed a dead letter as regards all broken haired breeds. Were it not that the said regulations are persistently broken, and ignored in spirit if not in the letter thereof, it would be impossible to bench such dogs in decent trim.

Those who are "in the know" are perfectly well aware how fashionable "patterns" pertaining to these terriers are produced, and how it is that their legs appear to be (whether they are or not) plumb straight, with bone carried down to the feet. Run the hand down from elbow to pastern, and in nine cases out of ten, a most marvelous transformation will unfold.

Trimming Dogs

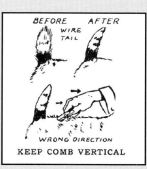

BEFORE AFTER
WIRE TAIL

WRONG DIRECTION
KEEP COMB VERTICAL

It is highly unreasonable to think those entering into competition with their dogs would not want to present them in the best form possible, providing they intend to win. Livestock fairs have existed since the Middle Ages and by the Nineteenth Century it was not only accepted, but expected, that the sheep or cow for public display would be much cleaner and sweeter smelling than the raw material on the farm. Yet, for some reason—perhaps because dogs had for eons been kept solely for the work they could do with little regard to appearance—any grooming of exhibition canines was viewed as contrary to their overall improvement.

The argument by those with smooth coated breeds that their dogs were always shown in a natural state has never been true. In his book from 1881, Vero Shaw describes at length the show ring preparation of Bull Terriers. This directive not only included the removal of whiskers and shaving the inside of the ears, but the "blueing" of the coats, as well. Admittedly, these are minor alterations in comparison to the complicated toilette of a Poodle, but alterations, nevertheless. And the Poodle, trimmed into fantastic patterns since time immemorial, was always allowed an exemption to the ban on trimming. Unfortunately, allowing exceptions for any breed puts those making the rules on an extraordinarily slippery slope for there can be no logic put forth which justifies trimming in one breed while forbidding it in another.

Poodle
Trimming Chart
1891

One of the things which organized canine governing bodies have repeatedly proven they cannot do well is keep up with the trends and changes in grooming styles created by the exhibitors. Presentation techniques are fostered by competition and a winning animal shown in a particular manner is sure to have imitators to follow. While most true breeders draw the line at outright faking such as hair dyes and surgical alterations, the onus of enforcement has been put on the backs of exhibitors and judges, rather than being routinely policed by the official regulatory body. The average exhibitor is generally not willing to publicly question the integrity of friends and fellow competitors. Furthermore, no training is provided to assist adjudicators in determining faked specimens. Consequently, even though judges have full authority in the ring and their decisions are final, few, if any, are willing to put their reputations on the line in such situations.

Dog shows started out, in England at any rate, as a leisure time hobby. There was no way anyone could have anticipated the sport would develop into an industry where people expected to make a living either as breeders, professional handlers, professional judges or in related capacities associated with an endless array of ancillary market products. Nineteenth Century rules based upon the ideal concept of sportsmanship can never

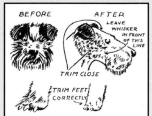

BEFORE AFTER
LEAVE WHISKER IN FRONT OF THIS LINE
TRIM CLOSE
TRIM FEET CORRECTLY

hope to have an impact on a system which has run away with itself and is driven by show wins. Thus, while many rules regarding "proper" presentation are still on the books, they cannot be uniformly enforced.

Perhaps, in the end, Edgar Farman was right—the best solution may be to publicly announce that faking is being permitted, thus leveling the playing field for all. He certainly would have been horrified to know that the Fox Terrier trimming illustrations shown were from a popular booklet written by a judge, Forest N. Hall. And if we must question whether 19th Century concepts of sportsmanship are still relevant, in the same vein we must seriously discuss the real purpose of the dog show today. If the principal vehicle for selecting breeding stock (if that is what really occurs at a dog show) is, by its very nature, today more than ever, artificial, then it only follows that the preparations for such competition will be of the same character.

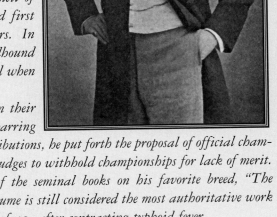

Edgar Farman was a London lawyer but is better known to us through his active involvement in dogs, being associated with the Kennel Club, of which he became a member in 1893. Farman was elected to the Committee in 1896 and was the driving force behind many significant changes in the sport. He was the first to support the formation of a Ladies' Branch of the Kennel Club in 1896, which finally became a reality in 1899. At various intervals he served as editor of the "Kennel Gazette," the last time just before his death in 1905. He also helped expand the power of the KC to include all dog shows, with the Licensed shows being the result, and it was he who suggested the formation of a Council of Representatives. Farman was also a founding member and first Honorary Secretary of the Association of Bloodhound Breeders. In that capacity he supported the establishment of the Bloodhound Trials, although he suffered a broken leg at the very first trial when kicked by a horse.

Farman believed all dog breeds should be shown in their natural state and was the principal advocate pursuing the barring of cropped dogs from show competition. Among his other contributions, he put forth the proposal of official championship certificates and formulated the rule which allowed judges to withhold championships for lack of merit. Particularly thorough and detail oriented, he wrote one of the seminal books on his favorite breed, "The Bulldog, A Monograph," first published in 1899. This volume is still considered the most authoritative work on the subject. Farman died in January, 1905, at the age of 42, after contracting typhoid fever.

say. The whole practice is

A Fraud on the Public.

I have never heard anything more forcibly condemnatory of the practice of trimming, although the gentleman in question did not make his statement for that purpose. Does it not mean, in other words, that the public, who know nothing of this artificial preparation, are induced by the appearance of such dogs at shows to buy them, or puppies bred from them, or use them as sires, and are thereby cheated out of their money for dogs which, when their coat is grown to its natural and normal state, are 'valueless'? Why, I hear, even the King had an experience of the kind. His Majesty acquired a certain dog, not a hundred years ago, and at once took an immense fancy to it. The animal was shortly afterward taken to the Royal Kennels, where it naturally received proper brushing and grooming, and was not again seen by His Majesty for a short time, but, lo and behold! When he next saw the dog, he did not know it, and, in fact, refused to acknowledge that it was the same animal at all."

"Anyhow," we added, "that the majority of these dogs are shown in this deceptive manner seems to be proved by the before mentioned judge's further statement:

"If, indeed, such a condition (by which he evidently means showing the dogs in their natural coat) is insisted upon, we venture to predict that half the fancy will go out of the breed."

"And," retorted Mr. Farman, "the very best possible event which could happen in the interests of the public, and, to my mind, the interests of dogdom."

"Now, to come to the critical point," we observed. "We have no doubt it is the desire of the Kennel Club

To Discountenance Such Deception,

as it must be detrimental to certain breeds in particular, and the reputation of dog showing in general. What do you, who have a long and intimate experience of Kennel Club Committee work, estimate is its power to stop what is an acknowledged fact by those 'In the know,' and may become a public scandal; also, what should be the action of members of the Kennel Club Committee who are particularly concerned in these breeds?"

"The Committee," explained Mr. Farman, "has plenty of power, if its majority will only exercise it. In fact, it is in a unique position, as every exhibitor under Kennel Club Rules or Regulations hands himself over bodily and agrees to the publication of his misdeeds in the official organ, the *Kennel Gazette*. I consider that in these days the cause of the faker has obtained a lamentable foothold. The stumbling block is the

Unholy alliance

with such a thing as 'legitimate trimming'."

"We recollect that in a chapter you wrote in the last edition of the *Dog Owner's Annual*, you say that you would

Allow Faking,"

"Ah, there you have it," was the prompt reply. "Yes, I would, as things are at present, and if they cannot be stopped, allow faking, and publicly announce that it is allowed. Then everybody would be placed on the same level. The novice would know where he is, and have a sporting chance with the old hand, and, provided he is a good barber, or employs one, have an equal chance with him. Besides, exhibitors of certain breeds would be able to do openly and honestly what they now do secretly. The public, too, would know what to expect of a dog after being purchased, namely,

A Complete Transformation."

Questions for Consideration

1. Do euphemisms for altering a dog's natural appearance make the procedure so described acceptable?

2. Farman takes a hard-line approach that all trimming is faking. Does this seem reasonable? Is bathing a dog altering its "natural" appearance?

3. What is a dog's "natural" appearance?

4. Farman states that any preparation for show which alters the dog's natural appearance is committing a fraud on the public. Does the public have a right to expect that the dog they purchase will look like those which are expertly groomed and presented at a show?

5. Farman declares that allowing faking in all its forms would level the playing field for the amateur and professional alike. Does it make any difference what methods are used to prepare a dog for the show ring? Should "faking" be allowed?

6. Because various breeds have vastly differing preparation procedures for exhibition, who should make the determination of what is allowed? Who should enforce these regulations, and can they be adequately policed? Should breeders and exhibitors of one breed have any say in the grooming practices of another?

7. Should allowable grooming practices for exhibition be "levelled down" to that of those who cheat to win? Should quality dogs be forced to compete against dogs which have been deceptively presented?

8. Are dog shows about breeding better dogs or artificially preparing them for exhibition?

9. Is it reasonable to create rules which determine "faking?" What is your definition of the term? Is it possible to create rules which unethical persons will not attempt to circumvent? Is "faking" still an issue today?

10. What would you suppose is the "moral standard" of the dog show world?

The Dog As Celebrity

George R. Krehl

"The Stock-keeper"
1891

"Strange all this difference should be,
Twixt Poodledum and Poodledee."

The Black Poodle Achilles

It is well the majority of our readers are familiar with the appearance of a show Poodle or, seeing the bizarre animal on our front page, they might suppose this journal to be the organ of the naturalists, and the picture a likeness of the last addition to the Zoological Gardens. So much are the common characteristics of the canine species disguised by the hirsute adornments of a prize Poodle, that we should advise their owners always to include in their list of tricks that of "speaking" or "asking," as the fact of the creature's being able to bark would serve as evidence of its being really a dog. Achilles belongs to the type usually known as the corded or Russian Poodle, and we believe we are correct in saying that the greatest number of them is to be found in Poland. At all events, we remember that when, a season or two ago, Poodles were the rage in fashionable circles, when the masher of the period was attended by

CH. ACHILLES
Artist, R. H. Moore
1891

his Poodle, as fancifully attired as his master, and so like master like dog were they, that both wore bangles and high collars—Well, in those days, the Poodles that were imported in flocks for Vanity Fair came from Poland, so we were told by Monsieur Felix, who appeared able to command an inexhaustible supply. Monsieur Felix, in spite of his foreign prefix, was as extreme an Englishman as any of the very highly commended trio, Brown, Jones and Robinson. And he was also an excellent clown, though, in speaking of him in that tense, we do not intend to imply that he has forfeited his existence or forsaken his merry profession. If Felix were doing "a turn" at the circus with his clever dogs, he was always sure of a hearty reception, and we have seen his labours in the ring better received than those of many a judge in the dog show, though there may be some of the others who are even bigger clowns.

These Poodles imported by Felix in droves, came from Poland, and arrived in the rough, and, like diamonds, were cut and fashioned out into park pets. Very rough, dirty and brown, shaggy and smelly they were on arrival,

146

George R. Krehl was probably one of the most influential people in the dog fancy in the late 19th Century and until his death in 1903 at age forty-six. As editor of "The Stock-keeper," he was clearly dedicated to excellence, surrounding himself with expert writers and artists as contributors to his paper. "The Stock-keeper" contained such depth of knowledge on all matters canine that it was the most widely read and imitated kennel newspaper on both sides of the Atlantic. Krehl became a member of the Kennel Club in 1891 and was nominated numerous times to serve on the Committee, a position he always declined on the basis of conflict of interest in his capacity as a member of the press. Krehl left "The Stock-keeper" in 1902 to form "The Illustrated Kennel News" with E. B. Joachim. That paper continued publication until March, 1918.

Unlike many of his contemporaries who had backgrounds in the Sporting breeds, Krehl favored the Hounds and was the first true expert on all Non-Sporting dogs. He had a discerning eye for exquisite type and quality and only the best was good enough for him in the breeds he owned. He was particularly associated with Bloodhounds, owning at one time the famous Ch. Cromwell; Borzoi, importing many from Russia; Beagles, in which with E. B. Joachim he produced the first Beagle champion in 1891, the bitch, Ch. Lonely. One of his proudest possessions was the medallion seen on his cravat which was given to him by the Prince of Wales when Krehl presented him a pair of Basset Hounds. Krehl was also among the four people responsible for introducing the Schipperke to England. Although not an active breeder of Bulldogs, the Bulldog Club made him an honorary member as he never failed to attend and report upon what appeared to be the considerably less than stereotypical, staid, Victorian dinner parties which the club held. Krehl is the person who coined the term, "French Bulldog," when, as a joke, he put a sign on his bench at the Crystal Palace show in 1893 which said "French Bulldogs of British Origin" to describe the six Toy Bulldogs entered which he had recently imported from France. Krehl was a Charter Member of the Toy Bulldog Club and supported the move to have them be true miniature Bulldogs. Thus, he favored the rose ear and was adamant in fighting against any recognition of the bat eared variety whose advocates, much to his consternation, adopted the name he had invented in jest. It was the only battle in dogs he ever lost.

Krehl was considered an "all-round" judge but he never accepted an assignment in breeds with which he had no association. He was consistently critical of those judges whom he felt, irresponsibly and to the detriment of the sport, would accept appointments in any breed to which they were assigned. As early as 1891 he is on record advocating breed examinations and calling for the development of a system to certify judges. He was not opposed to the "professional" judge but felt that the so-called "amateur" judge, which he considered himself, was unfairly disparaged and that any arguments advanced to state that one group was more knowledgeable than another were self-serving and due to ignorance of the language. "But, if these gentry, who distort the Queen's English, will look upon the word, 'amateur' they will find it means one who loves and cultivates any art or science, but does not follow the one as a profession." There is no doubt that George R. Krehl truly loved and cultivated dogs and we are fortunate that his vocation and avocation were one in the same.

Schipperkes, MIA AND DRIESKE
Owner, George R. Krehl
Artist, R. H. Moore
1889

Caricature

Dog Show at Islington

Bloodhound. Exhibited by Ald'man Saveloy.

Black Poodle

Champion Grabber. Defies caricature.

Champion Alligator. To be continued.

White Collie. Exhibited by
H. M. The Queen. Bred to points.

Well-trained dog (Skye Terrier).
Exhibited by Sir Edward Watkin.

Because a century later we live in a culture which, besides being considerably more jaded, has hundreds of leisure time options, it is difficult for us to fully grasp the high entertainment value that could be extracted from a dog show by the average person. Breeding dogs for show purposes tends to favor selection of exaggerated features, thus, the show dog is a natural subject for caricature. This was even more true during the Victorian era, for as new breeds were emerging there was a great tendency to breed for features so exaggerated from the "normal" canine that the most extreme dogs came to be considered the ideal for their respective breeds, in many cases becoming caricatures of themselves. Nevertheless, these charming drawings, from the versatile pen of George Krehl, appeared in "The Stock-keeper" in 1891 and still amuse us today.

Edwin Brough was considered the Bloodhound expert of his time and while his writings discussed the breed's history, remarkable scenting abilities and detailed instructions on how to properly train the dogs to utilize their noses, he said very little about breeding Bloodhounds for show, presumably because he did not envision this as a separate activity. In an article in "The Century," dated 1889, he does credit the dog show with saving the Bloodhound and many other breeds from becoming extinct. However, he adds, "I fear that dog shows and their attendant changes of fashion have done an immense amount of harm to some of our most useful breeds; but luckily the Bloodhound has been estimated most highly for his best and most characteristic qualities." This is an extraordinary statement for it was probably coincidental more than a decided attempt by judges to preserve traits specifically unique to the function of the breed.

However, Queen Victoria's "improved" Collies were a grand source of amusement at many shows. The Borzoi cross was introduced to change what were considered the Scotch Collie's "old-fashioned" head and coloration. Her Majesty's presentation on the bench of a pure white Collie was a sensational laughingstock to anyone who had seen Collies in action, knowing they had to be dark colored to be differentiated from the sheep at a distance. Since these dogs were not suited to do the work for which they were bred, the only polite thing to say was that they were, "Bred to points." Subsequently, white Collies became quite popular.

Cords

When corded Poodles were first introduced to the English show scene they created a sensation with the public. Just the promise in an advertisement that one of these exotically coiffed dogs would be exhibited drew great crowds and literally guaranteed the success of a show. Poodles were always exempt from the Kennel Club rules applying to preparing dogs for exhibition in that they were the only breed in which trimming of the coat was permitted. However, as pointed out in Krehl's article, maintaining these extreme coats required extreme preparations which were, in fact, prohibited; specifically, leaving oil in the coats during judging. This issue came to a head after the Toy Dog Society's Show in 1903, when the Reverend R. V. O. Graves protested three of the Poodles. Graves and his wife were well-known Poodle breeders but he claimed he had no personal feelings in the matter; simply wanting a ruling in regard to preparing Poodles for exhibition. The Toy Dog Society did not uphold his objection, stating there was nothing in the Kennel Club Rules as printed in the judging schedule to guide them. The Rev. Graves appealed the decision to the Kennel Club. After taking testimony from numerous Poodle breeders who were of the unanimous opinion that it would be impossible to show Poodles without the use of oil because their cords would break, the Kennel Club Committee upheld the appeal.

CH. THE ACROBAT
Owner, Mrs. K. Graves
1905

This was the beginning of the end for the corded Poodle as an exhibition animal and they rapidly diminished in popularity up until WWI. After the war there was little interest in reviving this time consuming and complicated grooming technique on a large scale basis. This important ruling cleared the way for the curly-coated Poodles favored by the French, which until this time could not get much of a foothold for championships in English competition against the corded dogs. A reflection of this difficulty was realized in a previous ruling, also in 1903, which gave the curly-coated Poodle separate variety status in show competition. Because the corded Poodle is a traditional form, it is still permitted to be exhibited in this fashion today, although very few people ever attempt to undertake the work entailed in the preparation and upkeep of these coats. And certainly, not since the turn of the century has anyone evaluated Poodles on the length of their cords.

and it required no mean tonsorial ability to turn one of these into my lady's darling with the face and cheeks clean shaved, leaving a Napoleonic moustache and goatee, and on the head a tuft to be tied up with ribbons, and legs carved fantastically into black sticks and matador puff balls; from midway in the back also bare, save two more balls on the hip points, and the tail treated like the legs. The shaggy coat had been combed, brushed, twisted, coaxed, and 'pickled,' until it hung in long spiral jet black cords, glossy and redolent of thine incomparable oil Macassar. One thing more was required to complete a perfect Poodle's get up, viz., the silver bangle to be worn as an anklet round the pastern joint. To prevent this slipping off an ingenious contrivance with an elastic band was employed. When society became poodlerised, clipping and shaving became a lucrative occupation—at the head of this industry we must place Mr. Brown, of Paddington, who excelled all his brother artists in quaint designs and superior finish. He was known as "Gobbler" Brown in his Varsity days (by the way, friends who may not have seen him for years, will be glad to hear that he is hale, fat and hearty). A week ago we met an old friend, and after having expressed our admiration of his own cheery good looks, we turned our attention to his companion, a handsome black Poodle, which was skillfully carved out in the latest mode, and on the loins the hair had been so deftly clipped and carefully left as to represent the "Gobbler's" crest and monogram. "That was done by Brown," we said. "You've hit it in once!" was the delighted acknowledgment. *Now this is fame.* If other artists, such as painters, were not in the habit of daubing their signatures across their pictures, how many of us would be able to say on seeing them, "That's a Snooks!" or "One of Simpkins's?" But the moment we saw that picture of a Poodle we knew he had been done by Brown. It is a puzzle, which as far as we know Poodledum has never troubled itself about, why the aft part of a Poodle should be shaved. It would seem just as ridiculous to shave the fore part, but we doubt if coat as a covering be as necessary for the shoulders as for the loins. If it be done for coolness, why should the hindquarters feel the refreshing breeze and the other half of the body swelter in heat? A Frenchman whom we once asked to account for the custom gave us the explanation that it was to make the dog look like a lion. This tickled our fancy hugely, that the Poodle, the most comic of the canine race, should be shorn in the image of the King of Beasts. Clipping is much more affected abroad than here, and we shall never forget one day turning a corner of the boulevard, and encountering a big self-coloured St. Bernard clipped to resemble a lion. In England we have settled it among ourselves that the corded Poodle is the genuine article, but your Frenchman claims equal recognition for his sort whose coats are frizzy, crisp, and curly, as opposed to the long

cords of the so-called Russian variety. In France also the white Poodle is very popular, but here he is not much fancied. It is but frank to own to those who cannot even tell the difference 'twixt Poodledum and Poodledee, that the marvellous and curious occupants of the show bench are not quite dogs of nature. No Poodle, unkempt, uncared for, would develop such cords; the skin has to be kept constantly lubricated, and the crop as it grows assiduously attended to. There are

BRIGHTON SWEEP
*Curly-Coated Poodle
Owner, Mrs. Nichols Rudall
1902
This dog sports the silver leg bangle
to which Krehl referred.*

two members of the canine family whose hair approaches the wool of the sheep in its felting qualities, they are the Poodle and the Irish Water Spaniel. As the Poodle's coat grows, it mats or felts, so when the hair dries and leaves the body it remains a part of the cord, and thus these long rags or cords are made, and by care are kept clean and not unsightly. If all Poodles were as handsome as our illustration, they would not be a breed that one could recommend for companion dogs; as a matter of fact, Achilles, unless his ringlets are tied up for him, cannot walk far enough for the requirements of exercise. The beauty of Achilles has condemned him to a life of voluptuous enjoyment, whereby he has been able to render the breed some services. It would be but a sad reflection on this most intelligent breed to imagine, as many people do, that their intellectuality ends at learning tricks, which, however amusing, are of no use. This is not the case, for they are not only well adapted by nature for sport, but are commonly used for that purpose on the Continent. They make the tenderest-mouthed retrievers by land or water. We know one at present that is perfectly broken as ever a retriever could be, and, writing from memory, we believe him to be a half brother of Achilles.

R. H. Moore, *if not the premier canine illustrator of the late 19th and early 20th Centuries in Great Britain, was certainly the most prolific. During a career which spanned over forty years, Moore literally produced thousands of pen and ink drawings depicting practically every top notch representative of every known breed. George R. Krehl brought Moore to public prominence within the dog fancy by relying on him almost exclusively to create the artwork for "The Stock-keeper." Besides this weekly, Moore also contributed illustrations to the "Sporting and Dramatic News," "Animal World," "Fancier's Gazette," "Fox Terrier Chronicle" and "Good Words." He illustrated numerous books, including Charles Lane's "All About Dogs," published in 1900.*

The growth of the dog show sport soon spawned corresponding market interests to serve the fancy. These industries, in turn, required quality advertising directed at a burgeoning group of canophiles. Among Moore's many clients was the first commercial dog food manufacturer, Spratt's Patent, Ltd.

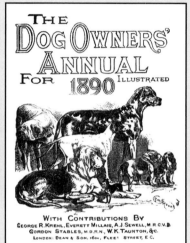

Everyone who has even a passing interest in dogs has seen numerous examples of Moore's works, published worldwide during his lifetime and still reprinted today because of their historical significance. Yet, Moore is now almost unknown, most likely because he rarely worked in color, creating very few of what would be referred to as "major works," in oil or watercolor, as did other British canine artists, such as R. Ward Binks or Arthur Wardle. A native of Northleigh, Oxfordshire, upon leaving school Moore apprenticed as a wood engraver but eventually gave up this medium, feeling the technique too confining. He then took up drawing as a profession, studying the figure and portraiture. However, he soon almost exclusively devoted himself to interpreting animals, particularly dogs.

As previously mentioned, the only pen and ink artist in America at the time who possessed comparable talent in interpreting the canine was G. Muss-Arnolt. Both artists created dogs which were anatomically accurate but Moore's dogs have a definite lyrical expressiveness, whereas Muss-Arnolt's dogs in ink possess a dynamic forcefulness. Surprisingly, unlike his contemporary in the United States, Moore was neither a breeder, exhibitor or judge. Nevertheless, he attended practically every major dog show in Great Britain in his capacity as a sketch artist. In reviewing the complete body of Moore's work a few earlier drawings are particularly significant in their depiction of rural dog shows. Further, his drawings were accurate representations of the dogs of his time. But most importantly, the oeuvre of R. H. Moore clearly indicates he was not only an expert draftsman, but a dog lover, as well.

Borzoi, Krilutt
Owner, The Hon. Mrs. Wellesley
1890
(n.b. — compare this drawing to that of the same dog on page 47. Describe and discuss the differences in interpretation).

The subject of our article is an old stager, or rather bencher. Before he came into Mr. Angell's possession he had been shown many times, but always in such bad condition that he never got higher than second. When Mr. Angell took his toilet in hand, a change came o'er the scene, and the dog than obtained the opportunity to prove what he could do. Since he made his first appearance when looking his best, honours of the highest have fallen to his lot, firsts, specials, champion prizes, etc. Mr. Angell's first win was when Achilles beat Champion Joe II at the Alexandra Palace. Achilles is a son of that grand dog Lyris, out of Mr. A. Chance's Begum. There were four prize winners in the same litter, one of them, Mrs. Taylor's Lyris II, won every time he was exhibited. Achilles is half brother to the Rev. Graves Champion Witch. He is the sire of some grand youngsters, which have won at the important shows. It appears rather like discovering a stable secret to give the length of Achilles' coat, but as Mr. Angell does not seem to mind his dog's best form being published, we will give it, for the benefit of Poodle breeders who have nothing good enough in their own kennels to test the merits of their prodigies; when they have reared a Poodle whose cords measure more than twenty six inches, they can try to beat Achilles.

Questions for Consideration

1. What has fashion to do with dogs and dog shows?

2. If particular fashion looks can only be obtained by artificial enhancements such as barbering, oils, hairsprays, etc., should we be concerned, or is this a matter for the individual parent clubs, exhibitors, and/or judges to determine?

3. As long as correct structure, type and movement play a significant role in the judgment of quality, does it make any difference what kinds of grooming techniques are used to create certain presentations? Why or why not?

4. How much importance should be given to the evaluation of non-structural qualities such as grooming techniques and/or handling presentations? Is breed ring judging supposed to be a forum for evaluating grooming? Is it the forum for evaluating handling?

5. Does extreme emphasis on coat, grooming and presentation inhibit the progress in a breed in regard to creating a uniform type? Give specific examples to either defend or refute this position.

6. Although the Poodle is renowned as a soft-mouthed retriever, the presentation of the dog's coat in the show ring is a traditional affectation which has no correlation to the functionality of the dog. Should this continue to be encouraged? Can you think of any other breeds which have an entirely different look for the show ring than for the work for which they were originally bred?

7. Granting that not all specimens of a breed will possess correct coat and coat texture, how much difference should there be between the appearance of a show dog and a representative of the breed kept for either working or pet purposes?

8. Are grooming techniques which are unique to certain breeds an important feature of breed type and therefore a priority in the proper evaluation of the dog?

9. Is there anything inherently wrong, i.e, either unethical or not beneficial, in exotic grooming presentations of certain breeds?

10. What is the difference between celebrity and popularity? Do individual dogs which attain celebrity status tend to increase the popularity of a given breed?

What Price Canine Syndicates?

G. Gordon Cook

"Popular Dogs"
1949

We use the term "syndicate" in a broad sense of the word. Such a syndicate is usually a group of persons enjoying some prominence in canine affairs—officials of kennel or breed clubs, amateur and professional judges and handlers, and so called breeding authorities who band together in the interest or in the ownership of a particular dog for the purpose of promoting said dog to stardom and/or advancing public acceptance of such dog's "get" or "produce" as the case may be.

The story is quite too long and involved for complete coverage in this release —rather, this is merely a further discussion of the subject hopefully tendered that it might alert the entire canine fancy's consciousness to the inherent dangers and evils of such syndicates and encourage a *vox populi* to the end that appropriate American Kennel Club controls shall be established before harm is done.

German Shepherd Dog
Doris vom Vogtlandshof
1949

Nothing is so devoid of news value or more suggestive of malcontented ramblings than an article which leaves the reader without substance into which to get his teeth, hence there follows names, dates, places and some few known particulars concerning a syndicate. This syndicate's scheme of untoward promotion of a German Shepherd bitch was thoughtlessly, indifferently, carelessly and/or artfully and deliberately devised by one or more of the persons interested in the success of the ill advised venture.

In the opinion of this writer there has been a transgression of the borderlines of AKC regulations and certainly of the concepts of propriety and good sportsmanship. It is unfortunate that this opening gun in support of principles should be fired from the ranks of any given breed fancy lest fanciers of other breeds take a "holier than thou" attitude toward the question—so fanciers of all breeds—you must understand that your breed is just as vulnerable. Take the question to heart for your own best interest and be quite aware that you too live in glass houses. The untoward promotion of certain dogs of numerous breeds is clearly in view. Remember that each of many judges are rated as eligible to pass upon many breeds. Remember the Group and Best in Show rings where so many of us hope to meet. If any of these points in the scheme of judging are vulnerable to the influences of a syndicate then all canine fanciers are open to exploitation.

Last year a German Shepherd bitch, Doris vom Vogtlandshof, was publicized in the *Shepherd Dog Review* as being an animal of great promise

How to Win Friends and Influence Judges

"I'M A JUDGE — WON'T YOU BUY A DOG FROM ME?"

1910

Since the beginning of organized dog shows there have been countless and never-ending complaints about the adjudicators' competencies. Despite high-minded platitudes to the contrary regarding sportsmanship, it seems we identify so strongly and closely with our dogs that for many, any loss, no matter how clinically rendered, is interpreted as a personal affront. Consequently, there must be some "logical" reason for a defeat. Quite amazingly, this process of discovery rarely gets around to the fact the winning canine may, indeed, be superior (or at least equal) to one's own. If inclined to believe all ringside gossip, the conclusion would have to be that even long established breeders who have produced generations of quality specimens, possess expert knowledge and unquestioned ethical behavior, transform into stupid, incompetent, senile crooks the moment they put on a judge's badge. Such hyperbole has always made the dog show judge an easy target for both artists and writers.

Since novice exhibitors hold judges in awe, it is a great temptation for a few to use that authority to promote their other canine activities, particularly in regard to selling dogs, as seen in the first cartoon from 1910. However, most inappropriate contacts usually originate with the exhibitor. With every form of mass communication now available to the entire population, today's judges are perpetually subjected to unsolicited communiques which are specifically designed to sway their opinions in favor of particular dogs. Because handlers and exhibitors unashamedly jockey for position at social events, send win photos, letters and e-mail, judges must work assiduously to protect their reputations as knowledgeable and honest.

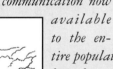

1931

1946

Conceding that human nature is not likely to change, how does one properly deal with those who insist dogs be appraised on other than their merits? In 1888, Edwin Brough faced a similar situation when judging Bloodhounds and simply exposed the guilty party in his official show report thusly: "In the Open Bitch Class Koodoo was decidedly the best; her owner had written to me soon after I was announced to judge, giving full particulars of her previous wins, etcetera, and I consider this in such bad taste that if I had had any doubt in the matter I should certainly have passed her over." There is no indication that Brough ever had to write such commentary again.

MY DOG, SIR

1884

Ch. Nornay Saddler *was one of the last nationally known canine celebrities in this country who achieved that status as a show dog rather than as a film star, such as Lassie or Rin-Tin-Tin. By the time Saddler was born in 1936, the Wire Fox Terrier had become the pre-eminent variety of the breed and it was almost impossible for a Smooth to defeat a Wire and advance to Group competition Consequently, interest in Smooths had declined dramatically. Imported from England at 11 months, Saddler was only actively shown for four years but won a total of 59 Best in Show awards, the all-breed record at the time. Further, he won the Fox Terrier Club of America's Grand Challenge Cup on six occasions. While remembered today as a fine example of the breed and a sire of over 30 champions, the real story is that Saddler's owner, James M. Austin, refused to exploit the dog for self-aggrandizement.*

Saddler could have easily been the first dog to win 100 Best in Show awards if that had been desired, but Austin's reason for exhibiting Smooths was to revive interest in the variety. The record was achieved when there were relatively few shows and no interstate highways. During his career, Saddler was only flown to one show on a private plane. Austin knew that Saddler's success forced judges to once again seriously consider Smooths for top awards and he realized this new-found interest in the variety would quickly diminish if other fanciers always had to be beaten by a practically invincible dog. As a result, except for the national specialty, Austin made it a policy to never exhibit Saddler again where he had previously won Best in Show. He also avoided showing under the same judges, if possible, once they had awarded the dog a Group first. As a result Smooths saw an upswing in both numbers and quality.

It is highly unlikely a dog could sell much gin today. This ad offered prints of Saddler for 10 cents each and all proceeds went to charities. Although artist Edwin Megargee painted this dog many times, the markings shown are not correct.

1941

During World War II, Saddler was an important canine fund-raiser for Dogs for Defense. At this time Austin allowed his dog's image to be used in various advertisements and increased Saddler's stud fee to $500 (up from $100), with all proceeds going to various charities, in particular, the American Red Cross. Saddler's name was even signed to a telegram with £50 sent to the top canine fund-raiser in England, the Bulldog, Ch. Bosworth Queen, whose charity provided services for victims of the blitz. Saddler died in 1948 at twelve years of age. James M. Austin had many other top winning dogs over the years, but during Saddler's lifetime he was able to demonstrate that it was still possible to display a true breeder's interest in improving and promoting one's favorite breed through sportsmanship, rather than a win at any cost attitude.

The seldom seen off-side of
CH. NORNAY SADDLER

CH. BOSWORTH QUEEN
Owner, Jimmy Knode

and was imported from Germany by Mr. Ernest Loeb, a professional handler of considerable reputation. Shortly thereafter, at the 1949 specialty show of the German Shepherd Dog Club of America, Inc., the coveted award, "Victrix," was delivered under somewhat questionable circumstances to Doris, purportedly owned by Mr. Loeb but later that same day disclosed by one of her owners as being the syndicated property of ten other persons prominent in the fancy and/or in the official family of the German Shepherd Dog Club of America, and further, that the gentleman, Dr. J. W. Sherer, who judged the bitches at the specialty, had a definite interest in Doris to the extent of having been appointed by the syndicate to supervise the bitch's breeding program—and that's quite an important interest, in terms of prestige if not in hard cash.

Right here it is appropriate to declare that nothing in this writing is to be construed as having been directed at the relative quality of the bitch, Doris. We like all good Shepherds and so let us never deny a welcome and a merited win to any Shepherd or other purebred canine, regardless of its ownership or place of birth. But let's not be dazzled by artifice or exploited by power practices.

Consider this: most of the then and now joint owners of the bitch as listed by Messrs. Rost and Cleveland in the April 1949 issue of *Popular Dogs*, were and are prominent judges and/or professional handlers.

What prestige and influence in promotion of this bitch's wins and puppies! Indeed, introduction of man power rather than of canine quality as the chosen avenue to wins and so one is led to conclude that the owners seem to lack confidence in their "find" from abroad to win on her own merits. Certainly the confidence of many of us has been shaken and we despair of getting desirable foreign blood through media which seems to place a higher value on wins than on the unguided quality that merits the wins.

Whatever the real or avowed intent of canine syndicates, it is clear that the practice of straw ownership of dogs within a clique of judges and professional handlers invites evils and the exploitation of that majority in the fancy who practice good sportsmanship.

Questions for Consideration

1. Are the Group and Best in Show rings necessarily the best forums for selecting future breeding stock?

2. How does one reconcile the question of quality when many of the top winning dogs at all-breed shows have never been exhibited or won top awards at specialty shows?

3. Agree or disagree. Many of today's top winning dogs are propelled to that status by people power rather than the ability to win on their own merit.

4. What is the purpose of campaigning a dog one has bred? What is the purpose of campaigning a dog if one has never bred any representatives of that particular breed?

5. Are dog shows about breeding better dogs or owning dogs which win?

6. Should limits be placed on the number of BIS awards a dog can win? Why or why not?

7. What is the exact purpose or value of rating systems which rank dogs according to how many dogs of other breeds they defeat?

8. Do rating systems encourage the breeding of generic show dogs rather than outstanding representatives of their breeds? Give specific examples.

9. How many people should own a dog, or be listed as owners of record?

10. Should judges co-own dogs with professional handlers? Should judges co-own dogs with anyone other than family members or *bona fide* business partners?

Bred-by-Exhibitor Class
Laurence A. Horswell

"Popular Dogs"
1949

At the June Delegates' Meeting, the impromptu discussion which followed the original proposal by John Oels, Delegate of the Bulldog Club of Philadelphia, that a "breeder's class" replace the Limit class, covered a lot of territory including eligibility of import, champions, etc., and the further question of restricting the handling of dogs in this class to their breeder-owners. The request was made that the AKC should secure an expression of opinion from the dog fancy on the sentiment toward setting up some such class as a regular class in place of the Limit Class.

Survey

Such a survey conducted by the AKC—of which the postcard questionnaire of the Dachshund Club of America membership was a part—produced the following expressions of preference:

Proposed Definition

With these data, the AKC Board of Directors has published in the November *Gazette*, a definition of a new Bred-by-Exhibitor Class for submission to the meeting of Delegates December 13, which at that time will require seventy-five per cent of the number present and voting to vote its adoption; and prior to adoption may be amended by a simple majority vote:

"Bred-by-Exhibitor Class shall be for all dogs except champions, six months of age and over, which shall be presently owned and exhibited by the same person or kennel who were the recognized breeders on the records of the American Kennel Club. The dog must be handled in the ring by the recorded owner and breeder or by a member of his or her immediate family." I should like here to discuss various aspects of this proposed amendment. I believe that there will be little disagreement in principle with the first sentence. With opportunities to show champions in the Open and Specials Only Classes, there certainly is no need for a restricted class for dogs which have won the title. The phrase "same person or kennel who were the recognized breeders on the records of the AKC," includes both registered dogs and such listed dogs as have had their owners and breeders recorded with the AKC and listing privileges extended by correspondence. I should

> *"This hardy perennial*
> —ENCOURAGING THE NOVICE—
> *is a pious slogan about which*
> *more is said in oblique efforts*
> *to advance other interests,*
> *than often is done actually*
> *to advance the novice*
> *with a worthwhile show dog."*

What is a Breeder?

Myrtle Kennels' English Setters
Owner, Mr. H. R. Barry
The goal of the breeder is not to produce one outstanding individual, but many quality dogs over a period of time.
1903

If difficulties exist in defining an "exhibitor," finding exactitude for the term "breeder" is perhaps more challenging. The AKC rules sensibly define a breeder as the person who owns a bitch at the time of mating. Unfortunately, this clinical definition for record keeping purposes fails to adequately differentiate between levels of involvement. The person who has bred only one litter is defined as a breeder in the same manner as another with decades of commitment. Further, one must seriously question whether any real breeders, in the best definition of the term, even exist anymore.

Before distemper vaccine became readily available in the 1930s the disease's high mortality rate required breeders to produce hundreds of puppies annually. However, this was not the primary reason for large scale breeding. At the dawn of dog shows, the goal was to fix type while making strides in breed improvement. Given the canine's genetic variability, this is not an easy task. Quite obviously, the desired result is more readily attainable when one has not just ten, but hundreds of puppies from which to choose. However, in today's society, large scale breeding is no longer considered socially acceptable. Any show person who admits to producing more than a half dozen litters per year will, no doubt, obtain a fair amount of quality dogs, but can also expect to be accused of running a "puppy mill." As a result, it becomes increasingly difficult to maintain a consistent level of type, let alone improve quality. This situation is further complicated by the fact that the dog's status has changed dramatically since the 19th Century. Dogs have become so anthropomorphized that many people view them as family members with the same inherent rights as human beings. Thus, the conscientious breeder's principal tool to maintain quality—grading animals—has come into question because pressure is brought to bear to keep all dogs produced alive, regardless of inherited anomalies, bad temperament or breed standard disqualifications. In most canine circles today, the word, "cull" is, indeed, a four-letter word not fit for polite society. As a consequence, the dog fancy is now burdening itself by spending large amounts of time and money to "rescue" poor quality surplus dogs, the majority of which were produced by "breeders" who had absolutely no pretensions toward canine improvement when they created their litters.

That the dedicated breeder is increasingly seen as merely the farmer to produce prize specimens for others to harvest is clearly evidenced by the endless touts in dog magazines which rarely credit the actual breeder. Today, many top show dogs are defined in terms of either the professional handler or the deep-pocketed owners and/or co-owners financing annual manic campaigns which designate the "best" dog as the one defeating the most animals of other breeds in Group or Best in Show competition. Yet, once the big winner is retired many of these co-owners automatically become "breeders of record" when offspring are produced, despite the fact that the only tangible evidence of their connection with a resultant litter is their signature on a piece of paper. The remarkable thing is that the breeders themselves don't differentiate. While many are quick to decry what they describe as "backyard breeders" or those who breed dogs for sale in pet shops, supporting a show system which evaluates quality based upon the amount of money spent is equally to blame for treating the dog as merely a commodity. When we elevate owners in name only to the status of dedicated breeders within the sport, simply because they have wide-open pocketbooks rather than particular expertise in dogs, it is rather specious to claim that the show dog is anything but a means to an end and subsequent talk of "improvement" is just more hot air.

assume that entry forms would be required to state the "owner of AKC record" for a listed entry to be accepted by show superintendents or show secretaries for inclusion in this class, in the same way that entries of puppies must state date and place of birth and names of breeder, sire and dam to be accepted for the Puppy Classes.

With respect to the second sentence of the class definition, restricting who may handle dogs in this class, during the discussion at the June Delegates' Meeting, it sounded to me as if considerable confusion stemmed from misunderstanding of the use of the word "exhibitor," many not realizing that the AKC defines exhibitors as the owners of the dogs being shown, but not necessarily the persons by whom the dogs are taken into the ring to be exhibited—the latter person actually "handling" the dog whether or not professional, or owner, or breeder. Restricting the handler to a member of the immediate family of the owner raises several questions.

Obviously not a novice, George C. Thomas, Jr., then Secretary of the English Setter Club of America, exhibits one of his Bloomfield Kennels' English Setters.
1900

Immediate Family?

First, who constitutes the immediate family? Mr. Bixby, AKC Vice-President, tells me that "immediate family" has for this purpose, been defined as including father, mother, brother, sister, husband, wife, son or daughter, but no grandparents, grandchildren, cousins, aunts, uncles or in-laws. At first, this sounds easy, but wait. As obviously a "kennel" as a recorded breeder-owner cannot have a father, mother, sister, brother, husband, wife, son or daughter, then this must apply to the immediate families of the individuals who singly or jointly own such kennels. Many kennels are registered in the name of husband and wife, which would set up two sets of fathers, mothers, brothers, sisters, and perhaps additional sons and daughters by previous marriages. I have sometimes noted in transfers of kennel names, that there are other forms of partnership involving two or even more individuals, each of whom would be entitled to a father, mother, brothers, sisters, husband, wife, sons and/or daughters as handlers, and registered kennels with four or five owners are not uncommon. What about dogs owned by syndicates? Such a bitch with ten registered owners could set up ten breeder-owners with her first litter of pups. The Westminster Kennel Club and other clubs have been owners and exhibitors of dogs. What about fire companies registered as breeder-owners of Dalmatians? Do the fathers, mothers, brothers, sisters, husbands, wives, sons and daughters apply to the officers, or to all the members or stockholders?

And what of the variations within the stated degrees of the immediate family—step-fathers or mothers, sons or daughters by informal or legal adoption, "natural" children, common-law husbands and wives? All these complications have appeared in the ranks of Dachshund breeders and owners, on a live-and-let-live basis. But would not this "immediate family" restriction force various issues before the AKC never contemplated in its original charter?

It would begin to look as if the AKC might find that registering litters had become the tail on a larger activity of registering human

Buy from a Breeder

The overwhelming popularity of dog shows quickly established that purebred dogs had significant monetary, as well as intrinsic, value. Consequently, in the tradition of medieval animal fairs, the show site became the most logical place to buy and sell dogs. For many years, sale prices could be listed in the catalog. Interested buyers would inform the show secretary or superintendent and sales would be transacted through the official office, thus insuring that the price advertised was the price paid. In this regard, dog shows provided a very useful service for prospective buyers. Dogs could be thoroughly inspected over the course of a public show and the buyer was saved a long trip to a far-off kennel. But, one could also haggle back at the benches as there were plenty of dogs sold at shows which were not advertised in the catalog. The ignorant and uninformed, particularly tourists, were easy targets to purchase these "bargains."

Even before the modality of the distemper virus was documented, wise breeders knew that large, transient canine gatherings had something to do with spreading the disease and rarely brought along puppies for exhibition. However, there were no prohibitions against this and whole litters of puppies from 6 weeks old and up would be sold at the shows. If one purchased a puppy directly from a kennel, most reputable breeders would replace it within a specified amount of time because dogs

were usually sold and shipped on approval. However, all dogs purchased at a show were "as is," even if obvious fraud could be proven. The most astute dog experts occasionally fell victim to such swindles. In 1890, E. B. Joachim purchased a Schipperke at a show only to discover at a much later date that it's chest had been dyed to cover a large white patch. But, when he brought charges before the Kennel Club nothing could be done. The seller, a Mr. E. Durant, stated he had purchased the dog only two weeks before he again sold her, claiming he was unaware of any alterations to the dog's appearance—and value.

Those who started dog shows presumed everyone was morally guided by honesty, fair play and sportsmanship. But, participation was open to all and many wanted to cash in on the canine's new found popularity. Thus, unless one knew with whom one was dealing, or had consigned a dog dealer as an agent, the probability of acquiring a show winner was remote. Consequently, many thousands of dollars, particularly American dollars, were spent on substandard dogs which were bought sight unseen. While many of these unfortunate deals involved Americans importing English dogs, plenty of local transactions foisted poor quality or sickly dogs on fellow citizens and foreigners alike. Dishonest deals thrive on the ignorance of the consumer and amazingly, in over a century of dog buying, the general public has not made great strides in learning about the breeds they wish to purchase. Consequently, the best admonition is still the oldest:

"Caveat emptor."

fathers, mothers, brothers, sisters, husbands, wives, sons and daughters, and adjudicating degrees of consanguinity—issuing identifications like the present certificates of officially determined canine height or color, with the addition of passport photos of the breeder-owners, and family tree diagrams with smaller photos, sample signatures and maybe fingerprints in the roots and branches to preclude unauthorized interchanges.

Discrimination?

And then we have the problem of discrimination, attempts to solve which have led to rules against dogs resting in their crates, against dogs resting along the route to the show if that makes them late at the gate, against exhibitors being charged different entry fees according to how many entries they have made, etc. Now some breeder-owners have more need of help handling their dogs than others, due to factors of age or infirmity, which ought not to handicap a dog from having his virtues exhibited in the ring as well as the next. And there are some breeder-owners who, through no fault of their own, have little or no immediate family in terms of father, mother, brother, sister, husband, wife, son or daughter, able and willing (in the words of John H. Lewis) to accompany them to dog shows and handle their dogs for them. Yet either of these variously handicapped breeder-owners may regard themselves victims of discrimination, if due to forces beyond their control they are not able to have the pride of their own breeding recognized by carrying their silks in the Bred-by-Exhibitor Class for lack of an eligible and willing

English Setter, Ch. Rock Falls Colonel, *the first to win* 100 *Best in Show awards. This remarkable achievement was attained with breeder/owner/handler William T. Holt.*

1953

jockey among their fathers, mothers, brothers, sisters, husbands, wives, sons and daughters.

Enforcement?

Second, how can such a restriction be enforced in practice without such family-tree identification cards as suggested above? (A) Not by judges, who certainly cannot be made responsible for examining conclusively into the identity of the breeder-owner, handler, and family relationships of every exhibitor who brings a dog into such a class; (B) Not by the stewards, who lack authority or time for such an inquisition as they exert themselves to get dogs into the ring with owners, handlers, or reasonable facsimiles or proxies, between duties of caring for ribbons, prizes and trophies, and marking the blackboard; (C) Not by the show superintendents or show secretaries, who lack authority or personnel to be present in every ring so to identify every exhibitor in these classes; (D) Not by bench show committees, for similar reasons; (E) Not by the AKC at the time of the show, for lack of field personnel, or; (F) Not by the AKC when the show records are processed subsequently in its offices, for by that time, it would be impossible to ascertain conclusively what person accompanied each dog into the ring, and it would require interminable correspondence to verify the *bona fides* of immediate family relationships; (G) Not by depending upon competitor protests before or while the class is being judged, for such protests would need to be adjudicated before the judging of the class could proceed, by judge, steward, superintendent, show secretary, bench show committee or AKC field representatives, with the same difficulties suggested in (A), (B), (C), (D), or (E)—not to mention the difficulties of exhibitors investigating the identities and family relationships of competitors, some of whom travel great distances, the potential ill-will inherent in such efforts to investigate, or the possibilities of collusion against which a sound, enforceable rule should clearly and specifically provide.

Confusion?

The effort to impose limitations upon who may handle a dog in a Bred-by-Exhibitor Class seems to me to stem from a confusion of motives: (1) Breeder-owners who lack confidence in their ability to handle the dogs they have bred as well as professional handlers, would exclude professional handlers. But there is no way to exclude a professional handler from handling entries of his own or his immediate family's breeder-ownership; (2) Any of us can name breeder-owners whose experience and skill at handling is great enough to meet and match professional handling all the way up to best in show competition, and these still would have this advantage over other breeder-owners; (3) The sentiment was expressed at the June Delegates' Meeting that a breeder-owner would desire and should be entitled to have the best representatives of his breeding handled in this class regardless of who handles them. The sentiment also was expressed that a Bred-by-Exhibitor Class would encourage the novice. This hardy perennial—Encouraging the Novice—is a pious slogan about which more is said in oblique efforts to advance other interests, than often is done actually to advance the novice with a worthwhile show dog. However, a breeder-owner certainly is not a typical novice exhibitor, and it seems a far cry to ring in this "novice" slogan to protect the produce of one breeder-owner from that of another; (4) The class should not try to encompass two purposes at once, combining bred-by-exhibitor with novice or amateur handling. If it is desired to have a class for novice handlers, it should be so designed and defined to protect against the seasoned amateur as much as against the professional handler. Two people have acquired a deserved reputation in Dachshund rings for conniving, and for crowding competitors, stepping on human and canine heels, etc.—one "professional" handler and one "amateur" handler-owner. A Bred-by-Exhibitor Class seems scarcely the place to try to protect the novice exhibitor from such advanced sportsmanship.

Without spinning this subject out too far, here are two further thoughts on this question of protecting the novice exhibitor. How long is a novice deserving of such protection? A novice dog can only win the Novice class only once—and even at that it must compete in the Winners Class without such protection. Would a novice amateur breeder-owner deserve protection from the breeder-owner whose experience embraces 100 litters? Fifty litters? Twenty-five litters? Ten litters? Five litters? When we were setting up the classifications for the Golden Jubilee Dachshund Specialty in 1945, one breeder-owner earnestly requested a separate class for puppies produced by that one kennel, promising to put up the prize money, and trophies and to secure a large entry for the class "because then no one else could win!" That would be real—if extreme—protection for the breeder-owner, or would it? Unless it is workable, even an AKC rule cannot provide every little thing the heart desireth!

If this presentation has explored the aspects of the new class from the sublime to the ridiculous, it is to stimulate thought now, before the December 13 meeting of the Delegates. Some definition of the new class is almost sure to be adopted at that time. The more forethought brought to bear at that meeting, the better the new class will work in practice.

Restrictions Unworkable?

We should not be stampeded by statistical polls or by slogans. If you go back to the tabulation, less than half of the clubs or people who received questionnaires and thereby had an opportunity to express their burning convictions, sent in replies favoring any restrictions whatever

The Fancy

Great interest in preserving and improving purebred dogs did not suddenly start in 1859 with the advent of dog shows. However, prior to this, except for the landed gentry who maintained dogs specifically for various forms of hunting, large kennels were rare. The only people who made their livings as dog breeders were generally the most disreputable in the kingdom. In fact, "the fancy," specifically meant those who either bred, kept, trained or purchased dogs and/or game fowl for fighting. In the late 18th and early 19th Centuries, the most notorious "fancier" was Ben White, who actually had an apprentice, Bill George. White's

"MR. PUNCH'S VISIT TO A VERY REMARKABLE PLACE"
Bill George's "Canine Castle" — 1846

establishment was located in a deserted section on the outskirts of London. He bred, trained and provided the majority of Bulldogs for baiting and many of the terrier crosses for fights at Westminster Pit.

The British have always had a knack for creating various blood sports and pugilistic events — even without the Roman influence. Under Queen Elizabeth I, bull baiting became a national pastime with matches being held in various locations every Sunday and holiday. Interest was still quite strong in the early part of the 19th Century. As it gradually waned, the fancy came up with more inventive betting events, pitting dogs not only against bulls or other dogs, but opposite rats, badgers, monkeys, bears and finally in 1825, lions. Lion baiting was the idea of fight promoter, Sam Wedgbury of Warwick. His match was well publicized and notices of it actually appeared in a periodical called, "The Sporting Magazine." However, on fight day, a large meeting of Quakers was being held in Warwick and they did everything in their power to prevent the contests on the basis of abject cruelty. The sheriff could do nothing for fear of the crowds and the bloody depravity which followed sickened many of the staunchest fight fans. Word of this spectacle quickly reached London and ordinances were passed to prohibit holding any animal fights in the city, and further, forbidding the raising of animals for them. Although Ben White's kennels were raided and closed down, he simply moved beyond the city limits and fights became underground activities. But public sentiment had been swayed against such "sports." In 1835 all animal fights were made illegal by act of Parliament.

About that time, Ben White died and everyone presumed Bulldogs would die with him. However, Bill George, who many times had been criticized by his master for making pets of the Bulldogs and spoiling them for fighting, decided to stay with the kennel business, renaming it "Canine Castle." He continued to breed Bulldogs, selecting for faithfulness and devotion — successfully eliminating the original combative nature. Bill George and his son, Alf, became active in the dog show world and most of the original show Bulldogs came from their line. One of the reasons the Bulldog quickly came to the fore at early canine exhibitions was because, apart from the ancient sporting dogs, it was one of the few breeds in which definite type was already well established. Within ten years, through his reputation for honesty, the quality of his dogs and the scrupulous way he cared for them, Bill George completely changed the public perception of the words "dog breeder" and "fancier." When "Mr. Punch" visited in 1846, the "Canine Castle" was a place gentlemen frequented. And by the time dog shows became popular, no one was ashamed to admit they were a member of "the fancy."

on who might handle dogs in this class. In that sense, those who favored the restrictions represented in the second sentence of the proposed definition can be classed as a minority of those who would be affected, and who had an opportunity to express themselves.

Also, it is just good common sense for a rule which introduces an innovation in the way of control over the identity and family relationships of exhibitors in the ring—where up to now every effort has been made to preserve a theoretical anonymity before the judge—to carry with it an explicit method for its enforcement, and not expect enforcement, like Topsy, just to grow.

Questions for Consideration

1. Horswell implies that the Delegate body relies upon spur-of-the-moment considerations rather than a logical thought process. Does it seem that the Delegates consistently seek simple solutions to difficult problems? Should last minute amendments be allowed to rules which have lasting impact on the sport?

2. What seems to drive the Delegates' decisions when they make significant changes to the dog show rules? Can the majority of fanciers ever hope to have their views properly represented when only a comparative handful of people have the ability to vote on important matters?

3. What is the official definition of an "exhibitor?" What is your definition of the term? Why would the official rule book have contradictory definitions of this term in regard to eligibility requirements for different classes?

4. Whose job is it to enforce the ownership and showing restrictions in Bred-by-Exhibitor Class? Who has the right to question exhibitors in regard to their relatives? Is it possible to enforce the eligibility rules of this class?

5. Should rules and classes be specifically designed to eliminate competition?

6. Some specialty clubs set up additional rules in their non-regular classes, such as Sweepstakes, to prohibit professional, or other than, owner-handlers. Do you agree with this principal? Elaborate upon your reasons.

7. Should breeders who, by handicap, infirmity or simply lack of skill or enjoyment in handling their own dogs be prohibited from entering them in certain classes?

8. Is there too much emphasis put upon handling and showmanship in the conformation ring? Give specific examples.

9. How would you describe and design the various classes available for competition?

10. How would dog shows change if bred-by-exhibitor variety groups and bred-by-exhibitor best in show awards were instituted?

11. If the points for "top dog" rating systems were computed to favor those animals competing in bred-by-exhibitor variety groups—instead of those dogs which were campaigned the most—how would dog shows change? Could such a change be an improvement?

12. Should there be limits on campaigning specials during the course of a year? If so, how would you structure these limits so they would be equitable?

13. How do you define the term, "dog breeder?"

14. What is the role of the breeder in the dog show sport today? What should that role be?

15. How would you characterize the general public perception of the term "dog breeder" today? Is it a positive, negative or vague impression? Elaborate.

The AKC—Incorporated

How to Make a Club a Business

"The American Field" and "Field and Fancy"
1907

Kennel Clubs Demand Recognition

The calm sea on which the AKC, Incorporated, so successfully launched by the AKC, Unincorporated, is already ruffled by an approaching squall—whether it will blow itself out or develop into a gale, time will tell.

The AKC was incorporated at a meeting held in New York on November 5, the incorporators being W. G. Rockefeller, A. P. Vredenburgh, M. A. Viti, H. K. Bloodgood, August Belmont, W. B. Emery, H. H. Hunnewell and G. M. Carnochan. A constitution was adopted and Mr. Belmont was chosen President, and Mr. Hunnewell, Vice-President, of the club. Then, on November 19, a special meeting was held. Twenty-three Delegates were present. All of the members of the AKC, Unincorporated, were elected members of the corporation, and their Delegates accepted as Delegates to the new club, and the Associate Members chosen Associate Subscribers. The incorporators then proceeded to the election of the Board of Directors, which under the provisions of the constitution of the AKC, Incorporated, is to consist of thirty persons, divided into five classes of six members each. Those of the first class are to serve five years from the annual meeting of 1907; those of the second class four years; of the third, three; of the fourth, two, and of the fifth, one.

The election of the Directors practically completed the incorporation of the AKC. All that remained was for the AKC, Unincorporated to turn over its property to the AKC, Incorporated, and this was done.

Now the Bull Terrier Club of America, as full of fight as the breed it represents, asks for a special meeting of the AKC to protest against the fact that the constitution of the AKC, Incorporated, is not in accordance with that of the AKC, Unincorporated, and against the fact that the proposed constitution was not shown to the rank and file before their Delegates were asked to turn over to the new organization their rights, title and interests in the old club. The Bull Terrier Club demands a revision of the newly adopted constitution, and calls attention to the fact that under its provisions no club whose Delegate is not one of the thirty Directors has any active representation in kennel affairs. It further lays emphasis on the fact that no Delegate who is not on the Board of Directors has any voice at any meeting, except the Annual, when he may vote for six Directors, and that no Directors are to be voted for till February, 1908. Attention is also called to the fact that the absolute control of all affairs is vested in an Executive Committee from whose action there is no appeal, even by the Board of Directors, and that this Executive Committee has entire control between meetings of Directors, and may meet whenever it chooses, only four members making a quorum. The Bull Terrier Club closes its letter with a strong protest

> "The only hope for American fanciers is getting the American Kennel Club back to the first principle —democracy— the plan on which it was started and the very life of the allied membership."

August Belmont, Jr. was the AKC's fourth President from 1888-1916. Although corporate accounts describe his reign as one of stability and installing sound business practices, careful analysis would more accurately characterize his management style as that of a bully. Belmont was responsible for reducing Delegate power from a democratic equal within the organization to a basically perfunctory position. It is hard for us to imagine the Delegates continued to keep both Belmont and Vredenburgh in office after repeated malfeasance. But, we must remember Belmont was in charge during the age of the robber barons, when wealth, above all else, was idolized in America, particularly in New York City.

Many details of Belmont's early life can be found in David Black's, "The King of Fifth Avenue," a biography of August Belmont, Sr. Best described as indolent, hot-tempered and not a scholar, August, Jr. spent most of his life trying to come out from under his father's giant shadow. Upon the elder's death, Belmont announced his "Junior" suffix was to be immediately dropped. Overly concerned about other's opinions, August, Jr. was always fending off what he imagined to be personal attacks on his dignity and position. However, the most shocking and revealing incident in Black's book regarding the younger Belmont's character involved the escape of one of his polo ponies. While loose, the horse kicked a boy in the face, leaving him unconscious for several days. When his father, a Mr. J. C. Tower, presented Belmont with a $25 doctor's bill, he refused to pay. A few days later, Tower saw Belmont on the train platform and again asked for the money. Belmont turned away and Tower called him, "a deadbeat and a fraud." Belmont then began beating him with his cane. A fight ensued. Tower filed suit for $10,000. Given the excessive amount of damages claimed, Belmont won, but upon the conclusion of events, sent Tower the original $25. At the same time, he also sent a note to Joseph Pulitzer, owner of the "New York World," telling him that under no circumstances was there to be anything in print stating he had paid the money.

Always involved with animals, Belmont was particularly interested in cock fighting and liked to let everyone know his gladiator fowl could trace their lineage back to the time of the Revolutionary War. From an early age he also kept dogs, principally Gordon Setters and then later, Smooth Fox Terriers. Unfortunately, Belmont was not a particularly careful dog man. For many years his dogs were not kenneled but allowed to run loose and breed at will on the Long Island family farm. On numerous occasions his father complained the stables were overrun with puppies. When his son did nothing about the situation, the patriarch was forced to order purges. Apparently, other dogs sometimes got into the mix. In 1878, August, Jr. wrote a threatening letter to dog show judge William Lort, who, because he did not believe some of Belmont's dogs to be purebred, disqualified them from competition at the Westminster KC event.

Yet, while Belmont's character flaws were obvious and severe, he did make some lasting contributions. In 1888, he suggested, and offered to cover against losses, publication of the AKC "Gazette." His principal motive for doing so was to eliminate negative reports in other papers. Nevertheless, the magazine is still in publication today. Belmont also had an eye for a sound investment and when no one else would take the risk on a new form of transportation, he stepped forward as the principal backer of the Interborough Rapid Transit (IRT) subway line in New York City. On opening day in 1904, nearly 150,000 invited guests rode the trains and later the general public gladly paid a nickel each to do so. Today, the Belmont name is most memorably associated with Thoroughbred horse racing. Belmont Park was built by, and named for, August Belmont, Sr. The younger Belmont is responsible for sparking his father's interest in racing and was later the breeder of both Fair Play and his most famous son, Man O'War. This great horse was sent to Saratoga as a yearling, the first time Belmont had ever sold any of his young stock at auction. But, Belmont did so because at age 60, he had volunteered to go to France as part of the war effort and help procure horses and mules for the army.

against thirty Directors managing the affairs of over one hundred and thirty clubs and several hundred Associate Members, and asks all the AKC clubs to join in a call for a special meeting.

Following the stand taken by the Bull Terrier Club of America, Delegates of the Collie Club of America, Russian Wolfhound Club of America and Bull Terrier Breeders' Association issued a call inviting Delegates of all other clubs to meet at the Ashland House, New York, Thursday, January 3, 1907, to review the recent actions of the American Kennel Club. That the actions of the AKC, Incorporated, were usurpative, unrepresented clubs assert, and many members of the latter have said they feel like doing what their loyal fellow countrymen did with the tea in Boston Harbor, once upon a time, and for the same reasons.

The American Field

August Belmont, Jr.'s best known Fox Terrier, BLEMTON VICTOR II. This dog won the American Fox Terrier Club's Grand Challenge Cup a total of 8 times. Artist, G. Muss-Arnolt c. 1895

Ashland Committee Meeting

Notwithstanding the warnings so often sounded, and danger signals displayed, apprising the true amateur dog fanciers of America that their interests in the American Kennel Club were being jeopardized, the ship of the AKC has struck upon the rocks of professionalism, and it now remains for the amateur fanciers to pull it off or let it go to pieces. Which shall it be?

The call for an informal meeting of AKC Delegates to protest against the usurpative methods of the American Kennel Club, Incorporated, which practically disenfranchised a great majority of the kennel clubs of America, was responded to by the Delegates of twenty-three clubs, who attended the meeting in the Ashland House, New York, last week Thursday.

That there was necessity for the meeting everyone who has kept posted on passing events knows. The consensus of opinion of those present was that certain officials of the AKC led by a non-elective official under the old constitution, to whit, the Secretary, held back cards on them and did not give the one hundred and thirty-odd Delegates to the AKC, Unincorporated, a square deal. Just who dealt the cards and engineered the deal no one wanted to say; but the meeting decided that amendments must be accepted by the AKC at its annual meeting next month, if the AKC is to continue to exist as an association of amateurs.

Dr. J. E. De Mund, who heartily supported the amendments, made the following statement to the Delegates present: "Secretary Vredenburgh said the amendments would only pass over his dead body. I do not think it was a remark in the club spirit that bands amateurs together who breed, show and talk dog."

The amendments referred to had been hand-delivered to the Secretary of the AKC by Dr. De Mund and Mr. R. S. Edson, to be sure they would be filed thirty days before the Annual Meeting, and one would suppose, from the Secretary's remark, that he considered himself the whole club.

Dr. De Mund said, further, "I am in the American Kennel Club for the purpose of promoting the interests of a sport, not of a trust, and if it is to be turned into a sort of a trust, I for one shall get out and devote my attention to my own club."

Mr. S. W. Maguire, Delegate of the Irish Setter Club of America, discussing the report on the incorporation of the AKC said, "The incorporators went forward, step by step, as steadily as

Dear Sir—I am in receipt of your instruction regarding the annual membership fee. I wrote you a year ago remitting my fee and at the same time tendering my resignation, and I would like to know if communications of that nature are ever submitted to the executive? I, at the same time, stated my reasons for not desiring to remain any longer a member of your club. I stated that if the kennel club, when soliciting memberships from men interested in dogs used by sportsmen, would show that they take an interest in the development of sporting dogs by encouraging field trials and field or other tests, I should be delighted to subscribe, but not when your club only encourages the breeding of effeminate specimens, and takes for its standard that poor, brainless imitation of humanity, the "dude," or encourages "rag chewing" in the press as to what length of legs a spaniel should have for field work, by men who would be worse startled at the discharge of a gun than their dogs, so little do they know of field work. No, show me that the kennel club intends taking a little interest in sporting dogs and I shall only be too pleased to renew my subscription or subscribe to any object that will add to the development of the sportsmen's dog.

soldiers. The reasons quoted may sound sweet on their ears. But what concerns us, who love the club of amateurs that has been quashed, are matters that have not been revealed. In the report of the AKC meeting of December 19, which put through the incorporation, I appear as one of the unanimous supporters of the act. If I had been at the meeting I should have opposed the action. I didn't know until seeing the minutes anything that had been done."

Considerable resentment was voiced because the control of the AKC had been taken away from the constituent club members and lodged in the Board of Directors, without responsibility to the Delegates. Directors are not now required to be Delegates of any club, some present officials not having any kennel interests. Under the existing system it would be difficult to change control, even though all the clubs might be a unit in opposition, for the reason that it would take years to install a new directorate, due to the incorporators naming the officers and directors, the latter with five-year terms.

Mr. S. R. Cutler, of the Bay State Kennel Club, announced his chagrin that, the morning of the meeting, he called at the office of the AKC to pay his club's annual dues, $10, and which Secretary Vredenburgh refused, because, under the new constitution, dues had to be paid by December 31. Mr. Cutler understood forty-nine clubs had been dropped on this account.

If the amendments to the constitution of the AKC, Incorporated, approved at this meeting, are adopted at the coming Annual Meeting of the AKC, Incorporated, constituent clubs will regain their constitutional rights and have something to say, through their Delegates, how the AKC shall govern its members and what disposition shall be made of the large cash asset ($30,000), that these clubs have built up in one way and another, the despotic transfer of which to the AKC, Incorporated caused such a just storm of protest.

If the amendments are not adopted, then what? The American Kennel Club, as a republican institution, is a necessity and should not be permitted to die. As a despotic institution, with autocratic officials, it would have no place on American soil.

The American Field

Narrowing Down

Dear Sir—I was one of the original incorporators of the American Kennel Club, and I attended the meeting where the new constitution was passed upon.

I regret to say that as I had already expressed my desire to be relieved of my duties as a Director and incorporator of the American

absolutely against the first principles of the AKC as it has been from the start, namely, that every club can have equal representation at all meetings of the club.

I may add, that as I have resigned as Delegate to the Duquesne Kennel Club, and as my successor will soon be appointed, I do not think it will be fair on my part to bind the Delegate of the Duquesne KC by any action I might take if I come to the next meeting.

G. M. Carnochan
Field and Fancy

Buying Success

From 1895-98, Ch. Go Bang amassed an enviable show record in England under the skillful handling of George Raper. His fame was such that Major G. M. Carnochan, a Wall Street broker, decided he must have the dog, at any price. The deal was consummated in 1898 for $2,500—the highest ever paid for a Wire Fox Terrier. After the money changed hands, Go Bang was entered in one last event before his trip to America, the Derby Terrier Show, where he was defeated by Barkby Ben. Afraid that another American would purchase competition for him, Carnochan told Raper he must have Barkby Ben, also. But, based on his recent win, and the owner's reluctance to part with him, the price had gone up substantially—to $2,500. Desperate to protect his investment, Carnochan bought the dog. Many British fanciers thought Carnochan had more money than sense, but in the end, he had made an extremely fortuitous purchase. First, he never allowed his two dogs to compete against each other. Consequently, Ch. Go Bang, a born show dog, was never defeated in the United States and did much to create interest in the Wire variety. However, his pedigree was unknown on his dam's side and as a sire, he only produced a few notable dogs. Barkby Ben, on the other hand, though not a showman, was significant in establishing "modern" type for Wires, siring dozens of winners in both England and America, including Ch. Cackler of Notts.

CH. GO BANG

Kennel Club (new), I did not pay a great deal of attention to it. But, this I will say—that while I heard that the new constitution enlarged the original eight directors to thirty, there was absolutely no mention made at the meeting, to the best of my knowledge, that the fact of there being thirty directors only, robbed all the other Delegates of a chance to vote at any but the Annual Meeting.

Had any such fact been mentioned, I should certainly have been against it, as it is

AKC—Democracy or Oligarchy?

President Belmont, of the American Kennel Club, Incorporated, was petitioned by seven Delegates of the AKC, Unincorporated, to convene a special meeting of the American Kennel Club, Inc., Saturday, February 9, for the explicit purpose of determining whether or not forty-nine clubs of the AKC, Inc. are still members of the AKC, this number having been notified that inasmuch as they had not paid their annual dues to the AKC, Incorporated, by

December 31, 1906, they were suspended.

The custom for years of accepting club dues as late as the Annual Meeting of the AKC in February of each year, in the absence of any notice to the contrary caused many clubs to hold off till the Annual Meeting this month, when their Delegates attending the meeting would pay the Secretary personally. However, it did not go this year, and as the Secretary refused to receive dues after December 31, many of the clubs stood suspended.

The reason for asking President Belmont to call the meeting is because the Secretary of the AKC, Inc., in replying to a letter from the suspended clubs, wherein they asked to be either placed in good standing by the Executive Committee, or be notified officially that they have not been suspended, stated that it had been "impossible to obtain a quorum of the Executive Committee" of the AKC, Inc., (four people!!) from which reply the clubs could derive no satisfaction and realized that they were down and out unless a special meeting of the AKC, Inc., were called to take action on the matter outside the "Executive Committee." If the special meeting is held the entire responsibility will be taken off the shoulders of the Executive Committee, and all clubs interested in the future welfare of the American Kennel Club should have Delegates present, that justice may be done to all clubs which have been so summarily dropped.

The American Field has received a number of letters in regard to the AKC incorporating as it did, appropriating the accumulated assets and forcing a closed corporation constitution on its members. Popular representation is a prerequisite, and authority to control the kennel affairs of America should not be vested in a practically perpetual Board of Directors, many of whom have no allied kennel interests. The board should be elected by the constituent club members of the AKC, if not annually, then for alternating periods of not more than two years each, and thus retain to the constituent club members the right of personal representation and direct participation in the management of the corporation their membership makes possible.

The only hope for American fanciers is getting the American Kennel Club back to the first principle—democracy—the plan on which it was started and the very life of the allied membership. Of late years the American Kennel Club has been drifting into an autocracy; feeling its strength, due more to the abiding confidence of those who were supporting it than from any other cause. The clique which craved life tenure of power, seeing the handwriting on the wall, incorporated an oligarchy, appropriated all assets, records and other property, and now asks the deluded followers, what are you going to do about it?

The American Field

Aftermath of the AKC Meeting

The New York show this year afforded an all-absorbing topic. This was kennel government. Many on the outside, by choice, considered that the government was entirely out of proportion to the work accomplished, that important duties have been neglected, and that vital matters pertaining to the interests involved and the dog's welfare have had to rely on individual effort, and that the growth has been in spite of the AKC's course.

"The revolt" makes the rank and file wonder what it is all about, and when Delegates have been asked to explain how such things could happen, some have been obliged to confess their ignorance of fundamental matters.

When the AKC was formed one provision with its significance was overlooked. It meant that in order to oust those who held the reins something like a revolution was necessary. Secure under this autocratic provision, it had been the policy to flourish a thong that looked like "harmony" whilst driving roughshod over everything. Not only the driver, but the page and grooms learned the use of the whip; it was used on the Pacific, it was tried on Canada, it was felt by every reformer, and when "Ashmont" came down

Correct Type and Good Breeding

Principally because of the American Civil War, dog fanciers in the United States lagged behind the British in developing organized dog shows. For many years it was also extremely difficult to buy top flight breeding and show stock. According to James Watson, the British coined the term, "American type," as a derogatory reference to canines not good enough to show in their homeland but which the less scrupulous gladly shipped off to the "colonials" at long prices. In fact, "type" quickly became the buzz word for any dog which was for sale.

However, it was very difficult for new breeds to gain a foothold in the United States. Initially, many breeds became known in this country only because British fanciers came here to exhibit; certainly not for the competition—for there was none—but in the hope of encouraging Americans to take up their favorite breed. One such introduction was the Bloodhound. Although the New England Kennel Club, founded in 1884, used a Bloodhound illustration for their logo, the breed was first exhibited in 1888, when the premier breeder, Mr. Edwin Brough, benched four of his dogs at Westminster Kennel Club. His hounds attracted a great deal of attention and one interested party was Mr. William Wade, editor of "Forest and Stream." Wade was a self-proclaimed expert

American or British?

Ch. Hands Up completed a successful show career in the USA, then competed in England several times, becoming a permanent export when the rabies quarantine was imposed in 1903. This dog achieved notoriety in the canine press as an American-bred Wire which could hold his own against the best British stock on British soil. But in fact, this Ch. Go Bang son was of straight British breeding. His dam, Belle Duval, was purchased by Reginald F. Mayhew from George Raper and imported in whelp. However, in contrast to AKC rules, the Kennel Club considered the owner of the bitch at the time of whelping, rather than mating, as the official breeder of record. Thus, Ch. Hands Up was technically, if not in reality, an American-bred dog.

on all breeds and, apparently not impressed with what the English could offer, began publishing numerous articles stating Bloodhounds really weren't superior in scenting ability to any American Foxhound, Setter, Beagle, and so on. He claimed the British were simply mired in producing the "wrong type." To back up his statements, he sent over one of his best Foxhounds the following year and arrogantly encouraged the British breeders to use this dog to "improve" their stock. Naturally, Wade was anxious to read Brough's opinion. "I saw Ran Tucker at the Alexandra Palace Show in 1889, and I took several Bloodhound breeders and one or two Foxhound men to look at him. I believe in saying nothing but what is good of the dead and would prefer not to criticise Ran as a Foxhound; but I do say it is rather cruel of Mr. Wade to say that he greatly resembles our Bloodhounds, and especially so when I remember that Mr. Wade's experience is limited to some Bloodhounds of mine—the four he saw on the bench." Wade later conceded that perhaps the two breeds were, indeed, different.

Nevertheless, issues of correct type are always more readily resolved than those of good breeding. In 1891, August Belmont exhibited in England and was shocked because most British fanciers didn't know—or care—who he was. One can only imagine his pomposity as "The Stock-keeper," besides reporting upon the AKC President's ill-humor and general rudeness, related that one of the principal entertainments of the show was people teaching one another how to "walk and talk like August Belmont." Outraged, Belmont informed editor George R. Krehl that he would no longer speak to him and that "The Stock-keeper" would be forever banned from the AKC offices. Obviously not overly distressed at the prospect of never again having to be in the presence of Belmont's temper tantrums, Krehl responded with a letter addressed to "Forest and Stream," in which he said, "In showing dogs one is compelled to mix with many people whom one is not obligated to know."

The AKC Offices
c. 1904

One purpose of a corporate office is to project an image to the outside world. In that regard, the AKC, founded in the era of private men's clubs, has always assumed the decor of exclusivity. With dark paneling and carpets, luxurious front office furniture, books, paintings and sundry objet d'art, one might presume an old-world stability that, in reality, is totally contradicted by the factual history and day-to-day management of the organization. The principal reason for this is because the Delegates have never taken full control of the AKC by demanding (and receiving) full accountability from the Board of Directors.

Although the Delegates successfully regained some power after the AKC's illegal incorporation, what was lost was the ability for representation to grow with the sport. When AKC re-incorporated, newly recognized kennel clubs no longer automatically became Member Clubs, having to fulfill stringent requirements and then eventually being voted upon by the Board of Directors. Thus, these "Licensed Clubs" were welcome to pay the fees necessary to hold AKC sanctioned events, but had no Delegate representation. This inequity was specifically detrimental to the West, for as the sport rapidly grew, representation and decision making for all kennel affairs was effectively maintained by the Eastern clubs. This imbalance still exists. Licensed Clubs now outnumber Member Clubs fully 3 to 1, and in combination with all other affiliated performance clubs by 7 to 1, but cannot vote for board members nor any dog show and registration rules which directly affect them. Consequently, the majority of today's dog show enthusiasts have no voice in the active management of their sport.

from New England with an overwhelming contingent, to insist on changes, the provision making the vote of the Delegates present ineffectual was the whip that was displayed.

This same method of ruling official dogdom has been introduced into the shows. It has not been ability, integrity or knowledge that has decided who shall judge, but much too often the question was whom the individual was in the

ring. Attempts have even been made to influence the press, and unless under the control of the clique, more rocks than roses have been put in the path of press representatives. When rottenness has been indicated, lack of ability or honesty made clear, or any degree of intelligent criticism offered, the word has gone forth, "he knows too much," and the stiletto has been used when the whip was disregarded. Thus has arisen the cry of "dog cliques," "dog rings," and "dog trusts." Whilst this was the face which could not long be concealed, things were going on behind the scenes—never intended for the light of day.

The revolt resulted, and with the once despised press as a factor, for wholesome conduct, for representation on a constituency basis, for proper authentic registration, for the use of the hoarded money by those who contributed it, for efficient judging, for progress, progressive reform, and the welfare of the dogs, with good will to all, fair play and a square deal for everyone in the game, the issue should be fought to a finish.

Save the AKC for its legitimate purposes, or the work such unions are intended for, but let it be worthy of the great army of enthusiastic kennel devotees who built it, worthy of the country and the age. It has been said that the schemer divided the cost of incorporation, and, if AKC is effectually taken out of the hands of this oligarchy, and the governed have a voice again, what will be done with those who so shamefully misused their office or their positions?

> *"When rottenness has been indicated, lack of ability or honesty made clear, or any degree of intelligent criticism offered, the word has gone forth, 'he knows too much,' and the stiletto has been used when the whip was disregarded."*

Nevertheless, as the incorporators did not use the charter within two years as is provided by the statutes, it is, therefore, undoubtedly null and void, with whatever is done under it.

"Manhattan"
The American Field

The Unexplained Explanation

The publication of Mr. Belmont's speech is nothing more or less than "hot air," though it may be easily seen that an appeal to loyalty is attempted. Certainly the AKC (Inc.) would have the Delegates go on in "the same unanimous and harmonious manner" that made it possible for them to obtain control of the club.

The idea of incorporating AKC is not a new one, but as there has been absolutely no kick on the Incorporating, only on how it was done, and how it was made the excuse for taking all power from the Delegates and thrusting a bitter pill down their throats in the form of a constitution so totally different from the old that they seem never to have been allied in any way, shape, or manner. As to the dangers of an unincorporated club I do not think them so great as this explanation would have us suppose.

"A half truth is a lie," and the whole truth was never told about the 1891 libel suit or Mr. Belmont's princely munificence. It is wonderful that though the club was really incorporated in 1903, no official action was taken or the old club dissolved till nearly three years afterward. If the dangers to an unincorporated body were so great one would but naturally suppose that it would be most desirable to have the property and papers and money of the old club transferred to the incorporated body as soon as possible. No one has explained this delay, but I think that we can all make some pretty shrewd guesses. To say that for the past five years the matter of incorporation has been given the greatest publicity is purest rot, if not something worse, as anyone who has been in dog politics will testify.

"A Disenfranchised Delegate"
Field and Fancy

Save the AKC

The Annual Meeting of the American Kennel Club, Thursday, February 14, was the most inharmonious in the history of the club, and at one period utter disorganization was threatened, and no doubt would have occurred had not two incidents arisen that prevented it. The first was the amendment to the incorporated constitution offered by President August Belmont, when bitter felling was running high on the part of the Delegates who felt the sting of disenfranchisement, after a battle of words in consequence of the proxies of certain clubs having been annulled and the action of the incorporators of the club at the discredited meeting of November 19, 1906. The protesting clubs were insistent on regaining their rights; the clique which had ensconced itself under the protecting arm of incorporation was strenuous in opposition. After many sharp verbal darts had passed back and forth, President Belmont poured the oil that stilled the troubled waters for a moment by his now noted conciliatory amendment:

"That the Annual Meeting of the club be held in February, and the regular quarterly meetings of the Delegates be held in May, August and November, at such time and places as the President may select, providing at least twenty days' notice be given to the Delegates."

The motion was seconded and carried unanimously. The first round in the fight for restoration of rights was thus gained, and the rainbow of hope for full restoration grew brighter forthwith.

Some cinders were still bright in the salamander of disenfranchisement and matters were warming up when a motion to adjourn was made. A tie vote resulted. The chair cast the deciding vote and the meeting stood adjourned.

This did not please the now partly disenfranchised contingent, and the second chapter remains to be written. Lawyers have been engaged on both sides, a test of strength will, in all likelihood, be had in the courts, and if the clique of incorporators are caught in their own trap it will not be a surprise to those who believe in the "square deal."

It is really too bad that such a grand organization as the American Kennel Club should be has had its timbers shivered by a clique of self-seeking autocrats. Whatever the result, confidence in certain officials has been destroyed, and they must be removed if the American Kennel Club is to fulfill its mission in American kenneldom.

The American Field

AKC Pot Still Boiling

The quarterly meeting of the AKC (alleged illegally incorporated), held May 2, proved to be not very different from what was prophesied—a family Incorporator's affair, and carried out on prearranged plans. After the meeting was over the probabilities of the whole matter going into court for settlement were stronger than ever. Instead of the Directors resigning and going through the form of re-election, they stuck with but a few exceptions, and there is only one way to prove which side is right in this contention—go to court, have the matter decided at once, and save the American Kennel Club and its membership from going to pieces. If the AKC Incorporators are so sure they are right, and if they have the good of the American kennel world at heart, why not enter into an agreed case and try the question out? What are they afraid of? Is not the interest of American kenneldom at stake? Have not clubs been disenfranchised? Have not other clubs, knocking for admission and recognition, been denied both? Where will this thing end if immediate decision is not obtained from a legal source —the courts? What is the use of filibustering, and who is responsible?

A resolution was adopted refusing to admit several clubs who had applied for membership, and who, in their applications, had specified their intention of holding shows this summer and fall. This refusal to elect these clubs means that the clubs will not be able to hold shows, as arranged, under AKC rules. The purpose of denial of membership would seem to be that

> "The American Kennel Club was organized for the benefit of all American fanciers, and that its affairs should be administered by officers chosen and elected by Delegates, instead of by a handful of self-seeking officials desiring perpetual control."

The United Kennel Club

Chauncey Zachariah Bennett *founded the United Kennel Club in 1898 as an alternative registry to what he believed was the AKC's emphasis on conformation-only show dogs owned by wealthy hobbyists. From the beginning, his goal was to provide a reliable registration service for the average man interested in preserving original working qualities, as well as conformation, of particular breeds. Bennett had been a clerk, then traveling salesman for the Desenberg grocery firm. He later formed the Bennett Novelty Works, manufacturing peanut-roasting machines. Obviously, this was not the glamorous Gilded Age background of those in charge of AKC. Initially, Bennett had little support and, certainly, no backers for his dog registry service. For two decades he pursued the UKC as a passionate hobby from his home in Kalamazoo, Michigan. A skilled mathematician, Bennett was the first to base a registry filing system on a numerical basis rather than by name of either the dog or its owner. Clearly a more logical method in anticipation of growth, the original system made UKC's eventual transition to computers relatively painless.*

Although AKC had already been in existence fourteen years prior to UKC's birth, registration of dogs was still a novel idea. The principal difference in initial concept between the two organizations was that AKC was first a show-giving organization, in which dogs must be either registered or listed in order to compete, whereas UKC's primary concept was providing reliable pedigrees and record keeping services to breeders, with performance events and shows as adjunct activities. Because many of the UKC's potential customers had no interest in showing their dogs as long as they could do the work for which they were bred, Bennett became a tireless promoter of the value of registered stock. As UKC gained acceptance and started to make slow but steady growth, the company made visible inroads into what AKC felt were registrations which should rightfully be theirs—even though most of these registrations were breeds the AKC didn't recognize. Nevertheless, by the mid-1920s, UKC had significantly expanded its events and AKC threatened fanciers with expulsion or being barred from AKC services if they exhibited their dogs at UKC shows. Bennett responded by encouraging exhibitors to show at both AKC and UKC events, stating that boycotting shows was of no particular benefit to the dog world. However, when AKC officials started referring to UKC as an "outlaw organization," matters finally ended up in court. The result was legal recognition that AKC was not the only dog registry in the United States. For many years following, the AKC refused to recognize the legitimacy of UKC pedigrees for those dogs which their owners wished to cross-register. This, despite the fact that UKC had always honored AKC pedigrees for anyone wishing to utilize their services.

From the beginning, UKC provided registry services for many rare breeds, or breeds not AKC recognized, such as the Toy Fox Terrier and the American Pit Bull Terrier (Bennett's original breed). Further, they were the first to register Black and Tan Coonhounds, American Water Spaniels and American Eskimo Dogs, among others. In 1905, their company magazine, "Bloodlines" was introduced and is still in publication along with two other periodicals, "Coonhound Bloodlines" and "Hunting Retriever." When Bennett died in 1937, UKC registered 30,000 dogs compared to 84,000 for AKC. UKC is the now the second oldest and second largest canine registry in the United States. However, because the AKC version of the dog show has developed into a more competitive forum where, in many breeds, a professional handler is almost a necessity, UKC conformation shows, which do not permit baiting or grooming in the ring, have never really attracted the entries or attention of the AKC shows. Nevertheless, UKC still sticks to its original intent of favoring the individual breeder/owner/handler. As of UKC's centennial year, this privately owned company, which has the luxury of operating as a business unhampered by a 19th Century men's club charter, continues to make steady growth with 10,000 performance, obedience and conformation events and over a quarter million registrations per year.

The Dog Trust

"Let dogs delight to bark and bite, for God hath made them so. But, children, you should never let such angry passions rise; Your little hands were never made to tear each other's eyes."
Issac Watts

*The West Coast dog situation
as portrayed by the
San Francisco Examiner
1910*

"The little children that head America's foremost kennels of blue-blooded dogs," was how the *"San Francisco Examiner"* described those in charge of AKC and the National Dog Breeders' Association when they took their battle to Federal court in 1910. From the beginning, AKC's "club of clubs" structure has never fully met the needs of the dog fancy, particularly breeders in the western United States. Initially, the few West Coast Member Clubs were geographically constrained to install East Coast residents as their Delegates. Further, when the show rules were changed to base championship points on the total number of dogs entered, and then late suggested, on the amount of prize money offered, it was almost impossible for anyone west of Chicago to attain a championship within their own area. These restrictions forced everyone, at great expense, to patronize the so-called "prestige shows" back East, as it was necessary to have one win at a 3-point or better show to attain a championship. Thus, the National Dog Breeders' Association was formed in San Francisco as a registry and show giving body, catering to West Coast dog fanciers.

The NDBA grew quickly and AKC's reaction was equally as swift. First, AKC formed the Pacific Coast Advisory Committee, ostensibly to represent the concerns of Western fanciers. In reality, the committee did little more than impose dictatorial restrictions on the westerners. For example, it was mandated that anyone using AKC's registration services could not exhibit their dogs, nor officiate, at other than AKC events, even though AKC did not license judges at this time. Then, under the guise of improving purebred dogs in America, but actually as an attempt to eliminate any competing canine registry, AKC successfully lobbied Congress to pass an act designating AKC as the official custodian of canine pedigrees. This meant that only dogs eligible for AKC registration could be imported duty-free.

Finally, a Federal suit under the Sherman anti-trust act was brought against AKC by W. E. Chute of San Francisco and Henry B. Lister, an attorney and President of the Marin Kennel Club. Mr. Chute, a well-known breeder and canine importer, had served as a judge for the Marin KC, under NDBA rules. Shortly thereafter, he received a letter from AKC informing him he was suspended and could no longer register any dogs nor exhibit at AKC shows. This ruling effectively put Mr. Chute out of business. The suit charged that AKC was only nominally involved in promoting purebred dogs, and had developed into a money making concern which had arrogated such powers and privileges to its officers and directors as to constitute a monopoly on the dog trade. Certainly, public sentiment was with the small breeders of the West, as opposed to the Eastern multi-millionaires in control of AKC, but there was never any real hope of winning this case. The AKC successfully argued that, after all, they were simply a "club," and as such, could make up their own membership rules.

somebody is afraid of too many votes to control—for be it known that the alleged illegally incorporated AKC is a closed corporation. There is something wrong in the logic advanced to keep new clubs from entering the exclusive precincts of the AKC stockade. Who is manning the ramparts?

The American Field

Courts to Decide AKC Status

The Ashland House Committee, so called, is composed solely of gentlemen who believe that the American Kennel Club was organized for the benefit of all American fanciers, and that its affairs should be administered by officers chosen and elected by Delegates, instead of by a handful of self-seeking officials desiring perpetual control, now that the AKC has a big cash asset and much valuable machinery in the way of records, etc. After trying every fair means to bring about a settlement, outside of the courts, of the illegal incorporation and seizure of the AKC assets and business machinery, the Ashland Committee is compelled, by the refusal of the usurping officials to submit the whole matter to a referee, to take the case into court for final settlement.

The American Field

Shall the AKC Survive?

The controversy that has been going on between the true amateur fanciers, who are the bone and sinew and active supporters of the American Kennel Club, and the professional officeholders and fanciers of the American Kennel Club (illegally incorporated), is still going on. The pity of it all is that the amateur fanciers and supporters have to struggle so hard to maintain their vested rights against entrenched schemers, entrenched because they are in possession of all the property—cash assets (nearly $30,000), furniture, fixtures, records and merchandise generally. All this property has been built up by amateur fanciers, for one purpose only, the advancement of the dog in America, and these fanciers are justified in their contention that this money should be used to further the interests of the dog in every way, not the least of which is the securing of the passage of laws in every state giving the dog a legal status, the securing of just and equitable transportation rates, punishing dog poisoners and thieves, assisting bench shows by personal participation, encouraging breeding by awarding high honor medals for dogs meeting AKC fixed standards, etc. There are many ways that the AKC surplus can be used to further canine interests, other than the building of a club house that not one member in a hundred, living three hundred miles from New York, will visit in a decade. The AKC should be national in every sense of the word.

The American Field

Dr. John E. De Mund, Delegate for the Russian Wolfhound (Borzoi) Club of America, emerged as the leader against August Belmont, returning a modicum of governing power back to the Delegates. A physician, De Mund served as AKC President from 1923-1932.

Will the AKC Reincorporate?

The American Kennel Club, Incorporated (wrongfully), apparently believes it the wisest policy to get under cover rather than have its dubious workings exposed by the limelight of publicity. At least, this would seem to be a charitable conclusion, in view of the AKC's reported action in avoiding court argument on the validity of the present incorporated club, which was set for the first week of this month. Some say that the AKC officials had their bluff, which they maintained up to the limit of time, called by the Ashland Committee, and what they did to avoid court argument was not a matter of wisdom or policy, but a startling, compulsory showdown.

Rather than expose to the public the inner machinations of usurping officials, it is reported and now so understood that the usurpative incorporators agreed to the Ashland Committee's demand that the AKC be reincorporated on a legitimate basis, that will insure just representation and give all accredited Delegates a voice in its management. It is now believed this will be done next month.

If so desirable a consummation of the disgraceful imbroglio of the past year should eventuate, and those responsible for the rupture shorn of power and relegated to innocuous desuetude, the American bench show world should be congratulated. If good is to result there must be a clean sweep of self-seeking, perpetual office holding individuals. If this is not done there will be constant friction that will result in one way only —the unselfish, non-office seeking Delegates will burn up with indignation and disappear; the rhinoceros-hided, office holding seekers will revel in their staying qualities and dictate the policies of the club.

The American Field

Questions for Consideration

1. What would you consider the optimum number for the AKC's Board of Directors?
2. Because AKC has a partisan board, i.e., board members are allowed to breed, exhibit and judge while in office, how can they possibly avoid the appearance of conflict of interest?
3. If AKC is to continue as a "club of clubs" shouldn't all affiliated clubs be entitled to Delegate representation? Defend your position.
4. How do you think the AKC would change if all affiliated clubs were allowed to have Delegate representation? How large should the Delegate body be?
5. Should Delegates be mandated to vote as their clubs direct them?
6. Is the American Kennel Club a business or an "amateur" organization? Elaborate.
7. If the AKC is an "amateur" organization, what justification can be put forth to pay board members for their attendance at monthly meetings?
8. If the AKC is a business, what justification can be put forth to only allow "amateur" fanciers to participate in the political process of the sport?
9. If the AKC is a business, what justification can be put forth to exclude from participation in the political process, those who also choose to make their involvement in the sport a business proposition, such as professional handlers, professional judges, superintendents and so on?
10. For whose benefit is the AKC run—anyone who owns a purebred dog, judges, handlers, breeders, pet shop owners, the AKC Board of Directors, the AKC staff, etc.? For whose benefit should it be run?
11. Does running the business of the AKC necessarily have anything to do with dogs?
12. If the AKC is a dog business, can it be optimally run by those who know little or nothing about the sport or who have little or no interest in dog ownership or dogs in general?
13. Do you think that the average dog show exhibitor has any real knowledge or interest in the political structure of AKC?
14. As long as most exhibitors can attend a dog show every weekend, do you think they care how the AKC is run?
15. Does kennel government adequately fulfill its mission to do everything to promote purebred dogs or does individual effort play a more important role in accomplishing significant contributions to the betterment of canines and the sport of dogs?

Judge the Dogs

The Hon. Mrs. Neville Lytton (Baroness Wentworth)

"Toy Dogs and their Ancestors"
1911

Besides the historical interest, I have tried to show the fancier how ridiculous and contemptible the present judging system appears to outsiders, who are not all as blind, deaf and stupid as they are given credit for. I want all those who read this to make up their minds once and for all to judge fairly and honestly for the sake of the dogs, whatever it may cost them in unpopularity with those who are less scrupulous. There are many fanciers who deplore the ways of the dog fancy as much as I do, but if they speak up they are put into Coventry and must say good bye to all hope of winning with their dogs. I shall take the bull by the horns as I do not belong to any club, so I owe no allegiance to anybody, though I wish every success to any of those bodies who may be working for the good of their respective breeds, and not to fill their own pockets.

> *"I WANT ALL THOSE WHO READ THIS TO make up their minds once and for all to JUDGE fairly and honestly for the sake of THE DOGS, whatever it may cost them in unpopularity with those who are less scrupulous."*

The judging of some breeds has long been a perfect farce; those in charge play into one another's hands, appoint each other as judges and report on their own dogs. Could anything be worse for the improvement of our breeds of dog? The results are disastrous. No wonder we get amazing exaggerations—no wonder type is lost and quality forgotten. No wonder respectable people are driven out of the shows. I have seen new breeders rise up with money and energy, full of kindliness, honesty, generosity and enthusiasm, and in six months they have been swindled out of their generosity, in eight months their kindliness has been bullied out of them, in ten months they have been forced out of their honesty, in twelve months their enthusiasm has turned to bitterness and they have either sold up their dogs and gone from the ring forever, or they have joined the various cliques of swindlers in desperation and become as bad as any of them. So bad a name do fanciers get that, as far as the outside world is concerned, one might just as well become a professional card sharper as a dog fancier! It is quite wrong that the fancy should be so regarded, but at times one is tempted to think that the devil is not painted a whit blacker than he is.

No one who has studied his breed, both as to points and history, is likely to belong to societies which, when they cannot get the old independent fanciers to judge their way, put in well-primed ignoramuses to award championships at important shows. The inevitable result of such a system is that the title of champion is no longer any guarantee of merit whatever, and most of the best people end by stopping out of the shows altogether, and that endless dissatisfaction, rows and ill feeling are created amongst exhibitors by the astonishing awards of people who ought to know better (and often *do* know better in their hearts) and the flagrant judging of the ignoramuses who, in spite of coaching, cannot even remember the dogs from one class to another.

To judges I would say, before accepting

179

the position, make up your mind decidedly that you do not care what your friends say of you. If you cannot do this, refuse the appointment. On starting for the show leave spite, jealousy, good nature, weak-mindedness, and all questions of personal advantage behind you. The judging ring is not the proper place for good nature or social amenities nor for the settling of old grudges. If your friends enter under you, make them clearly understand that they do so at their own risk, and that if they show dogs you have just sold to them (which is in the very worst taste) they must not expect any favoring. If you make this clear from the very first they will put up with your judgments with comparative cheerfulness, but if once you begin showing weakness or indecision, they will feel insulted if you do not favor them. With few exceptions, each exhibitor truly thinks his dog the best and it is the judge's business to decide on the matter and not to be influenced by the desire of his friends to secure first place. There are many people who "good-naturedly" favor friends by giving them undeserved prizes, yet these same people would no more dream of taking £5 belonging to a stranger and bestowing it on a friend than of robbing a mail coach or burgling someone's plate chest. This is, however, exactly what it comes to.

Exhibitors hate inconsistency, and if a man favors one type of dog in one class and another in the next class they get furious, whereas, if he knows what he wants and sticks to some standard of points which can be perceived as consistent, they may be cross, but will not accuse him of unfairness, and will try and enter under him next time the kind of animal to which he is evidently partial. This is the kind of judging that is required, and I want everyone who reads this to resolve henceforth not to be weak-minded as to friends or biased as to enemies, but to look at the dogs only. A good judge should hardly so much as see the face of a single exhibitor. His eyes are fixed on the dogs so that he can scarcely ever tell who has led them into the ring, and it stands to reason that the judge, who is always nervously glancing at the exhibitors, cannot but lose sight of the dogs and so miss many important points.

Novices should never judge at championship shows, as they are bound to make mistakes, and good dogs suffer most undeserved reverses at their hands. Novice judges should try not to be ridiculously puffed up with their own importance. Before they can lay claim to any respect or admiration they must prove their competence, and all they generally do in a first appearance is to prove their incompetence. Novices are usually like mirrors reflecting the last thing that has been put before them without any stable image of their own, or like water which is blown into ripples by every breeze. They are unconsciously biased by everything they hear, but are generally much too hopelessly confused in the ring to carry out much of what they go in intending to do. They find it very difficult to recognize the dogs, therefore if a novice begins by putting your dog back you will often change your luck by changing your handler, as ten to one the judge will not know the dog again in different hands. If a dog holds an unbeaten record, some judges will maliciously and wantonly put him down just to spoil his record, knowing that the defeat will be recorded and the elated winner will publish his victory to the four corners of the earth. Novice judges are very prone to indulge in this sort of

> "*E*xhibitors would make the shows much pleasanter for themselves if they would observe the good manners of ordinary life, but for some curious reason it is quite a common thing for respectable, well-mannered people to become rude and insolent as exhibitors. They seem to consider that the atmosphere of the shows absolves them from all the canons of decent politeness, which govern civilized human intercourse, and make themselves ridiculous as well as unpopular."

Mrs. Judith Anne Lytton *was the author of one of the most refreshing and outspoken dog books ever published, "Toy Dogs and their Ancestors." Even though the Edwardians fancied themselves much more modern and liberal than their Victorian predecessors, Lytton's direct, frank, humorous manner was not typical of the time. Her method of expression would have come in for much harsher criticism than it received in some reviews, but for the fact the work was the product of six years exhaustive research, authoritative and superbly written. The principal canine featured was the English Toy Spaniel, a breed she owned, bred and exhibited. The complete history of these charming little dogs was supplemented with numerous charts, diagrams and illustrations to help those who wished to breed and judge correct type. Also covered in great depth were sections on Japanese Spaniels, Pekingese and Pomeranians. It is interesting to note that Lytton adamantly felt the typical bow in the front assembly of the Pekingese was incorrect and that the legs should be straight, citing references of several old Oriental depictions. The other amusing "evidence" related was that in 1910 the Pekin Palace Dog Association actually offered prizes at their show for, "the most bow-legged and grotesque dog or bitch."*

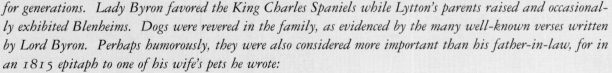

Judith Lytton was born into a literary family, being a great-granddaughter of the poet, George Gordon Lord Byron. Further, her family had kept Toy Spaniels for generations. Lady Byron favored the King Charles Spaniels while Lytton's parents raised and occasionally exhibited Blenheims. Dogs were revered in the family, as evidenced by the many well-known verses written by Lord Byron. Perhaps humorously, they were also considered more important than his father-in-law, for in an 1815 epitaph to one of his wife's pets he wrote:

> *"Alas, poor Prim,*
> *I'm sorry for him.*
> *I'd rather by half*
> *It had been Sir Ralph."*

Lytton's husband was the well-known portrait painter Neville Lytton and the illustration shown clearly indicates he had great ability to capture the character of his subjects. Pictured in ultra-feminine frills, we see a strong woman who is not afraid to take a bold stance in the outside world. Yet, at the same time, there is nothing crude or coarse in her demeanor. In looking at this portrait one would have to conclude that Judith Lytton was an exceptional woman, given the female stereotypes of the period. Another wonderful quality of the work is the depiction of Ch. Windfall, who became the breed record holder in his day with 13 Championships. To position a breed in which the correct head is of paramount importance with his back to the viewer is extraordinarily droll. Nevertheless, it reveals the dog's true temperament, for he was not interested in the admiration of strangers. Rather, he was utterly devoted to his mistress, never averting his eyes from her countenance.

showing off. Being for the first time in a position of trust and power, their heads are turned and they cannot resist abusing it.

Beginners think they can trust to their instinct, but this is all rubbish. Put them in the ring without a judging book and tell them to pick out the winners in several successive classes and you will soon see how they change their minds. Not one in a million has the natural instinct for harmony of proportion, which will prevent his making grievous mistakes, but even this millionth man cannot exist unless he has already had training of eye in some other way and has developed the faculty of critical comparison. You might as well expect to be a professional tea-taster by instinct as a judge of proportion without training, either conscious or unconscious. You must have the natural aptitude *as well as the training*.

A man who keeps and breeds ugly specimens himself is not suitable as a judge because he is accustomed to bad points and his eye gets spoilt. In order to be a good judge it is necessary to have a well trained eye and a decided character.

Judging requires a clear head and great firmness of mind. Decision can only be attained by knowing one's own mind. It is no use judging if you have no mind to know and are swayed by every whisper at the ringside. Don't be influenced by what other people may think of you. I have often heard a judge say, "Such and such a dog is not what I like, but I felt I had to put him up because his points are so remarkable." A man ought not to feel forced to put up a dog he does not like any more than he feels forced to buy it.

CH. WINDFALL
Blenheim English Toy Spaniel
Owner, Mrs. Judith Lytton
1904

This attitude betrays weakness of mind, and is almost invariably brought about by having constantly heard the dog publicly praised and not having nerve enough to boldly go against the tide of public opinion. But let me here again impress upon judges that they are there to teach and form public opinion and not to be guided by it.

If an enemy shows a dog under a judge he might want to allow him ten points to counteract his probable prejudice. But, a real connoisseur will not need to do this as he gets so enthusiastic over a good dog that he would not care a straw how much he hates the owner and often feels quite a glow of temporary sympathy for that person on account of his dog. It is policy to do good to those that hate you because in the long run they leave off hating you, whereas the dog fancying principle of an eye for an eye and a tooth for a tooth keeps ill feeling at boiling pitch. Pleasant manners and a willingness to do everybody any good turn in your power, go a long way to turning the wrath of exhibitors. Of course, I do not mean that you should be weak-mindedly soft and allow yourself to be bullied. Exhibitors would make the shows much pleasanter for themselves if they would observe the good manners of ordinary life, but for some curious reason it is quite a common thing for respectable, well-mannered people to become rude and insolent as exhibitors. They seem to consider that the atmosphere of the shows absolves them from all the canons of decent politeness, which govern civilized human intercourse, and make themselves ridiculous as well as unpopular.

Judith Lytton on Judging

> *"Judging requires a clear head and great fairness of mind. Decision can only be attained by knowing one's mind. It is of no use judging if you have no mind to know and are swayed by every whisper at ringside."*

Exhibitors have to reckon with many kinds of judges:

1. *The weak-minded, well-meaning man*, who never can make up his mind and gets hot and flustered and nervous, and makes the exhibitors cross and takes all the life out of the exhibits by having them lifted up and down and sent round and round the ring fifty times where once would suffice. This kind of judge almost invariably ends by awarding the prizes to the wrong dogs because, by looking at them too long, he loses the invaluable general impression of shape, style, and outline, and eventually makes his decision on questions of minute detail, which are thus given an importance beyond their actual value. Looking too long and too closely at a thing is a bad system as it tends to destroy all sense of proportion.

2. *The old hand* who is open to alter his decisions, according to the advantage he thinks he is likely to get, either in hard cash or in other ways.

3. *The equally old hand* who has a kink in his temper, who will put you up today and down tomorrow, out of pure spleen and biliousness, who is insulted if he is bribed and more insulted if he is not.

4. *The sensationalist*, who likes to turn everything topsy turvy.

5. *The ostentatious and self-righteous prig*—always blowing one's own trumpet.

6. *The jovial, happy-go-lucky man* who is always late, arrives in breathless haste with a flushed face and eager eye and has to catch an early train home. He hurries through his classes, loses his pencil, mislays his judging book, awards the stud dog prize to a bitch, gives the Pomeranian championship to a Pug and the open challenge cup to a litter, addresses the secretary as "My lad," shakes hands with total strangers, thanks everybody profusely and vanishes in a whirl of flurry, taking the slips of the last class with him and leaving everybody bewildered and gasping.

7. *The bully* who swears at the ring steward, insults the secretary, orders the exhibitors out of the ring if they dare so much as to sneeze without leave, frightens the dogs, reduces novices to hysterics, awards the prizes to the right dogs, and departs, saying he never saw such a cussed lot of wastrels in his life.

And finally,

8. THE RARE JUDGE, who knows his business, who is firm, courteous and dignified in the ring, punctual in getting there, who is rapid and decided in his awards and perfectly consistent and reliable.

> *"Judges are there to teach and form public opinion and not to be guided by it."*

Questions for Consideration

1. What is the real purpose of becoming a dog show judge? Do any of the types of judges enumerated on Lytton's list exist today?

2. Given the extraordinary numbers of dog shows annually and the fact that in most breeds, most of the time, the official judge is not a true expert, what exactly is the value of a championship?

3. Why should we give so much importance to so-called "prestige shows" if the adjudicators are not experts in each breed to which they are assigned? Is it in the best interests of the sport to continue to perpetuate the belief that awards at certain shows are of greater value than others, when that supposed value is perhaps more mythical than reality based?

4. Lytton stated the requisite natural "eye" was useless without the faculty for critical comparison and additional training so one could implement that knowledge. How should one go about getting this necessary training and who should be responsible for determining its structure and administering it? If you do not agree with the premise that any additional training is necessary to become a judge, is the quality of having an "eye" a self-determined evaluation?

5. While almost all judges claim to have a natural "eye" for dog flesh, how many do you suppose have the natural mental ability of critical comparison? Can you think of any occupation, craft, art, science, hobby, sport, etc., where anyone is designated an expert without any additional coaching, enhancing or expansion of their natural abilities? Do you think we have some judges who are just natural "canine savants" who need no additional training or study of the subject?

6. How many times should a beginning judge officiate at lower ranked events such as puppy matches and/or Open shows before being allowed to award championships and points?

7. Do most exhibitors want the dogs judged fairly and correctly or do they prefer a system which allows them to win as much and as often as possible, regardless of the merits of the dogs?

8. What percentage of judges do you believe to be blatantly dishonest? What percentage of exhibitors? What conclusions should one reasonably expect the general public to draw of a "sport" where one continually hears malicious gossip regarding the honesty/dishonesty of other breeders, exhibitors and judges from competing breeders, exhibitors and judges?

9. It has been said (but never supported by actual hard data) that the average length of time an exhibitor stays active in the sport is five years. Do you believe this statement? If so, is there anything which could be done to encourage new exhibitors to continue? Does this article give any insight which might lend credence to that supposition? Can you think of any reasons why someone would only want to be involved for such a short period of time?

10. From her experience, Lytton seemed to feel that, as a whole, the dog fancy consisted of a great many boorish, small-minded people whose motivations had less to do with the improvements of any particular breed of dog than with their own self-aggrandizement. From your personal experiences today, can you find any evidence to support this belief, or do you think these types of generally uncouth and unethical behaviors were strictly limited to the times in which she lived and wrote about?

Gems on Judging

"Popular Dogs"
1945

⭐ ⭐ ⭐ ⭐ ⭐

GEMS ON JUDGING

A Drama in Three Acts
(Thirteen Scenes)

Produced by the Professional Dog Judges Association

Opening Night—Wednesday
September 19, 1945
Ritz-Carlton Hotel
New York, N. Y.

⭐ ⭐ ⭐ ⭐ ⭐

Dramatis personae:

ANTON A. ROST..........................*A Moderator*
GEORGE F. FOLEY.................*A Superintendent*
PAUL PALMER........................*A Small Breeder*
     (REGINALD CLEVELAND, *understudy*)
MRS. SHERMAN HOYT..............*An Exhibitor*
LEONARD BRUMBY.....*A Professional Handler*
     (CLINT CALLAHAN, *understudy*)
JOHN P. WAGNER.....................*A Big Breeder*
W. L. KENDRICK...............*A Professional Judge*
E.D.KNIGHT........................*An AKC Director*
     (GEORGE HARTMAN, *understudy*)
W. ROSS PROCTOR...............*A Club Secretary*
ROLAND KILBON.....................*A Dog Writer*
HENRY D. BIXBY.........*The AKC Vice-President*

PROLOGUE

(Enter Mr. Rost. He goes to rostrum, holds microphone, delivers prologue.)

"Ours is a new organization. There are quite a few old-timers amongst us. None, we hope, too old to learn. Our primary purpose in organizing is to give the fancier able, comprehensive and instructive judging service."

(Exit Mr. Rost, after introducing George Foley.)

ACT ONE—Scene I

(Mr. Foley:)

"Judging isn't crooked, but I can't say there's nothing wrong with judging. The man who goes into a ring to judge dogs should know more than he has learned from living with a champion or a potential one. He must be fair. He must see every dog as one not owned by a stranger or a friend, but in comparison with its competitors. He must forget breed politics. I believe the favoring of friends and certain exhibitors is one of today's most pressing judging faults. Illustrating improved standards can aid judges. I still believe you can have better judging with some sort of planned educational program for judges. You can't do it with half knowledge or factions that split breeds into closely-knit groups."

ANTON ROST

(Exit Mr. F. Enter Mr. R., who introduces Reginald Cleveland.)

185

SCENE II

(Mr. Cleveland rises to read Paul Palmer's comments.)

"I tend more and more to lean toward the idea of almost universal use of highly-paid professional judges, plus a sprinkling of amateur breed specialists. I would like to see a group of professional judges retained by the AKC and member clubs on a year-round basis. I think they should do all the group and Best in Show judging and most of the breeds. I would like written critiques."

(Exit Mr. C. Enter Mr. R., who hands microphone to Mrs. Sherman B. Hoyt, the leading lady.)

SCENE III

(Mrs. Hoyt reads:)

"Before a novice judge obtains a license, he should have accomplished the following: Stew-arded with an expert at least six times, in his particular breed; judged at least six shows; be personally sponsored by two breeders, whose success and prominence are matters of official record; be sponsored by two all round judges approved by the AKC. I think that during this period, the established judge should be encouraged to comment and question his student judge. Could he not present his own opinion of such a steward to the AKC? I do not feel there should be any unpaid judges. A judge should be more than honest. He should be expert."

(Exit, etc., etc.)

SCENE IV

(Clint Callahan adjusts microphone and delivers Leonard Brumby's talk.)

"Our judging should be concentrated on breed judging rather than on group judging. No one can deny that if all breeds were well judged, then the group would be truly representative and the result of the group judging good. The AKC can remove its requirements that group judges should hold licenses to judge a large percentage of breeds in that group. Amateur judging should not require license. Professional judges should, in order to protect people purchasing their professional services. Amateurs should be encouraged to judge."

(Exit, etc., etc.)

SCENE V

(The microphone is raised for John P. Wagner, who declaims:)

"After a short apprenticeship in dogs, no one ever admits there is anything they don't know about them. They seem to feel that they will be ridiculed if they concede any lack of knowledge. I lay this weakness to the very superficial knowledge of many judges and fanciers plus the failure of judges to evaluate in their proper balance the fundamental qualities that distinguish excellent dogs—the tendencies of our judges to place emphasis on minor technicalities and to overlook animals as a whole... I believe a small committee should be appointed by the judges association to work out some educational plan that would be accessible to any fancier seeking knowledge."

(Exit, etc., etc.)

SCENE VI

(W. L. Kendrick, the next speaker, pronounces:)

"I would scrap none of the present machinery or systems. I have three suggestions; student judges to serve as stewards. Every applicant for a temporary license serve as a student steward three times before his application for a temporary license is in order. Require reports after each assignment. Establishment of the office of field secretary of the American Kennel Club. For many years I have thought it of great need to have an active representative of the AKC at every dog show possible."

(Exit, etc.,etc.)

SCENE VII

(George Hartman takes microphone to read E. D. Knight's notes.)

"I don't think you give election of a

Delegate much thought. It isn't the Board of Directors that run the American Kennel Club. It's your club. And now, for the Knight remarks."

"If the husbandry of dogs, including the basic principles of judging, were taught in our schools on the same basis as livestock activity of the 4-H Clubs, I have no doubt that many fine potential judges would be developed. I see little opportunity for drastic improvements without more definitely established courses of supply. Instead of

GEORGE HARTMAN having a reasonably uniform grounding in the fundamentals, most of our dog judges are like Topsy in Uncle Tom's Cabin; they just grew. The judging of dogs will, in my opinion, never cease to be a highly controversial subject in which emotion plays a leading part."
(Exit, etc., etc.)

SCENE VIII

(A club secretary, W. Ross Proctor, appears alone on scene.)

W. ROSS PROCTOR

"I happen to be a Pollyanna who doesn't advocate changing our present system of obtaining judges. Clubs do have a grave responsibility toward exhibitors that cannot be put on anyone else. They are the ones who pick the judges to pass on your dogs and mine. No judge can nominate himself. He must be asked and the Bench Show Committee of the show giving club does the asking. I can say it is possible to pick both competent and honest judges from the wealth of them available. If we all agreed every time, we all know there would be no dog shows, or at least, not more than one. And disagreeing with the judge's placings and arguing it out over a glass of beer can be a lot of fun."
(Exit,etc.,etc.)

"After a short apprenticeship in dogs, no one ever admits there is anything they don't know about them."

SCENE IX

(Roland Kilbon rises. Begins:)

"If some day you see a dog show where every judge interprets the standard as you think it should be interpreted, where the ribbons go just where you feel they should go and where all the spectators agree with every placing, you can be pretty certain that you have escaped hellfire and are in heaven! Much of the griping about the judging situation is traceable to plain poor sportsmanship. What is called for more than any particular change in the judging situation is the resurgence of sportsmanship among exhibitors. This should not involve condoning either incompetence or dishonesty."
(Exit, etc., etc.)

SCENE X

(No blare of trumpets, all quiet. Henry D. Bixby rises, looks at audience and notes:)

"The American Kennel Club realizes just as much as any of these speakers do the importance of a field man. Most complaints are not very much good. They come from newcomers in the field. There is bad judging. There is incompetent judging, and the worst thing of all, is the man who judges the owner of the dog and not the dog. Now, that isn't confined to amateurs or professionals. The good judges or the poor ones. They all do it at one time or another, just because they don't take their jobs seriously. Steward student judges have been tried with individual breeds and, like all other things, it hasn't worked out as well as we had hoped."

HENRY BIXBY AKC

ACT TWO—SCENE I

Intermission
(The Ritz Bar.)

Conversation is loud, mixed. The refrain: "Why that so-and-so didn't even look at my dog."

187

George _Foley_ It's a case of each one trying to tell, in the longest way, of the lousiest judging deal his own dogs ever got.

ACT THREE—SCENE I

(Back to Crystal Room.)

Question period. No room for repeating the queries. Most of them were directed to Henry D. Bixby and thus to the American Kennel Club. The answers—most of them—can be found in the nearest AKC rule book.

EPILOGUE

(Mr. Rost:)

"Nous sommes fini!"

Quick comment: Ideal setting. Unusually well staged and well handled by Producer Rost. Rost voice pleasant and tuned agreeably for microphone speaking. Talks serious, good. All interested, with everyone wanting "something to be done." A drama of much significance though some of the introductions were a bit like eulogies delivered over the earthly remains of the dearly departed.

Seen there—Crowd around 400. Handlers galore and the most representative press gallery since the Garden.

The First AKC Field Representative

Leonard Brumby, Sr., who piloted such greats as Ch. Nornay Saddler, also founded the Professional Handlers' Association. He took his new position at AKC in 1946 and died the following year. Field Reps are now an integral part of all AKC events.

Questions for Consideration

1. What do you feel is the most pressing problem with today's judging?

2. Foley favored a planned educational program for judges. How would you design such a program, what would you consider essential, and who should administer these educational events?

3. In this article, the creation of the position of AKC Field Representative was put forth. Do you feel the Field Reps play an important role in the efficient running of dog shows? Are they necessary? Would you expand or limit their present responsibilities? What should the qualifications be for their positions?

4. Kilbon felt that most complaints about judging could be attributed to poor sportsmanship and he also defined poor sportsmanship as tolerating incompetence and dishonesty. How much responsibility does the exhibitor bear in producing good judges and good judging?

5. Should those who choose to be "amateur" judges, i.e., not charging a fee for their services, be exempt from licensing (official approval) policies? If so, should there be limits on the number of times they should judge or the number of breeds they may adjudicate?

6. Should those judges who claim to be "professional" judges, i.e., charging fees for their services, be required to periodically attend educational events to retain their status as professionals in other fields of endeavor must do?

7. What do you think should be the minimum requirements for first time judging applicants? For those wishing to judge additional breeds?

8. Will it ever be possible for the system to mature to the point where further major changes to the approval system will not be routinely adopted? Why or why not? What do you feel drives the decisions which are made within the current system?

Judges Organizations
Francis A. Bigler

"Popular Dogs"
1945

Like the blinding light that floored Saul on the road to Damascus, it struck me one day that if some bright boy should form a professional judges association, and could weld it into a tight enough unit to assure concerted action, that association could come very close to running the dog game in its entirety. And the person who could control such an organization would become an individual of some consequence indeed. He would be the Petrillo of the Purebreds. He might even be able to thumb his nose at the AKC, upon occasion, with an amazing degree of impunity. Perhaps not a desirable state of affairs from the viewpoint of John Q. Public, who invariably furnishes the body when a body is to be booted about.

The all-round judge is a necessity to an all breed show. Even Morris and Essex can't put a fancier-judge in each of the 109 recognized breeds. At the average show, it is impracticable to have a fancier-judge in more than twenty breeds, usually much fewer. Someone must be obtained who can go through the motions of judging a great number of breeds, acting out the part of omniscience convincingly enough that the exhib-

> *"Another aim is said to be a closer co-operation with the Professional Handlers Association. Just as a digressing thought, a fellow told me recently that he thought co-operation between a few judges and handlers had already reached a high peak of efficiency."*

itors will depart without forming a posse. We can't get along without the all-rounders. It might not be entirely out of order to view with a bit of trepidation an organization of indispensible men. The fact that we believe the majority of these men to be honest and upright citizens may palliate the situation, but it also comes to mind that the majority of members of labor and other unions are honest and upright citizens, yet they have been known to become rackets, or I don't know my Pegler. A lot depends on who is in or who can eventually get into the driver's seat.

Such an organization now has been assembled, and does appear to be sliding smoothly down the gangways to a successful launching. This group can do the sport some good, likely; it can also do a great deal of harm, depending upon the person or persons who will formulate its policies, dictate its actions and play its politics. Unquestionably, if solidarity is achieved, it could be used to the great personal advantage of the few, if they were so minded, which is true of almost any organized group.

The fundamental purpose of forming any organization (unless it be strictly charitable, which classification scarcely embraces professional dog judging), theoretically, is to provide some benefit to the members. And the purpose of joining any such organization is to derive some benefit from membership. The Professional Dog

Championship Points

In 1900, the AKC presented to the fancy Alfred P. Vredenburgh's disastrously ill-conceived scheme for awarding championship points at dog shows, based upon the total number of dogs entered. Member Specialty clubs could automatically award 4 points for Winners in each sex, regardless of overall entry. All breed clubs needed an entry of 250 to award 1 point in each breed, up to the maximum of 5 points given at shows with entries over 1,000 dogs. Thus, dogs could attain championships without ever having defeated another member of their own breed. Worse, in keeping with the times, handlers were able to exact graft from the kennel clubs by refusing to enter their strings unless there were kick-backs. As there was nothing in the rule book requiring the owners to pay entry fees directly to the show secretary or superintendent, many handlers would collect these in advance from their clients and then make deals with the clubs to not pay any entry fees at all. In 1904, Vredenburgh "improved" upon his plan by suggesting the point schedule correlate with the amount of prize money offered. This would have made the situation for the majority of kennel clubs intolerable and did not pass. Eventually, the Delegates eliminated the entry fee inequities in the official rule book but it was many years before the point schedules were changed to reflect merit based upon competition within the individual breeds.

Handlers vs. Shows
"Rider and Driver"
1906

Those not on the inside have no idea what bench show clubs have to contend with in order to induce handlers to make entries at their shows. In great measure this was brought about by the clubs themselves by offering handlers inducements to attend their shows, and at the present time it is almost impossible to influence handlers to attend a show of their own volition. Many handlers now dictate their own terms. Clubs are asked to accept fifty or a hundred entries *gratis*, to help increase the number of entries. This concessionary practice is becoming more common and it is safe to say that few handlers attend a show unless they are offered inducements in the shape of a reduction of entry fees or a bonus to help defray expenses. Handlers are paid by the owners of the dogs which they handle and further, receive the winnings. There is no reason why they should expect more. It is an injustice to the clubs and to the other exhibitors.

At best a bench show club makes very little money; more frequently the balance is on the wrong side of the ledger; and why they should be called upon to cater to the handler is something difficult to understand. Handlers expect their prize money to be paid promptly, but how can this be possible if they fail to contribute toward making the show a success by paying their entries as others do? This practice of accepting entries free from handlers is becoming so prevalent that even many of the large private kennels are asking the same, and if it continues the time will come when nobody will pay their entry fees, and as a result it is going to kill the show business, for bench show clubs will become tired of going down into their pockets to make up deficits which should not be. The handler fraternity may not see this now, but if bench shows are killed their trade will suffer, and it will be practically a case of killing the goose that laid the golden eggs.

There is only one way to stop this evil, and that is for clubs to act in unison and absolutely refuse to accept entries for which the full amount has not been paid. Then if a handler refuses to attend because he is asked to pay a legitimate entry fee, let him remain away— his business will soon suffer in consequence, and in time he will see the error of the thing.

Judges Association can do its members much good, and quite legitimately. Lest anyone get an incorrect impression from this thesis, let me state that I consider the Association a quite legitimate enterprise, and if I were a professional I'd surely be among the first applying for membership. The point of this discourse is only to sound a warning note in pointing out the possibilities; no doubt you've thought of them, too, but have hesitated to broadcast your ideas because of the prospect of getting your ears pinned back to your shoulders next time you show under that man you've never been able to win under.

"Paid by the Day"

The aims of the PDJA, as published, read very well. The establishment of a minimum fee is, in itself, justification for organization. I could write a full page on the desirability of a minimum fee, and its advantages to exhibitors, show-giving clubs and superintendents, as well as to judges. Another aim is said to be a closer co-operation with the Professional Handlers Association. Just as a digressing thought, a fellow told me recently that he thought co-operation between a few judges and handlers had already reached a high peak of efficiency. I cannot at the moment picture any situation wherein co-operation between professional judges and professional handlers can be worked out to the benefit of the sport. Any official contact between judges and handlers should be through the American Kennel Club.

If a real "smart operator" happened to be directing the policies of the Judges Association,

he might have these things in mind: (1) To stage a propaganda campaign, selling the idea that all judging done by professionals is strictly on the up-and-up, and superbly competent; (2) To turn the flame-thrower on any person who dares to hint otherwise, now or in the future; (3) To make the obtaining of a judging license by a fancier-judge such a complicated and rigorous procedure that few would attempt it, tightening the hold of the professional on assignments; (4), (5), (6), etc., things with which I shall not sully your pure minds, dear readers. If you insist on details, please consult the AKC files on cases for which professional judges have been suspended, or at least brought to trial. It CAN happen here.

What I would like to see as one of the principal purposes of the organization, and which I seem to have missed in a hasty scanning of published material, is increased knowledge of breeds and better judging from the professionals themselves. While I have no way of proving it, I am willing to accept that some judges do have a competent judging knowledge of a great many breeds. But, using the judging of Boxers as a criterion, I'm inclined to accept in general the definition of an all-rounder given me by a professional handler some time ago, to whit: "A person who knows a few breeds thoroughly, can do a passable job in a dozen more, and guesses at all the rest."

Unless an unusual program of education with-

"Fishing for Prizes"
Although dog show handlers have not been the target of the artist's pen as often as judges, the cartoons shown appeared in "The American Field" in 1910.

"Paid by the Job"

191

Mr. and Mrs. Professional Handler

Mr. and Mrs. Alf Delmont were the first known husband and wife team to ply their trade as professional dog show handlers in the United States. For many years Alf Delmont had been the kennel manager for Tom Ashton, a breeder and judge of Fox Terriers in Leeds, England. Delmont had a natural talent for presenting dogs at their best, particularly coated dogs. However, as dog shows rapidly increased in popularity, opportunities to handle numerous breeds correspondingly diminished because the English system placed primary emphasis on breed judging. Thus, Delmont made the decision to move to the United States and become a professional all breed handler.

Settling in Devon, Pennsylvania, the Delmonts named their new establishment Leeds Kennels. In its day this kennel was considered a model for anyone wishing to study proper management of a large breeding, boarding and training business. The Delmonts set high standards and achieved a solid reputation for their ability to superbly condition and train dogs for the show ring. Although Mrs. Delmont was always listed as her husband's assistant handler, she took many dogs into the ring and was a successful breeder of Field Spaniels, Bulldogs and Irish

Terriers. She owned one of the top Irish Terrier sires, Rushford Meddler, and also the black Field Spaniel, Ch. Jubilee Prince. Alf Delmont handled all breeds but was particularly known as a terrier specialist. His business card was one of the first that stated the credo of the professional handler, "Remember, I show to win."

Apart from farming or the merchant trade, there were few respectable occupations in which spouses worked alongside each other in the earliest years of the 20th Century. Certainly, other than the circus or medicine shows (and some might claim dog shows embody many of those same qualities) cross country travel by women in a working capacity was virtually unheard

Leeds Kennels, 1904
The Delmonts believed dogs thrived on exercise and their establishment had numerous paddocks. Note how various client dogs were turned out together.

of. Nevertheless, dog shows provided a novel opportunity for women, as well as men, to make their livings handling dogs for others, although few women traveled extensively in the early years of the sport. Despite any glamour which might be supposed from this lifestyle, the Delmonts established their success through hard work and never showing a dog that was neither good enough to win nor at its best. The Delmonts created the earliest definition of the quality of service the fancy should expect from true professional dog show handlers.

in its own ranks is undertaken, the mere forming of an organization by professionals is not going to improve judging one bit, for the members are or will be those same judges who have been with us last week, last year, and for years back. If you didn't like some of them and squawked about them last year, you won't like them and will squawk about them next year. Or, it COULD be, if the organization is handled "right," if you squawk too long or too loud you may find yourself being poked in the

"EAR MASSAGE"

eye by a sharp stick.

Mr. Average Exhibitor, despite all the soft soap about the purity of judging now being ladled out, is more definitely interested than ever in seeing improved judging. He, more than anyone else, sees and feels the need for improvement.

Whittling it down, the Professional Dog Judges Association can do the game in general some good, or, under improper guidance and influence, it can become a terrible pain in the neck.

Questions for Consideration

1. What are the benefits (if any) to be derived from being a member of a judges organization? Is there any real need for judges organizations? For handlers organizations?

2. Should judges organizations consider the implementation of educational programs for their members and the fancy a primary obligation? If not, which group should be responsible for educating judges? Do judges need or benefit from educational opportunities?

3. Do judges organizations help improve the quality of judging? Cite specific examples.

4. Even more so now than when this article was penned, the proliferation of shows and the number of recognized breeds make the so-called "professional" or "all-round" judges indispensible in running a dog show. How much power could a professional judges group wield if they achieved solidarity? Why do you suppose this has not happened?

5. Should all judges charge a minimum or maximum fee for their services? If so, who should regulate this fee?

6. In a sport which supports professional handlers, professional judges, professional superintendents and provides a favorable atmosphere for dozens of related businesses to flourish, is the claim by AKC that dog showing is an "amateur" sport an antiquated notion?

7. George Hartman prefaced his remarks in the previous article by stating the election of Delegates was a very important consideration to the sport. However, professional judges are not permitted to become AKC Delegates. Is this AKC prohibition, which eliminates many of the most knowledgeable people in dogs from participating in the political process, in the best interests of the sport?

8. What benefits, if any, does the non-judge segment of the fancy derive from judges organizations? From handlers organizations? Elaborate.

9. Should judges co-own dogs with professional handlers? Why or why not?

10. How would you design the system of awarding championships to ensure that only dogs of real merit earn the title?

11. How would you design the judges approval system so that only those people of real knowledge and merit adjudicated?

The Baltimore Bubble

Laurence Alden Horswell

"American Kennel Gazette"
1946

Fanfare in the dog press heralded the prospect that at Baltimore, before Westminster, the Maryland Kennel Club would provide facilities for the Professional Dog Judges' Association to demonstrate how its leaders would operate a dog show. Having attended the Forum, and read its transcript, and having—I hope—a mind receptive toward progress which can be demonstrated to be more than agitation, I set forth for Baltimore unable to secure an advance copy of the judging program from the superintendent because of some delay in his receiving the breed timetable from the PDJA official in charge.

Saturday morning, at the show entrance, there were six tables where uniformed coast guardsmen checked incoming entries—one table for the breeds of each group. Exhibitor attendance was demanded for 11 A.M., judging to begin at 1 P.M. I have not an hourly breakdown of the ticket sales, but I was not impressed by any number of spectators during this two hour interval to justify requiring exhibitors and dogs to toe the line two hours before the judging—two hours which might have included lunch against the long afternoon, to lead without break into the evening judging.

What I did notice, from the superintendent's booth, was that the same demands were being made here as at other shows. The VIPs—or at a dog show should we change the army vernacular to V(ery) I(mportant) E(xhibitors)?—showed little originality in excuses for being late,

not wanting to bench their dogs, etc. These conversations recorded and transcribed at one show could be played back like radio station-break platter commercials at future shows, substituting modern electronics for a great deal of emotional energy. But this hypothetical patent reminds me a little of Amos' or Andy's comment on the impersonal announcement of successful artificial insemination, "Ain't that just too bad!"

The one o'clock judging started very nearly on time, with not more than the usual ten or fifteen minute delay. As Master of Ceremonies, the president of the Professional Dog Judges Association circulated from ring to ring, explaining to his judges and to the occupants of the seats reserved for student judges, how the judges would impart their comments. Good qualities, rather than faults of the exhibits were to be stressed, and to the imagination of the students would be left the corollary that aspects of a dog not favorably mentioned, might just possibly leave something to be desired.

I sat through several hound breeds in the afternoon. In the first class, when the ribbons were awarded, the exhibitors dashed out of the ring as usual. When the judge turned to the dogs to discuss them with the students, they had vanished. This was remedied by the MC adding to his instructions the following, which as far as I saw was strictly maintained during the remainder of the show. After the judge arrived at his decision, and placed a class, he first marked the judge's book and left it on the table. After that he usually discussed his placings before he handed out the ribbons.

The afternoon hound breeds had light entries as to numbers, but the proverbial high quality for small entries was maintained by producing the breed winners which placed first and second in the hound group.

The judge worked out a method of bringing the dogs near enough to the students so that their stance could be examined, and so that the exhibitors and the steward could hear the comments, which were clear to me and from which I derived considerable information.

"The words 'breed standard' were not mentioned in my hearing by any judge in discussing his placings. Phraseology could have been interpreted as Vox Dei in this respect."

Later I went to another ring where traffic was heavier. This judge handed out his ribbons as soon as he placed the dogs and marked his book, using only the brief interval between classes to comment on dogs which already had left the ring. In another ring, where afternoon traffic was light, the judge went into no more details than various paraphrases of: "I put this one up because it was better—or best." In another ring, one phrase led to considerable subsequent expression of exhibitor dissatisfaction: "I could place these two dogs either way...but for this or that reason I put this over that dog." More accurate and acceptable expression of the same sentiment probably would have been: "These dogs are so nearly even that the scales are tipped by this or that factor."

In the evening I sat under the MC himself while he judged Dachshunds. He followed scrupulously the technique outlined above, of marking his book and leaving it on the table with the steward while discussing the Dachshunds preliminary to handing out the ribbons. In this ring, the strip of rubber matting faced endwise to the students so that there was good opportunity

for the students to get the same perspective on gait—going and coming—as the judge himself, while the dog was under judgment. However, when placed, the dogs were lined up in the middle of the ring, and in talking to the students the judge's back was, most of the time, turned toward the exhibitors. This may explain why some of his remarks to the students were later quoted by exhibitors diametrically opposite to what I heard him say. The avowed policy of "speak no evil" put one judge in a dilemma from which he sought escape by saying, "The less I say about this one, the better," and that did not please the exhibitor, either!

The words "breed standard" were not mentioned in my hearing by any judge in discussing his placings. Phraseology could have been interpreted as *Vox Dei* in this respect. One off-record comment by a judge was that he welcomed the opportunity to get his reasons off his chest as he went along—an opportunity not provided under ordinary circumstances. Another judge volunteered when away from the ring, that he had re-read several standards before this show to fortify himself against possible questions. I believe that judges preparing to analyze their placings out loud will more likely than not be steadied in their judging by this prospect.

During the group judging, no comments were offered by any of the group judges, and no reason was given for reticence at this point in the show.

The exhibitors and the dogs were assembled in the ring before the identity of the group judge was disclosed by his appearance. The only judge visible in the ring until then was the indefatigable Master of Ceremonies, who waited only to beckon the chosen group judge and exit, smiling.

Even with a local group following each regular group, the judging adhered to its schedule of 30 minutes for each such pair of groups and the final best in show, and the rather anticlimactic best local dog in show, were over soon after ten o'clock.

So much for a narrative account. When it comes to estimating the desirability of repeating the great experiment, I do not know one voice that would be raised to that end.

Early Saturday afternoon it became apparent (and audible) that few if any exhibitors enjoyed being live targets for an instruction session, even if the comments were confined to the positive end of the critical spectrum—from good to better to best "in these and those particulars." Some exhibitors with vivid lack of confidence imagined all sorts of criticisms. I can't quote exact words until the *Gazette* is printed on asbestos. Others objected simply to having to wait in the ring "doing nothing—feeling like a fool" w h i l e the judge made his com- ments.

Before the end of S a t u r d a y afternoon, even the MC who had not yet been judging, had decided against the desirability of instructing student judges at an all breed competition. It took only a few minutes more to show that the suggested alternative of specialty shows would be no better, for these usually bring out breed entries and involve competition and emotional tensions to equal or exceed conditions at all breed shows.

This takes us back to the pattern of the German Shepherd judging classes, several of which I attended before the war. I remember that at these sessions, student judges had opportunity to go over the dogs in the ring, getting real "judge's eye" instead of ringside perspective, and the dogs and exhibitors had volunteered for the purpose.

Conclusion No. 1 seemed to be that student judging instruction and actual ring competition do not mix.

As for the timetable, exhibitors seemed to think that the two hours between 11 A.M. and 1 P.M. judging was taken out of their hides for no good reason, kept them from lunch, and length-

ened the day beyond the requirements for judging and gate, to support very doubtful if not mythical advantages of checking in dogs and tabulating absentees.

There were four rings in operation, and six professional all breed judges; two afternoon and two evening sessions, some of the rings occupied by successive judges and breeds without break for dinner. There were 761 dogs entered. Not counting the final evening for group judging this provided four rings from one to 10 P.M. Saturday and from one to seven Sunday, about fifteen hours. This would require breed judging at a rate of 761 dogs divided by 60 judging hours or about 12 or 13 dogs per hour. The schedule was calculated at the rate of 15 dogs per hour and was well maintained.

Conclusion No. 2 was that while conditions at Baltimore were more favorable than at the average show—with six professional all breed judges and two days to do 761 dogs—the schedule was well maintained and there was general approval of working by a definite schedule.

On whether or not there is advantage in not having group judges announced in advance, there are several comments. Even if licensed to do all breeds, most all-rounders are more definitely identified by background, experience and/or choice with the breeds of certain groups. Of the minority of exhibitors whose fortunes lead them often into group competition, many have more confidence in the judges so identified with the groups they show in. You hear again and again and again, "He's a terrier man, what is he doing in (or what does he know about) hounds?" with various transpositions of the groups.

When challenged on this point by one exhibitor, the MC responded in words as near to these as to make no difference in the meaning: (I lacked the advantage of having them electrically recorded.) "Serious competition is in the breed judging; the groups are put on for the spectacle; exhibitors should not take the ups and downs of group placings too seriously; any exhibitor is entitled to take his dog out of the ring when he sees who comes in to judge his group but the pressure of public opinion that to leave would be poor sportsmanship is relied on to keep exhibitors in the ring."—and it did.

I do not profess to know how many potential group contenders were attracted or repelled by the offer of this plan of group blindman's-bluff in the premium list. Many exhibitors who came to the ring and still could not tell until they were in the ring which of the six judges would officiate, expressed definite disapproval. There being six groups, done in order, and six judges, the choice of judges for the later groups diminished until for Group V it was a practical certainty after a terrier judge was designated.

I do know that there would be practical difficulties in trying the plan very often. The bill for fees and expenses of six professional judges for two days for a show bringing in 813 entry fees would not appeal to many show-giving clubs. Six all breed judges could not agree to judge no groups for a quarantine interval of time and distance very many times a year. To forswear judging all six groups for a month, and then judge only one of the six, is not a good way to approach the national goal of full employment. If individual judges are assigned for other groups at other shows, it would provide clues to the assignments.

And how much difference does it make by the end of the year? We hear examples of exhibitors following particular judges to small shows at unnatural distances for high placings. But an exhibitor of major league ambitions will encounter any or all of these judges within a season, and it might as well be at Baltimore, whether the encounter is anticipated with confidence or misgivings. I don't believe this is a field in which quarantine is any guarantee against contamination or re-contamination. At the Forum it was well said that there could be no unethical judging if unethical exhibitors provided no market for unethical judging. The Baltimore attempt to solve this problem might only accelerate efforts to cultivate group judges, suggesting that "bread cast over wider waters" "against the day" "when we shall meet again." I want it to be clear that these remarks apply only to the *theory* of having exhibitors and judges keep blind dates in the group rings—any similarity to living (or departed) personnel is strictly, unwittingly coincidental.

Conclusion No. 3 would be that conditions similar to having the six all breed judges at Baltimore seldom would exist; that secrecy would become increasingly difficult to preserve; that exhibitors have more confidence in some group judges than in others; that far-travelling large exhibitors can afford to make capital of playing such a slate across the board.

No comment on Baltimore would be adequate which did not refer to the enforcement of the benching rule. Here again we must note that the "VIE" perspective was very prominent. I could see that professional handlers had their work increased by having to circulate frequently past benches of their various breeds in various parts of the armory, in addition to feeding, exercising, grooming and exhibiting the dogs in their charge. On the other hand advance publicity for the show—part of the bargain between the show management and the public at the box office—sets forth the presence and display of prominent show dogs as one of the inducements for the spectators to buy their tickets.

One exhibitor objected to benching dogs on the basis that it was hard on the dogs' nerves to have curious spectators approach as close as regular benching permits. I heard mention of mild sedatives being used to calm high-strung dogs on the benches—leaving the dogs too calm to show with spirit when their turn came in the ring. Is not show temperament as much a part of the equipment of a show dog as show conformation, show training and show condition?

If any dogs are to be benched, and endure the strain of long hours of comparative inactivity and/or the unaccustomed stimulation of the sight, sound and smell of thousands of strangers at close range, while other dogs are sheltered from such strain by segregation from the public under conditions more favorable to conserving their physical and temperamental reserves, how can such inequality of competition be justified? Where in ascending the treadmill of competition does a "VIE" stake out a claim to preferential consideration?

Conclusion No. 4 would be to repeat the position of the AKC. The benching rule has been declared in effect by the AKC Board of Directors; this rule was adopted by the Delegates; and while it is on the books, the AKC administration is charged with its impartial enforcement.

Perhaps one more observation should be included. The AKC had an official representative at Baltimore. Many complaints arising from having judges comment on competitive dogs, and serious enforcement of the benching rule, could be and were investigated on the spot. Complaints are a well-recognized form of self expression; and the presence of a representative of duly constituted authority is the greatest deterrent to misbehavior.

Questions for Consideration

1. How would you plan a "perfect" dog show? Would you designate any actual shows as "perfect" or close to it? What differentiates these shows from others you have attended?

2. Is it reasonable to expect judges to give significant commentary on their placements without training in the area of verbalizing reasons?

3. How important is knowledge of a particular breed standard in critiquing an entry?

4. If judges knew they would be required to give logical reasons for their placements do you think they would spend (more/less/about the same) time studying breed standards?

5. What is the primary difference between breed judging and Group judging?

6. Should Group judges be required to give reasons for their placements or are the Groups merely in the show for spectator appeal?

7. If you were specialing a dog, would you enter shows at which the Group judges were not announced until just before Group judging? Why or why not?

8. Who should be in charge of educating judges? How would you design a system which would insure all judges have accurate and adequate knowledge of the various breeds?

9. How much emphasis should we continue to be put on Group competition when only a minority of exhibitors ever compete at that level?

10. Do you think educational events for student judges could be successfully combined with official dog shows? If this were done on a routine basis would exhibitor objections to public critiques diminish?

11. Wouldn't the quality of a judge's explanations remove all doubt concerning his or her particular knowledge of a given breed?

12. If the purpose of dog shows is to select breeding stock, shouldn't exhibitors expect—and want—knowledgeable criticism of their dogs?

Judges by Examination

H. F. Gibson

"The Kennel"
1911

When I first suggested the scheme to my Committee of appointing judges by examination it was favourably received, and I had their consent to put the same into operation, but my first attempt was not successful as no one came forward with the two unshown dogs required for the purpose, but when it becomes more generally known there should be no trouble in that respect. I have since received letters from many good authorities expressing their whole-hearted approval of the idea.

I want it to be clearly understood that I should like the matter ultimately to be brought to the notice of that august body, the Kennel Club, when the subject has been freely discussed and criticised by Great Dane fanciers of recognised standing whose views would carry weight. A few practical demonstrations would convince skeptical people of the advisability of clubs adopting the principle of having qualified judges only to officiate at shows.

It should be quite optional for persons who have already judged on several occasions, and thus gained additional knowledge of the breed by experience. Nevertheless, I feel sure that the majority of our best judges would not decline an invitation to submit to an examination especially if the Kennel Club issued to successful candidates a diploma or certificate of merit. Would-be judges would greatly appreciate the honour of being awarded a certificate of distinction bearing the seal of a registered specialist club, or prefer-ably that of the Kennel Club.

> *"There are far too many persons appointed to judge at more or less important shows, whose knowledge of the breed they adjudicate upon is very meagre."*

I would suggest the following rules to govern these examinations: (1) That each specialist club should nominate two experts; (2) That the Kennel Club be asked to appoint a referee to superintend the proceedings at all the four centres, and, if necessary, act as arbitrator, or, as an alternative, he should be mutually selected by the specialist clubs; (3) That meetings should be held once a year in London, Birmingham, Manchester and Leeds; (4) That the two visiting judges in charge of the examinations should hail from another town; (5) That applications should be made to one of the respective clubs for such visits; (6) That the number of candidates in each examination should be restricted to six, and that it should not be necessary to be a member of any particular club, but club members should take precedence; (7) That a small entry fee of, say 5 shillings, be charged to club members (extra to non-members), in order to help defray the expenses of the visiting judges; all extra charges to be met by the specialist club holding the meeting; (8) That printed slips for the use of candidates should be supplied by each club; (9) That two unshown dogs (preferably harlequin and brindle) should be used for the purpose; (10) That each candidate should orally name the different parts of the dog; (11) That each candidate be required to write on the slip provided the good and bad points of the dogs, giving his reasons, and that, taken by comparison as if it

Evaluating Varieties

In listing his parameters for testing prospective Great Dane judges, H. F. Gibson suggested the two animals presented for examination be unshown and, surprisingly, of different color varieties. To maintain clarity in the permitted hues, conscientious fanciers do not interbreed brindles and harlequins. As a consequence, the Great Dane supports separate but similar gene pools, which have diverged somewhat, although today all varieties produce competitive quality representatives. However, in Gibson's time, disparity in relative quality between colors was much more pronounced. Because of closed breeding populations, accurate inter-variety judging will always remain a challenge. This is especially so when varieties are divided by size, as in Poodles or American Eskimo Dogs, for each entrant generally has its own set of variety identifiable faults and virtues, in addition to those it possesses as an individual. If interbreeding is allowed and the varieties routinely occur in most litters, distinctive variation in conformation generally seems less pronounced in those breeds with coat varieties.

While judges are always admonished to evaluate the "total dog," that totality includes breed specific temperament—extremely difficult to assess in the show ring unless aberrant behavior is displayed. Surprisingly, while it is acknowledged that physical traits are genetically based, the fancy is generally loathe to admit any distinct qualities of temperament are inheritable. Yet, one would not select an English Setter to herd sheep. Further, while in some breeds specific colors are gene linked with luxurious coats, little credibility is given to experienced breeders emphatically stating a certain color produces dogs which are more "outgoing" and another color dogs which are "reserved," within the same breed. But, until accurate testing procedures are developed to explore the genetic basis of temperament, these empirical distinctions will continue to be categorized as no more than environmentally induced, individual behavior patterns—or pejoratively, as anthropomorphism.

To utilize Gibson's test, these two St. Bernards were selected for evaluation. Contemporaries from 1899, the zenith of the St. Bernard fancy, the Rough is of English breeding and the Smooth, American. (To preclude any further bias for prospective judges in this exercise, identifications are to be found in the illustration list). What is the difference, if any, between examining, evaluating and judging a dog? Name the various anatomical features of the dog. Should all judges be expected to have this knowledge? How should this expertise be determined? Evaluate each dog individually, first in the context of general canine conformation and then as a St. Bernard. Does the St. Bernard standard give preference to either Roughs or Smooths? What faults and virtues do these two dogs share in common? What are their principal differences? Which do you believe the better overall dog? Place the dogs, giving your reasons. In breeds with which you are not familiar, is it easier to list faults or to discuss virtues? If it is difficult to enumerate and discuss breed specific virtues, is one ready to expertly judge a particular breed?

Evaluating Change

In most breeds, comparing dogs from the past and present on an equal basis to determine which representative is "best" is almost impossible. However, careful study allows one to see where improvements have been made and also (sadly) when valuable features of type have fallen by the wayside. Domestic dogs are selected for traits which their owners deem most beneficial. Consequently, human beings determine the rate of development based upon numerous factors, including the strength or weaknesses of a written standard, distance which separates breeders, the influences of fad and fashion and, in the case of working or hunting breeds, the environmental conditions which affect their particular vocations.

The written standard is one yardstick to measure breed progress, or the lack thereof. However, certain breeds, such as the Greyhound, are of such ancient origin that a written standard has done little to alter their centuries-old appearance, simply because their form is almost entirely determined by function. Nevertheless, ill-conceived or poorly written standards subject breeds to vague and/or inconsistent judging decisions and frequent revisions in the written concept of the ideal, thus impeding steady advances toward a common goal. Distance between breeders is certainly critical in creating the written ideal. Numerous examples can be cited in which breed standards vary significantly from one country to another, with each group insisting upon authenticity of their particular verbiage. In the case of Great Britain and the United States, the rabies quarantine, which went into effect in 1903, stopped a free interchange of dogs. In almost a century of subsequent reproduction many breeds now display a decided variance in physical manifestations. Some interpret these differences as detrimental, arguing those in the "country of origin" should have full authority to determine the universal standard for any given breed. But, quite a few breeds came into their "modern" forms in other than their so-called country of origin. Still others have unknown homelands or hail from locations where there are no interested fanciers. Such nationalistic logic would suffice if all were to adhere to the original written standards. But, there is no evidence that modern fanciers, whom by happenstance were born in the same country as the ancestors of their dogs, have superior insight into the minds of a breed's long-dead founders in charting the course for improvement.

Once again, you are asked to evaluate two breed representatives, both champions. The first Beagle was

English, circa 1897, and the second an American-bred dog, from about 1904. Though the breed standards differ somewhat, the Beagle is considered a Foxhound in miniature on both sides of the Atlantic. Can you clearly identify both dogs as Beagles? Why or why not? Do you notice any obvious changes in style, form and type in less than 10 years? Do you notice any exaggerations? To what would you attribute the visible differences in structure and substance—hunting conditions in England and the United States or show ring competition? How would these dogs compare with the breed today, each in its own country? Would they be competitive in the show ring? How much variation in the interpretation and expression of correct type should be allowed?

201

were a "match," he should name the better of the two dogs; (12) That only one candidate at a time be admitted into the room; (13) That the public be admitted into the room; (14) That the name of the candidate should not appear on the slip, but that the secretary in charge should, after receiving it back, number the same, the identity being kept entirely to himself; (15) That the names of the successful candidates only be announced in the press, and not those who have failed; (16) That persons who have once failed should be given an opportunity of trying again at the next or following meeting; (17) That diplomas or certificates of merit be granted, signed by the referee, two visiting judges, and the secretary, bearing, if possible, the KC seal; (18) That the specialist clubs should send a list of the names of these successful candidates to the Kennel Club Committee, so that they may place the same on a Register of Judges.

There are far too many persons appointed to judge at more or less important shows, whose knowledge of the breed they adjudicate upon is very meagre. In most cases their appointment is the result of some connection with a club desirous of showing its appreciation of services rendered either as President, or because they have been liberal supporters.

Finally, I would strongly recommend the specialist clubs to send a list of all their competent judges to the KC, as I feel sure that sooner or later it will become necessary for the KC to assume control over the appointment of judges at all shows; it would then put a stop to promiscuous or indiscriminate appointments being made of so many incompetent judges.

Questions for Consideration

1. Who should be allowed to adjudicate at dog shows? What do you believe the qualification criteria should be? How would you define the term "breed expert?"

2. As long as a candidate has passed a procedural test and is in good standing, should there be any other restrictions placed upon judging qualifications? Wouldn't the market place quickly determine the "best" judges?

3. Whose responsibility is it to insure that all breeds are fairly and correctly judged?

4. What types of examinations should be instituted for prospective judges? Should these examinations include evaluating live dogs? Why or why not?

5. Should judges be required to take regular re-examinations of breeds for which they are already approved?

6. Which groups would be best able to establish and fairly administer any such tests—the official regulatory body, parent clubs, local specialty clubs or judges organizations?

7. Should dogs selected for live examinations be unshown animals? Why or why not? What about puppies, veterans or dogs not in show condition? How critical to the validity of the test outcome is the quality of the breed representatives utilized?

8. To fairly and equally assess credentials of candidates, shouldn't all judging applications be assigned a number when received and be discussed simply on their merits, rather than on personal biases, intentional or otherwise?

9. If judges are required by the regulatory body to pay for continuing education, such as breed seminars, aren't the so-called "amateur" judges, in effect, being forced to pay for their participation in the canine political process if they serve as Delegates? Conversely, should "professional" judges continue to be denied participation as Delegates simply because they choose not to absorb all the costs involved in their hobby? Is such a situation constructive or conducive to advancing the sport of purebred dogs?

This feature first appeared in 1945 and rather than the author didactically telling how the dogs should be placed, readers were invited to respond with their critiques. These dogs were drawn by animal illustrator Arthur Schilling, best known for his exquisite paintings of fancy fowl. The respondents to this quiz were Fox Terrier breeders Elizabeth Carruthers and Forest N. Hall, who was also an all-round judge.

A.   *B.*   *C.*

D.   *E.*   *F.*

Elizabeth Carruthers' Placings
First: Dog D

Easily the best of the six in my opinion on Fox Terrier conformation. Can give away to all the others: better balanced in quarters, tail set, better through the loin; better formed in ribs. Its neck comes out of the right place and the ear, although carrying more leather is better placed. Wins easily.

For Second, Third and Fourth, I have some trouble because it is a case of balancing faults, either because the drawings differ or in real

*Elizabeth Carruthers with two of her
home-bred Fox Terriers.
The Wire Fox Terrier,
CH. HETHERINGTON KNIGHT STORMER
and a Smooth puppy,
HETHERINGTON BLACK ANGEL
1938*

life, trimming presents three distinct styles, so I place:

Second: Dog C

I make him better behind and though slightly longer cast, he is better in elbow, shoulder and neck. I like his eye placement better and he is not as cheeky, he perhaps gives away a little in set on.

Third: Dog E

Although I make him straighter in stifle, I make him truer there, his tail set is better, topline more level, shoulder is better, fronts about equal. Although his neck is thicker, his head is set on better, and not so Borzoi-like, though perhaps as cheeky.

Fourth: Dog A

For reasons stated above.

Forest N. Hall's Placings

First: Dog E

A short bodied one, plenty of substance, excellent ear carriage and expression, sufficient length of head for his length of body. This is the kind you would expect to find loaded in shoulder, and might come towards you with his elbows out. He should be especially strong in hindquarters, and is the type that should sire a good one.

Second: Dog D

This little bitch crowds Mr. E. There is evidently more refinement, but we doubt if she has the spring of ribs, or quite the Fox Terrier expression, but is worthy of competition, and may be a shade better in shoulder. She doesn't look quite as good in feet. The depth of the pad can only be told by sense of touch, and not merely by taking a look, even if we had the actual dog before us.

Third: Dog C

This fellow does not appear to have the length of head equal to that of number one, and he seems to be a trifle longer in body and it is quite evident he doesn't have the spring of ribs. In my opinion, he does not have the correct type of Fox Terrier ear. The E dog has the real ear and the bitch a trifle too much of the V type, while this C dog has a lifted ear of the Airedale shape— nothing exaggerated, but not as pleasing in the ear as the two above him. Please compare ears on my 1 and 4. You could transplant these ears on either dog and it would never be noticed. Therefore, I believe, the first dog will have a great deal more Fox Terrier expression. Note the "come-kiss-me" look on C.

Fourth: Dog A

We put fourth place. Not a bad champion and could beat some very good dogs. However, he isn't as cobby as the first two, and probably not as good in head. Otherwise, a sound, honest dog.

And How Would You Judge These Bulldogs?

Has the dog show impacted and affected the development and appearance of various breeds? While the Bulldog standard remains virtually the same as when it was officially penned in 1875 (USA, 1890), modern dogs have changed in appearance. How does one reconcile these differences? If Bulldogs are a breed with which you are familiar, place the class and give your reasons. However, no one should leave this book without a lecture on Bulldogs. Therefore, if you admit to knowing little or nothing of the breed, secure a standard and learn by answering the questions posed as you judge this class. Unlike Schilling's Wire Fox Terriers, these

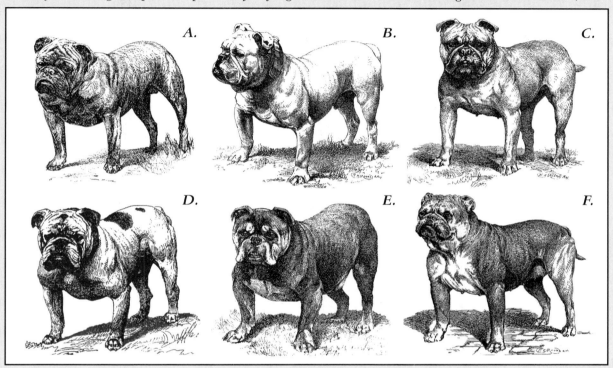

Bulldogs, drawn by R. H. Moore, represent portraits of actual dogs which graced the English show rings from the late 1880s-1890s. Remembering that the Bulldog standard states, "due allowance should be made in favor of the bitches," illustrations C and F are representatives of the preferred gender.

Describe each Bulldog in terms of its general conformation and then in relation to the requirements of the breed standard. Describe the overall body proportions of B and C. Do all these Bulldogs possess heads which meet the minimum requirements for size? Which Bulldog has the most broken up face? Which Bulldog has a "perfect" ear set and "perfect" ears (or very close to it)? Which Bulldog has the deepest brisket? Describe the front assembly of F and the rear assembly of C. Would all these Bulldogs move in an "unrestrained, free and vigorous" manner? What does the standard say in reference to the tan markings on E? Do these Bulldogs display distinctive features of type which are not commonly seen today? Which of the following traits do all these dogs share in common (more or less)? (1) deep stop; (2) broad, well cushioned muzzle; (3) broad underjaw; (4) well sprung ribs; (5) roach or "wheel" back; (6) low set tails; (7) well muscled hindquarters.

Are all the required characteristics in a breed standard important? In what specific ways are today's Bulldogs different, changed or improved from these representatives? Would any of these Bulldogs be competitive in today's show ring? Why or why not? Place the class and give your reasons.

Bonus Question: *Which of these show Bulldogs was the top winner of this group? (Answer below).*

Bonus Question Answer: F, CH. QUEEN MAB

And How Would You Judge These Borzoi?

Prior to the Revolution in 1917, the various Russian Hunts kept large packs of native Wolfhounds. Over time, distinctive differences, particularly in heads, were developed which immediately identified a dog's ori-

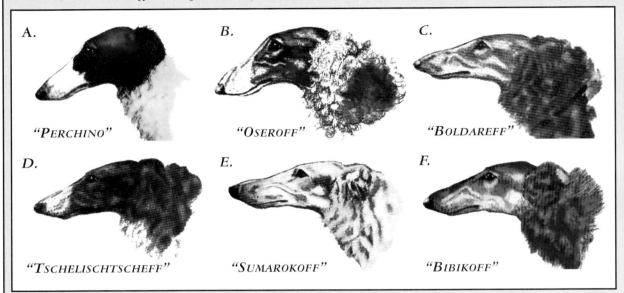

A. *"Perchino"*

B. *"Oseroff"*

C. *"Boldareff"*

D. *"Tschelischtscheff"*

E. *"Sumarokoff"*

F. *"Bibikoff"*

gin. Pictured are representatives from various established packs. Judge these Borzoi against the current breed standard. Do these dogs express different types or merely allowable type variations? Is there one particular head which predominates in the ring today? In your opinion, which heads are the most similar? Dissimilar? Elaborate and enumerate the exact differences and similarities among these heads.

Questions for Consideration

1. The Russian Masters of Hounds believed each distinctive head type was associated with specific characteristics such as color, coat quality, conformation and temperament. In your opinion, is this an accurate conclusion, not only in Borzoi, but other breeds as well? If true, does such knowledge aid the judging process or is it merely anecdotal information?

2. Do some breeds have a wider range of acceptable variation in correct type than others?

3. How critical is it for the adjudicator to be familiar with the various expressions of correct type within a particular breed? How does one acquire this knowledge?

4. Is an understanding of a breed's history, development and change over time relevant to judging dogs which are in the ring today? Why or why not?

5. For those wishing to judge dogs, is comparative study, analysis and commentary upon various drawings of dogs a worthwhile exercise? What are the advantages of such classes? The disadvantages?

6. From reading the critiques, is it possible to determine the priorities of both Carruthers and Hall in judging Wire Fox Terriers? Do both seem able to give meaningful justifications for their placements? How would you place this particular class?

7. While both placed the same four dogs, the placements varied between Carruthers and Hall. Should this be interpreted to mean one was right and the other wrong, or is there room for informed differences of opinion regarding the relative merits of a class of dogs?

True Judges Are Born, Not Made

E. J. Lewis

"American Kennel Gazette"
1929

Of all the functionaries connected with a dog show, the most important is the judge. The thought that is uppermost with all followers of shows relates to judges and judging. More differences of opinion are held and expressed on this subject than on any and all others. There are perhaps as many shades of opinion in this regard as there are active fanciers. In fact, the whole matter rests in opinion. Even the decisions of the judge always rest in opinion, and are received with opinion as to their correctness.

Judging propositions may not be capable of demonstration. Controlling views vary from time to time, but the changes made do not immediately greatly affect either matters of procedure or results attained. The conflicting opinions relate chiefly to the qualifications and disqualification of judges, the mode of their selection and the performance of their duties.

The true judge is born, not made. His first qualification is an appreciation of the breed before him and the capacity to appreciate, if possessed at all, must be inborn. The judge of dogs, then, is an artist and he deserves to rank with the poet, the painter, the sculptor, the musician and the inventor. None of these can we measure by ordinary standards. Each must have in his mind a conception of his art before he applies his pencil, brush, bow or chisel.

So must the judge of dogs have a concep-

> *"The term 'all-round judge' does not have a very definite meaning and does not imply any particular degree of skill. In strictness, it can only mean one who is willing to, and does, undertake to adjudicate every recognized breed. He may be a specialist in them all, or he may have particular ability in none."*

tion of the ideal of the breed before he can indicate the individual most nearly approaching that ideal. True, each breed of dogs has its standard, but it represents merely the technique of the art. The poet does not scan his lines to see if they express his sentiment, the picture artist does not apply a scale to his canvas to see if his proportion is correct and the connoisseur of dogs does not consult the standard to learn what impression a certain dog makes on him, nor does he apply a measuring instrument to determine whether his proportions are correct.

There is a popular view, entitled to serious consideration, which is not in accordance with the one above expressed. That view is that almost anyone of ordinary intelligence, with a knowledge of canine anatomy and the nature of the services required of the breed, may, with the assistance of the standard and its scale of points, do a reasonably satisfactory job of judging. Not being able to disprove the statement, I am inclined to concede, rather than admit, its truth. Even in such a case a natural sense of proportion is essential.

Should a judge, qualified by education rather than adaptation be obliged to adjudicate a number of breeds with large classes, the process would be laborious, tedious and exceedingly wearisome, not only to the official, but to the exhibitors and spectators. Clubs, after employing artificial judges for a few times, even with a mod-

The Original Dog Show Judge

William Lort, with his imposing stature, flowing beard, wild shock of hair and commanding presence, was a formidable and well-known figure at many of the earliest English dog shows. Though not the first to judge, he was a compelling force who successfully established the authority of the dog show adjudicator. In an age before written standards existed, he judged the dogs, "at a glance," quickly assessing their overall proportion, condition and quality, based upon his knowledge of breeds of the time.

Lort enjoyed a nationwide reputation as the ideal Victorian man's man—educated, well-spoken, interested in all sports, brave—yet possessing the "gentleness and thoughtful kindness of a woman." His national renown was such that when this photograph was published in 1884 the caption read, "There is no occasion to put a name to this portrait." He was considered a model family man, marrying early and raising 12 children.

Lort attended medical school, becoming a surgeon as his father before him. Taking parental advice to see the world before establishing his practice, he set off for the wilds of the American Rocky Mountains. With only his knife and gun he lived off the land with the fur traders. Making some important geological discoveries along the way, the US Congress named him an "Associate of the House." Next, he traveled to Brazil and then tried his hand at whale hunting off the Labrador coast. On one of his trans-Atlantic voyages he leaped overboard during a storm, rescuing the captain from drowning, afterwards taking command of the ship, when all hope of weathering the gale had been abandoned. This love of adventure lasted throughout his life. A championship swimmer and diver, in his late fifties he won a two mile ocean swimming meet off Brighton against men half his age and in his sixties went on another Arctic exploration trip.

Certainly Lort's celebrity status contributed to his judicial popularity, but his credibility was established through experience and success in both horses and dogs. He became a member of the Kennel Club in 1876 and besides originating the Stud Book for Pointers and Setters, was one of the earliest recognized breeders of Irish Setters and black Field Spaniels. Practically all exhibitors who had early success with these breeds could trace their dogs' lineage back to William Lort's stock. Lort eventually gave up exhibiting, but occasionally entered his dogs in field trials. He believed that in judging, breeders could make important contributions, contending in that capacity their work should be characterized by self-sacrifice, devotion and correctness in awarding prizes to only the best animals.

In the ring Lort's manner was always dignified, quick, decisive and final. Too quick for many of the also-rans, but it was said he was seldom, if ever, wrong. However, he was a warm personality, always willing and able to discuss the finer points of quality canines. Nevertheless, he would not tolerate any debate regarding his decisions. When dog shows began the exact role of the canine adjudicator was not firmly fixed. William Lort's innate bravery and decisiveness, combined with his expertise in dogs, were significant factors in establishing the dog show judge as someone with absolute authority to pass judgment on the merits of the entrants—without question.

"AN EARLY DOG SHOW"
This show was typical of those at which Lort would have judged.
Artist, R. H. Moore

erate degree of satisfaction, will eagerly seek for those who speak with the authority of connoisseurs, and not as statisticians.

Unless you have special ability and inclination in the line of dog judging, you will find it a profitless and thankless field of employment. In all walks of life and in all manner of undertakings, a skilled artisan is occasionally called upon to perform duties for which he is not fully prepared. In such a case he must either "go it blind," or consult the authorities for such assistance as he can find. Undoubtedly the latter course is the correct one for him to adopt. Occasionally a judge of dogs, through no fault of his own, encounters in the ring an unexpected problem. It is then no discredit to him if he stops and examines the standard. Usually it will point the way out of his dilemma.

> *"A popular view is that the best, and perhaps, the only true way to acquire judicial qualifications is by experience and service as a professional handler... and it may be questioned if the partisan occupation of a handler tends to develop that degree of open-mindedness so necessary in a judge."*

Occasionally, however, he will encounter a provision similar to the following, which is found in the standard of one of the popular breeds:

"The proper width of skull necessarily depends on the combined length of skull and muzzle, for what would be a thick or too broad a skull in one dog is not necessarily so in another of the same actual girth, but better supported by length of muzzle. It must also be considered in conjunction by clearness of outlines of cheeks and jaws."

This provision is meaningless to the novice. It means very little to me, although not altogether a novice in the breed under discussion. What it may mean to the experts is known only to them. However, the paragraph above quoted illustrates and emphasizes the truth that special knowledge is necessary to a correct interpretation of the standard.

A specialty judge is one who can expertly judge a particular breed and is recognized and endorsed by the official club for that breed. Whether that endorsement is a guarantee of high ability depends upon the care used by the club in selecting its judges. However, the welfare of each breed rests with its breeders, who speak through their organizations. We cannot go back of their decisions, whether we like them or not.

The doubt is occasionally expressed if one can properly judge more than one breed, as though capacity in one inhibits it in another. No doubt there are those who thoroughly appreciate a single breed, but cannot, or at least do not, go further. Doubtless, also, such cases are extremely rare. The fact that a number of judges have been endorsed by a dozen or so specialty clubs as being competent judges of their respective breeds, refutes the claim that one's ability to judge is limited to a single breed. And yet it must be admitted that he is specially gifted who appreciates all breeds to the extent that he can expertly judge them.

The term "all-round judge" does not have a very definite meaning and does not imply any particular degree of skill. In strictness, it can only mean one who is willing to, and does, undertake to adjudicate every recognized breed. He may be a specialist in them all, or he may have particular ability in none. His status is not officially established but depends upon popular demand and recognition by show giving clubs.

There is a school which holds that one cannot be a good judge unless he is a successful breeder. As well maintain that one cannot enjoy a good dinner unless he is a good cook. The task of the breeder is the harder. He must know not only the ideal of the breed, but also how to produce it. In other words, the successful breeder must be at once a scientist and an artist, and probably a good business man as well, while the judge may merely be a master of the art. It is a

The Born Judge

George Raper, whose nick-name, "The Irrepressible," matched his vivacious personality, was regarded by many as a born judge. He was easily the best known member of the canine community, worldwide, in his day. Born in Yorkshire in 1846, he acquired his first dog, a Fox Terrier, in 1861. His father Tom was an expert Greyhound slipper who had been associated with successive Waterloo Cup wins. Thus, Raper grew up not only with dogs, but dogs of great value and quality. As a young man George Raper apprenticed in the drapery trade but his love and interest in dogs was so compelling that he decided to go into the rather unheard of business of being a dog dealer and a judge. He was also an active breeder and exhibitor, having success with every breed he owned, particularly Bulldogs, Greyhounds and Fox Terriers.

A frequent exhibitor, Raper never took advantage of his status as a professional judge by showing anything other than good dogs, nor did he ever publicly question another fancier's awards within the ring. His written show reports were always well received for their candor. Furthermore, he consistently and publicly pointed out the virtues of his competition. This reputation for fairness and honesty served him well. One of the positive effects was that many Americans entrusted Raper to purchase top quality dogs of various breeds for them, knowing that the animals sent would be exactly as represented. Consequently, he was able to sell dogs at record breaking prices to fanciers across the pond, particularly Fox Terriers.

The first professional judge of international reputation, Raper adjudicated in every country that held dog shows during his lifetime. He served several times as a circuit judge in America, frequently crossing the Atlantic throughout his career. An influential judge, he inadvertently secured the establishment of the French Bulldog breed when judging at Westminster in 1897. In the absence of a written standard Raper awarded all prizes to quality dogs with rose ears, judging them as Toy Bulldogs, completely ignoring the American fancier's stated preference for bat ears. Outraged, the disenfranchised exhibitors set about to write the first standard for the breed.

A popular drawing card at any show, Raper only ever missed one assignment—in 1906, at age 60, when the San Francisco earthquake destroyed the show site. He returned the following year to fulfill the engagement. At that event he was the after dinner speaker and made light of his much-fabled "eye" for a dog. Commenting that he had sold many Fox Terriers which could go to ground he told the audience that over the years he had acquired many Bulldogs that would eventually go to ground, too. Asked to explain this strange phenomenon he stated that Bulldog development was so unpredictable that even as an expert he had made numerous mistakes. Since there was no market for poor quality Bulldogs he admitted that when his eye had failed him he was forced to put many Bulldogs into the ground with his shovel.

Always willing to help the novice, Raper told a story of a new exhibitor who waited outside the ring after an assignment to speak with him. Raper approached and asked if he wanted any information about the dogs which had just been in the ring. "Well," said the man, "it's like this. You never even looked at my terrier, and I sent you a ham. Didn't you get it?" Recognizing that the exhibitor had been told by others that judges expected presents he responded, "Oh, yes, the ham came all right; but, you see, the man whose terrier won sent a whole pig." Having shocked the exhibitor he then proceeded to take the time to explain where his dog failed when compared to really good specimens of the breed—and advised him that it was never necessary to send gifts to an honest judge.

matter of common knowledge that some of our most celebrated judges have been conspicuous failures as breeders. We can go no further than to say that the occupation of breeding does not unfit one for the duty of judging.

A judge usually possesses a dog of his own, but it is more as an outlet for his feelings and sentiments than as a professional necessity. Indeed, that ownership is as likely to prove a handicap as an assistance. Our hearts do not go out to our dogs by reason of their approach to breed perfection, but for qualities of disposition and temperament which are worthless in the ring. The devoted companion of field or fireside might well make an unperceived impression on his master which could not be left behind on entering into the ring.

I do not find in the standard of any breed a given number of points assigned to devotion, nor is it even made a requirement, and yet, without this quality, no dog serves the true purpose of his existence.

A popular view is that the best, and perhaps, the only true way to acquire judicial qualifications is by experience and service as a professional handler. The exponents of this view seem to have somewhat the better of the argument, at least so far as it relates to a judge of all breeds, but their position is far from proven.

The requisites of an acceptable judge are unquestioned integrity, natural adaptation, interest, familiarity with the standards and observation and experience in the exhibition of dogs at shows. While it is possible to have this experience without being paid for it, it is rather unusual for one to devote his entire time for several years in following shows around just for the fun of it, or to prepare for the very improbable event of being invited to officiate as a judge.

A referee of a boxing exhibition need not himself be a prize fighter; the ablest advocates in the courts of law have seldom attained high distinction as judges; and it may be questioned if the partisan occupation of a handler tends to develop that degree of open-mindedness so necessary in a judge.

If we were to concede that the best preparation for the profession of judge of all breeds is active service in conditioning, handling and exhibiting dogs for others, it must not be forgotten that one must be well along in canine knowledge before entering upon a successful career as a handler, and once having secured a large and profitable clientele in his profession, will wisely hesitate to give it up for the rather precarious one of judging. But so long as the judge of a specified breed is competent to pass upon it, it is a matter of indifference to the exhibitor whether he be a specialist or an all-rounder, professional or amateur, and when, where and how he acquired his skill is wholly immaterial.

"Confidence in the unbiased decisions of the judges is the foundation of the institution. When that foundation crumbles, the superstructure will surely fall... Perhaps proceedings where life, liberty or property are at stake are of more importance, but it is not more essential to a court than to a dog show that its adjudications should be respected."

The dog show, like every other institution, is in a constant state of evolution and transition. I am told that the present tendency is toward the increased employment of breed specialty judges. While this is probably true, there is no perceptible diminution in the demand for all-rounders. Many all breed shows are held each year and as they are at present conducted, each requires the attendance of at least one judge who is competent to pass on the merits of any and all breeds.

The increasing demand for breed specialty judges is always met by an increased supply. It is the proper ambition of every breeder-exhibitor to become a recognized judge of his favorite breed, and he is willing to devote much pains to fit himself for service, without hope of financial reward. There can be no over supply of these judges. Competition among them never becomes a serious matter, as their business success in no way depends upon their being called upon to judge.

The situation of a judge of all breeds is quite different. He cannot afford to qualify himself for the exacting services required unless he is to receive a handsome remuneration for his time. It is not well that he should be called upon to officiate frequently in the same territory, and thus his profitable clients are soon exhausted. It can easily be seen that the all breed shows demand a larger number of these judges than they are able to support. And here is perhaps the most perplexing problem facing the institution.

An oft suggested solution is to remove the disability placed upon handlers and dealers. This would be much like jumping from the frying pan into the fire. It is not a challenge of either the integrity or the ability of these persons to insist on their continued disqualification. Like all other persons, judges are human beings, and are subject to the influences which affect ordinary mortals.

Should a person be permitted to act in the dual capacities of judge and handler, he might feel under some constraint whenever, as judge, he met in the ring a client seeking a favorable decision. The general presumption is, of course, that his client would have an advantage over his competitors. The fact might easily be otherwise, and in his anxiety to avoid not actual favoritism, but its appearance he might be impelled to resolve all doubts against his client. There should be no such doubts to resolve.

A judge should be absolutely uninfluenced by any desire other than to place the dogs in the order of their true merit, and in his awards his duty to the breed should be his sole consideration. But even though he be entirely free from personal influence, it would be impossible to convince the exhibitors of the fact. As it now stands, there is enough suspicion in relation to judges' awards, without adding a practice which would further increase it. Confidence in the unbiased

decisions of the judges is the foundation of the institution. When that foundation crumbles, the superstructure will surely fall. Self-preservation requires the retention of the present rule of disqualification. It does not stigmatize or disparage any class to which it relates. The judge of a court is not permitted to receive a fee for legal services, nor to determine the cause of a former client, a blood relative, or business associate.

This rule has been tested by long experience, and is not considered as a reflection on the practice of law, a disapproval of business undertakings, nor a disgrace to be of kin to other members of society. Perhaps proceedings where life, liberty or property are at stake are of more importance than those we are now considering, but it is not more essential to a court than to a dog show that its adjudications should be respected.

During the progress of a show the judge is responsible to no one. Only one requirement is made of him—that he shall be on hand at the appointed day and hour, and enter his awards in the official judges book. Should he be absent, the judging may proceed without him, but there are no rules as to the manner in which he shall do his work and there must not be any. Each must use his own discretion, if discretion he has. If he were hedged about with rules of procedure or subjected to instructions from the superintendent or show committee, he would not be a judge but a mere clerk.

Probably the views, certainly the perceptions, of no two judges are quite the same. Some may unconsciously stress soundness and condition. Others may as unconsciously overlook these points in emphasizing quality, type and character. When two judges place given dogs in different order, shall we say that necessarily one has erred in his placings? No, rather that each has brought out different points of excellence, or differently penalized certain defects.

There is at least the suggestion of a movement to secure uniformity of judging, and to compel judges to interpret breed standards in a particular way. A judge cannot be compelled to

The Courteous Judge

Congratulations

Samuel L. Goldenberg doffs his hat to congratulate one of his winners at the French Bulldog Club of England show in 1913. While it may be possible to debate whether the ability to judge dogs is an inborn or environmental trait, many times one can also put forth the same argument for common courtesy in the show ring—of both judges and exhibitors.

Before moving to France in 1908, Samuel and Edwiga Goldenberg resided in Riverdale-on-Hudson, New York, making significant contributions with French Bulldogs and English Toy Spaniels. Certainly, the Goldenbergs each had that elusive "eye" for a dog. In 1904 on a trip to France they purchased a young pup which they named Nellcote Gamin. This remarkable dog became the "father" of the French Bulldog breed in the United States. From Mrs. Lillian Raymond-Mallock the Goldenbergs bought the English Toy Spaniel, Ch. Darnall Kitty, a British import. Under judge George Raper she was named Best in Show all breeds at Westminster in 1904. Sadly, although Kitty was undefeated in either country she never produced any offspring, having been killed in a freak accident while playing with a French Bulldog at the Nellcote Kennels in 1905.

In the year prior to the judging assignment illustrated, the Goldenbergs had traveled to Cherbourg, France to board the "Titanic." One of the reasons they were taking a voyage to New York was to attend the French Bulldog Club of America's annual specialty show. In 1911, Mr. Goldenberg had judged the event and drew the largest entry of Frenchies at any show ever held in the world. An active member of the FBDCA, he agreed to serve as one of three judges for a special $500 point match scheduled with the 1912 show. Probably because the Goldenbergs had crossed the Atlantic so many times they knew the ship was in grave danger after hitting the iceberg and immediately went up to the deck. According to accounts in both the "New York Herald" and the "Kennel Gazette," with the help of Mr. Bruce Ismay, Goldenberg assisted his wife into one of the first lifeboats to leave. She begged her husband to join her, but he refused, stating the order had been given for, "women and children first." When the boat was lowered it was only about half full and Mrs. Goldenberg cried out to her husband, "For God's sake, say good-bye to me!" Noticing that there were no women in the vicinity, Ismay called over one of the ship's officers, whereupon they seized Goldenberg and threw him overboard.

He managed to swim to the lifeboat and was pulled to safety.

The "Carpathia" arrived in New York City on April 18th. With one day to regain his composure, Goldenberg attended the FBDCA specialty at the Waldorf-Astoria on April 20th. His balloted selection for the match was Ch. Gamin's Riquet, the eventual winner. Apparently, for the truly courteous judge, nothing short of death would be a valid excuse to ever miss a judging assignment.

CH. DARNALL KITTY

CH. NELLCOTE GAMIN

do anything, and such an attempt is foredoomed to failure. When the inhabitants of the earth all speak the same language, worship at the same shrine, and vote the same political ticket on election day, then we may seek for men with exactly the same views as to the merits of dogs. Until then we may possibly be obliged to follow our present plan of depending, not on the judgment of a single judge, but on the consensus of opinion of a number of judges.

The judge's autocratic power ends with the closing of the show at which he officiates. His authority to judge is not a right, but a privilege, conferred by the show giving club with the approval of the License Committee of the American Kennel Club. The License committee is invested with almost unlimited discretion in giving or withholding its approval. It would not be well for this committee to make public its reasons for its action, and it does not do so. We are sometimes quite curious as to why the privilege is denied in certain cases, but we cannot learn unless the applicant chooses to inform us. It is really not our business, and no good would be accomplished by satisfying our curiosity.

If a judge wishes to score the dogs by points, he may do so, but it is not obligatory. The final decision is what counts, and the manner of reaching it is exclusively in the province of the judge. If the decision is correct, its correctness justifies the method. If it is wrong, nothing will justify it.

It is very effective if in every class the dogs are arranged in the order of the awards, yet to require this of the judge would be to interfere with his free agency and possibly disturb his mental process. It is also impressive if dogs, after having been placed in a given order, are promptly placed in the same relative order when they meet in another class. Judges there are who recognize each dog on its subsequent appearances, and who remember precisely what the previous order has been.

Others, perhaps as skillful, but not so gifted, must again carefully go through the process of weighing the merits and defects of dogs already placed, or consult the book. It has been said that the latter is bookkeeping, not judging. Perhaps so. But what is the judge with an ordinary memory to do? Why should he wary the patience of exhibitors and exhaust his own energies by rejudging, when it may be avoided by reference to the book and placing them as before? A sound memory is a convenient thing, and a valuable asset to a judge, but he is in the ring to judge the dogs, not to display a remarkable feat of memory.

Another judge, sure of his opinion and confident of his ability, may judge each class as though it stood by itself, and care not a whit if the position of two or more dogs is reversed. He can explain this by saying that a dog showed better in one class than the other. Can any one say, for this reason, that such a judge is not the equal

An Eye For...

"A Grand Old Faker Buys
an Irish Cup — 1884"
Artist, Archie Gunn
For some, it may not be necessary
to have an "eye" for a dog — if — one has
a good memory for faces.

For the second edition of "The Book of the Scottish Terrier," Dr. Fayette Ewing asked many of the old time breeders to write down their reminiscences. George Davidson, the Honorary Secretary of the Scottish Terrier Club (Scotland) wrote a section entitled, "The Fathers of the Breed," in which the following excerpt appeared.

Mr. Andrew Kinnear, Kirkcaldy, the owner of the Seafield prefix was in his day one of the most successful exhibitors. He bred a number of champions. I reckoned that he could put a dog in the ring in better condition to catch the judge's eye than any man of his time. Nobody knew a Scottie better than he but strange to say he was an absolute failure as a judge. He only judged on one occasion and I recall his telling me of his experience in that capacity. He said, "When I got in the center of the ring and saw the dogs round about me I absolutely did not know a good one from a bad one and I made a perfect mess of the job. I soon discovered I was not cut out to hand out awards but I had sense, which some I could mention have not got—I never took on the job again."

of the one who remembers, or the one who copies from the record? I think not.

Must a judge, on discovering that he has by inadvertence wrongly placed the dogs in the class, continue to make the same error in the classes which follow? Hardly. On a race track, because a horse wins one heat, it does not follow that he shall be accorded the other. If a dog shows well in one class, and sulks in another, is it not proper that he be rewarded and penalized accordingly? To ask the question is to answer it.

Shall the judge make a written report, and give his reasons for his decisions? Yes, if he chooses to do so, but little is to be gained by it. Those who witness the placings scarcely need it, and those who do not see the dogs in the ring are not much enlightened by it. The mind of the judge should not be distracted by thinking up alibis and excuses to incorporate in his review. Again, there are often exhibitors who feel that they have not received sufficient recognition. To them it is sufficient humiliation to receive a white ribbon, or possibly none at all; but when they read the judge's critique that the dog was unsound, of foreign type, a poor shower, or in wretched condition, they are likely to feel that it is insult added to injury. The judge has done his full duty when he has handed out the ribbons and

entered the awards in his book. To require more would detract from his dignity, impair his usefulness and be of no benefit whatever.

From various sources comes the complaint that the judging situation is unsatisfactory. It is impossible to tell how much of the criticism contains merit, and how much arises from the disappointment of defeat. It would be idle to claim that our judging system is perfect. It would be equally absurd to assume that any system that could be devised would give universal satisfaction.

It is significant that the dissatisfaction is least in evidence at the larger shows, where the ablest and most discriminating fanciers are in attendance, and that it is most loudly voiced at and after the petty and minor shows, where the presence of well informed exhibitors and visitors is accidental, or at most, incidental, and where the operations are conducted with the least formality.

This suggests that the dissatisfaction comes more from the situation than from the judging. Before we condemn the system, or any feature of it, would it not be well to improve the situation, so far as possible, by exercising more care in preparation for and in the operation of dog shows?

Questions for Consideration

1. The writer claims there is little to be gained by asking judges to give critiques and written reports of their award winners. Does this claim have merit?

2. Who are the most important people at a dog show? The judges, superintendents, field representatives, professional handlers, concessionaires, club members, spectators or exhibitors? Justify your position.

3. Who benefits from procedural rules and for whom are they designed? Do you think procedural rules interfere with a judge's thought process as the writer implies? Should judges be allowed full liberty to make their decisions in any manner they deem fit?

4. Lewis contends that procedural rules reduce adjudicators to the position of mere clerks. In countries other than the USA, stewards assume most of the bookkeeping responsibilities. Should the role of the steward be modified to assign them more responsibility in the ring?

5. Should professional handlers be allowed to judge while still actively engaged in their trade? Why or why not?

6. The writer states that while most people believe professional handlers have the best training to become all-round judges, they might not have developed an open mindset of knowing the difference between an outstanding breed representative and a dog that can win. Do you agree or disagree?

7. If you agree that experience as a professional handler is the best training for becoming an all-round judge then shouldn't the official regulatory body monitor this trade and set up qualification standards and requirements?

8. If the regulatory body refuses to take responsibility for monitoring professional handlers, can it reasonably and rationally defend itself against claims that this group receives special treatment when applying to judge? What is a professional handler?

9. Is vast experience with dogs the same thing as judicial ability?

10. Because opinions of the ideal in any breed change over time, the author contends it is not possible to evaluate the quality of an individual's judging in terms of awards but only the concrete criteria relating to the qualifications for judging. Is it possible to objectively evaluate the quality of judging? If not, then why would it be necessary for a regulatory body to approve judges at all?

11. Would you characterize a written breed standard as concrete criteria?

12. Lewis believes knowledge of breed standards is not necessary as long as one has a conception of the ideal. Can the concept of the ideal be based solely upon independent criteria or personal opinion?

13. Does having an "eye" for a particular breed necessarily correlate with having an "eye" for all breeds?

14. While the writer maintains one is born with a set of ephemeral qualities which create a competent judge and no amount of training will instill these properties in those not so gifted, the majority of the examples he put forth refute his premise. Defend your opinion on this topic with specific examples. *Example:* Name the judges whom you think have or have not a "natural" eye for a dog (yourself included, if you currently judge).

15. Are dog show judges (select one): artists/scientists/neither/both/don't know?

16. Were dog show judges made of sterner stuff back in the "good old days?"

If You're Thinking of Judging

H. W. Lacy

"American Kennel Gazette"
1925

Old stagers in the dog game have always maintained that no one could really judge a dog unless he were a breeder and had shown himself capable of appreciating what a good dog should be by owning and exhibiting the best. That would seem to be good reasoning. It may have sufficed in those older days, but we have not time today. We must get along and attain our goals without pottering. Yet, in our hurry and crowding of shows, are we not too apt to forget the responsibilities that rest on the shoulders that bear the "ermine?"

How many of the best judges of horseflesh ever bred a horse? Some of the keenest judges are merely dealers. It is their business to know horses. The art critic is in the same boat. It is his business to know pictures. He could not, perhaps, paint the side of a barn, but he could pick out the flaws in some other fellow's work.

I have watched old breeders fool around in a ring of dogs, and struggle in a mental whirl that was distressing to see. The perspiration of perplexity has poured from them! Why? Because they were lost in a maze of detail. They had considered detail so much in breeding—striving to attain this or that important point, or eliminating this or that fault—that their mind was surcharged with responsibility.

The old idea that it requires a lifetime to know dogs has evaporated into the mists of the past. It all depends upon the assimilative capacity of the aspirant. One must be willing to learn in order to learn. Years ago we had to search diligently for our judges. Now they grow on every bush. The great changes brought about in our shows—the great popularity of the one day show, the extravagant classification that takes no heed of time, and the increase in breeds—have all tended to change the rhythm of the old shows.

We must have judges to cover the breeds. The day of the long endurance runs in judging is about ended, except perhaps for the three-day events; and even then exhibitors weary of the tension. What is the consequence? The increased number of shows encourage the invitation of individuals to take on breeds before they have even won a Winners' ribbon!

In those old days an invitation to judge was a very serious proposition. It was an undertaking. Today, it would seem, an invitation to judge is accepted by some as one would treat an invitation to dinner or other social function. This idea is strengthened when one looks over the lists of names of those who have assumed, and others who would assume, several breeds with which they can have no judicial affiliation, or with which they can take no personal interest. This is

James Mortimer's Fox Terriers,
SUFFOLK RISK AND SUFFOLK TOBY
Artist, G. Muss-Arnolt
1890

the most serious condition that confronts our dog world today.

The License Committee is struggling with the problem and is subjecting the myriads of applicants to a process of elimination—tryouts. If these neophytes please, if they are asked again and yet again, if it becomes apparent they are cut out for the work, then they are placed permanently on the woolsack. Under present conditions, probably there can be no better system. And as soon as the old-timers have passed on, there will be nobody to care.

At the same time, judging should, and must be, seriously considered. The most go-ahead fancy in the world today, that of the German Shepherd Dog, emphasizes this need by the ardent way in which it is tackling the judicial question, going further than any other breed enthusiasts have ever done in establishing schools for the education of judges, under approved and tried mentors. I do not say this will solve the problem, but it will help. The reason for doubt is individual adaptability.

The eye for form and the ability to differentiate the merits of a bunch of dogs are naturally developed by practice and study. In the early days, when Westminster was but five years or so old, and the American Kennel Club had not even been thought of, there were but three men who could be possibly considered as all-round judges, and there were no specialists. They were Mr. Kirk, a Scotsman living in Toronto, primarily a spaniel man, but with a general knowledge of most of the breeds of that day; James Watson, a newspaper man who fiddled with the Collie and Cocker Spaniel, but who could not then be considered much of a judge, and Mr. Mason, who had just come over from England with a big team, and with more experience as an exhibitor and judge than all the rest put together. At that time there were about as many shows as

there were judges!

James Mortimer's little caravansary near the Battery, in New York, was the rendezvous of half a dozen dogologists, chiefly coachmen interested in terriers and toys, who would spend the time in the little bar while their folds were at services in Trinity Church, a few blocks away.

In this way, and as an exhibitor of a Bull Terrier, Mortimer had become known as a doggy man and naturally became acquainted with Charlie Lincoln, the Foley of his day, and superintendent of the New York show. In 1883, Lincoln was running the first show at Pittsburgh, and Mr. Kirk was to judge the show. At the last moment he wired that indisposition would prevent his coming, and things were in a fix. It was suggested that Lincoln try Mortimer. As a forlorn hope, Lincoln telegraphed and Mortimer consented. I saw him off on a judging career that accumulated a record which spread over nearly thirty-five years.

Although, naturally, many of the breeds upon which he had to pass were little more than known, Mortimer's work generally was endorsed, and the only contretemps that occurred was when someone handed Mortimer a slip of paper as the Black and Tans came in for judgment. Mortimer glanced at it, and put it in his pocket. Feeling in this breed ran a bit high at the time, and it was supposed that the paper was a steer.

No matter what was on that paper—and no one really ever knew but those concerned—a controversy for months raged regarding what became known as "The Pittsburgh Piece of Paper" in the columns of *Forest and Stream* and *The American Field*.

Those were the days when judging was taken very seriously, and the judge was expected to know what he was about, for his errors would surely be criticized in the doggy press. Those also were the days when controversies over ring deci-

> *"The old idea that it requires a lifetime to know dogs has evaporated into the mists of the past. It all depends upon the assimilative capacity of the aspirant. One must be willing to learn in order to learn."*

James Mortimer was every bit the colorful character described by Harry Lacy—and more. At a time when there were only five people in the United States actively exhibiting Wire-Haired Fox Terriers, Mortimer did everything possible to promote the variety. At the shows he superintended, Wires were always benched in a prominent place and their classes well supplied with expensive trophies. Mortimer is also responsible for bringing the Great Dane to show recognition and perhaps this is why he was so particularly stunned and angry when he was not chosen by the Great Dane Club of America's members as the World's Fair judge in 1893 (see page 31). Because an employee had been severely injured removing a Great Dane from a shipping  crate in the early 1870s, Superintendent Charles Lincoln refused to accept any further Great Dane entries. Although Danes continued to be exhibited without incident under such names as "German Mastiff," "German Boar Hound" and "Siberian Bloodhound" (see page 74), this ban stayed in effect until Lincoln's death in 1884. Having imported several Great Danes for his clients, Mortimer cleared the way for their approval, and the breed was first exhibited under its official moniker at Westminster in 1886.

No one ran a dog show as professionally, efficiently and expertly as James Mortimer. In fact, he originated many of the basic procedures and show rules which we take for granted today. To begin with, because he liked to eat his meals at regular hours, his shows ran on time. The seemingly obvious idea of having bench numbers match the catalog numbers was his doing. He also was the first to require exhibitor armband numbers so spectators, who did not know the individual dogs, could follow the judging and mark their catalogs. Show dates were originally granted by AKC without any consideration as to whether clubs would be in competition with each other for the same dogs. This soon became a serious problem and Mortimer proposed the idea of the corresponding date calendar. This innovation allowed everyone to plan in advance, knowing particular shows would be held at approximately the same time each year. In concert with this came his most far-reaching idea, however, the invention of the "show circuit."

More than any other factor, the show circuit dramatically changed the nature of dog shows in America, in that it firmly established the need for both professional handlers and professional judges. Dog shows could now be held almost continually and a dramatic increase in entries and new shows resulted. However, very few owners could absent themselves from their regular employment to such an extent to either show or judge. As a result, the professional "circuit judge" came into being. Because the superintendent customarily selected most judges, these circuit judges would be the same for a season, with only an occasional foreign or local judge thrown in. Resultant complaints generated by this system were numerous; in particular, the circuit was the official birthplace of the still-heard gripe that professional judges only put up professional handlers. Repeated questions were raised regarding the circuit judges' knowledge and/or competency to adjudicate all breeds. But the most serious objection was in relation to the actual health of the dogs. After being shipped on a train, dogs would be benched for four days, exercised only on lead, then loaded up to ride the rails to the next town. Drafty show venues, sudden changes of diet, careless handling by freight companies, lack of adequate exercise and exposure to disease led to the deaths of many show dogs. Of those that survived, very few ended a long season of shows in the same fit condition they had been in when they started.

Always smoking a cigar whether superintending or judging, Mortimer had many chinks in his armor, but enjoyed the company of exhibitors and, in most cases, this seemed mutual, as detailed in one of his show reports from 1888. "Czar should have been second; he won the prize for the best American-bred Great Dane, a fact which so elated his owner that he bedecked his stall with American flags, and wanted to treat the whole show to champagne. I dissuaded him from pursuing such an expensive course, but joined him in privately discussing a bottle of Mumm's Extra Dry in honor of the event."

James Mortimer judging Chow Chows at Belmont Park
1912

been famous by contrast. One of his failings—at least to my mind—was his overweening delight in upsetting some sure thing. No other judge ever did this as much as Mortimer and kept his popularity. In a certain sense, it became a great asset to Mortimer in that the exhibitor felt, no matter what his luck under Mortimer might be that day, the next day, with the same dogs in the ring, Mortimer might be liable to reverse the placing.

He was essentially a judge that considered the dog on the day it was exhibited. It was what he was going to do with the dog, and not what he had done. To what extent this trait ruled his work I might mention the case where he once made two famous Bull Terriers equal firsts, and then, two hours after, gave one the special over the other! And all the satisfaction the enquirer got was an, "Oh, well!"

Another failing in Mortimer's judicial work, especially in later years, was the obsession to find a new dog, and if it was owned by some ordinary outside exhibitor, so much the better. All these failings, as we may term them, arise from individuality of character, and Mortimer had this in marked degree.

He was also more than ordinarily jealous of his work as a judge, would brook no correction or questioning, and by pure force of personality compelled acceptance of his verdicts. In summing up, if asked the outstanding features of his work as a judge, I should say observance of standards (as he often remarked, "the standards were his Bible"), absolute confidence in himself, and a jealous regard for his position that assured the exhibitor of an honest decision.

Why do I relate all this around one man? Because, in the first place, Mortimer was a char-

sions would rage for months, and really furnished about the only excitement in the long waits between shows! Mr. Mortimer usually was in the thick of it, and held his own with the tenacity and ability that marked him so conspicuously in his later years.

In a discussion of judging dogs in America I must necessarily speak of the influence and methods of this man, whose personality was so conspicuous. Mortimer was an epoch maker, and he could run a show as well as he could judge it. He was the most methodical judge we have ever had. He would pursue the even tenor of his judgment, even if darkness fell before he had completed his classes. At Lenox, once, the glare of the automobile lights had to be thrown on his ring in order to finish his work.

Listen, you superficial judges of the day, it was one of Mortimer's tenets to examine carefully every dog in the ring, no matter what was its casual merit. He was very literal in his judging, and this came of his placing the standard ever before him. One cannot be a good judge and flout the written standards. I am taking Mortimer as an example because, through his strict adherence to standards, he became a national figure, and one who probably did much to advance the progress of dog fancying in America.

Mortimer had faults or he would not have

acter that will never be seen again in America, for the conditions that made him have changed completely; and again another reason is that in pointing out some of his failings, I would better impress on the new judge the avoidance of these wherever possible. And thirdly, the efficient and methodical way Mortimer went about his work, giving every dog a thorough tryout and chance to do its best.

If ever there was a judge who, in looking over his candidates, literally absorbed each into his mental retina, it was this man. He never forgot or missed his dogs as some of our so-called all-rounders today are apt to do, and have done. As a commentary on the changes that have come about, Mortimer, were he alive today would have to choose whether he would run the New York show or continue as a judge! But it would have been hard to make that decision. If he decided to judge, the dog world would have lost one of its greatest superintendents. If he decided to run shows, one of the greatest judges that ever stepped into the ring would have been missing. And, if Mortimer had to make the decision, he would have chosen that which was for the best for the game.

Questions for Consideration

1. Is it necessary for one to have been a successful breeder and exhibitor in order to be a successful judge? Elaborate upon your reasons.

2. Lacy maintains that good judging abilities do not necessarily correlate with lifetime involvement in the sport. He also implies that good judges are not born that way but their ability is grounded in assimilative capacity and willingness to learn; that an eye for form and the ability to differentiate the merits in a class of dogs are acquired by practice and study. Do you agree or disagree? Give specific examples which support your opinions.

3. Lacy states that the reason for failure in attempts to educate judges is a lack of individual adaptability. Are dog fanciers as a whole generally resistant to changes in the approval system? Is it possible for the system to advance?

4. What role should education play in the development and approval of dog show judges?

5. In 1925, AKC recognized only 69 breeds. Lacy believed the most serious problem confronting the dog world was that of judges accepting assignments in breeds in which they had limited interest, affiliation or knowledge. Currently the number of recognized breeds has increased over 100 percent. What are the numerical limits of breeds any one person can be expected to know thoroughly and judge well? Should limits be put on the number of breeds for which any judge can be approved?

6. Given Lacy's contention that the ability to judge is a learning process, is it possible that one can know all breeds thoroughly and judge them well? To what percentage of the dog fancy would you ascribe this ability? How many breeds do you believe you could judge, not just competently, but expertly?

7. According to Lacy, in 1925, a significant part of the approval system was based upon in-the-ring tryouts of new judges. Is this a valid method to establish competency? How would you design an ideal judges approval system?

8. Mortimer is hailed as one who did much to advance the progress of dog shows in America principally because of his methodology in judging procedure and strict adherence to the breed standards. How important are these two factors today?

9. Is judging "on the day" a valid method or is it just an excuse for inconsistency?

Benched Shows

"Popular Dogs"
1950

CH. MASTERPIECE *can be seen in the ring at the Mascoutah Kennel Club show in Chicago, 1897. Above, the same dog. Artist, George Ford Morris*

If it were not for the tearing of a leaf from the office calendar the end of the year would likely slip by most people as it does over the new litter of puppies which knows that the year's real change comes with the spring. When we think of a change we usually think of it in terms of progress. Along this line let us stop to analyze the decision of a few clubs to revert to the plan of unbenched shows.

Is an unbenched show a sign of progress? Back in the early days all shows were unbenched, with dogs in boxes or on leads all day or lying at the feet of harassed owners sitting around the exhibiting ring.

Alva Rosenberg, a most highly respected judge and the one selected as the Judge of the Year for both 1947 and 1948 states:

"An unbenched show lacks glamour—it detracts immeasurably from a spectator's viewpoint and takes from a show one of its prime reasons for existence. It is not conducive to bringing new fanciers to the fold and with older kennels dropping out of existence each year we need reinforcements. A dog show is an exhibition where people come to see dogs and I use the word 'see' in the fullest sense.

A birds-eye view of a handful of dogs standing in fixed position is not what the public expects or wants. If they (the public) are ever to really interest themselves in dogs let the dogs be

222

On the Bench

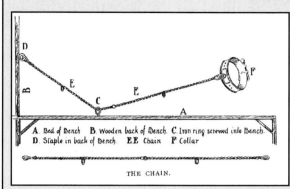

A. Bed of Bench B. Wooden back of Bench C. Iron ring screwed into Bench.
D. Staple in back of Bench. E.E. Chain F Collar

THE CHAIN.

While some may remember benched shows as glamorous events, their problems and virtues were discovered by trial and error. Most early benched shows lasted four days, with superintendents caring for the dogs. At larger British shows and in America, superintendents employed staff managers who hired young boys from the local area to be "runners." Each manager had charge of a set amount of dogs and his runners were responsible for exercising the dogs twice a day, feeding, watering, disinfecting and keeping assigned areas clean. Superintendent Charlie Lincoln had a strict set of rules for his employees and any drunkenness resulted in immediate dismissal.

In the late afternoon, all spectators were required to leave exhibition halls while employees cared for their charges. Unfortunately, accidents were frequent, as "The Stock-keeper" reported in 1892. "During the time that all visitors were asked to step outside the show at Derby on the first day, one of the Dachshund exhibits slipped off its bench and hanged itself. It is about time that show managements gave their attention to the possibility of such fatal accidents, for they have been rather frequent of late. It should be the duty of bench stewards to see the exhibits are tied up with the proper length of chain." Amazingly, it took more than ten years to produce a simple and logical solution. In 1905, Mr. L. Allen Shuter suggested the introduction of a swivel bolt in the bottom of the bench. This allowed all dogs to have adequate chain to turn around but not enough length to jump or fall. His concept was drawn by Mr. Harding Cox and the Kennel Club Committee made the new design mandatory.

Sawdust covered floors can be seen in the picture of the 1897 Mascoutah Kennel Club show. Most early show venues were similar—drafty, dark and dusty. Consequently, colds and sore throats were common exhibitor and spectator afflictions. In the 1890s the theory, for women at least, was that the fashionable décolleté dresses were to blame. But, in "The American Field," a Pittsburgh physician claimed, "The causes of sore throat (at shows) stem from the fact that where many women are gathered together, the clamor of tongues is so great that it is necessary for one to raise one's voice to be heard and get a word in edgeways."

more accessible. Let them have a close-up view—possibly a chance to even touch! The thrill of putting his hands on a champion and sometimes getting a responsive wag of the tail can often convert a casual observer into a real show dog enthusiast. Then they realize that under his skin the show dog is really just like the old farm dog they so fondly recall. Gone is the idea that blue ribbon dogs are automatons which stand or move as their handlers see fit to direct them.

The unbenched show usually proves a disappointment to them—they leave with a feeling that they have been cheated. They see a dog show advertised 'five hundred dogs—one hundred different breeds' never noticing or, if they do, not

knowing what the words 'unbenched show' mean. They have a few hours to spend at a dog show and they feel that in that time they can not only see the breed or breeds they are most interested in but get acquainted with breeds whose names, though fascinating, are quite unknown to them. Chances are that they see none of these breeds unless they happen to be in the judging ring at the time. Result: a resolve not to attend any more dog shows and the loss of a potential dog fancier.

If we must have unbenched shows let us confine them to specialty shows where the attendance as a rule is comprised almost solely of seasoned fanciers. But for all-breed shows, whether large or small, I say let us have benched shows."

223

Feeding the Show

The creation of readily available commercial dog foods in the 19th Century was a direct result of the growing popularity of dog shows. Large packs of hounds and sporting dogs kept by the wealthy had always fared well because they were given regular diets of bread, milk and horse meat. But, most other canines subsisted on whatever scraps were offered. Formal competition soon brought to light the necessity of proper conditioning, necessitating dependable, convenient and healthy dog rations. As most early shows lasted four days, commercial manufacturers quickly realized the advantage of providing their products free to fanciers who would be likely to purchase them in the future.

The first large commercial concern catering specifically to the show animal trade was Spratt's Patent, Limited, founded by James Spratt. Spratt was an electrician, spending most of his early life in Canada, installing and improving lightning rods. After extensive traveling, he finally returned to his homeland and rather late in life, more as a job to keep busy than as a career, he decided to purchase a small manufacturing company and started making commercial dog biscuits, livestock and poultry feed. If timing is everything, Spratt was fortuitous, because his company was in its infancy when 14 year old Charles Cruft was hired in 1866. Cruft had trained as a manufacturer's jeweler but found the work too sedentary. Nevertheless, that training in attention to detail, along with his energy and organizational skills, allowed him to quickly rise to General Manager at Spratt's. Under his skilled watch the company grew to be the largest of its kind in the world. Cruft suggested to Spratt that providing feed and benching services at dog shows would be a wise move for the company, encouraging the dog show clientele to purchase their products. Spratt agreed, and the company was the first to form a Show Department, of which Cruft became the head. In that capacity he visited and personally managed innumerable shows of all kinds throughout the United Kingdom and on the continent. This symbiotic relationship between dog show enthusiasts and the major dog food companies still exists today. Manufacturers are well aware that those who raise quality purebreds demand and are anxious to buy the best available food for their dogs. Fanciers are cognizant of the expense entailed in hosting quality dog shows. Thus, corporate sponsorship of the fancy exists on many levels, from the actual underwriting of various canine events and publications to generous donations for scientific research, scholarships and related endeavors.

After 20 years of service, Cruft made special arrangements with Spratt's to superintend and hold shows on his own under their sponsorship. His first such event was the 1886 Terrier Show at the Royal Aquarium. Acting as manager or show secretary, or both, at many shows promoted by others, Cruft's expertise was so great that he was in constant demand. Events under his management set record breaking entries. Eventually, he decided to stage his own extravaganza. Cruft's dog show quickly became the most successful and largest in the world. Today the show hosts over 20,000 dogs. Of all contemporary canine events, every died-in-the-wool dog fancier considers Crufts, now run by the Kennel Club and no longer with an apostrophe, to be the premier attraction to attend at least once, if not annually.

Spratt's advertisement, 1891
Artist, R. H. Moore

Charles Cruft

The Dog Show Concession

It did not take Spratt's Patent, Ltd. too long to realize dog shows created a captive audience which was not only interested, but had the expendable income to purchase canine livery. As part of their agreement in providing the benching and dog food at shows, Spratt's was always given a prominently placed display booth. Besides their famous biscuits, they soon offered chains, collars, leads and combs. The ancillary market business mushroomed from that point. Clubs soon noticed that by soliciting vendors they not only provided a service to their exhibitors and spectators but also generated more money for their organizations by renting booth space.

In England, vendors were not only a common sight by 1900, but expected to be present in great numbers and variety for a show to be considered a first class event. "The Ladies' Kennel Journal" gave a full report of the wares available at the 1900 Ladies' Kennel Association fixture. Next to Spratt's was the Bermondsey firm selling wicker hampers, shipping boxes and dog houses. Then, Dobson and Sons, displaying fine gold and silver jewelry fashioned in various breeds. Ornate trophies which they had created on commission were also on view, including the Golden Dholpore 500 Guinea Cup. Occupying a prominent position was "The Stock-keeper," with the latest weekly issue of the paper and a large doggy book stall. Among the various kennel supply companies, Jeyes' Sanitary Compound did a brisk trade, in part because their products displayed the Royal Warrant, the best endorsement possible.

While vendors also existed at American shows, those who provided other than essential services were not common until after 1905, when Mrs. Lillian Raymond-Mallock received press attention selling such things as canine motif jewelry, porcelain figurines and fancy collars at the Toy Spaniel Club show. All proceeds were to benefit the club. It was soon discovered that dog show people are not generally collectors but accumulators, willing to buy anything of any quality which has an image of their favorite breed upon it.

Oddly enough, while catering to every canine whim, very few of the earliest shows (and surprisingly, many of the dog shows still held today), provided food service for the people present, including judges. This was a serious concern and constant complaint of exhibitors. No one, especially women, relished the prospect of leaving their dogs unattended on the bench while wandering about a strange town in search of a proper hotel or suitable café. However, any show of real merit not only had food vendors and a separate luncheon for judges and stewards, but always established either a Ladies' Tent or Ladies' Lounge. There, women could escape the constant activity and dog show crowds for a few minutes and be guaranteed respite—while enjoying a civilized cup of tea.

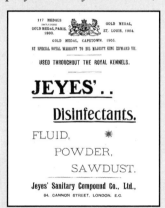
Artist, Marguerite Kirmse
1913

Judge Anton Rost, veteran all-rounder, who is considered an authority on all breeds, replied to our inquiry, "I see no possible advantage in an unbenched show excepting perhaps a monetary one, and here are just a few of the advantages of the benched shows: (1) convenience to the dog himself; (2) convenience for the paid admission guest in locating dogs; (3) convenience for the runners in locating dogs to be judged; (4) appearance of the show; (5) comparative safety of dogs and visitors."

Mr. Rost goes on to describe exhibitors who sit at the ringside with their dogs, something which often results in dog fights or distracts the attention of the dogs being shown. "I can see no possible excuse for an unbenched show unless the building has not sufficient space to hold the benching or if there is no benching available," he concluded.

Louis J. Murr, popular all-rounder, who also has had experience with unbenched shows wrote, "My opinion in regard to benched and unbenched shows is as follows: (1) Unbenched shows are all right if there are less than 200 dogs but suitable shelter for the dogs should be provided in case of bad weather or hot sun; (2) I do not favor unbenched shows indoors regardless of number; (3) I sincerely believe and approve of benched shows at all times; (4) I do not think that the number of rings makes much difference if the ring stewards and assistants are experienced."

An item in connection with the expenses of running a dog show which is seldom thought of is insurance. Since the cost of an insurance premium is based on the hazards involved, and since the hazards of someone getting bitten or of dog fights (one dog may permanently injure another), are greater at an unbenched show, the insurance cost is likely to be more. Recognizing the fact that some clubs stage unbenched shows without any insurance coverage at all, it can easily be seen that the officers or any individual member of a club could be held liable should an accident happen or a dog bite someone. In an unincorporated club any and/or every member can be held responsible should someone have grounds for a law suit.

Questions for Consideration

1. What exactly does the public expect to see when they attend a dog show?
2. Is there any proof that benched shows are more convenient or safer for the dogs, exhibitors and/or spectators?
3. What are the advantages and disadvantages of a benched show? An unbenched show?
4. How do benched shows compare with today's cluster shows in terms of convenience to the dogs, exhibitors and spectators?
5. When this article was written in 1950 there were 321 all breed dog shows held in the United States. That number has now climbed to over 1,500. Do you think this tremendous growth would have been attainable if all clubs were required to have benched shows?
6. Since most people participate in dog clubs on a hobby/volunteer basis should they be required to stage large, expensive benched shows when it is much cheaper both in time and money to have an unbenched show?
7. Which type of show do you prefer—benched or unbenched? Why?
8. Hasn't the market place pretty much determined the viability of the benched show?
9. Are benched showed a relic from a slower paced, bygone era?
10. Would the few remaining benched shows in this country continue to exist without significant financial support from various dog food companies?

The Dog Show as a Judge Sees It

James W. Spring

"Popular Dogs"
1928

Breeding purebred dogs is a sport. The dog show provides the place where the dog which you have bred may be exhibited and be shown to be more perfect or less perfect than a dog bred by one of your competitors. The decision must be made by someone, and in this particular form of sport it is made by a judge, so called, who is believed to be competent to determine the merits of the dogs which come before him.

The selection of a judge rests, in the first instance, with the bench show committee appointed by the club or organization which is giving the show where the dogs are to be exhibited. If the judge is incapable of doing his work well he is not to be blamed. The blame should be placed where it belongs and that is on the committee which appointed him. As soon as he is selected, however, whether he be professional or amateur, gently born or otherwise, rich or poor, he is the judge, and his antecedents and personality should be forgotten. The show giving club owes him a distinct duty, and this, in many instances it does not perform. I do not refer to the specialty club giving a show for one breed only. I have in mind the all breed shows, where many judges are selected and officiate. They come from every walk of life, but they were chosen, it is to be hoped, not because of their social connections, but because of their ability to judge dogs.

The bench show committee spends most of its energy in persuading a judge to consent to give his time and services and then proceeds to forget his existence, unless by chance he fails to appear at the time and place appointed. The place where he is to do his work may be many miles away from his home. It may be a small town or city where he, like any other stranger, is ignorant of the transportation facilities with which the bench show committee is well acquainted. He does not know where the show is to be held, and if the distance from his home is so far that he is obliged to spend a night or so, he is without knowledge of which are the good hotels and which the poor ones in the small town or city where the show is given. Does the bench show committee give him any light on this problem? It does not.

The judge must get to the show in the morning as best he may, spend his morning judging, and then, when the noon intermission arrives, what provision is made for luncheon?

The Ideal Folding Kennel

MARTINDALE PATENT.

as approved by leading Veterinary & Canine Surgeons.

WHEN IN USE.

WHEN NOT IN USE.

When not in use the Kennel can be folded to about ⅓ of its total height, and easily packed in a dress trunk for transit. It is neat, light and durable, and in sickness its sanitary advantages and accessibility to the patient have made it find great favour. **Made in various sizes.** **For Toy Dogs from 10/6.** Prices vary according to size required. Large Folding **HAMPERS** for Dog Shows also supplied.

Write for full particulars to the Sole Makers,

THE SUSSEX BASKET INDUSTRY Ltd.,

Manufacturers of Cane and Wicker Goods,

Worthing. Crawley Down, and Tunbridge Wells.

The first manufactured folding crate — made of wicker
1911

227

Traveling with Dogs

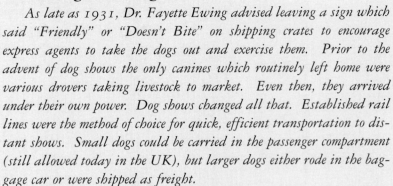

As late as 1931, Dr. Fayette Ewing advised leaving a sign which said "Friendly" or "Doesn't Bite" on shipping crates to encourage express agents to take the dogs out and exercise them. Prior to the advent of dog shows the only canines which routinely left home were various drovers taking livestock to market. Even then, they arrived under their own power. Dog shows changed all that. Established rail lines were the method of choice for quick, efficient transportation to distant shows. Small dogs could be carried in the passenger compartment (still allowed today in the UK), but larger dogs either rode in the baggage car or were shipped as freight.

For many years dogs could travel loose, needing only a strong leather collar with a nameplate and a tie chain. As dog shows became more numerous express companies eventually insisted upon secure shipping crates. In England the material of choice was wicker. Lightweight, cheap and versatile, the canes could be woven into innumerable styles which also allowed for some modicum of ventilation. But, it was impossible to utilize this material in the United States principally because freight handlers here were more commonly referred to as "freight heavers." The wooden "Field and Fancy" crate shown was quite popular because it could withstand this type of abuse. Further, the advertisements claimed that because there was a "full 1/8 inch space" between the slats this crate provided adequate ventilation for all breeds. Yet, it was not uncommon for show dogs to be injured or die during shipping. Considering the hardships the dogs endured in transit it is a wonder any survived at all. Besides train travel, many rode steamers across the Atlantic. Literally thousands of dogs were imported to the United States from Europe and England prior to WWI. Most of these dogs traveled on cargo ships, including bitches in whelp. In 1893, James Mortimer imported from Germany the famous Great Dane, Cesar Hansa. Heavy seas occurred and the ship arrived several days late. When the dog was finally delivered to the show and taken out of his crate it was discovered he had sustained a broken hindleg.

Unless owners or handlers traveled with their dogs they were sent directly to the show secretary or superintendent. Unaccompanied dogs were in the complete care of the show committee who took the responsibility of packing the dogs off to their next destination. Express companies picked up and delivered dogs via horse drawn wagons. Baggage cars were normally not ventilated (let alone air conditioned) and luggage was routinely piled up around the crates. Consequently, many dogs died from heat stoke or suffocation. In Great Britain there were less extremes in temperature and shorter distances to travel than in the USA, but if an unexpected heat wave struck show secretaries could expect disaster. This occurred at the Bulldog Club show in 1891. The show secretary, Mr. William Sprague, reported to "The Stock-keeper" that of the first seven crates he opened, three contained dead dogs. It could only be hoped express agents would feed and water the dogs. Some railroad employees were hesitant to open the canine coffins pictured here and risk attack by an animal desperate to escape. However, such attacks rarely occurred. Show dogs of the last century invariably had sound, stable temperaments. Fear of injury and, in particular, fear of rabies was so great that any display of canine aggression resulted in an immediate death sentence.

Shipping dogs by train correspondingly declined as more people purchased their own automobiles. After WWII the majority of exhibitors actually did travel with their dogs to shows. This increased amount of time spent with one's dog greatly contributed to canines no longer being viewed as valuable livestock, but as important members of the family.

You Are Invited to Judge

John H. Bull

"The American Field"

1893

One of your correspondents a short time back complained that certain gentlemen who promised to judge at the Bexar Field Trials of 1893 failed to show up or even mention their inability to officiate. This was ungentlemanly to say the least, but probably these men were treated as was a Denver sportsman who was requested to act as judge last year, and made all preparations for so doing. This was Mr. Earnest F. Thomas. Mr. Thomas expressed his willingness to officiate, though it was a long and hard trip from Denver to San Antonio (fifty-four hour's ride on the train), and would necessitate at least seven days' absence from business. Not hearing from the Bexar Club regarding transportation, etc., Mr. Thomas wired their Secretary (Mr. Chabot) asking whether they intended sending transportation; and adding, if so, that he (Mr. Thomas) would stand all other expenses, such as hotel, etc. Mr. Chabot replied by mail saying they had secured other judges. This letter was dated two days before the trials, showing conclusively they had expected Mr. Thomas to take seven days from business at an expense of one hundred dollars for the thankless job of judging their trials. Now, is it not customary for associations of this kind to pay judges' expenses? Do you not think the Bexar Field Trial Club acted very discourteously toward Mr. Thomas? In my humble opinion the Bexar Club will never be much until it broadens its views and acts the gentleman.

Frequently none. He finishes his work in the afternoon or evening too late to catch a train to leave for his home. What provision is made for his entertainment while in the small town or city? If he is not personally known to the bench show committee or prominent members of the club no provision is made.

It is a simple thing to remedy all this. I have been judging for a good many years. I have judged at one time or another at most of the shows held in the East. I know many of those who play a prominent part in this dog game of ours, but, nonetheless, I have had my fair share of unpleasant experiences. What the fate must be of a less well-known person who is good enough to give his services to judge I dislike to think. The winter shows are about to begin. If any resolutions are to be made and kept for the New Year I suggest that bench show committees resolve to look after their judges.

A judge may find it lonely even in New York or Boston. It is conceivable that he may not know the good hotels in either of these cities. I make the suggestion for what it may be worth that the show committee appoint some members of its club whose duty it shall be to look after the comfort and entertainment of each of its judges. We are beginning to learn that a show will not function properly unless good stewards are appointed to assist the judges. Why not add to the steward's duties, the one of seeing that his judge is taken care of after the latter reaches the city where the show is to be held? It would contribute to the pleasure of both and make the show more popular. Boston does this, indirectly, it is true, but, nonetheless, it is a fact that no man who judges at Boston is left at loose ends. Other cities can do the same and with profit.

A contrast to the way in which the judges are taken care of in Boston was afforded by a trip that I took not many years ago to a middle New York State show. I arrived in the city close on to

The Good Old Days?

As we now have the ability to cross the country within a few hours it is almost impossible for us to really grasp the inherent dangers of travel in the United States, not so long ago. The following obituary graphically illustrates what were the almost routine risks of travel in the early years of the 20th Century.

California Comment

"The American Field"

1907

Another death of a sterling character in West Coast dogdom shocked the fancy, when Express Messenger Charles F. Charles lost his life in one of the worst train wrecks which has happened to the Northern Flyer in many years. The train, late, was tearing along at a terrific rate over a roadbed softened by heavy rains on the morning of February 3 when several coaches left the rails. The express car telescoped and was thrown with a chair car into the soft mud of a grain field. Immediately after the cars left the rails the mail coach crashed into the rear end of the express and hurled the safe Charles had so often defended against the side of the car, pinning him under its weight against the wall.

One presumes there would be plenty of questions regarding the safety of train travel after reading an article such as this. Railroad ads were common in all dog magazines at the turn of the last century.

It was only two years ago that "Charley" Charles withstood an attack on his car by bandits near Eugene, Oregon. The robbers forced the door and when he refused to come out and began shooting they threw a stick of dynamite with a lighted fuse attached into the car. Charles picked up the bomb and, putting out the fuse, threw it out of the door. The highwaymen desisted and fled. Following the attempted robbery of his car in 1901, the Wells-Fargo Company gave Charles an appropriately inscribed gold medal in token of his valor and also presented him with $1,000 as a reward against the bandits on this occasion. Nine years before this episode, at Ceres, in Stanislaus County, Charles and another messenger stood off what was believed to have been the notorious Evans-Sontag gang. He was given a gold watch by the company for his faithful service at this time and was sent to Arizona as shotgun messenger to protect the company's interests in the mining districts, where the Grant Wheeler Gang was then operating.

He was the type of messenger not met as often as sportsmen would wish, and dogs traveling in care of Charley Charles received all the spare time he had on his hands. He knew all the bench show and field trial handlers, and whenever any of the boys had a dog to ship they tried to get it off on Charley Charles' run, knowing it would receive the same attention they could themselves bestow. He used to write on the crates of dogs belonging to his friends, "I had him out every chance I got," and anyone thus learning his pet came through with Charley Charles had no further misgivings about the dog's condition.

Charles had been in six wrecks and four holdups and was probably the best known and most popular messenger in Wells-Fargo service on the coast. He was a crack shot on quails and ducks and was devoted to Setters, Cockers and Fox Terriers, which he had exhibited at several shows. A man of great personal magnetism, frank, cordial and fearless, Charley Charles had a host of friends in the dog world and their sympathy goes out to his wife, daughter and sisters in this hour of their terrible loss.

The Realm of the Dog

F. Freeman Lloyd
"The American Field"
1907

Walter B. Johnson of New York, being interviewed this week in reference to the dogs he saw while abroad in England and Ireland, said he was particularly struck with the large number of Scottish Terriers, which now appear to be the fashionable terrier companion in London, so far as his observations went. As he was in the metropolis at the height of the season, his remarks are worthy of note. It is true there were many Poms to be seen, but principally in carriages. Scottish Terriers, to use his words, "were all over the place"—on the pavements, in the parks and chained up outside the fashionable West End stores, under the charge of commissionaires.

But perhaps the greatest sight of all for anyone who takes even an ordinary interest in dogs, was a return to London of King Edward VII and his consort from a visit to the country. Crowds lined the route, the royal personages being cheered. After the King and Queen came the gentlemen and ladies in waiting, the immediate rear of his turnout being brought up by a private omnibus full of dogs, under the charge of two Buckingham Palace kennel maids. There were Fox Terriers, Irish Terriers, Scottish Terriers and Japanese Spaniels. As all the dogs were standing up on the seats looking out of the windows, and apparently interested in the now more than jovial multitude, the superintendent of the coming Bryn Mawr Kennel Club show remarked that he had never seen a more comical sight in his life. Where the King and Queen go, their dogs also go.

midnight before the first day of the show. I had the forethought to write to a hotel to obtain a reservation for a room and bath. No one met me at the station. No one met me at the hotel. The reservation had not been made, and there was no room in any hotel that night—at least, so I was told. I called up the superintendent of the show on the telephone and found out that was the least of his troubles. I obtained a room. I judged the show. I have crossed that city off my books.

I have in mind another show in western Massachusetts. I was met at the station, given a delightful room in a good hotel, had breakfast and a car took me to the show grounds, which were some distance from the city. I started work and from that time on I was left to my own resources. No provision for luncheon had been made for the judges. By the time I had finished my morning classes, the food had given out.

Fortunately, I met a friend who had a motor car and we went back to town and lunched at the hotel. In the afternoon I went on with my remaining classes, knowing that if I could finish by a given time I could get a train back to Boston that evening. If I missed that train there was not a chance of returning and this meant another night away from home and another day away from business. I tried to find someone on the bench show committee to get transportation back to town, but the committee was busy. They had gotten me to the show and their dogs were judged. Taxis were unheard of in that particular neck of the woods. I got back to town and just managed to catch the train. Perhaps you think that I will judge at that show again—not if I am in my right mind. I can go on in this strain for pages and every other man who has judged in the last twenty years can relate similar experiences.

Poisoned

After being named best champion bitch at the Mascoutah KC show in 1892, Ch. Irene and another Great Dane owned by Mr. Helmerle, Roland, arrived at their next destination dead. Both were the victims of poisoning, en route. Larger breeds were most likely to be injured or die during shipping because many express agents were terrified of them. Shipping fees were paid in advance and railroads transported dogs entirely at the owner's risk. Even if neglect or maliciousness could be proven, there was little recourse because dogs had no monetary value in the eyes of the law. However, dog shows significantly increased public awareness of purebred dogs as valuable personal property. By the end of the 19th Century numerous court decisions confirmed this concept.

Great Dane, CH. IRENE
Owner, Carl Helmerle
Artist, G. Muss-Arnolt, 1892

I have finished my little sermon and hope that it may make an impression on some bench show committees for the coming year. If it does, a start will be made towards keeping the sport we all like from going under. It means work for the bench show committee, it means thought and it may cost something in money, but it will repay far more than it costs.

Questions for Consideration

1. The author states that show committees are ultimately responsible for bad judging because they select those who officiate. Does this seem to be a reasonable statement? Why or why not?

2. What do you believe are the prime motivating factors in selecting judging panels for dog shows? What do you think these criteria should be? How would you structure an "ideal" judging panel?

3. Since this article was written, travel conditions in the United States have improved tremendously and most show committees routinely appoint a hospitality chairperson. Whose responsibility is it to entertain judges? What should judges expect in the way of provisions, entertainment and remuneration? What should clubs be expected to do in terms of providing for the needs (and demands) of their judges?

4. Are there any shows at which you have adjudicated which have not entertained or taken care of your needs as you might have anticipated? If so, how did you handle the situation so that the club could make improvements? Would you officiate for these clubs in the future? Would you inform other judges of your problems with these particular clubs?

5. If you have served on any show committees, are there any judges whom you felt were excessively demanding or unreasonable? If so, how did you handle the situation so that peace could be attained? Are there any judges, whom because of their uncouth or unco-operative behavior you would choose never to invite again? Would you inform other clubs of your problems with these particular judges?

6. How much traveling should dogs be subjected to in their owners' quests for achieving honors on various rating systems? Should there be limitations on the amount of shows in which dogs can be campaigned once they have attained their championships?

Prize Money vs. Ribbons

"Field and Fancy"
1906

We see that some of our exhibitors have had their knives into the ribbon shows recently on several occasions. But do they stop to consider, when they say we must have money for owners to win, where the money is to come from or who is to put it up? It is easy to say that "they" must put it up, but so many amateur show promoters have been bitten that the "they" is distinctly scarce. We can obtain money from novices and enthusiasts in new places just so many times, and then the game is up. Conditions are not the same here as they are in the British Isles, where so much greater a proportion of the public is interested in dogs, and where, before a show comes off in a district the hat can be passed around to the county squire, the country gentleman and the hotel keeper and be filled with sovereigns enough to start a show fund. There, the prize money is often subscribed before the show opens. But in America some are very much interested in dogs, while the great majority are not, and do not care and would look upon the hat being passed around for a subscription to a dog show in their city as a great imposition. So, consequently, our world is a world within itself in America and has to be supported by the doggy people themselves, and we cannot see the logic that demands that one section of the dog world should feed the other, or

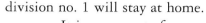

division no. 1 will stay at home.

It is some sort of recognition that is required just now of the fact that we must help ourselves and each other at the same time and be ready to help the whole, that will save dog showing and dog shows from extinction. If the wealthy owners cannot afford to go to shows unless they can win the money subscribed by men much poorer than themselves, why, then, the poorer of the fraternity and those of moderate means had better divide the responsibility between them and hold dog shows for sport.

It is very easy to say we must have money shows; but will someone devise some good and feasible way of getting this money so that no one in the fraternity shall lose by it? We are quite aware of the hardships of shows without prize money, but we are also aware that most of the suckers that were born to put up money for others to win have come, lived, died and been buried. Does it ever occur to many that in most of our large cities there have been shows running at a loss, the money for which has been largely subscribed by willing amateurs and young men hardly out of their teens? And this money has been lost, time and again, without much squealing; and as often as not an exhibitor can be seen doing

Ribbon Shows

1890 Prize Card for the Bulldog Club, Inc.
Artist, R. H. Moore

The challenge method of awarding championships requires the winner in each sex in every breed be designated first in Challenge Class, regardless of whether or not any entrant has already attained its championship. Today, this system is almost universally recognized as the best method to insure quality when awarding the coveted title of "champion." (Major exceptions are the Canadian Kennel Club and the American Kennel Club). The challenge system was particularly fair to large and small shows alike, as championships were based on quality, not quantity of competition. Further, these awards were not automatic. Judges were expected to withhold any awards for lack of merit. Later, as shows increased in Great Britain, it became necessary to designate a limited amount of certificates available for each breed within a calendar year to maintain a high level of quality in those dogs adjudicated champions.

From its inception, the AKC roughly followed the English system for awarding championships, requiring three first prize wins in the Open Class, then in 1898, Winners Class. In 1884, the year AKC was founded, 11 all breed shows were held. By 1900, that number had dramatically increased to 24, along with 3 independent specialty shows. Except for the AKC's arcane club of clubs structure, there was no particular reason at that time to change the system. Unfortunately, the few large clubs which controlled the organization realized that if dog shows continued to increase there would soon be no need for the average exhibitor to attend their events. Consequently, a point system was instituted for all shows, based upon total entries. Thus, a show with 250 entries could award one point and the maximum number of five was given at shows with 1,000 or more dogs. Ten points were needed for champion status, with a three-point win required. This proposal was represented to the fancy as good for the sport. It was claimed a championship would be unattainable within a reasonable time unless a dog won against breed competition, but this was not true. Previously, unless there was a minimum entry of five in any particular breed no awards were recorded. This new system not only awarded points to all designated "Winners," regardless of breed entries, but created an extraordinary hardship for new clubs in remote areas. Most shows lasted four days and the expense to host one was significant. Because an exhibitor's outlay of time and money was the same whether one point or five, many by-passed the smaller shows. As a result, these clubs started offering colorful rosettes and streamer ribbons instead of prize money so they could afford to hold their one and two point shows.

The wealthy clubs initially thought these ribbon shows a rustic laughingstock and were amazed anyone would waste their time where no money or valuable trophies were awarded. Surprisingly, it was discovered most exhibitors liked these colorful mementos and were actually showing their dogs for sport, pleasure and as a social event. Dog shows continued to increase in number and by 1904 there were 37 all breed shows and 7 independent specialties. Entries also dramatically increased. Again, the larger clubs attempted to consolidate power by proposing points be based on the amount of prize money offered—an astounding $2,000 being necessary for a one point show. Had it passed, the death knell would have sounded for many kennel clubs. As a result, ribbon shows were here to stay, becoming mandatory awards at all AKC events. In response to a request from superintendent, George Foley, standardized ribbon colors and the 2"x 8" size were established in 1916.

The Age of Trophies

These trophies offered by the Mastiff Club of America represent typical Victorian work—heavy and ornate with exquisitely chased Mastiff relief images.

1893

When shows were held in taverns or sitting rooms, determining the "best" dogs was a pleasant way to spend an evening with friends. However, traveling to a neighbor's home or the town pub entailed a lot less effort than traversing the countryside with one's dog. If formal canine exhibitions were going to attract quality competition from great distances it was imperative that worthwhile and valuable prizes be offered. Thus, at the very first show for Pointers and Setters in Newcastle-on-Tyne, expensive guns were offered to the top winners. While firearms were appropriate prizes for hunting dogs, the dog show quickly expanded to include all breeds. Thus, more suitable commemorative awards were needed and the presentation trophy became the prize of choice (next to money).

Initially, many of these ornate silver or gold trophies were offered outright. Yet, sportsmanship as a conceptual ideal quickly fell by the wayside with the realization that dog shows were open to all. With an honest judge in the ring, a complete outsider had as much chance of winning the top prize as those who had donated it. As a direct result, many valuable trophies began to appear with complex restrictions. Dozens of extravagant and expensive trophies would be listed in premium lists to attract competition, only for entrants to discover these prizes were only available to club members. Others required numerous wins over several years before being claimed. Still, it was difficult to leave a show empty handed as clubs generally accepted any trophy offered with any requirements needed to win them. These awards came to be known as "specials" and were offered apart from the regular classes or championships. Dogs were not required to compete in the regular classes and could be entered "for specials only" if their owners desired. Awards for such things as the "best brindle Great Dane," or "best Spaniel exhibited by a Lady," or "best Fox Terrier owned by a club member, said dog never having won a first prize in any competition, save puppy classes," soon clogged the prize lists until adjudicating "specials" routinely took longer than the regular classes. In fact, at the 1897 Ladies' Kennel Association Show, Charles Lane needed an extra day to determine all the various prize winners for Pugs, necessitating contestants be present in the ring over three days.

Incredibly, while it was originally thought an absolute necessity to offer expensive prizes, once the concept of championships became established it was discovered that most true breeders considered the Winners award or Challenge Certificate the most valuable commodity, gladly competing for those honors, regardless of any other inducements. This fact, along with a decline in master silversmiths, two World Wars, the Depression and a dramatic increase in the price of silver, ended most superfluous awards. Overdone Victorian silver gave way to the less ornate, then silverplate, and finally, dog shows endured an incredibly long period when plastic winged victories reigned supreme. A few specialty clubs still display original hardware at their national shows, despite the ever increasing financial burden of maintaining museum quality pieces. As a result, historic awards are characterized by their scarcity and the committed organizations which have diligently preserved these truly special links to the past.

lots of kicking about getting the other man's money, or not getting it, and does not seem to care to take his share of the risk of a show.

Before we start to abuse the bridge that is helping out dull times and is carrying us over the river, i.e., the ribbon show, let us remember that without these ribbon shows the dog fancy may soon die out altogether in America, and that it is only kept alive in a great measure by volunteer labor and by the generous donations of a few willing amateurs in the different cities that we visit on the circuit. Before we condemn ribbon shows and say we must have money, let us, for decency's sake, stop and consider whose pocket it is we want to clean out. It is because some of us have not tried to get up shows that we have not stopped to consider whose money it is we want to win.

The Ladies' Kennel Association (USA) put up many thousands of good dollars in prize money, and lost it without a kick before they went in for ribbon shows; and it is doubtful if with the ribbon show they came out even. Is it polite to tell these ladies, who have done so much for our dog show world, that we will not attend their shows or exhibit unless we can go on sapping their pockets? Politeness and proper feeling should keep us quiet and help us to see the rights of the thing.

Buildings suitable for holding shows can be obtained in England for sometimes a fifth of the cost of a building in America, or sometimes for nothing. Judges in America demand more, for distances are greater and they have to be away from home so much longer; traveling expenses are much higher, and all things connected with shows, including benching, labor, etc., are so much higher here than in the British Isles that no comparison can be made. Even a ribbon show with us costs a lot of money, labor and time to get up. The money shows are on the wane in many places with the ribbon shows filling the gap and saving dog showing from ultimate extinction. We say that it is better not to burn the bridge that carries us over the river.

Questions for Consideration

1. What do you think is the most important consideration for those entering dog shows—the prizes, whether ribbons or money, the competition, the judge or other factors?

2. Are dog shows as they are now structured a sport, or are expensive trophies, awards and prize money necessary to induce competition? Do you think most experienced exhibitors would still attend shows if no prizes were offered other than championship points? Would novices continue to attend?

3. How would you design the perfect system of awarding championships?

4. Would you still exhibit if there were no Group or Best in Show competition and all judging ended at the breed level? Why or why not?

5. Does Group or Best in Show judging contribute to individual breed advancement?

6. Do you regularly donate trophies and prize money to various specialty and kennel clubs?

7. Who should be responsible for providing and paying for trophies and awards at shows?

8. Would shows have more appeal to the public if large amounts of prize money were regularly offered to the top winners?

9. The writer of the article claims that a greater percentage of the population in Great Britain is more interested in dogs and dog shows than in America. Do you agree or disagree?

10. To generate more revenue, the AKC continues to approve more and more events such as back-to-back shows. Currently, all breed and specialty shows combined total over 3,000 per year. What is the saturation point for numbers of shows before they adversely compete with each other or the quality of champions radically declines?

People and Dogs

Selected News Items

1890-1923

The First Woman Veterinary Surgeon

We desire to congratulate Miss Aleen Cust on the proud distinction of being the first lady enrolled as a Member of the Royal College of Veterinary Surgeons. Miss Cust has been a Member of the Ladies' Branch of the Kennel Club since 1900, and decided to take up veterinary work, to which end she passed through the full curriculum of four years work at the Edinburgh Veterinary College, and was greatly disappointed when the College declined, on the grounds of sex, to grant the diploma. Miss Cust, however, determined to practice in the West of Ireland, where she was also, for ten years, Veterinary Inspector under the Galway County Council and the Department of Agriculture in Ireland. During the War she was appointed by the War Office to a responsible position in the Bacteriological Laboratory of a Veterinary Hospital. The passing of the Sex Disqualification (Removal) Act has now settled the question, and on December 20th, 1922, Miss Cust was duly admitted MRCVS, on which honour we again beg to offer sincere congratulations.

The Kennel Gazette
1923

Miss Aleen Cust and her Chow Chow, SUNFLOWER
1901

Miss Alger Wins Automobile Race

Demonstrating her superb management of automobiles, Miss Lucile Alger, who owns the Red Brook Kennels, at Great Neck, Long Island, beat Mr. George Edward Kent, of Roslyn, in a most exciting race there.

Miss Alger drove an eight horsepower Renault, and, although accompanied by a chauffeur, managed the car herself. The course was twelve miles in length, extending from Great Neck to Roslyn. The start was made at two o'clock in the afternoon from the Great Neck League, and the course was covered in just twenty-four minutes.

In the first three miles of the course Mr. Kent, who also drove a Renault, led by several lengths. Miss Alger cried to the chauffeur to, "Give her her head!" and gripping the steering rod, bent over her machine and sent it whizzing past her opponent. She maintained her lead to the finish, and arrived a winner by two minutes.

Miss Alger, who is the daughter of a wealthy retired English army officer, occupies an elegant summer residence on the shore front with Miss Marian M. Grace, daughter of the late Mayor Grace. Her entries of Poodles have always won first prizes at the dog shows.

Field and Fancy
1904

The Death of Miss Anna A. Marks

It is with the keenest sorrow and deep regret that we have to announce the death on

December 14 of Miss Anna A. Marks, at South Beach, Connecticut. Never has there been a more enthusiastic sportswoman, a better judge of her well loved St. Bernards and a truer friend than Miss Marks. Her death is a sad loss to the dog world and to all those who knew this fine woman.

Miss Marks was born at Willowmere, her father's beautiful estate on South Beach, and from early childhood she showed a marked fondness for

Willowmere St. Bernards
Owner, Miss Anna A. Marks
1905

all animals. When she grew up she started in a small way what has become under her supervision the great Willowmere Farm and Kennels. Here on this beautiful place she raised and bred some of the best known St. Bernards in America. It is unnecessary to go into detail of all the winnings that the Willowmere Kennels have done. Some time ago it was unjustly printed by a rival of Miss Marks that she only won with the dogs that had a reputation before she owned them. This was a libel pure and simple, and to quote from a letter which the writer received from Miss Marks only a few weeks ago, she said:

"It is a queer thing that the great(?) sires which I have bought for my stud have failed as sires. I have not bred one good dog from any of them. All of my promising youngsters and all of my old or young champions were home bred and purely of the Willowmere strain."

This is absolutely true. She only won

with those of her own breeding.

Miss Marks really loved her dogs and horses (she also had a large stable), and it was, indeed, a pleasure to visit this remarkable woman and see how clearly she understood and how skillfully she managed this enormous establishment. She did much for the breed of St. Bernards in America and was the largest exhibitor at all the big shows in the west. Miss Marks was always of a cheerful disposition and a good loser.

A "nervous breakdown" was given as the cause of her death, but those who knew the true story know this to be only partially the cause. She had a big heart, and financial reverses came after the death of her father. Then, following this sad event, although having been left an equal share of his vast wealth, came litigation and severe opposition from her family, who tried in every way to compel her to cease breeding and showing "her dear friends," as she always styled her dogs. The odds were against her. The strain was too much, and continual worry finally laid to rest the noble type of a true American Sportswoman.

Field and Fancy
1906

George Jarvis Kills Himself

Mr. George Jarvis, of New York City, committed suicide last Thursday by shooting himself in his home at 1015 Washington Avenue. Mr. Jarvis, who was a retired member of the Fire Department and most active in Republican politics, was for many years a noted breeder and exhibitor of Pointers. Probably the most famous dog owned by this old-time fancier was the great Ch. Lad of Kent, a dog that has left a name that will always be noted in the annals of his race, for he was invincible, and won right and left all over the country. Since he exhibited this dog, Mr. Jarvis has owned several flyers, and only at the last New York show he won third in the Puppy class with Chappie of Kent, a most promising youngster, that has the honor of being the last dog ever led into the ring by his now lamented master.

During the recent hot spell that has oppressed this city Mr. Jarvis had continually complained of the heat, and it is thought that the weather, combined with a recent illness, made him despondent and led to the sad act, which robbed the fancy of a valuable member. The night before he killed himself he slept on the front stoop of his house, hoping to escape the heat. At breakfast time his wife called him, and as he passed through the house he killed himself. His death will shock the fancy, and the sympathizers with his widow will be legion.

Field and Fancy
1906

Helen Keller

Readers of *The Stock-Keeper* have from time to time gleaned intelligence of the wonderful child Helen Keller, who, though blind, deaf and dumb, can both read and write, and so hold communion with her many friends. The little girl's love of dogs has been her special password to the affections of doggy men here and elsewhere. It was recently related in these columns that Helen's own favourite dog had been killed, and expression was given to the feeling of sympathy excited by such sad news, by an offer to purchase another Mastiff to console the bereaved little maiden. Before the offer could be accepted, kind-hearted Mr. Wade (editor of *Forest and Stream*), who, in spite of his belligerent quill, has a soft place under his waistcoat, had sent a four footed envoy of compassion, which now wears Lioness's collar. The English gift was forestalled, but the gratitude of its intended recipient is no less fervid, as is shown in the letter which I enclose, and which I venture to think is so graceful in feeling and expression as to excuse my offering it for publication.

Institution for the Blind
South Boston, Mass., March 20, 1891

My dear friend Mr. Krehl—I have just heard, through Mr. Wade, of your kind offer to buy me a gentle dog, and I want to thank you for the kind

Pointer, Ch. Lad of Kent
Owner, George Jarvis
Artist, G. Muss-Arnolt
This top winning show dog was one of
Muss-Arnolt's favorite subjects, having been sired
by his own dog, Ch. Bracket
1893

thought. It makes me very happy indeed to know that I have such dear friends in other lands. It makes me think that all people are good and loving. I have read that the English and Americans are cousins, but I am sure it would be much truer to say that we are brothers and sisters. Many friends have told me about your great and magnificent city, and I have read a great deal that wise Englishmen have written. I have begun to read "Enoch Arden," and I know several of the great poet's poems by heart. I am eager to cross the ocean, for I want to see my English friends and their good and wise Queen. Once the Earl of Meath came to see me, and he told me that the Queen was much beloved by her people, because of her gentleness and wisdom. Some day you will be surprised to see a little strange girl coming into your office, but when you know it is the little girl who loves dogs and all other animals, you will laugh, and I hope you will give her a kiss, just as Mr. Wade does. He has another dog for me, and he thinks she will be as brave and faithful as my beautiful Lioness. And now I want to tell you what the dog lovers in America are going to do. They are going to send me some money for a poor little deaf and dumb and blind child. His name is Tommy, and he is five years old. His parents are too poor to pay to have the little fellow sent to school; so, instead of giving me a dog, the gentlemen are going to help make Tommy's life as bright and joyous as mine. Is it not a beautiful plan? Education will bring light and music into Tommy's soul, and then he cannot help being happy.

From your loving little friend,
Helen Keller

I feel that as the destination of any donations would not now be in a purely doggy direction, *The Stock-Keeper* would hardly be consistent in inviting the same, but there can be no reason against my offering personally to take charge of subscriptions, however small, which kind-hearted and gentle readers of the paper may be prompted to send, as an outward and visible sign of their interest in this child, to whom dogs are even more dear than to us, who can see their beauties, hear their voices, and tell them our thoughts and wishes.

> *Helen Keller's love of dogs continued throughout her life. She introduced the Akita to the United States, receiving one as a gift after a visit to Japan. That puppy died from distemper but a littermate, Kenzan-Go, shown here, was sent as a replacement in 1939.*

Your obedient servant,
George R. Krehl
1, Hanover Street, London, W.

P.S.—I have sent contributions from two friends and my own, for Helen Keller's "Beautiful Plan" and will forward others as received to *Forest and Stream* (U.S.A.) where they will be acknowledged.
The Stock-keeper
1891

Sango—The Kentish Fire Hero
Although the Beagles and Bloodhounds formed the leading features of the Brighton Dog Show in August last, Mrs. Wells' black Field Spaniel "Sango" excited considerable attention. This dog has formed a show in himself at various canine exhibitions, and is now "on view," with his progeny, at the Brighton Aquarium.

Sango's sire died in battle whilst accompanying his master, Lieut. Paget, in one of our African wars, and his grandsire was the celebrated prize winner Dan. His title of the "Kentish Fire Hero" arises from the following episode, which we take from a country paper:

"What might have been a disastrous fire was averted through the remarkable sagacity of a faithful spaniel dog. It appears that Mrs. Wells retired to rest, extinguishing the gas in the kitchen, and leaving a small jet burning at the foot of the stairs—there were no other lights in the house. About eleven o'clock, Mrs. Wells was awakened by the violent scratching of the dog at her bedroom door; she scolded the animal and told it to lie down; the dog, however, continued to howl piteously. Mrs. Wells, feeling that something unusual had occurred, stretched out her arm to reach the handle of the door, when the dog bounced into her room, frantically whining, seized hold of her, and dragged her from her bed on to the landing leading to the kitchen stairs, when he ran downstairs and then returned at a rapid rate several times. Finding Mrs. Wells did not go downstairs, the dog repeated his dragging, and jumping on her shoulders forced her forward down the stairs, when he sprang forward with his feet and pushed open the kitchen door. Mrs. Wells then found the kitchen full of smoke and flames. Finding the fire had been caused by a melted gas-pipe, she turned off the gas, and with great presence of mind, without waiting a moment, covered the flames with wool mats and the like, and did not relax her energy until the conflagration was extinguished. Mrs. Wells then examined the room and found that the gas pipe had melted along the ceiling leading to a hole through a cupboard and close to her bed, which, in a few moments, would have been ignited. It was through this hole the escaped gas had entered, and the smoke, which had nearly suffocated Mrs. Wells; and without a doubt, but for the timely warning of her faithful guard (especially as Mrs. Wells was quite alone), she would have perished in the fire. The value of this timely action on the part of the dog cannot be overestimated, for the water that supplied the town had been turned off at twelve noon during the day, and therefore the supply was limited; the house, also, is in the centre of a terrace. The agent investigated the fact, and sent his report to the insurance office interested. This office showed its appreciation of the dog's sagacity by affixing the official stamp to a magnificent gift of a collar, with the Company's own inscription. A subscription for a belt and harness from Sango's admirers was headed by a handsome donation from Her Royal Highness the Princess Leiningen."

Black Field Spaniel, SANGO
Owner, Mrs. Wells
1890

Sango's diploma was exhibited at the recent Great Dog Show at the Crystal Palace. Sango is a member of the Royal Humane Society and the Society for the Prevention of Cruelty to Animals, and like some of Mr. T. D. Dutton's St. Bernards, has made collections for various charitable purposes.

The Dog Owner's Annual
1890

Questions for Consideration

1. Are dog show people the only ones with whom you routinely associate?

2. Do you know any details of the lives of those whom you regularly see at dog shows—their vocations, accomplishments or families? Do you have any interest or concern about their personal problems?

3. Do you view dog show people as acquaintances, friends or competitors?

4. If your toughest competitor died tomorrow would you consider it a loss to the breed and the sport, or would you be glad to have an opening for the alpha position in the pack?

5. Do you enjoy the people you meet at dog shows?

6. Do you have any other interests besides dogs?

7. Does your family have any interest in your dog show hobby (or profession)? Would they prefer you didn't own any (so many) dogs?

8. What would happen to your dogs if you were to die tomorrow?

9. Would your family members have any interest in preserving photographs, trophies, books or other canine historical items you have collected over the years? Would they simply dispose of them as valueless?

10. Why do you keep and show dogs? If there were no longer any dog shows would you continue to keep dogs?

11. Can you give any reasonable explanation for canine behavior which we label heroic?

Fashions in Dogs

"Field and Fancy"
1904

It is the ever changing fashion in non-sporting dogs that possibly makes the work of the breeder much more difficult than it otherwise would be. The Greyhound lives and improves and greater numbers are bred every year from the British Isles to California, because of the sport they afford, and their market value is increasing instead of diminishing. The same may be said of Pointers, Setters and Foxhounds. Spaniels are one of the handiest of the dog tribe to the European shooter, but do not find so much to do here, yet they are raised in large numbers and find ready sale. The Beagle is another dog that is continually on the increase and will continue to increase, for he is one that can give us a great deal of sport, and yet, is easily kept and is kind and gentle. But it is the purely fancy dog that has his ups and downs and the fact that he is a purely fancy dog, perhaps, leads to his deterioration in some cases. For, not being used for sport, he does not lead the rugged life that the dog by nature was intended for, and consequently, is in danger of running downhill as to strength of constitution and so loses many old admirers. Great families of peculiar excellence spring up in certain breeds and carry all before them, but the blood runs out at last, and then the breed suffers,

A fashionable Manchester Terrier on the bench at the Birmingham show, 1877. Most show venues were cold, dark and damp. Confined to their benches, many breeds needed jackets to keep warm. Thus, the public impression of all show dogs as spoiled, pampered pets was born.

for other less fortunate strains have been starved out by the overwhelming distinction gained by the big kennel or family aforesaid. The small breeder and the small owner, who keeps and breeds his or her dogs for the pure love of the thing is probably the most potent factor in keeping alive what, at the time, are the unpopular breeds.

Why certain breeds of dogs enjoy greater popularity at one time than at another is hard to fathom, and the rise and fall of breeds is hard to gauge. A breed goes down for a time, and then it is suddenly remarked by those looking on that this breed is coming up again, and the why and the wherefore is not always so apparent. Small things turn the scale and the advent of one or two enthusiastic fanciers into the ranks of a certain breed seems to work like magic.

Artists have been known to bring dogs before the public through the means of a celebrated picture or by a series of these. It is probable that Sir Walter Scott did as much for the dog with his pen as any other writer, and the Dandie Dinmont and the Scotch Deerhound owe him a great deal; and, in fact, it may be said that he practically made the Dandie Dinmont a fancy dog. We may call John Leech one of the fathers of the Skye Terrier. Vandyke handed

242

down to us some of the Spaniels of his period. Briton Riviere gave us dogs of the correct types and his Collies were the best seen up to that time and created quite a sensation. Du Maurier made good use of the big St. Bernard and give us good specimens of the breed. Hogarth painted dogs of different varieties and helped the early history of dogs. Landseer helped the Deerhound and the Collie, though Landseer's pictures are not valued as highly now as they were twenty-five years ago, and his types of dogs were not quite as accurate from our point of view as those of some other artists. Still, Landseer did a great deal for the dog in his day and for sport in general. The black and white New-foundland bears the name of Landseer to this day though the breed seems to be running out. But, as it was clearly a manu-factured one, the manufacture should be possible again; in fact, quite as possible as the resuscita-tion of the Irish Wolfhound.

In America we seem to lack the enterprise of the English fanciers in tak-ing up new breeds. Is it because we lack poets or artists to bring them forward, or is it a curious phase of our kennel history that the most promi-nent breeds today in America are the old breeds or breeds that have been in the fancy for a long period? There should be a big field in this coun-try for bringing out such distinctive and typical breeds as the Chows, the Pekingese, the Schip-perkes, Skyes, Dandie Dinmonts, Sheepdogs, Basset Hounds, and the poor old Mastiff, who can now only muster up, as a rule, an entry of one. Of the many foreign breeds that are possible and that obtain big entries in Great Britain we hardly ever touch, and even there, the importation of new breeds has not yet reached the climax, but has been stopped by the quarantine laws. There are pure breeds scattered about the earth today or at least families of dogs of distinctive outline and characteristics, that have only occasionally found their way to British dog shows, but have never been seen at all in American shows. When a breed is on the upgrade, we throw all our energies into making that the breed of the day and it is a case of, "To him that hath more shall be given," and the favorite for the time being gets it all. We do little to broaden the dog fancy and to make exhibitions of dogs really interesting to the public, and then wonder why the public does not care to pay one dollar to see the same old thing every time.

The public likes change and sensation, perhaps more so today than ever before, and to this may be attributed, perhaps, the fact that a breed will become the fashion for a time and run away with all the cash. But is it to the health of the fancy or to the credit of those within the fold that we, instead of steadying the turn of the wheel, also help to push this along and kick the breeds on the downgrade still further down the hill? Our present day energies are concen-trated upon running breeds to extremes and our thoughts are concentrated when getting up a dog show upon seeing how many entries we can get from Tom, of a certain breed, and how many we can get from Harry, of the same breed most probably. But, when a member of the committee suggests that it would be a good idea to have some classes for the more rare varieties or the more or less unpopular dogs the reply is made that this class will only draw a "few" entries. Our club officers are forgetting the public who are expected to pay entrance money at the gate in order to make the show "pay" and the committee, in the first instance, has economized upon the very thing that the public wants to see —the rare varieties.

Our dog world is very small for such a big country, and we are like a dog making his bed in the straw for the night; we turn round and round in the same spot till we have made a comfortable place to sleep, and then we lie in that one spot and wonder that the public gets tired of seeing us

> "*We do little to broaden the dog fancy and to make exhibitions of dogs really interesting to the public, and then wonder why the public does not care to pay one dollar to see the same old thing every time.*"

Fashioning a Breed

*Irish Terrier, Ch. Brickbat
Owner, E. A. Wiener
Artist, R. H. Moore, 1889*

The idea of recording each individual breed's history developed concurrently with the concept of officially recognizing as unique the various canine forms. But, according to Darwin, most breeds lacked an exact history because they developed as regional creations. Such was the case of the Irish Terrier. The native red or wheaten-colored terriers of Ireland had been part of the landscape for centuries. It is generally believed they descended from the same stock as the Irish Wolfhound, being similar in outline, overall proportion, coat and color. Before the advent of dog shows, 60 pound Irish Terriers were not uncommon, lending plausibility to this theory. Certainly, the unflagging courage necessary to hunt wolves exists in Irish Terriers as, pound for pound, they are universally acclaimed as the most ferocious vermin killers extant.

Although a scale of points had been drawn up in 1870, Irish Terriers were exhibited for over 20 years without the benefit of a written standard. Thus, judges were at liberty to put up dogs which they "liked" until the breed no longer resembled the original terriers older fanciers remembered. By 1879, Irish Terriers had been further decimated by extensive cross-breeding with Scottish Terriers. George Krehl had a reputation for promoting and advancing rare breeds and was shocked at these changes. "To call the Irish Terriers of today miniature Wolfhounds would be sarcastic; the majority of them are sour-faced, yellow-eyed, black muzzled, chumpy-headed, and thickly built, and utterly unlike anything else so ugly as themselves. Of course, this is only our own simple and inexperienced opinion, which judges and connoisseurs of the breed are at liberty to dismiss with contempt. They may prefer the thick-legged clodhoppers; we still linger on the memory of the graceful and symmetrical Terriers; rather light in build, and with only proportionate bone to carry their weight." Krehl took up the banner for the Irish Terrier, initiating the Irish Terrier Club (England) and further assisting in writing the breed standard. The best account of these activities comes from "The Dog Book" by James Watson. Watson recalled that of the ten committee members, four or five had been active exhibitors while only a few were breeders. He classed himself and Krehl as exhibitors, although he (Watson) had imported, showed and also whelped the first litter of Irish Terriers in America in 1880-81. Because Watson and Krehl were professional writers they had control of much of the standard's final wording. Twenty years later, Watson described their efforts as those of well-intentioned amateurs. "In the standard, there are many indications of the fussy faddiness of the beginner in expounding inconsequential details, such as a negative penalty for white toe nails and for anything over a speck of white on chest. We were one of the aforesaid beginners." Watson also stated that after finally going beyond trivialities they started breeding "real terriers," although the written reference to nail color remains a relic from the past. For his part, Krehl was adamant Irish Terriers would have natural ears. The Kennel Club endorsed this ban and cropped Irish Terriers born after 1889 were barred from show competition, the first breed so designated.

As editor of "The Stock-keeper," George Krehl was in a position to give Irish Terriers prominent publicity, including numerous cover drawings of quality specimens. When studying all these illustrations by R. H. Moore collectively, it is clear that Krehl's energy and forceful personality helped bring the resultant dogs more in line with his particular remembrance and vision of the Irish Terrier as a lithe, refined and active animal. As a result, Irish Terriers gained worldwide popularity. In essence, the real history of the Irish Terrier began with their revival in the late 19th Century, when concerned enthusiasts fashioned a written standard, thus preventing this unique breed from disappearing into obscurity.

The Fashionable Dog Show

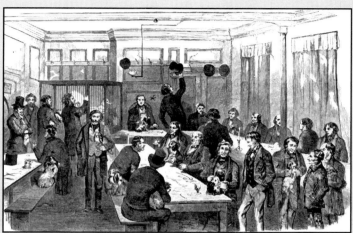

Dog shows were the catalyst to change the appearance and character of many breeds. Equally, the resultant competition radically altered the appearance and character of the dog shows themselves. We can well imagine the enjoyable nature of this gathering at the Eight Bells in 1851, as these gentlemen prepare to spend the evening discussing the finer points of the King Charles Spaniel over a pipe and a pint. With the beginning of formalized dog shows in 1859, the focus quickly changed to that of a major social gathering lasting several days, where one went not only to see, but be seen. Without intending to romanticize the past, it can be clearly documented that each passing year has produced less talk about dogs than about winning. While the specialty clubs can still maintain an educational atmosphere at a more relaxed pace, the increase in numbers of all breed shows and the rush to see who can win the most in a year have rapidly homogenized most events. Still, given the innate competitive nature of human beings, one wonders how long dog shows would have lasted if the discussion were only about dogs and never about devising systems to tangibly "prove" one canine better than another.

Until WWI, dog shows were important public promenades. According to "The Stock-keeper," if you were an American "swell" it was extremely critical to let people know you read the London newspapers. Thus, many attending the evening opening preview of the Westminster KC in 1891 arrived toting macintoshes and umbrellas on their arms in mild weather—because it had been raining in London that week. The very first dog show held within a hotel was the premiere specialty of the French Bulldog Club of America in 1898. This exclusive, invitation-only event at the Waldorf-Astoria in New York City included a dinner party and ball room dancing. Three major newspapers covered the soirée and numerous columns were devoted to the socialites' fancy frocks. The American public certainly doesn't consider attending a dog show "fashionable" anymore. Today, one would be hard pressed to find the majority of exhibitors in anything but casual, functional attire. Yet, one of the remarkable oddities of the American dog show scene is that there have always been concerted attempts, which have been put into the rule book at various times, to designate certain shows as more "fashionable" or more "prestigious" than others. Nevertheless, some of the most successful shows in this country are not necessarily the largest, nor do they offer anything more than competent judges, excellent show venues and courteous club members—very similar to the conviviality which would have been found at the Eight Bells in 1851.

in the same place. If we could find a way of making dog shows popular and of spreading more breeds than one at a time the dog fancy might progress and the public come to see them. "Will it pay?" is too much the cry and we think of just a few select ones that are making their living at the game. The amateur and the purveyor of rare breeds gets the cold shoulder, often by getting no classes for his breed or perhaps only one. Then this breed is dumped in with a "lot" to a judge who knows nothing about it, and the awards are ridiculous. We want exhibitions as incentives to breeders, and we want the public's money at the gate to pay the bills, but we too often just think of our own little inner circle and then blame the public if they do not come to our dog shows when we have only been working for our own interests and have thought nothing about the public till it

Fox Terrier Fads

A. H. Clarke

"The Fox Terrier Chronicle "
1892

CH. RESULT
Owner, A. H. Clarke
Artist, Arthur Wardle

Probably nothing is so harmful to any breed or variety of animal as the fads which periodically set in for their supposed improvement. At one time coat was the great fad and one constantly saw good terriers put back in the prize list because their coats were considered too straight and smooth (!). No matter how soft so long as they had plenty of it, and this was carried to such an extent that one saw terriers at every show with heavy spongy coats which afforded them no protection and which a shower of rain would very soon drench them through. This went on for a considerable time until a breed was established of fluffy, soft-looking dogs with great open feet and spongy thick legs, long bodies and heavy ears—the very opposite of what a real hard terrier should be.

The next fad was "front, legs, and feet." Everything else was ignored for the time being; no use the looker-on saying, "He has a bad head and ears," or, "I don't like his hindquarters." The reply was always the same, "Look at his front!" And they did look and talk and rave about fronts until a man thought he had produced a wonder if he brought to a show a puppy with a narrow weedy front (the less space between the forelegs, the better). What matter if this apology for a terrier had flat ribs, straight shoulders and long shelly body? It did not put him back. On the contrary, he was for the time the idol of exhibitors, and won all before him. One thing I have always marvelled at is how a judge can shut his eyes to bad hindquarters; but this is now constantly being done, and a terrier with a narrow front, straight proppy shoulders and absolutely badly-formed hindquarters (straight stifles, hocks turned in, and tail set-on badly), would be placed over a terrier with a moderately good front, but beautifully formed everywhere else. I am quite sure the only way to improve a breed is for judges to go in for good all-round animals, and then we shall get uniformity.

And why are big terriers encouraged? Why should we go on giving prizes and encouraging breeders to ignore size and, so long as they can win, bring terriers to our shows which could not possibly go to ground (at least in the shires) and are only fit to course rabbits at a sporting public? We don't want these leggy whippety terriers. We want a compact dog, well ribbed (yet with liberty), good clean hard bone, short hard thick coat and a varmint head and ears—and it is doing the breed an injury to encourage these giants. I should also like to make my grumble against heavy coarse terriers. We want activity in a terrier and lissomeness, so that he can turn and squeeze past a tight place in following a fox, and not a cloddy animal which would stick fast in an earth and be more trouble getting out than the varmint you were pursuing. To obtain this activity and litheness we must have quality bodies, and quality legs and feet. The smart active athlete, not the powerful ploughman. Or, to take another simile— a blood hunter and not a half-bred cart horse. I don't know how these fads are started, but certainly they are the very worst things which possibly could befall a breed.

was too late. A dog show to be interesting and instructive to the public should be an all round exhibit of as many varieties of dogs as we can get together. Some breeds will pay and some will not, but fortunately there are quite a few advocates of certain breeds in America, as elsewhere, that do not care if the game pays them or not, so long as they think they get a fair show and an opening as good as their neighbor. We work our dog shows backwards, as far as the public is concerned; and as far as the ultimate spread of the different breeds is concerned, we make little progress. Those within the fold, seeing what little it takes to bring a breed into fashion, might bend their energies somewhat to preventing fashion—when it is running away with a certain breed—from running down three or four others with it.

This Yorkshire Terrier was exhibited at Birmingham, 1877. Small size, beautiful steel blue and gold coloration and ability of the silky hair to grow to extreme lengths made the Yorkie one of the first breeds of fashion.

A fly wheel on a machine is a useful thing. When a novice or a band of enthusiasts come to bring forward a new variety they should have the right of way till they have succeeded or failed. That fashion ruins the dog fancy we have ourselves largely to blame, for not looking after our own interests better and seeing to it that breeds that hang fire for a time don't drop out altogether. As a rule we within the fold are the most short-sighted of all and give the parting kicks to the departing favorites of the last few years.

We have boomed one variety of sheepdog, and honor to him, but there are at least six or seven, if not more, varieties of the sheepdog equally clever that have never appeared at all in America up to now. Just think what it would lend to a dog show if we could advertise that on exhibition were many different exponents of the several varieties of sheepdogs with a competition at the end of the show to see which country could produce the best in the field. We have none of this,

though our vaudeville shows get more wonderful every day. Verily, our dog shows are slow things, and the exhibitor may well yawn and drag out a weary four days at most of them, for if the visitor has seen one, he has seen the lot, as they are managed today. We do not want a boom in one breed, but we want a boom in all breeds and we want a shake-up all 'round. But, we are a slow, humdrum and unprogressive lot and we expect the public not to know, so we do the ostrich act, again and again.

Dog shows, as run now, are of no possible interest to anyone but the exhibitor. We are, as a rule, not even breeders, for we let the purchaser get all the prizes, and if the purchaser sets up a fashion in buying, as in coats or hats, we do not steady the wheel and keep our dog shows balanced, but let fashion run away with us and then wonder that the public tires of it.

What we need is that dog shows should be interesting and all breeds should have a look. If we do not know many of the foreign breeds we could at least try to learn and put up those to judge them that know the most about them. Fashion in certain breeds has put us to sleep, and we wait silently for the next boom instead of setting the fashion and making the public take a genuine interest in what we do. There is little doubt but that a few sporting shows for ribbons, with good classes for all the known breeds, would bring out entries if the same facilities were extended to all breeds alike as to the capabilities of the judges. Our present policy at dog shows of allotting the most popular breeds to certain experts that are, in many cases imported at great expense, may be a good thing for the inner circle, but does it advance the dog show as a whole? No; it kills the public interest. The expense cannot be carried all the way through, and perhaps a cheap man is detailed for the odds and ends and these go home to stay there. Thus, the interest in the future shows is lessened to the public who pay the gate money. Fashion makes our dogs and unmakes many of them, but in letting it run riot entirely with all our breeds we are not very far-seeing and are spoiling our own sport and the dog fancy at large. Fashion only puts the money in one direction while it lasts and weakens all the rest. By dropping our hands and running with the crowd, for the time being, we ruin our own business, when our object should be to keep up as many breeds as possible at the same time. Dropping classes because a breed is under a cloud for a time and giving twenty-five classes to one breed because popular, and denying one of these twenty-five to another breed that is trying to gain a footing, are all forms of social suicide as far as we are concerned and help fashion to kill our business. Fashion is a good servant, but a bad master for the majority and very costly at all times to the average run of mankind.

> *"Dog shows, as run now, are of no possible interest to anyone but the exhibitor. We are, as a rule, not even breeders, for we let the purchaser get all the prizes."*

Questions for Consideration

1. Is it more difficult to breed a continued and consistent level of quality in breeds which do not have a corresponding performance function? Justify your position.

2. Define the following terms as they relate to dogs: (1) fashion; (2) fads; (3) breed improvement; (4) breed progress; (5) popularity.

3. Is it beneficial to the sport to recognize and promote as many breeds as possible?

4. If breeds decline in popularity and eventually die out should we be concerned? If we are concerned, what should we do to prevent this? Considering how all breeds originally developed, couldn't we, at a future date, recreate these breeds—or at least credible replicas—if interest in such breeds were to revive?

5. What (if any) is the correlation between a breed's history and the interpretation of correct type within the show ring?

6. If we agree that even rare breeds have value, how would you design the judging system to ensure they were always expertly and properly judged?

7. Are you aware of any particular breed standards which ascribe penalties for traits which no longer occur within the breed or are now considered inconsequential? Elaborate.

8. What should the qualifications be of those who undertake to write a breed standard? What should the qualifications be of those who are appointed to revise a breed standard?

9. How much of an impact on a breed and its subsequent popularity can one motivated person generate?

10. How much of an impact on a particular breed and on the sport in general occurs when a long established kennel is disbanded? Is this effect positive or negative? Elaborate.

11. The writer claims that if you have seen one show, you've basically seen them all. Do you find this to be true?

12. What is the main motivation for running shows from the show giving club's perspective?

13. For whom are dog shows designed—breeders, exhibitors, professional handlers, judges, show giving clubs, superintendents, the AKC or the general public? For whom should they be designed?

Scientific Breeding

G. Muss-Arnolt

"The American Field"
1892

There are many breeders, but of what kind? Being so very little *au fait* in the present *status quo* of the Great Dane, it really puts me under great obligation for this kind of information! I wish to impress my ideas about a pedigree and poor specimen vs. no pedigree and a good specimen. It has so much value to me that I certainly would not buy the best dog living, except for show hippodroming, if I could not ascertain, from reliable authority, where he came from, that is, what line of conformation, characteristics, temperament, etc., his ancestors had. Pedigree certainly does not create a dog, but for heaven's sake, how idiotic a man must be to breed to an absolutely pedigreeless dog, wasting every advantage of breeding for what he considers correct type. One might just as well let the bitch run loose when in season; the chances of getting a good one would be just as much. This very carelessness, this absolute lack of the true breeder's instinct and principles in our breeders has kept the Great Dane back. He ought to be—considering the length of time he has been in existence as a breed—the most true and typical dog that is bred; but he will never gain public favor as the best large dog of all kinds —no ornament, no cripple, but an eminently spry and intelligent companion—till we learn to

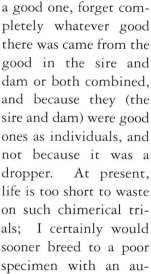

breed with full knowledge of breeding principles.

How would it be, if a Pointer or Setter breeder bred to a good dog, which had no pedigree whatever? Only a fool would attempt it. Some of these people, who swear that a dropper is the best hunting dog, because there once existed a good one, forget completely whatever good there was came from the good in the sire and dam or both combined, and because they (the sire and dam) were good ones as individuals, and not because it was a dropper. At present, life is too short to waste on such chimerical trials; I certainly would sooner breed to a poor specimen with an authenticated pedigree than to the *beau ideal* of a show dog without any proofs of breeding—unless somebody else had tried the dog on more than one bitch with good results—which would give a sort of indirect safeguard against too much risk.

The question, "What is a pedigree?" has incensed my wrath against this very vital stumbling block when the answer is, "Simply for the benefit of the buyer, so that he knows what strain he gets." Yes, very simple, indeed, if it were not the all-important point that nobody can be severe enough against those worthless pedigrees of Nobody's Caesar, Mr. So-and-So's Pasha, etc. Of course, it is the owner's own affair if he is satisfied

Dogs and Science

THE NEWARK MAD DOG SCARE — 1888
This cartoon spoofed rabies hysteria. Horses, people and Bulldog wear chain mail to prevent bites. Others opt for stilts to keep out of harm's way.
Artist, J. A. Ricker

The fatal nature of rabies and its direct association with canines has been documented since ancient times. Because the modality of the disease was unknown, keeping dogs as pets was always considered a risky proposition. Consequently, very few breeds served other than strictly utilitarian purposes for centuries. Under these circumstances, it seems incredible that dog shows became so enormously popular in the 19th Century, decades before an effective rabies treatment was available. But, faith that nature could be mastered through science was a Victorian hallmark. If a cure was not currently available, one soon would be. In 1885, nine year old Joseph Meister, who had been attacked by a rabid dog, was brought to Louis Pasteur. The father of five children, three of whom died of typhoid fever, Pasteur knew only too well the anguished pleas of parents willing to do anything to save their child.

Treated with Pasteur's new and untested vaccine, the boy lived. Within the next year, 350 people were vaccinated, all but one surviving.

However, an effective canine vaccine would not be available for many years. There was no question the booming trade in purebred dogs exposed more canines and people to the disease. Furthermore, we must remember that while dogs were common, they were not commonly seen in public prior to dog shows. For those who had grown up with an ingrained fear of rabies, encountering so many dogs casually paraded about was a terrifying experience. An actual reported case within a community put all dogs under suspicion. Public hysteria was easily ignited by any dog acting the least bit odd. To quell these fears, various laws were enacted. The most ill-advised were those requiring all dogs be muzzled, under the theory that if the animal couldn't bite, it was safe. Incredibly, all sporting breeds and hound packs—those dogs most likely to encounter rabies vectors in the wild—were exempt. Herding dogs, however, were required to be muzzled, despite the fact most refused to work when so encumbered. Even tiny household pets needed muzzles when in public. Such unreasonable legislation caused an uproar. In fact, the Ladies' Kennel Association (England) was initially founded as the Ladies' Anti-Muzzling League. When it became evident muzzling laws were unenforceable, besides doing nothing to prevent the spread of rabies, Great Britain instituted quarantine laws. Thus, after 1903, the free exchange of show dogs from the rest of the world to England ceased.

Even after Pasteur's work became publicly known, ignorance and fear of rabies continued. Many of the most knowledgeable dog people refused to admit the disease was widespread for fear of additional restrictive legislation which would impede their hobby and/or traffic in dogs. "The American Field" reported the following statements from the February, 1892 AKC Delegates' Meeting. "Secretary Vredenburgh called attention to the appeal made by Mr. Elliot Smith for a contribution to Paul Gibier's Pasteur Institute, referred at the previous meeting to the Advisory Committee. Mr. Anthony moved an appropriation of $50. Seconded. The motion was opposed by a number of the Delegates, the consensus of opinion apparently being that such action would show a recognition by the American Kennel Club of the existence of rabies, or hydrophobia, and of its belief in the efficacy of the Pasteur cure. On motion the matter was laid upon the table." There is no indication this motion has ever come off the table, but hopefully, the fear of scientific advancements and their ability to aid purebred dogs has been lessened.

At the time, canine health was not the primary interest of most scientific research and generous financial support necessary for progress was only available for diseases which also occurred in humans. Fortunately, or unfortunately, as the case may be, both species share many maladies. However, one particular disease which human beings do not contract is canine distemper. This literal canine plague was responsible for the deaths of thousands, crippling or impairing the health of countless others. Considering that prior to vaccinations roughly 50% of all adult dogs and 80% of all puppies exposed to the disease would die, one has to be in awe of the persistence of dedicated breeders who carried on, repeatedly losing their best dogs. Arthur Croxton Smith in his book, "Dogs Since 1900," related selling the third pick of a Bloodhound litter for only seven guineas. That dog became Ch. Hengist, described as one of the better hounds of his day, but Smith said, "I had two better ones in the same litter which promised to make a name for themselves, but distemper thought otherwise."

Well into the first quarter of the 20th Century no cure for distemper was in sight. A significant movement in that direction began with the foundation of the Animal Health Trust in England, devoted to scientific research into animal diseases, with a separate canine division established at Newmarket. But, progress was still painfully slow in providing a distemper cure. Finally, in 1923, Harding Cox and his brother Horace put forth an initial contribution and through the pages of their magazine, "The Field," appealed to the public for meaningful sums of money to donate specifically for distemper research. Their stated goals were to firmly and finally ascertain the disease's cause and then create an effective canine vaccine. Sufficient funds were quickly raised and "The Field" Distemper Council was established with the cooperation of the Medical Research Council. Sir Patrick Laidlaw and Dr. G. W. Dunkin were put in charge. They effectively proved a healthy dog could be immunized for life against distemper. A commercial prophylaxis became available in the 1930s.

Yet, scientific advances sometimes take the form of a double-edged sword. Dog shows overwhelmingly succeeded in creating public interest in purebreds. Before preventative vaccines, the heartaches were of such magnitude that only those passionately dedicated to a favorite breed, and determined to produce quality, became active fanciers. Because effective vaccines allowed more puppies to survive, most old-time breeders scaled back their breeding programs. Concurrently, to fill a growing demand for pets, commercial breeders appeared. All their dogs were for sale, regardless of quality, including those animals which were unhealthy, unsound and unstable—and eventually allowed to reproduce. Over several decades large scale "puppy mills" have increased the regulatory body's bottom line to such an extent that issues of true canine quality now seem opposed to registration numbers (revenue). As a result, the general public increasingly believes purebred dogs to be inferior to mixed breeds. It is not enough to host social events for canine health programs when the registry has the full power to demand a modicum of health criteria be met before a dog is allowed to be bred. "To do everything to advance...purebred dogs," must include instituting all scientific advances which convince the public to reasonably expect the dog they purchase is not merely registered, but healthy as well.

Numerous distemper "cures" were touted long before effective vaccines became available.

1903

What is a Pedigree?

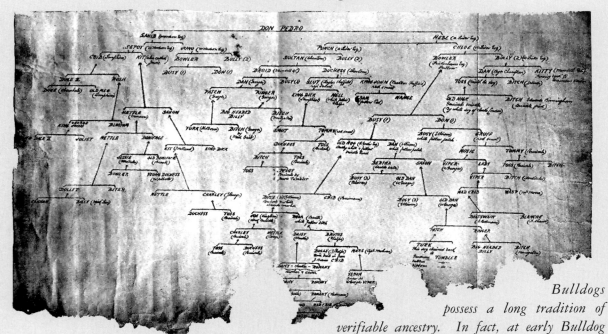

Bulldogs possess a long tradition of verifiable ancestry. In fact, at early Bulldog exhibitions, silver collars were awarded as specials for the longest pedigree. These genealogies were further enhanced by an extensive pictorial record and the oral history of long-time breeders. Such resources proved a distinct advantage, not only in understanding the characteristics of individual ancestors, but as an aid in fixing breed type. Don Pedro, whose pedigree is shown, was whelped in 1882. His pedigree went back several times through Ch. Crib and beyond to such dogs as Romanie, whelped in 1862. Although comparing a puppy photograph to an engraving, we can clearly see extraordinary similarities in head type. While Don Pedro never attained premier show ring honors, astute breeders knew the qualities and traits of his progenitors. Thus, he was utilized at stud, siring several notable champions.

*ROMANIE
Owner, R. J. Lloyd Price*

For the average person, one of the fascinations of owning a purebred dog is the written pedigree, documenting a blue-blooded ancestry. Initially, buying a well-bred dog helped one identify with the aristocracy, although to most purchasers, generations of canine ancestors are merely fancy names on paper. But, they are a necessity to reassure pet owners their dogs are of quality and royal background. Considering how extremely important a verifiable pedigree is to those acquiring a purebred dog, it is remarkable the AKC devalues the worth of this commodity with printed disclaimers stating the company only, "Records the parentage" and "cannot guarantee the health and quality of dogs in its registry." In fact, as a private entity, AKC has full authority, if not an obligation, to institute enforceable health, quality and identification requirements for each dog bred, exhibited or utilizing the registry. Responsible dog breeders in the 21st Century should not be constrained by 19th Century breeding systems or antiquated rules, especially when daily scientific breakthroughs at the molecular level will lead to the elimination of numerous canine maladies—if all members of the breeding population are required to be tested.

*DON PEDRO
Owner, W. H. Sprague*

with only names on paper, but any man who accepts such a pedigree, fully knowing how unreliable it is, cannot be called a breeder, as producing puppies by mating any kind of a dog and bitch is not breeding in the way that I understand the term, and it is only a severe loss of time, money and to the detriment of any kind of breed.

I shall be happy if I get the chance to see a good Great Dane when I judge, being absolutely disinterested at present in Great Danes, as far as owning one is concerned. I keep only hunting dogs and mostly Pointers, but I have been associated with and have owned good Great Danes from childhood up. Well do I remember my first little scare and the subsequent confidence I had in my father's old Danube, on whose back I fell asleep after a long romp together, when my brother, like all boys bent for mischief, crept up from behind and pinched Danube's tail severely. The old dog, like myself, was asleep and from the sudden pain turned around and took my whole face in his huge jaws. Although under the circumstances it would have been quite excusable if he had snapped, he realized immediately the correct cause and withdrew his fangs without even scratching me and commenced licking my face instead, as a kind of atonement for his mistake. In this beautiful temper of the well-bred Great Dane lies his greatest value; but to avoid many a shocking accident it is the absolute duty of every breeder to fully know the pedigree of his dogs, nay, not only know their pedigrees, but also the different peculiarities of their most prominent ancestors, so as to breed, what I term, scientifically. No one can have satisfactory results in any other way except by accident.

Questions for Consideration

1. What is the purpose of a pedigree?
2. What is scientific breeding?
3. How critical is selection for correct, breed specific temperament?
4. Do you think most dog fanciers make much of an effort to find out anything more about their dog's ancestors than individual show records?
5. Do you believe so-called "puppy mills" are detrimental to the advancement of purebred dogs? Why or why not? If you believe they are detrimental, how would you eliminate mass commercial breeding yet, at the same time, provide adequate numbers of dogs to satisfy the public demand for purebred pets?
6. If a registry organization such as the AKC is chartered "to do everything to advance...purebred dogs," do they have any obligation to make significant demands upon those utilizing the registry to insure that dogs used for breeding purposes are tested clear of specific inheritable diseases?
7. What specific actions could or should the AKC institute to insure the public can acquire quality purebred dogs?
8. Should various breed parent clubs establish minimum health criteria to be enforced by the regulatory and show giving body to prevent animals from either becoming champions, being specialed or being bred before they have tested clear of specific problems? *Examples:* Irish Setters for progressive retinal atrophy; Labrador Retrievers for hip dysplasia; Scottish Terriers for von Willebrand's disease, etcetera? Why or why not?
9. If we don't demand healthy breeding stock, is future canine improvement possible?
10. If we cannot, will not or simply don't care whether or not purebred dogs meet minimum health standards before they are bred, then what, indeed, is the real purpose of dog shows and dog breeding?

Shows and Breeding Value

R. E. Nichols ("Great Dane")

"Bulldogs and Bulldog Men"
1908

By offering prizes for competition, dog shows have greatly stimulated the production of improved stock, and thus done grand service to the breeding interest. But, shows have so multiplied of late that the inexperienced owner stands today in danger of placing prize winning before breeding quality.

Under the existing system a judge can only adjudicate on what he sees in the show ring. He must judge entirely on outward appearance, without regard to such vital matters as constitutional vigour, prepotency and the ability to produce healthy and profitable offspring. Hence, the improvement resulting from dog shows has not always been upon desirable lines and the method of judging practised has sometimes culminated in degeneration in valued breeding character. It is well known, for instance, that some successful prize winners are unable to properly nourish their own progeny, despite every advantage humanly possible, and that yet others are sterile or breed only with menace to life.

Prizes are unquestionably a stamp of quality, but of *showing* rather than *breeding* quality, and we ought to give much greater weight to breeding value, which is either not perceptible in the show ring, or is apparent only in a limited degree. To many buyers and sellers the fact that a dog has won such-and-such prizes is now seemingly all sufficient. To the dog shower, pure and simple, it really is all sufficient, for the show ring

> *"Any method of awarding prizes for breeding stock that takes no account of even the actual capacity to breed at all is OBVIOUSLY a far from perfect method."*

is undoubtedly the proper place to choose dogs for showing; but to the breeder it is of vastly greater moment to know what an animal is capable of breeding and what its ancestors have bred, for he is concerned with the quality and quantity of puppies, and cannot therefore afford to give too much weight to prizes awarded on a system that must in many cases interfere with the perpetuation of healthy offspring. Breeding stock should be primarily kept for breeding; and the ultimate end of all good breeding is increased and better quality *production*. The breeder requires that at least as much attention must be paid to breeding performance as to prize winning. Show ring honours are an advantage to him if not permitted to prejudice his *breeding*, but they do not ordinarily justify his buying or retaining animals which fail in productive capacity.

Too much dependence is usually placed on mere prize winning as an indication of breeding value, and, in consequence, novice breeders frequently purchase at fancy prices stock that is practically worthless for breeding purposes. Indeed, under existing conditions, it is easily possible for even experienced owners to unconsciously assess show successes too highly. The show ring method of selecting dogs for breeding is opposed to the laws of good breeding. Prizes for breeding stock should be awarded for constitution and prolificacy, and for the quality and health of the offspring under existing conditions

254

Breeding for Tomorrow
William J. Brainard, Jr.
"Popular Dogs"
1951

The next time we think about breeding another litter, it might put us in the right frame of mind to think of the great breeders of the past. These were not men of little substance, nor seekers after shortcuts to a hit-and-run sort of accomplishment. They built strongly. The proof of their successful efforts is readily available for all to see today. Nothing is more simple than breeding animals. Nothing more difficult than breeding superior animals. Every so often, some spectacular individual, bred by the take-a-chance system, is at that moment deservedly cleaning up the show rings. If—if, these would only breed true—but the ones we have watched never have. No matter how great the blood, some just do not make the grade.

If your purpose in breeding dogs is to produce "show dogs," then you are saying, in reality, you are interested in the highest quality, the greatest absence of fault in conformation, the essence of type, the personification of true temperament, and all the other characteristics of excellence, plus elegance. You recognize right away that the perfect animal has yet to be produced, but you have a picture in your mind. We must give some analytical thought to the job for which the particular dog was intended, and decide the relative importance of the different parts of the apparatus which enable him to function. But, so often we see animals in the show ring, failing acutely in a fundamental, and seeing more and more failing in the same one or two, we wonder if proper consideration is being given to structural composition.

I must say my little word upon "quality." Once you have seen it, there can be no argument. A while back, we overheard a casual character carrying on about a certain terrier then being promoted in the ring. "Look at the quality," was the theme. Sometimes we wonder how many think of quality as a lack of substance. When we have all the rest, and quality in every part, we are ready to go places. Refinement, elegance, the look of eagles, coupled with the substance to get the job done, and the functional parts to do it—then we are coming closer to the ideal pattern. But just because we are faced with a delicately chiseled head, a neat ear, a clever throat latch or neck placement, is no reason to throw the book away in exultation. Quality is the lifeblood of the breed's future, but it cannot be a thing apart from the functional. Quality covers every part and exudes from the whole.

If we are worthy of the dogs we have inherited, more thought above and beyond our own immediate success or failure in the show ring is needed. It may not be entirely complimentary, but unless the judge can find some reason to withhold the ribbon, there must be a winner in every class, in every breed and group, in every show. There is a great tendency to breed to the dog of the year, the local champion or anything handy for about as good a reason. In so doing we dissipate at least some of the heritage of the past. As part of the great dog breeding tradition we must give more care and thought to breed improvement. The names of countless champions are only lines on paper. Few in history will always hold a point of pride. If you could breed ten generations, gradually working towards the picture in your mind, and then finally be rewarded with a real one which would do the breed, as well as your name, some lasting good, how satisfactory that would be. Progress seems to come from thought and effort and perseverance. Let us continue to make breed progress.

Improvement and Uniformity

When James Watson visited the Nutley, New Jersey kennels of Mr. and Mrs. Philip B. Adams in 1904, he remarked that the Boston Terriers pictured on the left were a rare sight — one of the most uniform teams he had ever seen in the breed. Quite a comment coming from the man most adamantly opposed to breed recognition in 1891. Having seen Boston Terriers develop from the ground up, Watson was aware of the initial diversity with which breeders had to work. He personally witnessed great strides made in breeding with each subsequent generation. In that comparative context, his pronouncement of uniformity was probably correct.

The term, "improvement" implies an advance to a better state of quality. Such advances are always more noticeable in newly recognized breeds where much remains to be accomplished. Initially, the goal is to identify and keep positive characteristics while eliminating obvious faults. This is not an easy task, especially when each parent can only give 50% of all its qualities — good, bad or indifferent — to each puppy. Consequently, canines are much easier to change than improve. Reflecting this difficulty and acknowledging the ease with which words on paper may be added or erased, numerous breed standards bear witness to repeated revisions, matching the concept of the ideal to dogs already in existence.

Maximum canine improvement means uniformity, or relative sameness, of all available breeding stock. Arthur Croxton Smith voiced the opinion that such canine perfection had been attained in Greyhounds and various Foxhound packs prior to WWII. As a direct result of positive 19th Century economic and social conditions, these breeds were kept in large numbers. Masters of Hounds not only had the luxury of choosing the best puppies from dozens of litters, but later selecting superior breeding stock on purely functional criteria — those dogs which had proved their worth in the field. Nevertheless, the hardships of worldwide conflagrations forced many packs to disband and this high level of uniformity disappeared. As a result, many Foxhounds and Greyhounds seen in the show ring after WWII could no longer be considered as typical specimens of a uniform group, but, more accurately, as incidental individual breed representatives. Smith felt that without the pack system these breeds would never again attain the quantity of past overall perfection.

Present day fanciers would pronounce the 1959 Boston Terrier team pictured below as not only improved, but more uniform than the 1904 dogs. They have elegant, well-formed heads and a striking sameness in size, substance and markings (n.b. — the Boston Terrier standard allows three distinct sizes). These dogs clearly exhibit the preferred terrier-like conformation as opposed to their predecessors' Bulldog-like characteristics. Yet, when viewing the lack of forechests, narrow front assemblies placed too far forward and poor feet, one could argue for uniformity of faults — the antithesis of improvement. However, 40 years later, that is an extremely unfair and unwarranted assessment of their overall quality. Time is such a significant factor in evaluating dogs that we can never properly compare the past with the present. Barring a favorable mutation, each generation of dog breeders is limited by the qualities of the individual dogs available within their contemporary gene pool. For this reason alone, if improvements are to continue, it has to be pleaded that those holding dog shows should determine how to evaluate genotypes, in concert with phenotypes.

as well as for external conformation.

The present system of judging conduces, too, to certain physical characters being assessed above their real value, either because they are fashionable at the moment, or because the lack of them has been indelibly impressed on the judge's mind by some previous personal experience. Fashion in dogs is as inexplicable as it is in ladies' dresses; but since, as previously stated, the ultimate end of breeding is reproduction of desired characteristics, no breeder can afford to neglect the cultivation of fashionable points, even when clearly of no utility to the animal nor of any special beauty, provided always that they do not exclude what is of greater value. But, when fashion and sentiment are pushed to the extreme of actually prejudicing real and valuable breeding quality, then they degenerate into purely mischievous fads, tending to deterioration and to failure. The breeder, unlike the casual buyer who seeks only the pride or pleasure of possession, must value the dog, not merely for its apparent individual character, but primarily for its ability to transmit to future generations its useful qualities; and any method of awarding prizes for breeding stock that takes no account of even the actual capacity to breed at all is obviously a far from perfect method.

If, therefore, dog shows are to encourage to the greatest possible degree the general improvement of breeding stock, it is evident that —at least in some classes—the judges must be guided in their awards by reliable records of breeding performance, as well as by physical conformation, thus ensuring proper recognition of the best producing as well as the best showing animals. Equally obviously, individual effort can accomplish but little in this direction. It is essentially a matter for the organized energy of good breeding associations, with time and money available for putting their own houses in proper order by promoting purely breeding competitions amongst their members. Every step in the right direction is ground gained. And though the difficulties may appear insurmountable at the outset, each little stage accomplished will make the way plain for further improvement. Even individual enterprise can help, since the donors of special prizes can always, if so minded, make them specifically breeding awards.

Questions for Consideration

1. What is breed progress?
2. Are there any limits to breed improvement? Can you name any breeds in which the quality is so uniformly high that little room for improvement exists?
3. Is there a difference between selecting show dogs as opposed to selecting breeding stock?
4. What is quality in reference to show dogs? What is breeding quality? Do these terms designate the same thing? Should they?
5. If dog shows are about selecting future breeding stock, why do you suppose there is not more interest in brood bitch, stud dog or futurity classes?
6. If dog shows are about selecting future breeding stock, what purpose to that end is served by Group competition?
7. If dog shows are about selecting future breeding stock, how would you design the system of awarding championships to insure that the best show winners were also the best available breeding stock?
8. If the method of awarding championships takes no account of actual breeding capacity, how can we claim dog shows are about selecting breeding stock?
9. Do you think selecting future breeding stock is the primary objective of most dog show exhibitors?

Look Forward

A. Harold Stocker

"The Kennel Gazette"
1906

SWEEPING ALONG
Artist, G. W. Goddard
1878

Saving Time vs. Training Dogs

Most scent hounds are generally hunted in packs, but the Bloodhound's unique work usually requires dogs to be run singly or in couples. Edwin Brough believed the best results came from training each dog to work alone. "It is, of course, a great temptation to 'save time'...but this method spells failure as a rule, and the bulk of the work should be done singly. The hounds which are slowest in speed or in nose are apt to throw up their heads and simply run with the leading hound or hounds instead of carefully working out the line each for himself." This problem is clearly illustrated in the wood engraving of Lord Wolverton's Ranston Bloodhounds.

It is something to be thankful for that Bloodhound breeders have apparently at last arrived at the conclusion that another outcross* is imperative. When seventy-five per cent of young hounds never reach maturity, and of the remaining twenty-five per cent, at least half are useless for any serious hunting because a long day makes them lie down and wish to die; then, in the opinion of any sound hunting man, not absolutely blinded by prejudice, it is about time some fresh blood was introduced.

There are two half-bred hounds now at the public stud. The first is Boatman, bred by Mr. E. Brough, by Baxter, a Bloodhound, ex Frivole, a Vendée Nivernaise Griffon, who was imported by Lieutenant Colonel Joynson. I have never seen Boatman hunt, but he is a fine hound, though he was rather too strong an individual for a pack hound on the clean boot, hence his being drafted by the Dumfrieshire Otterhounds. He is now the property of Mr. Frank Rayner, Haddington, N. B., who tells me he is a grand hound on the clean boot. Boatman is the sire of Hybla and Hamo, winners at the last field trials of the Association of Bloodhound Breeders (held in Warwickshire in 1903); also of Diadem of Craigweil, a very good hunting hound, and many others. The second is a dog hound of my own breeding, Dreadnought of Craigweil, by Torpedo of Craigweil, a Bloodhound, ex Dauntless Lady of

NOTE: Today, with closed breeding populations, an outcross is defined as a mating between two animals of the same breed which share no ancestors in common within four generations. For purposes of this article the term refers specifically to utilizing two distinct breeds. —AMH.

Edwin Brough, *whose name was synonymous with Bloodhounds during his lifetime, is still revered as the consummate authority on the breed. Born in 1844 and living 85 years, very little is written about Brough's personal life, although he eventually gave up his kennel due to declining health. However, one account added he could normally be seen early in the morning—a tall, white vestured figure taking as many as 40 Bloodhounds and a Nubian milk goat out for a romp along the sandy banks of Scalby Beck at his estate, Wyndgate, near Scarborough. Brough acquired his first Bloodhounds in the 1860s and, after the founding of the Kennel Club, registered a bitch named Clotho in 1874. From that point on, all the hounds he bred had names starting with the letter 'B'. Brough joined the Kennel Club in 1876 and was one of the original founders and first president of the Association of Bloodhound Breeders. As early as 1880, Brough advocated official man-trailing tests for Bloodhounds and the first trials were held in 1886.*

At the close of the American Civil War, Union soldiers destroyed many large hound packs found in the South, partly because popular stories described vicious "Bloodhounds" (most of which were actually Mastiff/Foxhound or Great Dane/Foxhound crosses), sent out to track down and maim runaway slaves. Consequently, there were no established Bloodhound kennels and none had ever been exhibited in the United States. In 1888, Brough decided to introduce the breed to America, exhibiting four of his hounds at Westminster. Brough's dogs were of such outstanding quality and attracted so much public attention that an exception was made to give them separate breed classification rather than relegating them to the Miscellaneous Class. Thus, Ch. Barnaby was the first Bloodhound best of breed winner in America. Later that same year, in an attempt to find Jack the Ripper, Ch. Barnaby and kennelmate, Ch. Burgho, were sent to London. Unfortunately, no agreements could be met regarding such things as insurance and the dogs were returned to Brough before being put into service. Nevertheless, in several test runs the Bloodhounds demonstrated they could significantly aid police in finding criminals. During the time they were kenneled in London, no further murders occurred. Sadly, the killings resumed immediately after the dogs were gone and these crimes were never solved.

Arthur Croxton Smith described the Brough years as the Golden Age of Bloodhounds. He felt one reason for his success was that he kept two lines in his kennel. He stated Brough was extremely interested in working abilities and a "zealot" on performance, not tolerating unsoundness in legs and feet in his own dogs. As a result, Smith said Brough possessed the most uniform collection of dogs with real hound quality that he had ever seen, claiming they were more remarkable in that regard because they were not exaggerated. Unlike many of his contemporaries, Brough disagreed with the premise that show dogs were useless for their work and actually credited the dog show with saving the Bloodhound from extinction, as they had become quite scarce by the 19th Century. "The greatest benefactor to the ancient race is the man who breeds intelligently, and supports both trials and shows, but there will always be people who are unable to devote time to both, and the trialer should remember that he will always be greatly indebted to the showman, and the showman should bear in mind that he owes the excuse for his existence to the trialer. Both are equally interested in maintaining the true type, and their conception of the ideal hound should be the same. Of late years it has become a fashion in some quarters to profess that dogs of any kind, which are successful on the bench, must necessarily be useless for work and the belief is sometimes most strongly held by those who have not specially distinguished themselves in breeding exhibition animals...Doubtless there are good workers which have not sufficient type and quality for the bench, but many of the most successful show hounds have proved themselves the best workers also, when they have had opportunities of showing their capability, and this is only natural to expect."

Bloodhound Outcrosses

Lewis B. Strong

"The American Kennel Gazette"

1906

WITCHCRAFT

A mistaken impression has prevailed in America that Bloodhounds have been purely bred—that their blood was uncontaminated by that of any other breed for centuries. As a matter of fact, I have been unable to discover any authentic Bloodhound pedigree that went back further than about sixty years, beyond which time Bloodhound pedigrees, so far as I know, do not exist, so that prior to that time we really know little of their purity or impurity of blood. We do know that during these last sixty years Bloodhounds have been crossed several times with other hounds, and that the Bloodhound of today, instead of having been injured in appearance by these numerous outcrosses, is a far more beautiful hound than in the early days when Landseer painted him.

In spite of the invigorating effects of several outcrosses, the Bloodhound remains one of the scarcest and perhaps the most inbred of all English dogs. I should hardly think that they can survive another half century of inbreeding as close as the past fifty years, and I think that, unless Bloodhound breeders take the subject strongly in hand, there is danger that the Bloodhound may in time become extinct, exterminated by inbreeding. The only remedy I can think of, besides refraining from inbreeding, is for English and American breeders to boldly make outcrosses, so as to get a liberal infusion of new blood. Experience shows that in making these Bloodhound outcrosses type is quickly recovered, thanks to the impressive power inbreeding gives—champion hounds have been bred even in the second generation of an outcross.

I will briefly describe the various Bloodhound outcrosses up to the present day:

The first few were made by mating a Bloodhound with a New Forest bitch. New Forest Hounds, or Talbots, were, like the Southern Hound, an English breed, now extinct, that somewhat resembled the Bloodhound. I have no precise information about their origin, but have heard they have been bred by keepers in the New Forest for hundreds of years to track wounded game.

The two first Bloodhound-New Forest crosses were made some fifty years ago and each of these crosses brought into the world a half-bred hound named Hector. One was owned by Mr. Wakefield and the other by Mr. Nichol. No Bloodhound exists today that does not hark back to these two hounds. Several years later we find that the grand dam of the celebrated Druid, born in 1862, was Malwood, who was bred by the keepers of New Forest—the presumption being she was of the New Forest breed. Druid's descendants can be found very

DRUID
The first champion Bloodhound

many times in every modern Bloodhound's pedigree.

In 1876 Mr. Nichol made his well known cross between the Bloodhound Victor and Mr. Nevill's New Forest bitch Countess. The puppies seem to have been poor specimens. The worst of them was a bitch called Restless, described as very small and bad throughout. When bred, however, with Captain Clayton's Bloodhound, Luath XI, Restless gave birth to a litter that was probably the best ever bred in England until that time. It contained four champions, Napier, Hebe, Belladonna and Diana. It is well worth remarking that these surprisingly fine hounds were but three-quarters pure and that their dam was one of the worst possible Bloodhounds.

ROSEMARY
Owners, E. Brough & J. Winchell
Artist, G. Muss-Arnolt
1890

Mr. Edwin Brough, the best authority on the Bloodhound says, "This outcross was so successful that it would be impossible to find today a purebred Bloodhound without some of this blood in its veins."

The next outcross was made by Mr. Edwin Brough in 1881 by Bravo (out of the Luath XI-Restless litter) and Clara, a purely bred Southern Hound. From this litter a bitch, Rose, was mated with the Bloodhound Ch. Nobleman and one of her puppies, Rosemary, was sent to America. I remember seeing Rosemary, a very small and very plain bitch. In spite of her plain appearance, however, she was a wonderfully good brood bitch, and bred for her owner, Mr. Winchell, the two well known American champions, Victor and Jack Shepard. Before leaving England, Rosemary, bred to Burgho, produced Blazer and Barbara Allen, winners of many first prizes. I have myself seen or owned many of Rosemary's descendants, and have noticed their superiority in vigor, owing to their slight infusion of new blood.

About the same time, or a little later than Mr. Brough's cross, Mr. Mark Beaufoy made an outcross between a Bloodhound and a French Hound named Babylone, that was a mixture of three breeds of hounds—the St. Hubert (now extinct), the Vendée and the Bloodhound. The English Champion What's Wanted was descended in the third generation from Babylone, and was the dam of Ch. Wandle Warrior, a grand hound often shown in New York and Boston. This dog was the sire of Mr. Winchell's Rallywood and Rallywood has been, I think, the sire of more good puppies than any hound that we have yet had in America.

The only other English outcross of which I know is that recently made by Lieut. Col. Joynson, who mated a Bloodhound with a Griffon Vendée. I hear that this cross is "not

CH. WANDLE WARRIOR
Breeder, A. Croxton Smith
Artist, G. Muss-Arnolt
1902

quite sufficiently matured for description yet."

There remains for description only the outcross that I made in 1899 by mating an American Foxhound, Bones, with the Bloodhound bitch, Black Patti. This outcross has been, as yet, of little practical importance, as our breeders have fought shy of it, perhaps because it was a domestic production and not an English one, and it has been but little dispersed. There is probably nothing so good in America for Bloodhound outcrossing as our own Foxhound, many of which strongly resemble inferior Bloodhounds.

American Foxhound, Bones

Bones had shorter legs than a Bloodhound and was whiter in color. It was difficult to breed out these short, white legs, but in other respects type was quickly regained. The bitch Stalwart, shown in the picture, was half Bloodhound and half Foxhound. Her puppies, by a Bloodhound, were consequently three-quarters pure, and two of them were excellent hounds. One of this litter was again bred with a Bloodhound, and the puppies, which were seven-eighths pure, were, some of them, of fine quality. A beautiful seven-eighths bitch from this litter, Witchcraft, was bred with Mr. Winchell's Rallywood, and one of the puppies of her litter was the hound Ch. Magician. This hound has in his skin the blood of every one of the English outcrosses mentioned in this article except Lieut. Col. Joynson's. Far from showing want of type, however, he is as good a Bloodhound as I have ever seen; in fact one of the three or four best, and his two brothers, Blackfriar and Valiant, are nearly as good. He is remarkable for his vigor and hardiness and has recently come out of the distemper with flying colors. He has, as yet, bred but one litter, but in this litter are some puppies of the very finest quality.

I no longer own him.
I wish I did.

American Foxhound/Bloodhound cross, Stalwart

Ch. Magician
1906

Craigweil, Otterhound. He is a grand hound all through, with immense strength behind the saddle, and though this is only his first season, he is quite exceptionally good in the field, and has already proved himself a wonderful stayer. He is bred from the best hunting stock on both sides. This is a point which breeders should be very careful about, because if a hound has hunted regularly and hard for one season at least, then surely the soundness of its constitution is proved, otherwise serious regular hunting would have killed it. Let anyone who does not believe this or who considers it a fad take two couples of inbred show hounds, and if he can by his genius persuade them to hunt at all on a cold line, let him give them a good stiff season, and see how many of them can stand it. If a single hound is alive at the end, he will be lucky indeed.

I have no doubt that I shall be set down as a faddist who ignores type, and thinks solely of the hunting powers of the breed, but this is not entirely true. I do frankly confess, I take the view that Bloodhounds are a great sporting breed, and should first and foremost be bred for hunting. I am just as keen as anyone on the preservation of type, but I say most emphatically, that the man who is a dog show man solely (whether from choice or from dire necessity), has no business to go in for any sporting breed, certainly not Bloodhounds, because he has no opportunity of knowing from personal observation in the field what points are of paramount importance, and in what particulars certain hounds

BABETTE
Breeder/Owner, Edwin Brough
Artist, R. H. Moore
1889

> "*The man who is a dog show man solely (whether from choice or from dire necessity), has no business to go in for any sporting breed.*"

excel, and what their chief faults are. He therefore falls back on an endeavour to get that exaggeration of the show points of the breed which shall make his hound more of a freakish monstrosity than anyone elses; and to gain the object he is obliged to practice continued inbreeding which Mr. W. Arkwright has so aptly described as out and out folly. Bloodhounds suffer considerably from the fact that the vested interests are so largely in the hands of the dog show people.

There is another point which I would implore Bloodhound breeders to remember, viz., that in using a stallion hound who has at least one season's regular hunting to his credit, they are not only using a hound, the soundness of whose constitution is proved; but puppies got by such a hound are far more likely to hunt well, than those by a hound who never hunts at all, or only hunts spasmodically. This is well shown by the decision of the Association of Masters of Foxhounds who should know what they are talking about.

The Kennel Club is, I am certain, quite ready to rank the Bloodhound as a hunting hound as soon as the hound himself and his owners are ready, and in this connection I would point with gratitude to the fact that at the Kennel Club Show, and, indeed, elsewhere, Bloodhounds have been kenneled like the hounds they are, and judged as they should be in a proper hound ring. In addition I gratefully acknowledge the permission from the Show Committee for my hounds to be taken away from the late Kennel Club Show at the end of the second day, a privilege accorded to

More Than A Dog
Country, Modernity and the Individual

"Past and Present"
South London Bulldog Society prize card.
The Bulldog had successfully risen from an
unsavory past to become what the Victorian
man aspired to be–a gentleman.
Artist, R. G. S. Mann
1898

Today, committees writing or revising breed standards generally confine their descriptions to physical conformation which can be evaluated in the show ring. Consequently, breed specific temperament and character traits have been generically reduced to the readily discernible, such as "friendly," "lively," or "intelligent." However, the Victorian era was remarkable in its ability to routinely assign metaphoric or symbolic meanings to the mundane. For a few select breeds, most notably, the Bulldog, Smooth Fox Terrier and Bloodhound, early fanciers not only described the correct appearance of an ideal specimen, but purposefully ascribed corresponding character qualities, as well. What is remarkable is these temperament characteristics were not always limited to what a breed was, but what it was expected to become.

Since ancient times the dog has represented unconditional love, devotion and willingness to serve its master. The Roman designation, "Fido" (I am faithful), clearly acknowledged this unique cross-species bond. Yet, the phenomenon of assigning additional, breed specific, anthropomorphic attributes to canines was a reflection of the overall optimism of the Victorian age. The great majority of our known breeds were developed during the 19th Century. In breeding dogs for specific conformation and abilities it is not surprising that most original breed standards, which were English in origin, incorporated Victorian sensibilities of order. Thus, corresponding character traits were consciously delineated.

In a society sanctifying the virtues of "work," it was initially difficult to justify time spent on the relatively new Victorian concepts of "leisure time" or "hobbies." Idleness was reviled and a breed lacking utility was doomed to disappear. Such was clearly the case with the Bulldog after 1835. Yet, in one of the most extraordinary sales pitches of the 19th Century, devotees proclaimed it, "The National Breed," representing English tenacity and pluck. Almost overnight, the justification for preserving this cultural icon for "Country" was in place. It was well known early Bulldogs possessed extreme loyalty to their masters, indomitable courage and such imperviousness to pain that only death prevented them from carrying out their assigned duty. Coupled with that, however, was unparalleled savagery. Though Bulldogs were selectively bred for centuries for ferocity, the Victorians believed character was a matter of choice, influenced and limited by environment. In other words, the Bulldog was capable of becoming virtuous. Numerous late 19th Century accounts exist which seriously claimed the Bulldog's former unsavory attributes were a product of mingling with "bad company" and that by placing the dog within a civilized environment he would become better through the association. Unacceptable temperament, though on the wane, was not uncommon when the breed standard was penned in 1875. When the Americans wrote their version of the standard they incorporated the then optimistic description of correct Bulldog temperament as, "equable and kind, resolute and courageous (not vicious or aggressive), and demeanor should be pacific and dignified. These attributes should be countenanced by the expression and behavior." The Bulldog was officially mandated to rise above its bad upbringing–and it did.

The 1851 Exposition in England not only paid homage to the Industrial Revolution but publicly proclaimed the Victorian belief that, through science, life would only get better. Further, "modern" man, having

More Than A Dog
Country, Modernity and the Individual

successfully harnessed the environment, was now in control of his own destiny and for the first time in the history of the world, had the necessary tools to achieve his dreams. This Victorian definition of modernity is what the Smooth Fox Terrier represented. Show specimens of the breed were always referred to as "modern." In the breed standard their appearance was likened to the most up-to-date equine equivalent, a "cleverly made hunter." Literally the sports car of its day, a well-bred hunter was an essential middle class accoutrement when many of the private Hunts became country clubs toward the end of the 19th Century. A good looking Smooth Fox Terrier was also an important accessory, for it indicated to your associates in the city that you had the wherewithal to ride to hounds on a regular basis. The modern Fox Terrier was designed to be a mirror of its owner—adaptable to either city or country life with innate resourcefulness and a love of sport, besides being elegant, stylish and amiable. Most significantly, this was the first breed to which known principles of "scientific breeding" were actively applied and discussed. Competition among fanciers to produce the best was keen and the level and intensity of planned inbreeding carried out for numerous generations would be attempted by few today. But, the selection criteria of these skillful breeders obviously worked. Besides producing a consistent level of outward physical conformation and type, the Smooth Fox Terrier remains relatively free of many inherited genetic diseases which plague numerous other purebreds.

What Country provided and Modernity achieved was, surprisingly, one of the first cultures which valued and encouraged the contributions of the "Individual," even to the point of tolerating eccentricities in those who focused on productive work. Further, though in control of the environment because of scientific advances, the Victorian individual still had a foundation of spiritual strength to guide daily decisions. Among the highest possible attainments was to put oneself in the service of others for no personal benefit or gain. This quality was designated as "noble." Only one breed, the Bloodhound, could represent such a level of character. While wild dogs hunted to survive and various domestic dogs hunted for sport, the Bloodhound was best at an activity which provided no particular benefit in canine terms—trailing man. When breed standards were first being written, it was impossible to discuss Bloodhounds without simultaneously referring to the one person most clearly associated with them—Edwin Brough. Although it is known that Dr. J. Sidney Turner made some contributions to the Bloodhound standard, Brough defined this inner-directed hound as, "extremely affectionate, neither quarrelsome with companions nor with other dogs. His nature is somewhat shy and equally sensitive to kindness or correction by his master." The expression, appropriately, "is noble and dignified, and characterized by solemnity, wisdom, and power." Unlike other scent hounds, the Bloodhound was never considered a pack hound. In his writings on training the breed, Brough always emphasized that each individual dog had to puzzle out its own trail alone, weigh the evidence, reach its own conclusions and then proceed with steadfast patience, never giving up on the trail. The implicit reward, for the ideal Victorian individual, was not some tangible, earthly memento of the achievement, but experiencing and completing a well-run journey.

While today, in our fast-paced age, it is laughable to think a Smooth Fox Terrier, or any other dog, could be a simile for modernity, the Bulldog is still the metaphor for never giving up and tenaciously doing one's duty. It resolutely persists as the icon for England. The Bloodhound has largely been supplanted in its work by faster dogs, but is still considered the best and most reliable cold trailer. And the description of magnanimous behavior—"noble"—remains the highest compliment anyone could hope to have ascribed to oneself as an individual in our society, or any to come.

CH. BURGHO
Artist, R. H. Moore
1899

The Life Span of Show Dogs
"Field and Fancy"
1901

A subject that will bear consideration, and really requires serious thought, is the ever growing shortness of life evident in some breeds of our domestic or show dogs. The dog is supposed to be an animal that might be hale and hearty at 12 years of age, and would live to 15 or 16 years or over, but we hear of breeds, popular on the show bench, averaging about 6 years, and a dog of that age may look very old. In other cases we hear of certain families of dogs that do not live beyond the age of three or four years, three being nearer the limit than four; and in some cases two years might really strike the average. If dogs were bred from, whose age limit is about three years and at the most six years, it, of course, necessarily follows that the progeny inherit the weakness of the parents and mature quickly, are in their prime, we might say, for a year or two years, and at four years of age are beneath the ground.

The evolutionary background and history of the carnivores place the cat, the dog, the hyena, the civets, etc., very close together, and suggest that all come from the same parent stem, with probably the dog as the oldest form, though this is merely conjecture. But, it is a fact that the carnivores, among which the dog is included, are a hard working race, living active hunting lives and taking a lot of exercise. The question of early mortality and deca-dence among the dog tribe is occasioning considerable anxiety in the minds of some breeders; but as many of our fanciers come and go, staying in the fancy a short time and then giving place to others, the subject has not been given the prominence it deserves.

Should many of our most prominent races acquire the character of being very short lived, their financial value will depreciate accordingly, and such breeds as acquire the worst reputations in this line will suffer the most. The time has come to call a halt in breeding pup-pies from a short lived strain.

BLUEBERRY *and pups*
Breeder/Owner, Edwin Brough
Artist, R. H. Moore
1899

all hunting hounds.

I have found a great many faults with the show hound pure and simple, and more, perhaps, with his owner. What remedy is there? Well, only one as far as I can see, but I fear there is no prospect of its being carried out whilst the vested interest is with the dog show man. Briefly it is this: I think that after a certain date, say two years hence, no Bloodhound over the age of two years should be allowed to compete at any show unless it held a certificate of proficiency in hunt-ing the clean boot, won at an open field trial of either the Association of Bloodhound Breeders, or the Bloodhound Hunt Club, or other recognised authority. No possible objection could be raised to this proposal, except by the dog show man, who cares not one single jot for the nose and hunting instincts of the breed.

All true sportsmen, all sound hunting men, and, without exception, everyone who genuinely loves the Bloodhound for the reason for which it was originally differentiated and bred, namely, for hunting, would welcome the adoption of this proposal with open arms; for it would be the death of continued inbreeding, inasmuch as the in and inbred show hound which could not hunt, and thus could not win his certificate, would be utterly valueless. Whilst of all other hounds we should know that at any rate every single one had some idea of hunting and the best looking and most typical would still be the show winners.

Questions for Consideration

1. Do various breeds represent more than just physical variations of canine form?
2. Should those interested only in show qualities participate as active breeders if they own breeds which have a corresponding performance or working function?
3. Does it harm the fancy in general, and specific breeds in particular, when they are bred strictly for show purposes without concern to original working qualities?
4. Should there be radical divergence in appearance and temperament of show dogs and performance dogs of the same breed? Why or why not?
5. If we concede that breeding for show means breeding for a winning phenotype which can reasonably be expected to reproduce itself, why should we bother with hip x-rays, eye checks and so on, if the show dog does not display any clinical symptoms which would eliminate it from competition?
6. Since normal dogs generally live only to an age of 12-15 years, why spend time or money to eliminate inherited conditions? Isn't it easier to just acquire another dog?
7. Do you think show dog longevity is a problem? What is the average age at death of your favorite breed? Do you consider this normal? If not, what do you suggest be done to correct the problem?
8. Since show dogs would continue to be judged and awarded prizes based upon their individual breed standards, would breed type be lost if meaningful outcrosses to other breeds were allowed?
9. If outcrosses to different breeds were permitted, who should make the determination to proceed and state which breeds could be utilized—the AKC, the parent clubs or responsible breeders? Who would establish the criteria to justify an outcross?
10. What is a responsible breeder?
11. Because closed breeding populations exist in the majority of recognized breeds—most from between fifty to over one hundred years—many breeds now have a high incidence of inheritable diseases. Should outcrosses to other breeds be considered at this time to maintain viability, especially in some of the rarer breeds?
12. If an outcross to another breed would eliminate or significantly reduce the incidence of conditions such as bloat (gastric torsion) or inheritable diseases, don't responsible breeders have an obligation to consider this option if, indeed, the goal is breed improvement? Or, would it be easier to wait for the canine genome to be mapped out and then solve all the problems on the molecular level?
13. What is a purebred dog?

The Utility of Dog Shows

"The Field"
1894

The question has often been asked, "Have dog shows improved the canine race or otherwise?" This can well be answered in the affirmative. Something like thirty-five years ago the first dog show was held, the *locus in quo* being far away north, at Newcastle-on-Tyne—a sorry and meager affair compared with the huge gatherings which now take place periodically in London, Birmingham, and in some other large provincial towns. At the inaugural exhibition there were fewer than seventy entries, and Pointers and Setters only were represented; now a show to be of high repute must include from five hundred to a thousand or more dogs, of which there will probably be about forty varieties. Somehow or other, the purely sporting animals nowadays do not muster in the same numbers as those that are generally understood to be the more fancy dogs, although, at the Birmingham gathering, which will shortly be held, the display of the former is the finest which takes place in the kingdom. This seems rather odd; but it has been the fashion to show sporting dogs in Curzon Hall, yet there is no reason why they should appear more strongly there than elsewhere, unless it be because the Birmingham Show is the oldest establishment of its kind, and actually dates back to the same year as that in which the first show of all took place. Anyone visiting the larger exhibitions for the first time must have noticed the number of spectators present and the generally business-like way in which they go about their pleasure. Many of them are no doubt exhibitors themselves, and there are numerous keepers and assistants in charge of the dogs. All ranks and conditions of men and women intermingle with each other, and the fancier in corduroy may be seen in conversation on some knotty point of a favorite Toy Spaniel with a woman in furs and velvet. At a dog show all appear to meet on the same level; in the ring, where the awards are made, and outside it, where the criticisms are freely hatched. This general leveling up has its advantages, for it puts the common fancier on his best behavior, and, whatever his language and manners may be among his everyday companions, at the dog show they are all that the most exacting might desire. Here he is improved in his surroundings, and after a visit to the Crystal Palace

THE KENDAL OTTERHOUNDS
at the Birmingham, England show
1877
No longer required to do their original work, the few remaining specimens of this breed exist principally as show dogs.

Death Makes Equals of the High and Low

And, as Victorian England and the rest of the world soon discovered, dog shows had the same omnipotent power to bring together in a public forum royalty and commoner, men and women, amateur and professional. Constrained for centuries by a rigid class structure, the concept of not only mingling, but actually competing on an equal basis with all strata of society, was revolutionary. A commonly held Victorian belief was

The Terrier Show

This illustration depicts people and events at the Terrier Show held at the Royal Aquarium in 1886. This was the first show superintended by Charles Cruft.

Top: Mrs. Jackson and "Bluebell" her drop-eared Skye; Mr. G. Raper's dog "Raby Baffler."

Middle: The long and the short of it. Irish Terrier Fanciers Billy Graham, Mr. C. J. Barnett. Mr. T. Maxwell, Mr. G. Raper, Mr. Humphrey di Trafford. Mr. H. di Trafford's Champion Wire Hair Terrier "Barton Wonder." Three prominent prize winners— The Rev. Fisher's 1st Special— Smooth Fox Terrier No. 103; 236—Mr. Maxwell's "Welsher," winner of first prize and cup; The outsider, "Little Jim Smith."

Bottom: Mr. Hodges holding forth on "Dandie Dinmonts." Along the row.

Biographies of some of the people depicted here by artist, Archie Gunn, can be found in Charles Lane's, "Dog Shows and Doggy People," published in 1902.

that one could improve by associating with one's "betters." This was the principal rationale put forth to justify such an uncommonly egalitarian social event as the dog show. Although top winners could be purchased, wealth was no guarantee one could breed a good dog. Royal ancestry was no guarantee one would win. Charles Lane was the first person to publicly adjudicate any of Queen Victoria's canines. Her attendant made it quite clear to him whose ownership the dog was, but Lane simply judged the dogs, awarding Her Majesty's entry a second prize. In the end, the "betters" with whom everyone was associating were the dogs. With love and loyalty for their owners, regardless of class, canines successfully elevated their own social and legal status in a manner no other animal has ever been able to attain. And they did it by just being themselves.

or to the Agricultural Hall he may return home an improved man and act accordingly.

But it is not on this account that we write in defense of dog shows, but because they have had a very great influence in obtaining kinder treatment to the many varieties of the canine race. Before such exhibitions were invented by Messrs. Shortnose, Pape, and Brailsford—names, indeed, to conjure with so far as the better side of sporting matters is concerned—the dog fancier was a strange being. He might appear in many characters—a rough, with "Newgate knocker" and a Toy Terrier; or as a swell, with stiff-starched collar, heavy check trousers, and a Bulldog. Now he is found in sundry forms, but not one of them is remarkable; he may be clad as the respectable workingman, or as the clergyman. The "woman fancier," too, is there—ladylike and neatly attired in tailor-made costume of wholesome tweed; or as the workingman's wife in less fashionably cut garments. A time was when the poor dog got more kicks than half-pence; but the day came when he could win prizes for his owners. A kicked, broken-spirited animal had not so good a chance of taking the honors as the better cared for, sprightly, if you like, impudent, little pet, so the "kicks" were dispensed with, and the dog was fondled and well fed instead. He came to be looked upon as part and parcel of the household, and was treated accordingly. The Toy Spaniels, Toy Terriers, and many varieties of the other terriers live in happier times now than those in which their ancestors existed, for many of the best of these little dogs, though bred by artisans in London and other large centers, are well cared for and, because not pampered and over-fed, lead a happier existence than when they were removed to more aristocratic surroundings.

Some of our dogs still undergo the mutilation and pain of having their ears cut, but shows have decreased this operation to a certain extent. Pugs are not shorn of their aural appendages as once was the case, nor are Irish Terriers. Perhaps when the Bull Terrier and Black and Tan Terrier and English White Terrier clubs, to say nothing of those for the Great Dane and Yorkshire Terrier, become more humanitarian they will follow the exceedingly good example of the Irish Terrier club and adopt such measures as will abolish cropping in its entirety. The London and Birmingham fanciers now frequent the dog show instead of surrounding the dog pit, and find it more to their advantage and less to their danger to favor beauty in their dogs rather than ferocity. And so, less dog fighting is indulged in than formerly. This is not because the bench dog is less plucky than his cousin, for there is a story told of a celebrated Bull Terrier bitch belonging to the late James Hinks of Birmingham, which, after winning the chief prize at one of our metropolitan gatherings, fought a battle the same evening with a champion fighter, and killed her opponent.

To the shooting man, the country squire and sportsman the benefit dog shows have produced, and no doubt will continue to produce, is not so apparent. As a rule, he does not see the best dogs on the benches, so far as field work is concerned, for many a prize winner is useless with the gun, and the "beautiful neck, strong loins, unexceptional legs and feet, and lovely expression," of which the reporter is so fond of writing, are useless unless they are accompanied by intelligence and perfect olfactory organs. Neither of the latter can be distinguished in the ring. Thus the grumbler appears to have grounds for complaint, especially when his own dog, which may be fairly shapely to the eye and very nearly perfect over grouse and partridge, is beaten by his neighbor's, which, though more elegant in form, is absolutely gun-shy and worthless in the field.

> *"Were it not for shows and field trials we might not have to look far in advance when the commoner sporting dog is to be extinct, the sole survivor being the retriever in some shape or form."*

Dogs and the Environment

Over 100 years ago, the author of the main article stated dog shows could not shoulder the blame for the decline in numbers of sporting dogs, more profoundly ascribing this change to loss of supportive wildlife habitat. Today, we are fully inculcated to environmental issues, but in the 1890s, the destruction of game and extinction of species were relatively new concerns. The Industrial Revolution made Great Britain the wealthiest country in the world. Increased urbanization and improved farming methods not only reduced wildlife habitat but removed the need for the vast majority of citizens to put food on the table by hunting. While sport hunting still encouraged the production of dogs developed for specific game, their real decline was accelerated by major improvements in firearms. The dramatic advances in both accuracy and power of these new guns meant that commercial hunters could provide thousands of birds to satisfy an urban palate desiring wildfowl on the menu. The dogs needed for commercial hunting were rugged, tireless, utilitarian retrievers, which the author correctly predicted would become the most predominate of all sporting dogs.

As early as 1883, "The American Field" printed numerous pleas to end commercial hunting and called for the institution of controlled hunting seasons. However, although few were listening in 1859, Darwin had already documented how interactive relationships of various species within an environment have a direct impact on the survivability of other species. For example, he detailed how the number of cats within a district not only had an obvious connection to the number of mice, but also to the amount of red clover and local bee populations, as well. Further, Darwin stated that competition among domesticated animals may be even more stringent than in wild populations because human beings select for such things as economics, convenience and fancy. This loss of diversity for the benefit of increased production is clearly evidenced today when we note that the Holstein is the dominant milk producer and the Leghorn the primary commercial egg layer. Unfortunately, dog fanciers still fail to realize the implications these theories and trends have on the survivability of their own favorite canine breed or, for that matter, of all dogs into the next century.

In 1894 there were only 37 officially recognized dog breeds in the United States. Today, that number is 140 and still growing. In continuing to recognize more breeds, AKC registrations have increased overall, notwithstanding the figures for 1997, which posted a decline in 48% of all breeds recognized. However, this decrease is consistent with other trends indicating fewer homes owning dogs as pets in the United States. Each newly recognized breed is in competition for a favorable environment with those already in existence. And under the control of public mood or fancy, some breeds will inevitably supplant others. Consequently, those with annual registrations of under 100, if not under 1,000, may not remain viable. All sincere dog fanciers should sober up to the statistical facts that with increased competition for available owners, quite a few breeds stand more than an even chance of disappearing altogether by the middle of the 21st Century.

Incredibly, the uniquely extraordinary genetic quality of the canine—diversity—may contribute to its decline. This available variety tends to foster dog fanciers only interested in their favorite breed with little reality based concern that the health and viability of all breeds has a direct impact on the entire sport. Surely, after more than 100 years of showing dogs, the fancy must be expected to reach a level of maturity in which their interests are broadened beyond winning at the next show. However, even a concerned fancy, saddled with a registry body which defines canine progress as continual growth in registrations (revenue), will be doomed to failure unless urgent and relevant steps, beyond public relations window dressing, are taken to ask—and correctly answer—all serious questions regarding the survivability of dogs in the society and environment of the future.

The Loss of Diversity

CH. ECLIPSE
Artist, R. H. Moore

The White English Terrier belongs to a small number of "original" breeds which served as tap roots for many of our modern canine forms. Apart from the spitz and spaniel families, the Greyhound, Bloodhound, Bulldog, Mastiff and White English Terrier seemed to possess such dominant and useful combinations of conformation, temperament and unique inherent traits that knowledgeable dog breeders took great pains, not only to retain the original animals, but to automatically turn to them when they needed to infuse and fix desired characteristics into other breeds. Further, when these five breeds were crossed with each other the resultant variations were not nondescript mongrels, but distinct material from which could be melded new definite breeds.

Extremely common in and around Lancashire, the White English Terrier was a close cousin of the Black and Tans, or as we refer to them today in America, Manchester Terriers. Apparently part of the English countryside since time immemorial, this breed was frequently represented in late 18th and early 19th Century paintings and prints. Like the Manchester, there were definite size variations with the top weight about 20 pounds. While the Wire-Haired Fox Terrier originally developed from a separate source, in all likelihood, the White English Terrier, one of the most common stable dogs at the time, played a role in the creation of the Smooths. When bull-baiting became illegal in 1835, White English Terriers were the principal fountain head for the terrier side of the equation in the various bull-and-terrier crosses which developed, particularly the Bull Terrier.

After the disappearance of the White English Terrier, many later writers presumed, incorrectly, that the breed was a descendant of the Bull Terrier, rather than the opposite. While today's Bull Terriers have radically changed in head type, the confusion sprang from the superficial similarities of earlier stock to the older breed. To differentiate, the White English Terrier had a fuller, oval eye; less fill under the eyes; a squarer muzzle with stronger underjaw; more tuck-up in the body and, most notably, a tractable, affectionate temperament —completely lacking the warrior disposition of the Bull Terrier.

The White English Terrier is also one of the positively identified progenitors of the Boston Terrier. Although the White English Terrier was never common in the United States, at the turn of the last century Boston Terriers and Bull Terriers, including numerous Toy Bull Terriers (a great many of which were probably White English Terriers), were so popular in America that there was really no niche left for another similar breed. But, if the dog show can be credited with saving many breeds from extinction, the dog show rules in effect in England, conversely, led to the rapid demise of the White English Terrier.

More correctly, the reaction to the rules by the owners of White English Terriers was the primary reason for their disappearance. When cropped dogs were barred from English show competition in 1895, owners of the breed refused to comply, maintaining the breed had always been traditionally cropped and that the determination of correct presentation was the prerogative of the specialist club. The Kennel Club adamantly refused to make an exception for this ancient breed. Without the forum of the dog show for public display and championships, registrations rapidly dwindled as newly introduced breeds captured the public fancy. The last of the breed was exhibited in 1904, although the KC carried the breed on the roster until 1917. The White English Terrier did not merely disappear from public view—it became extinct. This extirpation was so complete that after World War I most new dog show exhibitors had never heard of a White English Terrier, let alone mourn the loss of a uniquely prepotent and important breed.

Still, it may be possible to have dogs perfect in appearance and as good in the field as natural ability and careful training can make them. Hitherto, shows have not been the cause of production of field dogs to any great extent, though some mighty bench winners in their day have performed equally mighty deeds in the field, and may such have from time to time sprung from the kennels of Mr. R. J. Lloyd Price, Mr. Purcell Llewellin, and other celebrities in their line.

Perhaps modern farming improvements and the general changes in the surroundings of shooting have had no little to do with any deterioration there may be in some sporting dogs of today, though we are not certain where this deterioration comes in. So the blame of that must not be laid at the doors of the dog shows, as is usually the case. Not half the number of Pointers, Setters and spaniels are kept now for shooting purposes as was the case thirty years ago. Human beaters, in the form of a score of Giles Scrogginses, take the place of the spaniels, and in many parts of the country the retriever has usurped the position of the Pointer and Setter. Birds of all kinds, barring pheasants, are wilder now than then. They appear to become more so every year, and "driving" is resorted to for both grouse and partridges where shooting over dogs once held sway. "Walking up," too, with retrievers "at heel," is likewise in vogue, while on few manors are the well-broken Pointer and Setter found, nor the teams of spaniels which drop promptly to whistle or to gunshot. Were it not for shows and field trials we might not have to look far in advance when the commoner sporting dog is to be extinct, the sole survivor being the retriever in some shape or form.

The gentle and interesting Scottish Deerhound is now having his nose put out of joint as a sporting dog by the Collie, and in some cases by the retriever; and the noble Bloodhound, with no work for him to do, will also have to survive and flourish under the aegis of dog shows. Sporting terriers can usually make room for themselves, while Foxhounds, Otterhounds,

Harriers, Beagles, and Greyhounds are not, so far as we know at present, likely to require the support of exhibitions to prevent their extirpation; for, if the hare in some places is becoming extinct, a substitute for her is found in the deer, which will afford to the horseman a greater amount of galloping, even if the hunting be not so good. Let disappointed exhibitors rail; let the conservative sportsman of a past generation grumble as he may at what he calls the "modern ruin of all dogs." Shows have not been without their influence for good, and in the future cannot fail to prevent, or at any rate retard, the extinction of some of our biggest, most sagacious, and handsomest varieties of the canine race.

Allusion need scarcely be made to the advantage of dog shows from a commercial point of view. The railway companies are aware of it, and do not consider it derogatory to canvass for the support of an exhibitor, so far as their line is concerned, on the eve of an important exhibition; but this purely trade side of the subject need not be discussed here.

Saved by the Show

According to Stonehenge, this hairless Chinese Crested was the only breed representative in England in 1866. Though there was no real interest in these exotics, dedicated breeders persisted in utilizing the dog show forum to keep them before the public. Finally becoming more numerous in Great Britain and America in the late 20th Century, they are now frequent competitors in the Toy Group, little changed in appearance from the image shown.

273

A Passion for Performance

Although after 1835 animal fights were illegal in Britain, rats didn't disappear. Consequently, no one objected to utilizing dogs to kill vermin, even at competitive events in the pit. The image shown of Ch. Ruling Passion was painted by Maud Earl. Eventually sold to Edgar Farman, this red brindle, under 45 pounds bitch was Best Bulldog in 1894 at the Bulldog Club, Inc. show. According to "The Stockkeeper," she missed this event in 1891. "Mr. Alfred J. Smith's Ruling Passion was absent from the Bulldog show in consequence of her face having been damaged by rats whilst endeavouring to beat the record."

Questions for Consideration

1. Have dog shows helped improve the appearance, functionality and status of the dog within society or not? Give specific examples for each category.

2. Is companionship a valid reason for keeping certain breeds? Is existing merely as a show dog an equally valid justification or must dogs be expected to perform a useful function? Is being a companion or show dog a useful function if it brings pleasure to the owner?

3. Because of the dramatic increase in numbers of dogs in competition, quality of competition and quantity of shows and performance events, is it a reasonable expectation to demand that any particular breed excel in both conformation and performance events designed to test original function?

4. How does one reconcile the gap in appearance and temperament which exists in several breeds between show dogs and those still performing their original function? In your opinion, is this gap more superficial than actual? If actual, which group is correct, i.e., entitled to proclaim they are maintaining and producing "true type?"

5. Is it possible to have a dog which is both correctly conformed according to its standard of excellence and still able to perform its original function? Which quality is more important? Are qualities of functionality and conformation mutually exclusive?

6. Are dog shows responsible for the "modern ruin of all dogs," or, as the writer contends are they responsible for the preservation of unique canine variations?

7. If breeds disappear because they are no longer able to perform their original work or have fallen from public favor, should we be concerned?

8. Could many of the very large dog show extravaganzas in existence today be more properly described as trade shows rather than dog shows?

9. In discussing the attraction of all walks of life to the dog show, the writer asserts the Victorian belief that associating with one's "betters" would improve character. However, less than 20 years later, Judith Lytton claimed that the fastest way to ethical compromise was to spend too much time with dog show people. How much of dog showing is actually about improving the various breeds and how much revolves around social interactions —good, bad or indifferent?

Past & Future of Dog Shows

"The Kennel Review"
1883

Exhibition of Sporting and other dogs, Holborn, 1861

There is nothing more commonly heard than the pessimist cry that dog shows are about played out. It is very generally felt that they are not, in themselves, in the mode of carrying on, nor in many of their concomitants wholly satisfactory. Thereupon, the disappointed and the querulous join with the rigid righteous and the dreamers after an impossible perfection in things mundane to set up a discordant howl that dog shows are going from bad to worse. We are not of those who take such a dismal view of these institutions any more than we believe them to be perfect of their kind.

Let us look back to the shows of former years, let us consider their initiation, the causes that produced them, the objects sought to be attained by them, their gradual development to their present numbers and extent, and see whether in what has been accomplished we cannot find some grains of hope for the future, even if we are not justified in taking a too strongly optimistic view of them.

Those who would inquire into the earliest dog shows must direct their research into what is so far as these institutions are concerned, prehistoric times. Long before Curzon Hall was built or the Crystal Palace was designed to enclose a world's fair, or its galleries turned into temporary kennels, dog shows were held in the snug parlours and smoking rooms of the taverns, and the same spirit of emulation was at work there that served to initiate the more public shows, from which have grown the monster gatherings of the present, and without which they would soon cease to exist.

We are often compelled to think that there has been rather too much high faluting about the object of shows being solely the improvement of the dog. Let us be thankful if the condition of dogs generally is ameliorated, and the several kinds improved by the influence of shows, direct or indirect; but at the same time let us be candid enough with ourselves to admit that there are several other objects, some of them

275

perhaps less worthy, that supply the stimulus that keeps these exhibitions going.

When it is remembered how universal a favourite the dog is, how close our relations with him are in sport, work and leisure, and the natural desire of most of us to possess the handsomest and the best, the why and the wherefore of dog shows is seen at a glance; and there can be no doubt that at first it was more to compare friendly notes and provide a good reason for a pleasant gathering, than with any very pronounced views of improving the dog, that they were at first instituted, and for some time, supported. That shows have tended to improve many of our breeds no one who has watched their development during the last twenty years can possibly doubt.

At one time, with the exception of a very few classes, there was nothing like uniformity of character met with, in some classes

"Dog Shows Then"
Artist, R. H. Moore

there was nothing but mongrelism to be seen, in others one or two specimens stood prominently forward as the representatives of a type, whilst the remainder of the class consisted of nondescripts. Now it is a rare thing at our principal shows to meet with a specimen that has not fair claims to rank as one of the kind of the class in which we find him exhibited, and the majority of classes now consist of fairly good specimens, thus showing the effect of the teaching competition has imparted in the family character they display. On the other hand, those who complain that utility has been lost sight of, and that the arbitrary standards set up have rather deteriorated than improved many breeds, are not without support to their opinions in existing facts.

Mastiffs, the grand, historic, broad mouthed dogs of Britain, that have ceased to bark or to pay sweetest welcome as we draw near

home, are not absent from shows where preference is sometimes given to preponderance of flesh over true character. Terriers who have lost their right to the name, because they will not go to earth, are exalted to premier honours because they are beautiful according to the prevailing fashion. And Collies that refuse to look at a sheep until Normanized into mutton, but are decorated because they are the mode, are not wanting. These are some of the evil things we have inherited from the past, or rather, they are the natural result of having allowed "fancy" full sway without some counterpoise or ballast in the shape of improved and educated judgment to check its extravagancies.

Against the past we have charges of unfair dealing and of favouritism between committees, exhibitors, and judges; many of which charges are gross exaggerations, and others unfounded, leaving but a very small percentage of the actively dishonest in the bulk of those associated with shows; but those mildewed ears have given a bad character to the whole in the opinion of those who cannot, or will not, discriminate. Happily the opportunities for practising unfairness diminish with time; exhibitors are more alive to what should be, and any flagrant dereliction of duty by a judge, or any gross miscarriage of justice through his incompetence is now quickly detected, and although we are still a long way from perfection, yet it is gratifying to know that we have now a very large number of competent judges, and an increasing number of exhibitors with keen eyes and improved judgment to detect an error.

Faking in all its varied and contemptible forms was at its rankest growth in the past; it cannot now fatten on the ignorance and credulity which once was its game and food. The faker is

Dog Shows—A Woman Remembers

The following appeared in Charles Lane's "Dog Shows and Doggy People." One of the earliest St. Bernard breeders, Mrs. Jagger began exhibiting in 1872. The first woman to judge any large breed in both Great Britain and on the Continent, she contributed many articles to the "Ladies' Field," "Bazaar," "Lady Exhibitor," and the "Ladies' Kennel Journal." She also penned several books on other topics.

Anyone who has owned one particular breed for thirty years knows the so-called improvements that have taken place in that breed. If thirty years brings changes in a breed, it has brought more startling changes in dogs and dog shows. A once primitive pastime has become a vast, organised business, demanding time, thought and money. An animal that was once valued at three-halfpence can now be sold for a thousand pounds.

The Bulldog that was formerly the companion of a type of Bill Sykes is in the front rank of canine beauties. The dogs of the shepherd and drover are the petted inmates of palaces. The Old English Mastiff has given place to the Russian Wolfhound, the Black and Tan Terrier to the French Poodle, the hardy Smooth Terrier to the long-haired monstrosity, and so on. Journals and newspapers devoted to dogs are as eagerly read as the daily newspaper and dogs and dog showing are now part of the present social life.

Perhaps the greatest change in dog showing from the days when they were held in obscure public houses has been the introduction of the feminine element. Lady exhibitors now own some of the best dogs, both in large and small breeds and are considered by many as reliable judges as men. After the breaking down of many hostile barriers they have been chosen to adjudicate upon their respective breeds without shocking "Mrs. Grundy." Since the introduction of the St. Bernard into England the breed has always been favoured by women, yet I was the first woman asked to judge the breed, as well, to judge any large breed. This was in Belfast as late as 1894, and the event caused a sensation at the time, the Press giving such headlines as "A Lady Going to the Dogs," "Advance of Women," and "Innovation in Dog Judging." Now I can judge without comment. Other ladies have followed in taking the large breeds, notably Her Grace the Duchess of Newcastle, Mrs. Horsfall, Mrs. Mansfield and others. In fact, female judges are now almost as numerous as men.

My earliest recollections of dog showing were the agricultural shows of the North, where dogs were only allowed on sufferance. Spratt's and Calabar's did not exist and pedigrees were not required. Wooden stakes were driven into the ground and the free air of heaven blew about the dogs. Another interesting item was that we were not allowed to either lead our dogs to be judged or be present during judging. I can, however, recall such old world shows as Penistone and Woodsome, where fine specimens of the canine race were exhibited, such as Mastiffs, Bull Terriers and the large Black and Tan Terriers, now so seldom seen.

In the earlier days committees of local agricultural shows had to look to gamekeepers and such ilk for canine knowledge and these men were appointed year after year. I can remember showing my dogs under several gamekeepers. Then I can recall such people as Charles Greaves, John Inman and Mr. William Lort. I was wont to look with reverent awe upon the latter, never dreaming that one day I, too, should myself, "don the ermine."

277

The St. Bernard Mystique

Albert Smith, the first traveler to ascend Mount Blanc, returned from his Alpine trip with two St. Bernards, but it was the Rev. J. Cumming Macdonna who popularized the breed in England. Early show catalogs generally listed breeds in order of size, from large to small. Pride of place almost invariably went to either Bloodhounds or St. Bernards, not because they were the largest but rather, they were considered the most virtuous. The heroic life-saving tales of Barry (whose stuffed remains reside in the Natural History Museum in Berne) and the other dogs of the Swiss monastery attained mythical proportions in England. The print shown, one of many copies of Landseer's 1820 painting, helped perpetuate this romantic notion. While today we breed dogs for a particular physical appearance, temperament or specific function, in Victorian times many breeds had the added quality of being metaphors for various character traits. Thus, the St. Bernard was actually viewed as a true canine Saint, for, as the stories go, they possessed the ultimate virtue of willingly laying down their lives to save human beings. Many people considered touching a St. Bernard on display at a dog show to be an almost spiritual experience and throngs of people were always about these dogs on the bench. In fact, because of the reverential attitude toward the breed, early judging schedules were created to accommodate the St. Bernard exhibitors, including holding up judging if certain big winners were not ready to be examined.

During the Victorian era St. Bernards were popularly portrayed as the canine icon of sacrificial virtue.

Naturally, the English set about to "improve" the breed. Sincerely believing that such a heroic dog would also possess the wisdom and nobility of a Bloodhound, St. Bernards were crossed with that breed for the specific purpose of introducing the deep haw and wrinkled brow which denoted those traits. Initially, it was also a necessity that the breed possess double dewclaws on the rear legs. The justification for this was to "prove" they were of Swiss descent, for all were told that these appendages were needed for the dog to walk on top of the snow. This fad lasted until Hugh Dalziel wrote a scathingly sarcastic article wondering why the supernumerary toes were not equally as necessary for the front legs, painting a verbal picture of the dogs plowing a trail with their heads in search of their victims. But, the one significant change which led to the St. Bernard being the first boom and bust breed in popularity was the quest for size at any cost.

The rationale, if it may be called that, for this selection process was the feeling that any breed so grand in spirit would, of necessity, need to be grand in stature, with an imposing, massive head. Soundness and activity were quickly exchanged for size. Fanciers, particularly Americans, were willing to pay any price for the largest St. Bernard available and entries of over one hundred were common at all major shows on both sides of the Atlantic. Finally, within thirty years, the unwieldy size of the breed with its concomitant expense to rear and house, the amount of space needed to keep them and the introduction of new breeds, made the once premier show dog an undesirable possession.

Nevertheless, the public had not forsaken the idea of owning a breed of heroic character. The Newfoundland soon filled the void and was immensely popular in nautically inclined Great Britain. It was said that once "rescued" by one of these dogs bathers took great caution never to step in the water again if a Newfoundland was nearby. One such case recounted was that of a woman swimmer dragged to shore against her will, her bathing suit shredded in the process and the dog happily presenting her to onlookers—in much less than modest attire.

not dead nor have his artful dodges ceased to disgrace and discredit dog showing, but his tricks are few and far between by comparison with what has been.

The great and rapid development of shows has brought into being another class that has exercised considerable influence, and that is the expert or specialist reporter. It would be a difficult question to decide whether these have done more harm or good. Taking them in the bulk we are disposed to think they have been a useful class; that some of them have been knavish enough is probably true, that many of them are extremely foolish and wanting in practical knowledge of what they write about, they themselves furnish abundant proof, but there are those among them who can equally well analyze the merits of a dog and the qualities and conduct of a judge, and to such we are often indebted. But, unfortunately, the mystic editorial "we" veils all alike, and the incompetent reporter is unworthily exalted, and the public confidence abused, whilst the able man suffers by the association.

Quite recently there has been an extraordinary development of what are termed special clubs—associations for the furtherance of the interests of the breed they affect. These now number over a dozen, and there is a promise of a considerable increase. It is becoming more and more the custom of committees in framing their schedules to consult these clubs, knowing that they not only add to the attractions of the prize lists, but exercise a very great influence in swelling the entries.

People usually expect a *quid pro quo*, and special clubs are not free from this human weakness. They ask, and with considerable force of reason, that the prizes they give for the encouragement of their breed shall be awarded by judges whom they approve, and that his awards shall be made in accordance with the standard of excellence recognized by them, and the result of this is that members of the clubs are, as a rule, elected to adjudicate on dogs owned by the outside public competing against dogs the property of the fellow members.

This state of things gives rise to comment anything but complimentary to the system and the club, even when the judge is not individually attacked. There is certainly too often grounds for complaint, and it is not to be wondered at, for however hard a man may try, it is difficult to free himself from the *esprit de corps* which club fellowship of this kind is supposed to engender. It is still more difficult to convince outsiders that they are truly competing against the club members on level terms.

Such are dog shows—so far as we have attempted to describe them—after twenty years of life, and, as we view them, they are still struggling to disencumber themselves from the results of early errors and the weeds of bad customs that have grown up with them. We have, over and over again, heard the cry that dog shows were on the wane and that their death knell would soon be struck, but, like most British institutions, they have shown, and are showing, a wonderful tenacity of life and give very strong evidence that our insular practice of gradual reform will better serve to improve their constitution and practice than any violent revolution. There never have been so many shows, with such wide and full classification and liberal prize lists as have already been and are announced to be held this year. No shows in the past have ever had the wide and the very substantial support given as is being afforded to those of 1883, and therefore, and especially

"Dog Shows Now"
Artist, R. H. Moore
(n.b.—depicted are the bench chains designed by L. Allen Shuter).

in the face of many deviations from past practice, it seems a fitting time, by the light of the past, to consider the future of shows.

We would unwillingly pass over without notice such vulgar abuses as the tricks known as "faking," by which, through one device or another, a dog is made to appear other than he is. But, unfortunately, the evil exists, and the detection of these frauds is too often left to everybody, with the natural consequence that crime remains undetected and unpunished. Since the abortive attempt of the Kennel Club to deal with the subject, people seem to have gone to sleep over it, and probably some may think the festering wound is not there because it has been covered over with a respectable looking soothing plaster.

But the evil is a real one, and at a future time we shall return to it. In the meantime, we say managing committees ought to bestir themselves to stamp out the evil thing. It is unfair to ask the judge to find out cases of faking. The competitor against the guilty party is the most likely to find out the cheat, but he shrinks from becoming informer on the condition that he must deposit a sovereign and lose it unless he can prove at least good grounds for his charge, and he may, and often has, other and more delicate reasons for refusing the task. We recommend that opportunities be given to parties, exhibitors or others, to call the attention, without disclosure of their personality, of the committee to apparent or suspected frauds, and that thereupon a committee of investigation should unostentatiously proceed to inquire into the case. One of the evil results of past practice has been, as we have already shown, to create types of dogs with certain features arbitrarily demanded by fashion and of no real value, but, on the contrary, detrimental to the usefulness of the animal in his natural work. Collies are an instance in point. So much has been sacrificed to coat that present day show dogs have coats that

"We are fully convinced that good looks and intrinsic good qualities may be propagated together, and to do so is the future work of dog shows and those who manage and support them."

would be a positive hindrance to work, and to get rid of a setter-like head and large saddleflap ears, with the demand for, "glossy black and rich mahogany or orange tan," advocated by some judges, reporters, and others a dozen years ago, breeders have run into the opposite extreme, and at the present rate of progress in the same direction we will soon have Collies with no heads at all.

The corrective for this is trials of ability in the management of sheep, for the encouragement of which the Collie Club is deserving of all praise. Trials in practical work according to their kind should be extended to many more breeds than are now subjected to such ordeals. If Bassets and Dachshunds are bred for generations for show purposes only, their unquestionably good qualities as workmen will be lost.

St. Bernard men insist on dewclaws, and assert that they will aid in supporting the dog in traveling over snow, but of what use can these supernumerary toes be to a dog that knows no change save from his kennel to the show bench? Terriers of various breeds are kept under conditions that thwart their natural propensities and distort useful qualities. Bulldogs are now bred so much for fancy points that, amongst other useful and, indeed, absolutely necessary attributes, the quality of courage, by which the race was long distinguished, is rapidly degenerating into an excess of nervousness, and their teeth, sacrificed to valueless attributes, will soon necessitate every exhibition dog being spoon fed. And so we might go through many classes showing the urgent need of some changes in our methods of improving the dog by bench shows.

We are glad on these considerations to see that the British Kennel Association are about to revive at Aston water trials for Newfoundlands and other dogs that may be used as life savers, and it is this utility view of the dog that we so strongly advocate should be sedulously cultivated, and a little consideration of it will show our readers what a wide field there is when the several breeds and their various services are taken into account, and it is the development of this class of work which we are of opinion should characterize the dog shows of the future.

We are perfectly aware of the objections that may be urged, and of the difficulties that are sure to be raised. There are people, and not a few, who always see a lion in the way when if they had but courage to go forward they would find the beast but a mouse. The question is, and it is of such serious importance, we beg of our readers to weigh it well—are we to cultivate dogs in agreement with certain descriptions of appearances, to total neglect of their best and most useful qualities? We think not, and we are fully convinced that good looks and intrinsic good qualities may be propagated together, and to do so is the future work of dog shows and those who manage and support them.

We have but touched on the future of dog shows, and space compelling us to close we defer consideration of other interesting points to be discussed in the future.

Questions for Consideration

1. Are dog shows important? To whom?
2. Do you believe dog shows have helped improve dogs?
3. The writer states that even though the original purpose of dog shows was for the improvement of the dog, many other social factors enter into their continued success. What are the three main reasons you attend, exhibit and/or judge at dog shows?
4. Does the dog press serve a useful purpose in the continuation of dog shows? Explain your reasons.
5. Is creating or modifying dogs for fancy points as opposed to enhancing useful function deleterious?
6. The writer feels it is unfair to place the onus on the judge to act upon incidences of faking. Whose responsibility is it (if anyone's) to do something about those who cheat?
7. In dog breeding, can good looks and intrinsic qualities be propagated together?
8. What issues regarding the sport of dogs do you feel are different today than those of the past? What issues remain to be solved?
9. Do you derive pleasure from being involved in the sport of dogs?

What do you envision as the future of dog shows?

Bibliography

BOOKS

Ackerman, Irving C. The Complete Fox Terrier: *Wire-Haired and Smooth Coated.* Orange Judd Publishing Co., New York. 1938.

Appleton, Douglas H. The Beagle Handbook. Nicholson & Watson. London. 1959.

Ash, Edward C. This Doggie Business. Hutchinson & Co., Ltd. London. 1934.

Barnes, Duncan, Editor and AKC Staff. The AKC's World of the Pure-Bred Dog. Howell Book House. New York. 1983.

Berger-Wheeler, Capt. F. E. A. The Bulldog Yearbook and Handbook, 1932. T. & W. Goulding. Bristol, England. 1932.

Black, David. The King of Fifth Avenue: *the fortunes of August Belmont.* The Dial Press. New York. 1981.

Bouyet, Barbara. Akita: *Treasure of Japan.* MIP Publishing. Montecito, CA. 1992.

Bowring, Clara and Monro, Alida. The Poodle. The Macmillan Company. New York. 1960.

Brey, Catherine F. and Reed, Lena, F. The Complete Bloodhound. Howell Book House. New York. 1978.

Brough, Edwin. The Bloodhound and its use in Tracking Criminals. The Illustrated Kennel News Co. London. 1902.

Brown, William F. Albert Frederick Hochwalt, *a biography.* A. F. Hochwalt Co. Dayton, Ohio. 1939.

Chadwick, Winifred E. The Borzoi Handbook. Nicholson & Watson. London. 1952.

Comminges, Waldner. Le Bouldogue Français: *son origine, son histoire, son élevage.* Librairie de Paris. Paris. 1933.

Compton, Herbert. The Twentieth Century Dog. Grant Richards. London. 1904.

Connett, Eugene V., Editor. American Sporting Dogs. D. Van Nostrand Company, Inc. New York. 1948.

Cooper, H. St. John. Bulldogs and Bulldog Men. Field and Fancy Publications. New York. 1908.

Cox, Major Harding. Dogs and I. G. P. Putnam's Sons. New York. 1924.

Craven, Arthur. Dogs of the World. Manchester, England. 1930.

Dale, Peter Allan. In Pursuit of a Scientific Culture: *Science, Art and Society in the Victorian Age.* The University of Wisconsin Press. Madison. 1989.

Darwin, Charles. The Descent of Man and Selection in Relation to Sex. 1871.

Darwin, Charles. The Origin of Species by Means of Natural Selection. 1859.

Deacon, Sydney. Show Bulldogs. Our Dogs Publishing Co., Ltd. Manchester, England. *c.* 1919.

Dunlap, Robert H. and Williams, David J. Veterinary Medicine: An Illustrated History. Mosby. St. Louis, Missouri. 1996.

Ewing, Dr. Fayette C. The Book of the Scottish Terrier. Orange Judd Publishing Company, Inc. New York. 1936.

Farman, Edgar. The Bulldog, *A Monograph.* The Kennel Gazette. London. 1899.

The French Bulldog Club of America and the

French Bulldog Club of New England. The French Bulldog: *History of the Origin of the Breed, Its Cultivation and Development.* Hamilton Printing Co. Albany, New York. 1926.

Hall, Forest N. Stripping a Wire. Ben Martin. Dallas, Texas. 1935.

Harris, Jose. Private Lives, Public Spirit: *Britain 1870-1914.* Penguin Books. London. 1993.

Harrison, J. F. C. Early Victorian Britain: 1832-51. Fontana Press. London. 1988.

Harrison, J. F. C. Late Victorian Britain: 1875-1901. Fontana Press. London. 1990.

Haynes, Williams. The Fox Terrier. Outing Publishing Company. New York. 1912.

Hochwalt, A. F. The Modern Pointer. 1917.

Horswell, Laurence Alden and Horswell, Dorothy Allison. Your Pet Dachshund. All-Pet Books. Fond du Lac, Wisconsin. 1954.

Jackson, Frank. Crufts: *The Official History.* Pelham Books. Harmondsworth, Middlesex, England. 1990.

Jackson, Jean and Jackson, Frank. Parson Jack Russell Terriers. Crowood Press. Ramsbury, Marlborough, Wiltshire, England. 1990.

Jaquet, Edward William. The Kennel Club: *A History and Record of its Work—1873-1905.* The Kennel Gazette. London. 1905.

Lane, Charles Henry. All About Dogs. John Lane. London. 1900.

Lane, Charles Henry. Dog Shows and Doggy People. Hutchinson & Co. London. 1902.

Lee, Rawdon B. Fox Terrier. Horace Cox. London. 1902.

Lee, Rawdon B. Modern Dogs of Great Britain and Ireland: *A History and Description.* Horace Cox. London. 1897.

Linderman, Joan M. and Funk, Virginia B. The New Complete Akita. Howell Book House. New York. 1994.

Lytton, The Hon. Mrs. Neville. Toy Dogs and their Ancestors: *Including the History and Management of Toy Spaniels, Pekingese, Japanese and Pomeranians.* D. Appleton and Company. New York. 1911.

Lowe, Brian. Hunting the Clean Boot: T*he Working Bloodhound.* Blandford Press. Poole Dorset, England. 1981.

McCandlish, W. L. Popular Dog Show Maxims: *Judges, Judged and Judging.* c. 1925.

McCandlish, W. L. The Scottish Terrier. Our Dogs Publishing Company, Ltd. Manchester, England. 1925.

Marples, Theo. Show Dogs: *Their Points and Characteristics. How to breed for Prizes and Profit.* Our Dogs Publishing Company, Ltd. Manchester, England. 1908.

Mattheson, Darley. Terriers. John Lane the Brodley Head, Ltd. London. 1922.

Meyer, Enno. The Bulldog. Orange Judd Pub. Co., Inc. New York. 1952.

Mills, Wesley. The Dog Book. T. Fisher Unwin. London. 1898.

Montgomery, E. S. The Complete Irish Terrier. Denlinger's. Middleburg, VA. 1958.

Muss-Arnolt,G., Motschenbacker, Dr. C., Lellmann, Professor D. Willfred and DCA Committee, Editors. Official Dachshund Standard of the Dachshund Club of America. Patterson Press. New York. 1904.

O'Neill, Charles, Editor. The American Kennel Club 1884-1994: *A Source Book.* Howell Book House. New York. 1985.

Ormond, Richard. Sir Edwin Landseer. Exhibition Catalog. Rizzoli. New York. 1982.

Reynolds, Don. Champion of Champions. Random House. 1950.

Ritvo, Harriet. The Animal Estate: *The English and Other Creatures in the Victorian Age.* Harvard University Press. Cambridge. 1989.

Sameja, Osiman. Yorkshire Terriers: *An Owners Companion.* The Crowood Press, Ltd. Ramsburg, Marlborough, Wiltshire, England. 1992.

The Schipperke Club of America. The Complete Schipperke. Howell Book House. New York. 1993.

Serrell, Alys. F., edited by Frances Slaughter. With Hound and Terrier in the Field. William Blackwood and Sons. Edinborough and London. 1904.

Shaw, Vero. The Encyclopedia of the Kennel.

George Routledge & Sons, Ltd. London. 1913.

Shaw, Vero. The Illustrated Book of the Dog. Cassell, Petter, Galpin & Co. London. 1881.

Shields, George O. The American Book of the Dog. Rand McNally. Chicago & New York. 1891.

Smith, Arthur Croxton. Dogs Since 1900. Andrew Dakers, Ltd. London. 1950.

Smith, Arthur Croxton. Sporting Dogs. Scribners. New York. 1938.

Stables, Dr. Gordon, Editor. The Dog Owners Annual Illustrated for 1890. Dean & Son. London. 1890.

Stables, Dr. Gordon, Editor. The Dog Owners Annual Illustrated for 1892. Dean & Son. London. 1892.

Sturgeon, A. G. Bulldogdom. Pearce & Gardner, Ltd. Chorleton-cum-Hardy. England. Third edition. 1923.

Sutton, Catherine. Dog Shows and Show Dogs: *A definitive study.* K & R Books, Ltd. Edlington, Lincolnshire, England. 1980.

Taylor, Major J. M. Field Trial Record of Dogs in America (1874-1907). Nicholson Printing Co. Pittsburgh, PA. 1907.

United Kennel Club, Inc. United Kennel Club, Inc. 1898-1997: *The First 100 Years.* United Kennel Club. Kalamazoo, Michigan. 1997.

Vesey-Fitzgerald, Brian, Editor. The Book of the Dog. Nicholson & Watson. London. 1948.

Vesey-Fitzgerald, Brian, Editor. The Domestic Dog: *An Introduction to its History.* Routledge and Kegan Paul. London. 1957.

Walsh, Dr. John H. ("Stonehenge"). The Dogs of the British Islands. Horace Cox. London. 1872.

Watson, James ("Porcupine"). The Dog Book: *A Popular History of the Dog, with Practical Information as to Care and Management of House, Kennel, and Exhibition Dogs; and Descriptions of All the Important Breeds.* Doubleday, Page & Co. New York. 1905.

Youatt, William. The Dog. Charles Knight and Co. London. 1845.

PERIODICALS

The American Dachshund
The American Field
The American Kennel Gazette
Animal World
Breeder and Sportsman
Canine World
The Century
The Chicago Field
The Detroit Times
Dog Times
Dog World (USA)
Fancier's Gazette
The Field
Field and Fancy
Forest and Stream
The Fox Terrier Chronicle
The French Bull Dog
German Shepherd Review
The Graphic
The Illustrated Kennel Magazine
The Illustrated Kennel News
The Illustrated London News
The Kennel
The Kennel Review (England)
The Kennel Gazette
Ladies' Field
The Ladies' Kennel Journal
The Lady Exhibitor
Leslie's Weekly
Man's Best Friend
Our Dogs
Pall Mall Gazette
Pet Dog Journal
The Philadelphia Press
Popular Dogs
Punch
Rider and Driver
The San Francisco Examiner
Sporting and Dramatic News
The Stock-keeper
Turf, Farm and Field
The World (USA)

Authors, Artists and Photographers

Illustration Credits

PHOTOGRAPHS

(3) *The Bulldog, A Monograph,* 1899; (8) (Collie) *Field and Fancy,* 1905; (Samoyed) *Popular Dogs,* 1928; (12) *The Bulldog, A Monograph,* 1899; (14) *American Sporting Dogs,* 1948; (16) (Mortimer)*The American Field,* 1893; (Belmont) *Field and Fancy,* 1906; (16, 17) (Terry) *Field and Fancy,* 1904; (17) (Tracy) *The American Field,* 1892; (Davidson) *The American Field,* 1892; (18) *Field Trial Record of Dogs in America,* 1907; (25) *The American Field,* 1892; (26) *The American Field,* 1892; (27) *The American Field,* 1893; (29) *The American Field,* 1893; (31) *The American Field,* 1893; (35) *The American Field,* 1893; (39) *The American Field,* 1892; (42) *The Bulldog, A Monograph,* 1899; (43) *Bulldogs and Bulldog Men,* 1908; (44) *The Bulldog, A Monograph,* 1899; (45) *The American Field,* 1893; (47) *The American Field,* 1897; (48) *Field and Fancy,* 1906; (51) *The French Bull Dog,* 1913; (52) (top) *The Kennel,* 1912; (bottom), *Le Bouldogue Français,* 1933; (54) (top) *Field and Fancy,* 1904; (bottom), Anne M. Hier, 1996; (56) *The American Field,* 1903; (57) (top) *The American Field,* 1903; (bottom) *The Kennel,* 1912; (58) (top) *The American Field,* 1888; (bottom) *Dog Shows and Doggy People,* 1902; (59) *The Complete Fox Terrier,* 1938; (62) #1, *The American Field,* 1903; #2, *The American Field,* 1903; #3, *The Kennel,* 1911; #4, *Field and Fancy,* 1905; #5, *The American Field,* 1892; (63) #6, *The Kennel Gazette,* 1904; #7, *Field Trial Record of Dogs in America,* 1907; #8, *The American Field,* 1903; #9, *Field and Fancy,* 1902; #10, *Field and Fancy,* 1905; #11, *The Kennel,* 1911; (64) #1, collection of the author, *c.* 1891; #2, *The Dog Book* (Watson), 1904; #3, *The American Field,* 1903; #4, *Field and Fancy,* 1903; #5, *The Kennel Club, A History, etc.,* 1905; (65) #6, *The Dog Book* (Watson), 1904; #7, *Field and Fancy,* 1904; #8, *Field and Fancy,* 1902; #9, *Field and Fancy,* 1904; #10, *Field and Fancy,* 1905; #11, *The French Bull Dog,* 1913; (66) *Field and Fancy,* 1903; (67) *The Kennel,* 1913; (69) *Popular Dogs,* 1946; (73) *The Kennel,* 1913; (75) *The American Kennel Gazette,* 1904; (76-77) (top to bottom, left side then right) #1, *The American Kennel Gazette,* 1904; #2, *Field and Fancy,* 1904; #3, *Field and Fancy,* 1904; #4, *Field and Fancy,* 1904; #5, *The American Field,* 1906; #6, *Field and Fancy,* 1904; #7, *Field and Fancy,* 1906; #8, *Field and Fancy,* 1906; #9, *Field and Fancy,* 1905; #10, *Field and Fancy,* 1905; #11, *The American Field,* 1906; #12, *Field and Fancy,* 1905; #13, *The American Field,* 1906; #14, *Field and Fancy,* 1906; #15, *Field and Fancy,* 1906; #16, *Field and Fancy,* 1905; (81) *The American Field,* 1891; (84) *Field and Fancy,* 1906; (93) *The American Field,* 1892; (97) *The American Field,* 1896; (98) ("Early" Fox Terrier) *The Fox Terrier Chronicle,* 1884; (Modern" Fox Terrier) *The Complete Fox Terrier,* 1938; (100) *The American Field,* 1903; (101) *The Scottish Terrier,* 1936; (103) *The Kennel Gazette,* 1898; (104) *The Scottish Terrier,* 1925; (106), (107), (108) *The Kennel,* 1913; (110) *The Kennel Review,* 1886; (111) (both) *The Kennel,* 1913; (113) *The Detroit Times,* 1957; (120) *The American Kennel Gazette,* 1935; (126) *Dog Shows and Doggy People,* 1902; (131) (top) *Dog Shows and Doggy People,* 1902; (bottom) *The Ladies' Kennel Journal,* 1897; (132) *Dog Shows and Doggy People,* 1902; (133) *The Kennel,* 1913; (134) *The American Field,* 1903; (135) *Field and Fancy,* 1905; (137) (all) *The Complete Fox Terrier,* 1938; (139) (top) *The Fox Terrier Chronicle,* 1898; (bottom) *The American Field,* 1903; (140) *The Kennel Club, A History, etc.,* 1905; (141) *The Fox Terrier,* 1912; (144) *The Kennel Club, A History, etc.,* 1905; (147) *The Bulldog, A Monograph,* 1899; (149) *Field and Fancy,* 1905; (150) *Field and Fancy,* 1902; (151) *Dog Shows and Doggy People,* 1902; (153) *Popular Dogs,* 1949; (155) (Fox Terrier) *Champion of Champions,* 1950; (Bulldog) *The Bulldog,* 1952; (158) *Field and Fancy,* 1903; (159) *The American Field,* 1900; (161) *Popular Dogs,* 1953; (166) *Field and Fancy,* 1906; (169) *The Complete Fox Terrier,* 1938; (171) Westminster KC show catalog, 1902; (172) *Field and Fancy,* 1905; (175) With permission of the United Kennel Club, 1998; (177) *The American Kennel Gazette,* 1932; (182) *The Dog Book* (Watson) 1904; (185-188) *Popular Dogs,* 1945; (192) (all) *Field and Fancy,* 1904; (204) *The Complete Fox Terrier,* 1938; (208) *The Kennel Review,* 1884; (210) *Field and Fancy,* 1906; (213) (left) *Dog Shows and Doggy People,* 1902; (right) *The French Bull Dog,* 1913; (220) *The Kennel,* 1912; (222) *The American Field,* 1897; (224) *Dog Shows and Doggy People,* 1902; (233) show ribbon, collection of the author, *c.* 1906; (235) *The American Field,* 1893; (237) *Ladies' Kennel Journal,* 1901; (238) *Field and Fancy,* 1905; (240) American Institute for the Blind, 1939; (252) (top) *Bulldogdom,* 1923; (lower left) *The Bulldog, A Monograph,* 1899; (256) (top) *Field and Fancy,* 1904; (bottom) *The American Kennel Gazette,* 1959; (259) courtesy of Dr. James W. Edwards, *c.* 1888; (260) *The American Kennel Gazette,* 1906; (262) (top, middle) *The*

American Kennel Gazette, 1906; (bottom) *Field Trial Record of Dogs in America*, 1907; (277) *Dog Shows and Doggy People*, 1902; (**Epilogue**) *The Twentieth Century Dog*, 1904; (**Back Cover**), collection of the author, Victoria Cabinet Studios, 1890.

ARTWORK

(**Cover**), (**frontispiece**), *The Graphic*, 1892; *(ix)* *The American Kennel Gazette*, 1906; *(x), (xi)*, *The Graphic*, 1892; (1) *Show Dogs*, 1908; (5) *The Bulldog, A Monograph*, 1899; (6) Toy Spaniel C of A show catalog, 1906; (7) *The American Kennel Gazette*, 1904; (8) (top) *The Stock-keeper*, 1891; (bottom) *The Fox Terrier Chronicle*, 1900; (11) *Our Dogs*, 1899; (13) *The Chicago Field*, 1877; (19) *The American Field*, 1893; (21) (left) *The American Field*, 1892; (middle) *The American Kennel Gazette*, 1892; (right) *The American Field*, 1892; (23) *The American Field*, 1893; (28) *The American Field*, 1892; (29) *The American Kennel Gazette*, 1899; (36) *The American Field*, 1892; (38) *The Fox Terrier Chronicle*, 1895; (44) collection of the author, c. 1891; (45) (top) *The American Field*, 1893; (bottom left) *The American Field*, 1892; (bottom right) *The American Field*, 1892; (46) (top) *Canine World*, 1890; (bottom) *The Stock-keeper*, 1888; (47) *Canine World*, 1890; (51) *The French Bull Dog*, 1913; (55) *The French Bull Dog*, 1913; (60) *Show Dogs*, 1908; (61) *Toy Dogs and Their Ancestors*, 1910; (68) *Pet Dachshund*, 1954; (70) *Popular Dogs*, 1949; (71) *Pet Dachshund*, 1954; (74) (top) *Leslie's Weekly*, 1877; (bottom) *The American Kennel Gazette*, 1904; (80), (81), (86), (90) *The World*, 1891; (95) *The Illustrated London News*, 1861; (96) *The American Field*, 1893; (97) *The American Field*, 1906; (98) (King Charles) *The Illustrated Book of the Dog*, 1881; (Scotch Collie) *The Dog* (Youatt), 1845; (English Toy Spaniel) *Show Dogs*, 1908; (Collie) *This Doggie Business*, 1934; (99) *The American Field*, 1892; (102) *Show Dogs*, 1908; (105) *The American Kennel Gazette*, 1899; (114) *The American Kennel Gazette*, 1899; (115) *Official Dachshund Standard*, 1904; (118) *The American Kennel Gazette*, 1950; (122) *Great Dane C of A Illustrated Standard*, 1945; (123) *Show Dogs*, 1908; (124) *The American Kennel Gazette*, 1950; (127) from a lithograph, collection of the author, c. 1835; (128) Anne Hier, collection of the author, 1997; (130) *All About Dogs*, 1900; (132) *All About Dogs*, 1900; (136) *The Graphic*, 1877; (138) *The Kennel*, 1913; (140) *The Kennel Club, A History, etc.*, 1905; (143) (top and bottom) *Stripping a Wire*, 1935; (middle) *The American Book of the Dog*, 1891; (146) *The Dog Book* (Mills), 1898; (147) *The Dog Owners Annual*, 1890; (148) *The Stock-keeper*, 1891; (151) (middle) *The Dog Owners Annual*, 1890; (bottom) *The Dog Owners Annual*, 1892; (154) #1, *Toy Dogs and Their Ancestors*, 1910; #2, *The American Kennel Gazette*, 1946; #3, *The American Kennel Gazette*, 1931; #4, *The Kennel Review*, 1884; (155) collection of the author, 1941; (157) *The American Kennel Gazette*, 1931; (160) *The Dog Book* (Mills), 1898; (176) *The San Francisco Examiner*, 1910; (181) *Toy Dogs and Their Ancestors*, 1910; (189), (191), (193) *The American Field*, 1910; (194) (inset) *The American Kennel Gazette*, 1954; (196) (ribbon) *The American Kennel Gazette*, 1954; (trophy) *The Kennel Gazette*, 1925; (197), (198) (insets) *The American Kennel Gazette*, 1954; (200) (top) *The Dog Owners Annual*, 1890; (bottom) *The American Kennel Gazette*, 1899; (201) (top) *The Dog Book* (Mills), 1898; (bottom) *The American Kennel Gazette*, 1904; (203) *Popular Dogs*, 1945; (205) (all except 'D') *The American Field*, 1890; ('D') *Field and Fancy*, 1905; (206) (all) *The Borzoi Handbook*, 1952; (208) *This Doggie Business*, 1934; (213) *The French Bull Dog*, 1913; (214) *The Kennel Review*, 1884; (217) *The American Kennel Gazette*, 1890; (219) *The American Field*, 1893; (222) *The American Field*, 1897; (223) *The Kennel Gazette*, 1905; (224) *The Stock-keeper*, 1891; (225) (top) *The French Bull Dog*, 1913; (middle, bottom) *The Kennel Club, A History, etc.*, 1905; (227) *The Kennel Gazette*, 1911; (228) (top) *The Kennel Gazette*, 1897; (bottom) *Field and Fancy*, 1905; (232) *The American Field*, 1892; (234) *The Stock-keeper*, 1891; (235) *The Ladies' Kennel Journal*, 1897; (239) *The American Kennel Gazette*, 1893; (241) *The Dog Owners Annual*, 1890; (242) *The Graphic*, 1877; (244), (245) *This Doggie Business*, 1934; (246) *Field and Fancy*, 1902; (247) *The Graphic*, 1877; (249) *The American Kennel Gazette*, 1945; (250) *The Kennel Review*, 1888; (251) *Field and Fancy*, 1903; (252) *The Dogs of the British Islands*, 1872; (258) *The Illustrated London News*, 1878; (260) *The Dogs of the British Islands*, 1872; (261) (top) *The American Kennel Gazette*, 1890; (bottom) *The American Kennel Gazette*, 1902; (263) *The Century*, 1899; (264) *The Bulldog, A Monograph*, 1899; (265), (266) *The Century*, 1899; (268) *The Graphic*, 1877; (269) *The Kennel Review*, 1886; (271) *The American Field*, 1893; (272) *The Dog Book* (Mills), 1898; (273) *Dogs of the British Islands*, 1872; (274) *The Bulldog, A Monograph*, 1899; (275) *The Illustrated London News*, 1861; (276) *Dog Shows and Doggy People*, 1902; (278) W. S. Smith, 1835; (279) *Dog Shows and Doggy People*, 1902; (281) *The Illustrated London News*, 1861; (**Tailpiece**), *The Graphic*, 1877.

Index

Including Text and Illustration References

Epilogue
Charles G. Hopton

"The French Bull Dog"
1913

It is unfortunate that some owners and exhibitors never seem to enter into the true spirit which should animate those in the sport of showing dogs. An exhibitor who elects to show his dogs before a certain judge should be prepared to accept, with a fair degree of equanimity, the results of awards that may be made. Judges who are dishonest or incompetent are so rare as hardly to be a factor worth considering. True, the judge may err; he may overlook the good points in your dog and fail to see the bad points of your competition. But, nevertheless, you have freely chosen to place your dog before him. You should be prepared to accept, with outward good grace at least, his decisions. Any other attitude is unsportsmanlike and not compatible with good taste.

Judges, almost without exception, faithfully and honestly try to be consistent, and are seldom influenced by any consideration save to make awards that fairly agree with their impressions of the dogs as they appear at the moment they are before them. A judge's reputation, of which he is naturally jealous, is at stake every time he officiates in the show ring. An award that cannot be successfully defended would do him more injury than it could possibly do any exhibitor.

What has kept the sport alive, and will continue to make it exciting, is the impossibility of knowing in advance what different judges will decide as to the merits of each exhibitor's dog. One not constituted by nature to view the whole matter from a true sporting spirit, and philosophically accept whatever fate has in store for him, had better stay out of the game. Such an individual loses the very essence of the sport, and extracts neither fun nor comfort out of it.

When due allowance is made for individual preferences, and the widely different opinions that may prevail about a particular dog of any breed, one can readily understand how one judge places a certain dog high, and another, perhaps equally competent, looks at the same dog on a different occasion and quite radically reverses the judgment of the other. At best, all standards of type will always be more or less susceptible to divergent and conflicting interpretations. Realizing this fact, how absurd and inexcusable are the contentions of some exhibitors in their criticism of judges who have failed to make awards to suit their individual opinions.

The seasoned show ring contenders have learned from experience that uncertainties are the rule, rather than otherwise, in the show ring, and are prepared to make proper allowances for all the factors which enter in the case and rarely impugn the personal honor of the judge, however far he may vary in his decisions, from their own judgment. The real simon-pure sports, who have survived many battles in the show ring, are seldom found bitterly railing against the judge. They take their defeats, however disappointed they may be, outwardly good-naturedly, realizing that after all, in ninety-nine times out of a hundred if a real mistake in judging has been made it was an honest one on the part of the judge. Men and women who are constituted to look at the matter in this light are the ones who stay in the game and, in the end, extract out of it the full measure of excitement and enjoyment.

*"Nevertheless,
Wisdom is vindicated
by all her children."*

Luke 7:35

FINE